Basic Conversational Russian

Basic Conversational

HOLT,
RINEHART and
WINSTON

NEW YORK

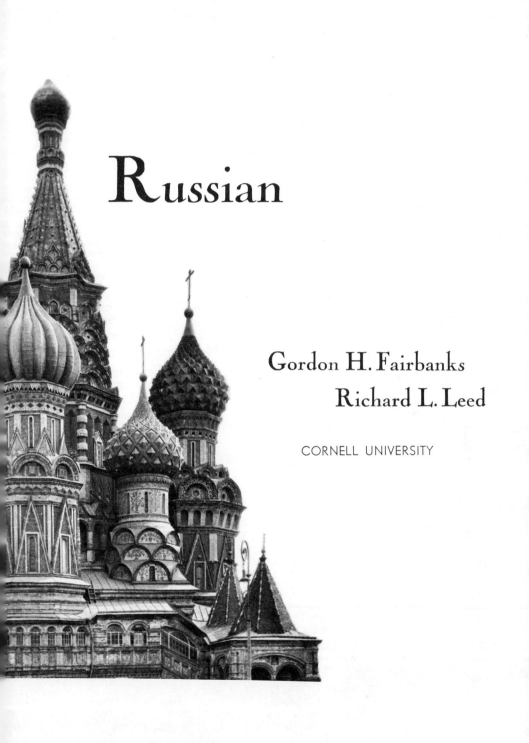

Russian

Gordon H. Fairbanks
Richard L. Leed

CORNELL UNIVERSITY

SBN: 03-019040-1

Printed in the United States of America

0123 40 98765

Introduction

Basic Conversational Russian is a beginning textbook, the aim of which is to provide the college or high school student with the basic speech habits necessary for control of spoken, conversational Russian. With the aid of recordings this book can also be used for self instruction. Those students whose ultimate goal is a good reading knowledge of Russian are advised to treat this course exactly as do those who wish to develop active control of the spoken language. There are a number of reasons for this: first, the most efficient method of developing thorough and fluent reading ability is to begin the study of a language by learning to speak it; second, the literature in a particular language cannot be appreciated unless one has the built-in capacity of contrasting literary style with the style of everyday run of the mill speech; third, one can never be certain that the ability to speak will not turn out to.be useful at some time.

The methodology assumed in this textbook is based on the familiar linguistic generalization to the effect that language behavior is to a significant degree a matter of habit formation. If the learner does not have habitual control of the pronunciation and grammar of the language, then in an actual conversation with a speaker of the language he will be too busy thinking about *how* to say what he wants to say; his ultimate goal in learning a foreign language is the full possession of the habits of pronunciation, grammar and lexicon so that he can free his mind to think of *what* he wants to say. It is therefore essential that the student devote most of his time to active practice *in* the language rather than to reading grammatical descriptions *about* the language. For the adult foreigner learning English, for example, knowledge of the fact that words of a certain shape add -s to form the plural is unquestionably useful, but he will have to practice quite a bit before he can use it automatically, without having to make a conscious effort.

INTRODUCTION

In developing habits through practice—in language learning—the following factors are involved: (1) *imitation* of a good model, (2) constant *repetition* of a particular activity, and (3) *regularity* of practice.

Two types of practice activity are provided in this book: memorization of dialogues and patterned exercise material for repetition.

DIALOGUES. The tape recordings or the native speaking teacher provides the model for the student to imitate. Normally, each student must repeat each sentence many times—and always after the teacher's model—before his performance is acceptable and properly reinforced. The student is then expected to learn the entire dialogue as an actor learns his role, i.e., at normal speed and with the same intonation as the model. The purpose of dialogue memorization is not merely to supply the student with a stock of useful everyday phrases, but to inculcate patterns from which further utterances can be produced by analogical word formations. Although the primary aim of the dialogue is the introduction of grammatical patterns, the language of the dialogues is typical of normal, connected speech, not of artificial grammar book examples.

PATTERNED EXERCISES. After each conversation and each grammar unit there is a set of exercises which are designed to drill the patterns previously introduced. Almost all of them are designed to be performed with books closed, using the oral cues of the teacher or recordings. Rather than testing the students knowledge, these exercises are to be practiced repeatedly until the student can complete his response within the time allowed by the pauses in the recordings.

The heart of the course consists of the above activities—dialogues for imitation and memorization and exercises for repetition and practice. In addition, the textbook contains a substantial amount of grammatical description. In spite of the bulk of this latter type of material, it should be borne in mind that grammar rules are useful only to the extent that they make oral practice easier and more comprehensible, ultimately leading to more fluent conversational ability. The student should not expect to be able to apply these rules successfully after mere study of the grammar units; it is far more advisable to proceed in the following order: (1) skim the grammar unit which follows a set of two conversation units before memorizing the dialogues, since the grammar unit contains a description of the new material presented in them,

(2) memorize the dialogues thoroughly, and (3) study the grammar unit in more detail in connection with oral practice of the exercises. Most of the student's homework will consist of practicing aloud, not in poring over paradigms and grammar rules.

The number of vocabulary items introduced in this course is severely limited, following the principle that the student's attention would otherwise be diverted from the main task of learning to manipulate the language freely, i.e., of internalizing the grammatical and phonological patterns.

Depending on the hours available per week this textbook may be covered in anywhere from one semester of a fairly intensive college course to two years of a less intensive high school course.

Review lessons, which occur after every six units, offer the student the opportunity of putting into practice what he has learned, by conversing in Russian about the topics suggested. The conversation topics in each review lesson are only suggestions and could easily be increased in number and scope. The important thing is for the student to avoid the temptation of trying to express ideas for which he does not yet have sufficient vocabulary or of trying to go beyond the limited grammatical constructions at his disposal. He should try to use all of the expressions and constructions he has practiced thus far, using whole sentences and parts of sentences from previously memorized dialogues, recombining them and manipulating them ad lib, and making analogies on the basis of patterns from the dialogues and exercises.

The tape recordings, available from the publisher, may be used effectively both in the classroom and the language laboratory, and are invaluable for self instruction. Eight native Russians serve as untiring models for student practice. They give natural performances of the dialogues and conversations and record many of the repetition and transformation exercises.

Acknowledgements

The authors wish to thank all of the people who have helped produce this textbook. We are very grateful to Miss Zoya Pavlovskis, who composed the first drafts of the dialogues. The criticisms offered by many elementary Russian students of Cornell University and by their teachers, all of whom suffered through mimeographed versions of the text, were most helpful. Several versions of the book were read by a number of Soviet citizens, whose help we gratefully acknowledge. Comments by S. Petrushin, Dean of the Lenin Pedagogical Institute in Moscow and by V. Maslov of the Philology Department of Leningrad University, along with tape recorded readings and comments by various university students, were invaluable in the principal revision of the text. A very thorough reading of the final manuscript by G. N. Tsvetkov, N. M. Khruleva, I. M. Suryaninova, V. M. Makeeva, G. N. Tsivanyuk, all speakers of Russian from the Soviet Union, proved to be of great assistance to us. Finally, our thanks to our typists, Mrs. Patricia Crabbe, Mrs. Margaret Curit and Miss Margery Carlson for their excellent work in preparing the manuscript for publication. Ultimate responsibility for the contents of the book of course rests with the authors.

G. H. F.
R. L. L.

Table of Contents

TABLE OF CONTENTS

Basic Conversational Russian

CONVERSATION 1

First day in Moscow

John Wright, author and journalist feels strange and bewildered on his first stroll in Moscow. He is glad when he recognizes in the crowd the girl who sold him a wallet that very morning.

CONVERSATION UNIT ONE ━━━━━━━━━

ENGLISH EQUIVALENTS

JOHN	[1] Hello.
GIRL	[2] Hello. How are you?
JOHN	[3] Fine, thanks. And you?
GIRL	[4] [I'm] fine too.
JOHN	[5] Tell [me] please, where [is the] restaurant?
GIRL	[6] The restaurant is here on the right.
JOHN	[7] Thanks. And what's that on the left? [8] [Is] that also a restaurant?
GIRL	[9] No, that's not a restaurant. That's a cafe.
JOHN	[10] And where's the station?
GIRL	[11] It's there across the way [opposite].
JOHN	[12] Thanks.
GIRL	[13] You're welcome.
JOHN	[14] Goodbye.
GIRL	[15] Goodbye.

NOTES

7 **Чтó** is pronounced either /štó/ or, more rarely, /čto/.
Это corresponds to both "this" (close to the speaker) and "that" (farther from the speaker).

9 **Ресторáн** — usually a large well-appointed eating establishment where full meals are served; **кафé** — serves light meals.

13 **Пожáлуйста.** Note that this word is used both in situations where English speakers say "please" and where they say "you're welcome".

ADDITIONAL VOCABULARY

пóчта   *post office*
/póčta/
гостíница *hotel*
/gaṣṭíṇica/

2

Первый день в Москве

ДЖОН [džón]	¹ Здра́вствуйте. [zdrástvuyţi.]
ДЕ́ВУШКА [ḑévuška]	² Здра́вствуйте. Как вы́ пожива́ете? [zdrástvuyţi. kák ví paživáyiţi?]
ДЖОН	³ Хорошо́, спаси́бо. А вы́? [xarašó, spaşíba. a ví?]
ДЕ́ВУШКА	⁴ То́же хорошо́. [tóži xarašó.]
ДЖОН	⁵ Скажи́те, пожа́луйста, где́ рестора́н? [skažíţi, pažálsta, gḑé ṛistarán?]
ДЕ́ВУШКА	⁶ Рестора́н зде́сь, напра́во. [ṛistarán ẓḑéş, napráva.]
ДЖОН	⁷ Спаси́бо. А что́ э́то нале́во? [spaşíba. a štó éta naḷéva?] ⁸ Э́то то́же рестора́н? [éta tóži ṛistarán?]
ДЕ́ВУШКА	⁹ Не́т, э́то не рестора́н. Э́то кафе́. [ṇét, éta ṇi ṛistarán. éta kafé.]
ДЖОН	¹⁰ А́ где́ вокза́л? [á gḑé vagzál?]
ДЕ́ВУШКА	¹¹ О́н та́м, напро́тив. [ón tám, napróţif.]
ДЖОН	¹² Спаси́бо. [spaşíba.]
ДЕ́ВУШКА	¹³ Пожа́луйста. [pažalsta.]
ДЖОН	¹⁴ До свида́ния. [da şᶹidáṇya.]
ДЕ́ВУШКА	¹⁵ До свида́ния. [da şᶹidáṇya.]

УПРАЖНЕ́НИЯ

(EXERCISES)

A. Read *Pronunciation Sections* **1** and **4.11** through **4.15**. Perform *Drills* **16** through **20**.

B. Say in Russian:

1. Hello. 2. How are you? 3. Fine, thanks. 4. And you? 5. [I'm] fine too. 6. Tell [me] please, where [is the] restaurant? 7. The restaurant is here on the right. 8. And what's that on the left? 9. Is that also a restaurant? 10. No, that's not a restaurant. 11. That's a cafe. 12. And where's the station? 13. It's there across the way (opposite). 14. Thanks. 15. You're welcome. 16. Goodbye.

C. Give the Russian equivalents:

1. Hello. 2. How are you? 3. Fine. 4. Fine, thanks. 5. And you? 6. I'm fine, too.

7. Where's the restaurant? 8. Tell me, please, where's the restaurant? 9. The restaurant is there on the right. 10. The cafe is there on the right. 11. The restaurant is there. 12. The restaurant is here.

13. Where's the station? 14. Where's the restaurant? 15. Where's the hotel? 16. Where's the post office? 17. The station is here. 18. The station is to the right. 19. The station is there to the right. 20. The station is across the way.

21. The hotel is there to the left. 22. The hotel is there to the left and the restaurant is here. 23. The cafe is there on the left and the restaurant is here. 24. The cafe is there on the left and the restaurant is there on the right.

25. Is that a post office? 26. Is that a restaurant? 27. Is that a restaurant on the left? 28. Is that a hotel on the left? 29. No, that's not a hotel; that's a station. 30. No, that's not a station, that's a post office.

D. READING EXERCISE

Listen to each of the following words and imitate it. Next, read aloud the list of words in order to become familiar with their written form.

а	*and*	от	*from*
там	*there*	то	*then; that*
мат	*checkmate*	ко	*to*
так	*so; right*	кот	*cat*
как	*how*	ком	*whom*
акт	*act*	ток	*current*
мáма	*mama*	том	*that*

In the following group of words the letters **д, п, л, г,** which are derived from the Greek alphabet, are introduced.

да	*yes*	по	*along*
до	*up to*	пот	*sweat*
дом	*house*	пол	*floor*
дóма	*at home*	пáпа	*papa*
дáма	*lady*	пал	*fell*
дáта	*date*	пакт	*pact*
дал	*gave*		
дóлга	*of the debt*		

лак	*lacquer*	гол	*goal*
лом	*scrap*	гóда	*of the year*
лáма	*llama*	глóтка	*throat*
лáпа	*paw*		
лáпка	*little paw*		
лáмпа	*lamp*		

6

CONVERSATION 2

A visit in a classroom

John, who is going to write an article about the pedagogical system in the USSR, has been invited to a school and visits a class.

7

CONVERSATION UNIT TWO _____

ENGLISH EQUIVALENTS

TEACHER	[1] Open [your] books, please.
	[2] Repeat this sentence after me.
	[3] Where is the letter from Ivan?
STUDENTS (in chorus)	[4] Where is the letter from Ivan?
TEACHER	[5] No, Basil (*diminutive*). [That's] not right.
	[6] Repeat [it] again.
	[7] Where is the letter from Ivan?
BASIL	[8] Where is the letter from Ivan?
TEACHER	[9] That's better.
	[10] Say the word "letter".
BASIL	[11] Letter.
TEACHER	[12] [Say] the whole sentence — Where is the letter from Ivan?
BASIL	[13] Where is the letter from Ivan?
TEACHER	[14] Right. Close your books.

NOTES

9 Так. The basic meaning of this word is "thus, so, that way".

ADDITIONAL VOCABULARY

учи́тель /učíṭiḷ/	*teacher* (male)	**студе́нт** /stuḍént/	*student* (male)
учи́тельница /učíṭiḷṇica/	*teacher* (female)	**студе́нтка** stuḍéntka/	*student* (female)

Посещение класса

УЧИ́ТЕЛЬ [učíṭiḷ]	[1] Откро́йте, пожа́луйста, кни́ги. [atkróyṭi, pažálsta, ķņígi.]
	[2] Повтори́те за мно́й э́ту фра́зу. [paftaṛíṭi za mnóy étu frázu.]
	[3] « Где́ письмо́ от Ива́на? » [gḍé ṗişmó at ivána?]
СТУДЕ́НТЫ (хо́ром) : [stuḑénti]	[4] « Где́ письмо́ от Ива́на? » [(xóram) : gḍé ṗişmó at ivána?]
УЧИ́ТЕЛЬ	[5] Не́т, Ва́ся. Не ве́рно. [ņét, vá̱şa. ṇiɣérna.]
	[6] Повтори́те ещё ра́з. [paftaṛíṭi yiščó rás.]
	[7] « Где́ письмо́ от Ива́на? » [gḍé ṗişmó at ivána?]
ВА́СЯ	[8] « Где́ письмо́ от Ива́на? » [gḍé ṗişmó at ivána?]
УЧИ́ТЕЛЬ	[9] Та́к лу́чше. [ták lútša.]
	[10] Скажи́те сло́во « письмо́ ». [skažíṭi slóva ṗişmó.]
ВА́СЯ	[11] Письмо́. [ṗişmó.]
УЧИ́ТЕЛЬ	[12] Всю́ фра́зу: « Где́ письмо́ от Ива́на? » [fşú frázu: gḍé ṗişmó at ivána?]
ВА́СЯ	[13] « Где́ письмо́ от Ива́на? » [gḍé ṗişmó at ivána?]
УЧИ́ТЕЛЬ	[14] Пра́вильно. Закро́йте кни́ги. [práɣiḷna. zakróyṭi ķņígi.]

УПРАЖНЕ́НИЯ

(EXERCISES)

A. Read the whole of *Pronunciation Section* **2** through **2.9** and perform *Drills* **1** through **9.**

B. Say in Russian:

1. Open [your] books, please.   2. Repeat this sentence after me.   3. Where is the letter from Ivan?   4. [That's] not right.   5. Repeat [it] again. 6. [That's] not right.   7. Say the word "letter".   8. [Say] the whole sentence.   9. Right.   10. That's better.   11. Close [your] books.

C. Make the following substitutions orally:
The . . . . . is there.

¹ station	⁵ teacher (f.)	⁸ cafe
² hotel	⁶ student (m.)	⁹ letter
³ restaurant	⁷ student (f.)	¹⁰ post office
⁴ teacher (m.)		

D. CHAIN PRACTICE
Student A will ask student B, "Where is the . . . ?" Student B will answer and then ask student C where something else is. Continue around the class and go as fast as you can. For example:

A. Где́ гости́ница? **B.** Гости́ница здесь. Где́ студе́нт? **C** Студе́нт здесь. Где́...?

E. READING EXERCISE
Listen to each of the following words and imitate it. Next, read aloud the list of words in order to become familiar with their written form. The letters introduced here look familiar but have sound values different from the corresponding English letters.

RUSSIAN: **р, с, н, в, х, з, у**
TRANSCRIPTION: /r   s   n   v   x   z   u/

рот	mouth	спорт	sports	тон	tone
рос	he grew	стул	chair	курс	course
róза	rose	стол	table	план	plan
рук	of arms	ну	well	хор	chorus
рост	growth	нос	nose	холм	hill
сок	juice	нам	to us	слух	hearing
сóда	soda	вот	here	звук	sound
сон	dream	вас	you	зал	hall
суп	soup	Вóлга	Volga	зóна	zone
		волк	wolf		

OTHER CONSONANT LETTERS: **ч, ш, ж, щ, ц, б, ф, й**
TRANSCRIPTION: /č   š   ž   šč   c   b   f   y/

час	hour	мýжа	husband's	бал	ball
чýда	wonder's	жал	squeezed	бóмба	bomb
чáшка	cup	жáба	toad	бáба	woman
чай	tea	жáжда	thirst	бой	battle
май	May	жар	fever	фáза	phase
лáйка	Eskimo dog	щýка	pike	фарс	farce
шум	noise	борщ	borsch	шкаф	cupboard
шар	ball	плащ	raincoat	торф	peat
ваш	your	бац!	bang!	шарф	scarf
наш	our	тáнца	dance's	факт	fact
шкóла	school				

GRAMMAR UNIT ONE

◐ 1. The Russian writing system

In the first three Grammar Units of this book the Russian writing system is presented. Contrary to popular opinion, the apparent strangeness of the letters used in Russian will not cause any difficulty. On the other hand the interrelationship between the sounds of the language and the letters used in writing them will require considerable study. It is not expected that you will immediately assimilate this discussion of the writing system in its entirety. You should constantly reread and study it as you work with the grammar of the language.

1.1 The Russian (Cyrillic) Alphabet

PRINTING	WRITING	LETTER NAMES	TRANSCRIPTION (*See Pronunciation*)	ENGLISH EQUIVALENTS (*See Pronunciation*)
А а	*A a*	a	/a/	*a* as in *car*
Б б	*Б б*	bé	/b/	*b* as in *bin*
В в	*В в*	vé	/v/	*v* as in *van*
Г г	*Г г*	gé	/g/	*g* as in *gun*
Д д	*Д дэ*	dé	/d/	*d* as in *din*
Е е	*Е е*	yé	/e/	*e* as in *yet*
Ё ё	*Ё ё*	yó	/o/	*aw* as in *yawn*
Ж ж	*Ж ж*	žé	/ž/	*z* as in *azure*
З з	*З з*	zé	/z/	*z* as in *zinc*
И и	*И и*	i	/i/[1]	*ea* as in *beat*
Й й	*Й й*	í krátkaya	/y/	*y* as in *yes*
К к	*К к*	ká	/k/	*c* as in *cat*
Л л	*Л л*	él	/l/	*ll* as in *pull*
М м	*М м*	ém	/m/	*m* as in *man*
Н н	*Н н*	én	/n/	*n* as in *net*
О о	*О о*	ó	/o/	*o* as in *story*
П п	*П п*	pé	/p/	*p* as in *pin*
Р р	*Р р*	ér	/r/	(Scottish trilled *r*)
С с	*С с*	és	/s/	*s* as in *sink*
Т т	*Т т*	té	/t/	*t* as in *tin*
У у	*У у*	ú	/u/	*oo* as in *mooring*
Ф ф	*Ф ф*	éf	/f/	*f* as in *fan*
Х х	*Х х*	xá	/x/	(*ch* as in German *ach* or Scottish *loch*)

[1] Pronounced /i/ as in **спасибо.** Cf. *Pronunciation Section* **4.21.**

Ц	ц	*Ц* *ц*	ce	/c/	*ts* as in *bats*
Ч	ч	*Ч* *ч*	čé	/č/	*ch* as in *chin*
Ш	ш	*Ш* *ш*	šá	/š/	*sh* as in *harsh*
Щ	щ	*Щ* *щ*	ščá	/šč/	*shch* as in *fresh cheese*
Ъ	ъ	*ъ*	tyórdiy znák		
Ы	ы	*ы*	i¹	/i/	*i* as in *bit*
Ь	ь	*ь*	mⱥxkiy znák		
Э	э	*Э* *э*	é abarótnaya	/e/	*e* as in *bet*
Ю	ю	*Ю* *ю*	yú	/u/	*ou* as in *you*
Я	я	*Я* *я*	yá	/a/	*a* as in *yacht*

1.2 Palatalized versus Plain Consonants

Most Russian consonants have two different pronunciations even though each consonant has only one spelling. These consonants may be pronounced PLAIN or PALATALIZED. The palatalized version is represented in the transcription of sound by a comma beneath the consonant symbol: e.g. PLAIN CONSONANT sound "t" = /t/:/brat/ *brother;* PALATALIZED CONSONANT sound "t" = /ṭ/:/braṭ/ *to take.*

1.21 Paired Consonants

The Russian consonants which are paired, that is, those which may have one of two different pronunciations—plain or palatalized—are:

П /p/ *or* /p̦/; **Б** /b/ *or* /b̦/; **М** /m/ *or* /m̦/;
Ф /f/ *or* /f̦/; **В** /v/ *or* /v̦/;
Т /t/ *or* /ṭ/; **Д** /d/ *or* /d̦/; **Н** /n/ *or* /n̦/; **С** /s/ *or* /ṣ/ **З** /z/ *or* /z̦/;
Л /l/ *or* /l̦/; **Р** /r/ *or* /ṛ/
К /k/ *or* /k̦/; **Г** /g/ *or* /g̦/; **Х** /x/ *or* /x̦/.

There is only one written form for each Russian consonant, and this written form gives no indication in itself whether the consonant is palatalized or plain. But the Russian writing system makes it quite clear whether the consonant is pronounced as palatized or plain in the following ways:

1) When the consonant occurs at the end of a word, and when it occurs before another consonant, Russian indicates that the consonant is palatalized by writing ь (called мягкий знáк) after the consonant. For example: final "t" is palatalized in the word for "*to take*" брать /braṭ/.

¹ Pronounced /i/ as in вы. Cf. *Pronunciation Section* **4.11.**

13

And: "s" before another consonant is palatalized in the word for "*letter*" письмо́ /piṣmó/.

2) When the consonant occurs before a vowel, a specific written form of the vowel is used to indicate that the consonant is palatalized. Each of the five vowel sounds of Russian is represented by two letters—one to indicate a preceding plain consonant and one to indicate a preceding palatalized consonant.

In the following chart are presented the two ways of writing each of the five vowel sounds in Russian. Note these carefully, for the choice of the written vowel indicates whether the consonant that precedes it is plain or palatalized.[1]

THE WRITTEN FORMS OF THE VOWEL SOUNDS

When a consonant which may be pronounced either palatalized or plain is followed by a stressed vowel: —the choice of the written vowel indicates in the written word whether the consonant is plain or palatalized.

VOWEL SOUND		This vowel indicates that the preceding "paired" consonant is PLAIN			This vowel indicates that the preceding "paired" consonant is PALATALIZED	
/i/	ы	бы́л	/bíl/ *was*	и	би́л	/ḅil/ *beat*
/e/[2]	е, э	кафе́	/kafé/ *cafe*	е	не́т	/ṇet/ *no*
/a/	а	ма́ть	/máṭ/ *mother*	я	мя́ть	/ṃáṭ/ *crumple*
/o/[3]	о	но́с	/nós/ *nose*	е, ё	нёс	/ṇós/ *carried*
/u/	у	лу́к	/lúk/ *onion*	ю	лю́к	/ḻúk/ *hatchway*

[1] This chart refers only to stressed vowels. Unstressed vowels will be considered in Grammar Unit 2.

[2] The vowel sound /e/ occurs very rarely after plain consonants. When it does it is usually written with Russian е: кафе́ /kafé/ *cafe*. The letter э is seldom used but when it does occur it is likely to be found in initial position: э́то *this, that.*

[3] After a palatalized consonant the Russian letter е may represent either the stressed vowel sound /e/ or the stressed vowel sound /ó/. To remove this ambiguity it is common practice in many textbooks to write the Russian letter е to represent the stressed vowel sound /é/ and to write the same letter with two dots above it, ё, to represent the stressed vowel sound /ó/. For example нале́во *to the left,* has the stressed vowel sound /é/, whereas ещё *still,* has the stressed vowel /ó/. This distinction in writing is only made to help the learner and is not usual in ordinary Russian books.

The Russian consonants **к**, **г** and **х** are always plain before the stressed vowel sound /a/, /o/ or /u/. These stressed vowel sounds are, then, always written **a**, **o** and **y** after the consonants **к**, **г** and **х**.

ка	/ka/	**га**	/ga/	**ха**	/xa/
ко	/ko/	**го**	/go/	**хо**	/xo/
ку	/ku/	**гу**	/gu/	**ху**	/xu/

The same three consonants are always palatalized before the stressed vowel sound /i/ or /e/. These stressed vowel sounds are, then, always written **и** and **е** after the consonants **к**, **г** and **х**.

ки	/ki̩/	**ги**	/gi̩/	**хи**	/xi̩/
ке	/ke̩/	**ге**	/ge̩/	**хе**	/xe̩/

To summarize: after the letters **к**, **г**, **х** only the letters **и**, **е** (indicating palatalization) and **a**, **o**, **y** (indicating plain) may occur. Or, to put it still another way: the letters **к**, **г**, **х** can never be followed by the letters **я**, **ю** or **ы** except for a few words of foreign origin.

1.22 Non-paired Consonants

Of the non-paired Russian consonants, three are always plain

ш /š/   **ж** /ž/   **ц** /c/

Three, also, are always palatalized:

ч /č/   **щ** /šč/   /y[1]/

Since all of these consonants are always predictably either palatalized or plain, the spelling of the vowel sound following the consonant is arbitrary and does not follow the pattern of the chart in section **1.21** above. Rather it follows the scheme outlined on the next page.

---

[1] The writing of the consonant sound /y/ will be discussed in Grammar Unit 2.

SPELLING OF THE VOWELS AFTER NON-PAIRED CONSONANTS				
VOWEL SOUND	AFTER Ш	AFTER Ж	AFTER Ц	AFTER Ч	AFTER Щ
/i/		и	и, ы¹		и
/e/			е		
/a/			а		
/o/			о, е (ё)²		
/u/			у		

⏺ 2. Articles

There are no words in Russian corresponding to the English articles *a, an, the*.

Э́то рестора́н. {That's a restaurant.
                {That's the restaurant.

⏺ 3. The verb *to be*

Where in English a present tense form of the verb *to be* occurs, in the Russian equivalent there is generally no verb.

Рестора́н нале́во.   The restaurant is to the left.

⏺ 4. Russian Nouns

Russian nouns have (1) gender; (2) case; and (3) number.

(1) GENDER. The Russian noun is either masculine, feminine or neuter. Since *masculine* and *neuter* nouns, in Russian, have greater similarities in forms and endings than do either to *feminine* nouns, we present them throughout this text in the order *masculine, neuter, feminine*.

MASCULINE:	Ива́н	/iván/	*Ivan*
NEUTER:	письмо́	/piṣ,mó/	*letter*
FEMININE:	де́вушка	/ḍévuška/	*girl*

¹ After ц the letter **ы** for the vowel sound /i/ occurs with the greater frequency: **отцы́** /atcí/ *fathers*. The letter **и** occurs here in relatively few words, usually borrowed from other languages: **цирк** /cirk/ *circus*. This difference in spelling is strictly arbitrary and does not indicate a difference in pronunciation.

² The distribution of the letters **о, е** and **ё** for the vowel sound /o/ is complex, and will be discussed in Grammar Unit 3.

(2) CASE. The Russian noun has six case forms: *nominative, genitive, dative, accusative, instrumental* and *locative*.

We will not introduce the Russian cases in this order, but once we have treated all of them, and in the reference materials provided at the back of this book, they will be so presented.

To illustrate, briefly, the use of the different cases: 1) The subject of the sentence is in the *nominative* case: **Ива́н** здéсь *Ivan* is here. 2) In many instances the noun which is the object of a preposition is in the *genitive* case: Где́ письмó от **Ива́на**? Where is the letter from *Ivan*?

(3) NUMBER. Most Russian nouns have *singular* and *plural* forms for each of the six cases.

5. Gender of Nouns

The classification of *masculine* and *feminine* agrees to quite an extent with the sex of the noun. For example, **Ива́н** *Ivan*, is masculine, while **де́вушка** *girl*, is feminine. But there are discrepancies, and an inanimate noun may belong to any of the three genders. For instance, while **письмó** *letter*, is neuter in gender, **рестора́н** *restaurant*, is masculine, and **гости́ница** *hotel*, is feminine.

You will find it practical to divide nouns into the three classes—masculine, neuter and feminine, on the basis of the pronouns that are used to refer to them. For instance, those nouns that are referred to by the pronoun **он** /ón/ *he, it*, you will classify as masculine; those referred to by the pronoun **онó** /anó/ *it*, you will classify as neuter; and those referred to by the pronoun **она́** /aná/, *she, it*, you will classify as feminine. Notice particularly that the endings of each of these pronouns is similar to the endings of the nouns: the masculine **он** ends in a consonant; the neuter **онó** ends in **-o**, and the feminine **она́** ends in **-a**.

Masculine

| Где́ студе́нт? | **Он** здéсь. | /ón/ |
| Где́ учи́тель? | **Он** здéсь. | |

Neuter

| Где́ письмó? | **Онó** здéсь. | /anó/ |

Feminine

| Где́ студе́нтка? | **Она́** здéсь. | /aná/ |

6. Nominative Case of Nouns

Russian nouns are generally given in dictionaries and vocabularies in their nominative singular form, and from the form given the gender of the noun may usually be determined:

Masculine   All nouns ending in a consonant letter are masculine: вокза́л *station*, Ива́н *Ivan*, etc.

Some nouns ending in the letter **-ь**, are masculine: учи́тель *teacher.*

Neuter   Nouns ending in **-o** or **-e** are neuter: письмо́ *letter;* кафе́ *cafe,* etc.[1]

Feminine   Nouns ending in **-a** or **-я** are feminine: фра́за *sentence,* студе́нтка *girl student,* etc.[1]

Some nouns ending in the letter **ь** are feminine: мать *mother.*

In subsequent discussions, feminine nouns ending in the letter **a** or **я** will be referred to as FEMININE CLASS I, and feminine nouns ending in the letter **ь** will be referred to as FEMININE CLASS II. It is not necessary to make a subdivision of the two types of masculine nouns because they have basically the same endings.

The nominative singular forms of the nouns you have met so far are:

MASCULINE	NEUTER	FEMININE I	FEMININE II
рестора́н	письмо́	гости́ница	(none)
вокза́л	сло́во	кни́га	
Ива́н	кафе́	фра́за	
студе́нт		учи́тельница	
учи́тель		студе́нтка	
		де́вушка	

⟩ 7.   The Uses of the Nominative Case

The nominative case is used as the subject of a sentence. For example:

Рестора́н здесь.   *The restaurant* is here.

It is also used as the complement of an equational sentence, e.g.,

Это **рестора́н.**   This is *a restaurant.*

УПРАЖНЕ́НИЯ (EXERCISES)

A. Read the whole of *Pronunciation Section* 6 and imitate the recordings of *Pronunciation Drills* **37, 40, 42, 43.**

B. Read all of *Pronunciation Section* 3 through **3.8** and perform *Drills* **10** through **15.**

---

[1] There are extremely few exceptions to this statement, and you must learn them as you meet them.

C. Listen to the following questions and answer them according to the model, using the pronouns **óн, онá, онó:**

MODEL: Гдé ресторáн?   **Óн здéсь.**

1. Гдé кафé?
2. Гдé гостúница?
3. Гдé вокзáл?
4. Гдé письмó?
5. Гдé учúтель?
6. Гдé учúтельница?
7. Гдé студéнт?
8. Гдé студéнтка?
9. Гдé Ивáн?
10. Гдé дéвушка?
11. Гдé кнúга?
12. Гдé пóчта?

D. Repeat *Exercise C* according to the following model:

MODEL: Гдé ресторáн?   **Óн тáм.**

E. Make the following substitutions orally:
Э́то.....

¹ restaurant	⁵ girl	⁹ Ivan
² hotel	⁶ student (two ways)	¹⁰ book
³ station	⁷ teacher (two ways)	¹¹ post office
⁴ cafe	⁸ letter	

F. Give the Russian equivalents:

1. Where's the teacher? (f)
2. She's here.
3. Where's the student? (m)
4. He's here, too.
5. What's that?
6. That's a letter.
7. Repeat that sentence.
8. What's that?
9. That's a restaurant.
10. That's a restaurant?
11. That's right.
12. Where's the station?
13. The station's over there.
14. It's over there across the way.
15. Say the word station in Russian.
16. That's not right.
17. Repeat, please.

G. READING EXERCISE

(1) Listen to each of the following words and imitate it. (2) Next, read the list aloud, while you cover the transcription. (As you do so, note the contrast between plain and palatalized consonants as symbolized by the мя́гкий знáк, **ь,** and by the spelling of the vowels.)

19

GRAMMAR UNIT ONE

Мягкий знак

брат	/brat/	*brother*	стол	/stol/	*table*
брать	/braṭ/	*to take*	столь	/stoḷ/	*so*
быт	/bit/	*way of life*	вес	/ɣes/	*weight*
быть	/biṭ/	*to be*	весь	/ɣeṣ/	*all*
дан	/dan/	*given*	полка	/polka/	*shelf*
дань	/daṇ/	*tribute*	полька	/poḷka/	*Polish woman, polka*
жал	/žal/	*squeezed*	Волга	/volga/	*Volga*
жаль	/žaḷ/	*sorry*	Ольга	/oḷga/	*Olga*

a VERSUS я

флаги	/flagi/	*flags*	раса	/rasa/	*race*
фляги	/fḷaɣi/	*flask's*	ряса	/ṛasa/	*frock*
		мать	/maṭ/	*mother*		
		мять	/ṃaṭ/	*crumple*		

ы VERSUS и

был	/bil/	*was*	мыл	/mil/	*washed*
бил	/ḅil/	*beat*	мил	/ṃil/	*nice*
быт	/bit/	*way of life*	выл	/vil/	*howled*
бит	/ḅit/	*beaten*	вил	/ɣil/	*twisted*

o VERSUS ё

мол	/mol/	*they say*	нос	/nos/	*nose*
мёл	/ṃol/	*swept*	нёс	/ṇos/	*carried*
		ток	/tok/	*current*		
		тёк	/ṭok/	*flowed*		

у VERSUS ю

лук	/luk/	*onion*
люк	/ḷuk/	*hatchway*

THE LETTER е

вес	/ɣes/	*weight*	неба	/ṇeba/	*sky's*
лета	/ḷeta/	*summer's*	нет	/ṇet/	*no*

20

CONVERSATION 3

On a street in Moscow

John stops a passer-by and asks him for information. He likes to practice his Russian and does it even though the man—and here he is in for a surprise—.

CONVERSATION UNIT THREE _____

JOHN	[1] Sir! Tell [me] please, [2] where's the Bolshoy Theater?
PASSER-BY	[3] There's the Bolshoy Theater, across the way (opposite).
JOHN	[4] I don't understand. [5] Please repeat.
PASSER-BY	[6] Do you see that building?
JOHN	[7] Yes, [I] see [it].
PASSER-BY	[8] That building is the Bolshoy Theater. [9] Do [you] understand?
JOHN	[10] Yes, I understand. [11] And where's the Kremlin?
PASSER-BY	[12] It's there on the left.
JOHN	[13] And what street is this?
PASSER-BY	[14] I don't know. I'm a tourist.
JOHN	[15] Well what do you know about that (what do you say)! [16] Aren't you a Russian?
PASSER-BY	[17] No, I'm an American.
JOHN	[18] You speak Russian very well.
PASSER-BY	[19] My wife's a Russian. [20] We often speak Russian.

NOTES

1   The terms **граждани́н** (*m.*) and **гражда́нка** (*f.*) are the normal forms of address among Soviet citizens. The terms **господи́н** (*m.*) and **госпожа́** (*f.*) are usually used by a Soviet citizen in addressing foreigners.

2   **Большо́й теа́тр** is the most famous theater in Moscow. The literal meaning of **большо́й** is "large, great".

ADDITIONAL VOCABULARY

гражда́нка /graždánka/	Miss, Mrs.	**америка́нка** /amiṛikánka/	American (female)
господи́н /gaspaḍín/	Mr.	**по-англи́йски** /pa angḷíysḳi/	in English
госпожа́ /gaspažá/	Mrs., Miss		

22

_____ На улице в Москве

ДЖÓН
[džón]

¹ Граждани́н! Скажи́те, пожа́луйста, ² где Большо́й
[graždaņín! skažíţi pažálsta, ģḑé baļšóy ţiátr?]
теа́тр?

ПРОХÓЖИЙ
[praxóžiy]

³ Вóт Большóй теа́тр, напро́тив.
[vót baļšóy ţiátr napróţif.]

ДЖÓН

⁴ Я не понима́ю. ⁵ Пожа́луйста, повтори́те.
[yá ņi paņimáyu. pažálsta, paftaŗíţi.]

ПРОХÓЖИЙ

⁶ Вы́ ви́дите э́то зда́ние?
[ví yíḑiţi éta zdáņiya?]

ДЖÓН

⁷ Да́, ви́жу.
[dá, yížu.]

ПРОХÓЖИЙ

⁸ Э́то зда́ние — Большо́й теа́тр. ⁹ Понима́ете?
[éta zdáņiya   baļšóy ţiátr. paņimáyiţi?]

ДЖÓН

¹⁰ Да́, я понима́ю. ¹¹ А где́ Кре́мль?
[dá, yá paņimáyu. a ģḑé ķrémļ?]

ПРОХÓЖИЙ

¹² Вóн та́м нале́во.
[vón tám naļéva.]

ДЖÓН

¹³ А кака́я э́та у́лица?
[a kakáya éta úļica?]

ПРОХÓЖИЙ

¹⁴ Я́ не зна́ю. Я тури́ст.
[yá ņi znáyu. yá tuŗíst.]

ДЖÓН

¹⁵ Да что́ вы́ говори́те!
[da štó ví gavaŗíţi!]

¹⁶ Вы́ не ру́сский?
[ví ņi rúsķiy?]

ПРОХÓЖИЙ

¹⁷ Не́т, я америка́нец.
[ņét, yá amiŗikáņic.]

ДЖÓН

¹⁸ Вы́ о́чень хорошо́ говори́те по-ру́сски.
[ví óčiņ xarašó gavaŗíţi pa rúsķi.]

ПРОХÓЖИЙ

¹⁹ Моя́ жена́ ру́сская. ²⁰ Мы́ ча́сто говори́м по-
[mayá žiná rúskaya. mí částa gavaŗím parúsķi.]
ру́сски.

CONVERSATION UNIT THREE

NEW NOUNS

You have met the following nouns in this lesson. They are listed here in the nominative case form and classified as to gender.

Masculine		*Feminine I*	
теа́тр	theater	у́лица	street
тури́ст	tourist	америка́нка	American (f.)
америка́нец	American (m.)	жена́	wife
Кре́мль	Kremlin	госпожа́	Miss, Mrs.
господи́н	Mr.	гражда́нка	Miss, Mrs.
граждани́н	Mr.		

Neuter		*Feminine II*
зда́ние	building	(none)

THE WORDS русский AND русская

The words ру́сский "Russian (male)" and ру́сская "Russian (female)" are in the nominative case but do not have the endings of nouns and will be discussed later (*Grammar Unit* **5:3**).

УПРАЖНЕ́НИЯ (EXERCISES)

A. Read *Pronunciation Sections* **4, 4.1,** and all of **4.2** through **4.25** and perform *Drills* **22** through **26.** Then perform these *Drills* in the following order: **16, 22,** then **17, 23,** then **18, 24,** then **19, 25,** then **20, 26,** in order to compare the vowel sounds in these positions.

B. Say in Russian:

1. Sir! Tell [me] please, where's the Bolshoy Theater? 2. There's the Bolshoy Theater, across the way (opposite). 3. I don't understand. 4. Please repeat. 5. Do you see that building? 6. Yes, [I] see [it]. 7. That building is the Bolshoy Theater. 8. Do [you] understand? 9. Yes, I understand. 10. And where's the Kremlin? 11. It's there on the left. 12. And what street is this? 13. I don't know. 14. I'm a tourist. 15. Well what do you know about that (what do you say)! 16. Aren't you a Russian? 17. No, I'am an American. 18. You speak Russian very well. 19. My wife's a Russian. 20. We often speak Russian.

C. Listen to the following questions and answer them according to the model:

MODEL: Где́ рестора́н? — **Он та́м.**

1. Где́ гости́ница?	6. Где́ письмо́?	11. Где́ тури́ст?
2. Где́ теа́тр?	7. Где́ студе́нтка?	12. Где́ америка́нка?
3. Где́ кафе́?	8. Где́ Кре́мль?	13. Где́ моя́ жена́?
4. Где́ учи́тель?	9. Где́ учи́тельница?	14. Где́ э́то зда́ние?
5. Где́ вокза́л?	10. Где́ америка́нец?	15. Где́ по́чта?

D. Give the Russian equivalents:

1. He is a teacher. 2. She is a student. 3. He is a tourist. 4. She is a teacher. 5. He is a student. 6. He is a Russian. 7. She is an American. 8. She is a Russian. 9. He is an American. 10. She is my wife.

25

E. Give the Russian equivalents:

1. The teacher (*m.*) is a Russian. 2. The teacher (*f.*) is a Russian. 3. The teacher (*f.*) is an American. 4. The teacher (*m.*) is an American. 5. The student (*m.*) is an American. 6. The student (*f.*) is an American. 7. The student (*m.*) is a Russian. 8. The student (*f.*) is a Russian. 9. The student (*m.*) is a tourist. 10. My wife is an American. 11. My wife is a Russian. 12. Robert is an American. 13. The girl is a Russian. 14. Ivan is a Russian and John is an American.

F. Give the Russian equivalents:

1. Do you understand?
2. Yes, I understand.
3. No, I don't understand.

4. The Kremlin's over there on the left.
5. The Bolshoy Theater is on the right.
6. The station is across the way.
7. What street is this?

8. Are you an American?
9. No, I'm Russian.
10. I'm not a Russian, I'm an American.
11. I'm not a Russian, I'm a tourist.
12. Are you a tourist?

13. Do you speak Russian?
14. Do you speak English?
15. My wife's a Russian.
16. My wife's an American.
17. The tourist is an American.

G. READING EXERCISE

Here are some words you have had in conversation lessons. Note the spelling of the palatalized consonants. First imitate them as you hear them and then read aloud.

спасибо	/spaṣíba/	здесь	/ẓḍéṣ/	большой	/baḷšóy/
где	/gḍé/	книги	/ḵníɡi/	вы видите	/ví víḍiṭi/
ресторан	/ṛistarán/	письмо	/piṣmó/	улица	/úḷica/
налево	/naḷeva/	учитель	/učíṭiḷ/	очень	/očiṇ/
гостиница	/gaṣṭíṇica/	всю	/fṣu/		

CONVERSATION 4

Meeting the guide

In the hall of the Ukraina Hotel Mary Smith from Boston meets the Intourist guide who is going to show her the city.

CONVERSATION UNIT FOUR ━━━━━━

OLGA	[1]	Are you Mary Smith?
MARY	[2]	Yes. And are you my interpreter?
OLGA	[3]	Yes, I am the interpreter.
MARY	[4]	What is your name?
OLGA	[5]	My name is Olga.
MARY	[6]	Pleased to meet you (Very pleasant).
OLGA	[7]	Are you an American?
MARY	[8]	Yes, I'm an American.
OLGA	[9]	You speak Russian very well.
MARY	[10]	I understand Russian, but I don't speak it very fluently.
OLGA	[11]	Are you from New York?
MARY	[12]	No, I'm from Boston, but my sisters live in New York.
OLGA	[13]	Are you here for the first time?
MARY	[14]	Yes, for the first time.
OLGA	[15]	We can take a trip around the city.
MARY	[16]	That will be fine.

NOTES

1 **Перево́дчица** literally means "interpreter".

4 **Ка́к ва́с зову́т?** literally means "how do they call you?"

NEW NOUNS

The nominative singular forms of the new nouns from this lesson are:

Masculine		*Feminine I*	
Нью-Йо́рк	New York	О́льга	Olga
Босто́н	Boston	перево́дчица	interpreter (*f.*)
го́род	city	сестра́	sister
раз	time		

28

Туристка и переводчица

ÓЛЬГА
[ólga]

¹ Вы́ Мэ́ри Сми́т?
[ví méṛi ṣṃít?]

МЭ́РИ
[méṛi]

² Да́. А вы́ моя́ перево́дчица?
[a ví mayá piṛivótčica?]

ÓЛЬГА

³ Да́, я́ перево́дчица.
[dá, yá piṛivótčica.]

МЭ́РИ

⁴ Ка́к ва́с зову́т?
[kák váz zavút?]

ÓЛЬГА

⁵ Меня́ зову́т Óльга.
[ṃiṇá zavút ólga.]

МЭ́РИ

⁶ Óчень прия́тно.
[óčiṇ pṛiyátna.]

ÓЛЬГА

⁷ Вы́ америка́нка?
[ví aṃiṛikánka?]

МЭ́РИ

⁸ Да́, я́ америка́нка.
[dá, yá aṃiṛikánka.]

ÓЛЬГА

⁹ Вы́ о́чень хорошо́ говори́те по-ру́сски.
[ví óčiṇ xarašó gavaṛíṭi pa rúsḳi.]

МЭ́РИ

¹⁰ Я́ понима́ю по-ру́сски, но́ не о́чень свобо́дно говорю́.
[yá paṇimáyu pa rúsḳi, nó ṇi óčiṇ svabódna gavaṛú.]

ÓЛЬГА

¹¹ Вы́ из Нью-Йо́рка?
[ví iz ṇyu yórka?]

МЭ́РИ

¹² Не́т, я́ из Босто́на, а мои́ сёстры живу́т в Нью-Йо́рке.
[ṇét, yá iz bastóna, a mayí ṣóstri živút v ṇyú yórḳi.]

ÓЛЬГА

¹³ Вы́ в пе́рвый ра́з зде́сь?
[ví f péṛviy ráz ẓḍéṣ?]

МЭ́РИ

¹⁴ Да́, в пе́рвый ра́з.
[dá f péṛviy rás.]

ÓЛЬГА

¹⁵ Мы́ мо́жем пое́хать по го́роду.
[mí móžim payéxaṭ pa góradu.]

МЭ́РИ

¹⁶ Это бу́дет о́чень хорошо́.
[éta búḍit óčiṇ xarašó.]

УПРАЖНÉНИЯ (EXERCISES)

A. Read all of *Pronunciation Sections* **4.3** and **4.4** and perform *Drills* **27** through **32**.

B. Say in Russian:

1. Are you Mary Smith? 2. And are you my interpreter? 3. Yes, I am the interpreter. 4. What is your name? 5. My name is Olga. 6. Pleased to meet you (Very pleasant). 7. Are you an American? 8. Yes, I'm an American. 9. You speak Russian very well. 10. I understand Russian, but I don't speak it very fluently. 11. Are you from New York? 12. No. I'm from Boston, but my sisters live in New York. 13. Are you here for the first time? 14. Yes, for the first time. 15. We can take a trip around the city. 16. That will be fine.

C. Give the Russian equivalents:

MODEL: This is a station — **Э́то вокза́л.**

¹ a letter
² a hotel
³ a student (two ways)
⁴ the Kremlin
⁵ a restaurant
⁶ a theater
⁷ a teacher (two ways)
⁸ a tourist
⁹ my wife
¹⁰ New York
¹¹ Boston
¹² Olga
¹³ an interpreter (*f.*)
¹⁴ a post office

D. Give the Russian equivalents:

1. Do you understand? 2. Do you understand Russian? 3. I understand. 4. I don't understand. 5. I don't understand Russian. 6. I understand Russian very well. 7. I speak Russian. 8. I don't speak Russian. 9. I don't speak Russian very well. 10. I don't speak Russian very fluently. 11. I often speak Russian. 12. You speak Russian very well.

13. Are you a Russian? 14. No, I'm an American. 15. Olga is an American. 16. Olga is an interpreter. 17. The interpreter is a Russian. 18. My wife is a Russian. 19. Ivan is a tourist. 20. Ivan is an American. 21. Ivan's not an American, he's a Russian. 22. My wife's not a Russian, she's an American.

E. READING EXERCISE

Read the following sentences aloud:

1. Где́ вокза́л? 2. Где́ рестора́н? 3. Где́ гости́ница? 4. Где́ письмо́? 5. Э́то рестора́н. 6. Э́то теа́тр. 7. Э́то Кре́мль. 8. Ива́н-студе́нт. 9. О́льга-студе́нтка. 10. Ива́н-ру́сский. 11. О́льга-ру́сская. 12. Ива́н-америка́нец. 13. О́льга-америка́нка. 14. О́льга-перево́дчица. 15. Ива́н-тури́ст. 16. Вы́ понима́ете? 17. Да́, я́ понима́ю. 18. Не́т, я́ не понима́ю. 19. Я́ понима́ю по-англи́йски. 20. Вы́ говори́те по-англи́йски? 21. Я́ говорю́ по-ру́сски.

GRAMMAR UNIT TWO

◑ 1. The Writing of the Vowels

It was pointed out in *Grammar Unit One* that there are two written letters for each of the five vowel sounds of Russian, and the first basic principle of the Russian writing system was expounded: a stressed vowel sound is written with one vowel letter to indicate that a preceding consonant is plain, and is written with the other vowel letter to indicate that the preceding consonant is palatalized.

To this point we have dealt only with *stressed* vowels. Now we shall consider the pronunciation of *unstressed* vowels and the way they are written in Russian.

1.1 The Pronunciation of Unstressed Vowels in Russian

Compare the writing and the pronunciation of the masculine singular pronoun of the third person: **óн** *he, it* = /ón/. Note: (1) the stem vowel is stressed; (2) it is pronounced /o/; (3) it is written **o.**

Now compare the writing and the pronunciation of the feminine singular pronoun of the third person: **онá** *she, it* = /aná/. (The pronoun is composed of the stem **он** plus the ending **a.**) Note: (1) the stem vowel is unstressed; (2) it is pronounced /a/; but (3) it is written **o.**

These words **óн** and **онá** illustrate shift of stress from the stem vowel **o** in the first word to the ending in the second. The shift of stress, in words, may also be from the ending to the stem. Compare the pronunciation of the letter **o** in the three neuter nouns that follow:

письмó	/piṣmó/	*letter*
окнó	/aknó/	*window*
BUT: слóво	/slóva/	*word*

In **онá** the "Basic Vowel" sound *O* of the stem weakens in pronunciation, to /a/ due to the shift in stress to the ending. In the neuter noun слóво /slóva/, the "Basic Vowel" sound *O* of the ending weakens in pronunciation to /a/ due to the shift of stress from the ending to the stem. This weakening of the "Basic Vowel" sound when stress is removed from it is a regular feature of the Russian language. In any grammatical form, whether stem or ending, the stressed vowel /o/ will automatically be pronounced /a/ if stress moves away from it.[1] A convenient way of stating this change is to say that the Basic Vowel *O* is weakened. We will, then, add to our transcription the symbol *O* (capital letter and italic type) which will stand for the sound /o/ when stressed and /a/ when unstressed.

---

[1] *EXCEPTION:* provided it does not follow a palatalized consonant. But, more about this later.

31

1.2   Writing the Unstressed Vowels

We have seen that the third person pronouns **óн** and **она́** have the Basic Vowel O in their stem, and that this vowel is pronounced /o/ when stressed and /a/ when unstressed. But note: stressed or unstressed, this Basic Vowel O is written as it was written when stressed: **óн, она́.** We conclude, then, that in Russian, unstressed vowels are written with the letter that represents the sound they would have if stressed. And we may now state that fact as the second basic principle of the Russian writing system: *A vowel letter in Russian represents the basic sound, that is, the sound it would have if stressed.*

This principle is not so strange for speakers of English as it might first seem, for it is the principle that is also employed in writing our language. For instance, a speaker of Russian might well ask why *metal* and *hospital* are spelled with *-al* rather than *-il* as in *civil*, since most Americans pronounce the endings for all three words in exactly the same way. If we were called upon to explain this and had considered the problem we would answer that the Basic Vowel *A* was pronounced /a/ and written *a* when under stress, as in *hospitálity* and *metállic*, and that the pronunciation of *A* weakened to /i/ when stress moved elsewhere in the word (*métal, hóspital*). But, that *we retained the spelling of the vowel as if it were under stress.*

The main difference between the Russian and English systems of writing basic vowels is that the Russian system is simpler and more consistent.

Consider the actual sound values of the five Basic Vowels in the various unstressed positions, as indicated in the chart which follows:

ACTUAL SOUND VALUES OF THE BASIC VOWELS IN UNSTRESSED POSITIONS[1]				
BASIC VOWEL	Initially and after plain consonant (except /š ž/)	After palatalized consonant and /š ž/	At the end of a word when after /š ž y/	BASIC VOWEL
I				I
E		/i/		E
A	/a/			A
O			/a/	O
U		/u/		U

[1] This chart is incomplete in several respects; partly because some speakers have minor variations in pronunciation, and partly because some words in the language deviate from the chart. The number of deviations in any case is extremely small and need not concern the beginning student.

For the writing of unstressed vowels, remember: unstressed vowels are written with the letter that represents the sound they would have if stressed. Therefore, for the writing of the unstressed vowels see the charts and explanation of the writing of stressed vowels already presented in Grammar Unit 1.

If you will study the section on pronunciation of vowels (*Pronunciation Section* 4) and also the preceding section on the writing of vowels, you will see that the vowel *sound* used in *speaking* depends, for the most part, on:

(1) the type of consonant sound that precedes the written vowel, and

(2) the position of stress.

On the other hand, the particular *letter* used in *writing* Russian vowels depends on:

(1) the type of consonant that precedes the written vowel, and

(2) the basic vowel that is to be indicated.

It does not depend on the position of stress (with the exception of the symbol **ё** which is not normally used in Russian books).

A very practical over-simplification for making the appropriate sounds when reading Russian from the printed page is the following statement:

(1) the letter **о**, **а**, when unstressed, are both pronounced /a/.

(2) the letters **и**, **е**, **я**, when unstressed, are all pronounced /i/.

(3) for details in final position and after the non-paired consonants **щ**, **ш**, **ж**, **ц**, **ч**, see the preceding charts.

In the following examples note the pronunciation of the unstressed vowels:

слóво	/slóva/	*word*
ýлица	/úḷica/	*street*
гостúница	/gasṭíṇica/	*hotel*
напрóтив	/napróṭif/	*opposite*
вокзáл	/vagzál/	*station*
кафé	/kafé/	*cafe*

1.3 Writing the Sound /y/

The only independent letter in Russian used to represent the sound /y/ is **й** (**й** краткое/i krátkaya/). This letter, however, is used only at the end of a word or before a consonant:

большóй	/baḷsóy/	*big*
открóйте	/atkróyṭi/	*open!*

33

Before a vowel, the presence of the /y/ sound is indicated by writing the vowel letter that is otherwise used to indicate that the preceding consonant is palatalized, thus: /yi¹/ = **и**; /ye/ = **е**; /ya/ = **я**; /yo/ = **ё**; and /yu/ = **ю**.

INITIAL /y/ + VOWEL

я	/yá/	*I*
е́сть	/yéṣṭ/	*there is, there are*
ю́г	/yúk/	*south*
ёлка	/yólka/	*fir tree*

VOWEL + /y/ + VOWEL

мо**я**	/mayá/	*my*
зн**а́ю**	/znáyu/	*I know*
понима́**е**те	/paṇimáyiṭi/	*you understand*
м**ой**	/mayí/	*my*

But, if /y/ sound + VOWEL is preceded by a consonant, how does Russian indicate the palatalization or plainness of the consonant? Very simply:

If /y/ + VOWEL is preceded by a palatalized consonant, the palatalization of the consonant is indicated by inserting **ь** (мягкий знак) after the consonant:

семь**я**   /ṣiṃyá/

If /y/ + VOWEL is preceded by a plain consonant, the plainness of the consonant is indicated by inserting **ъ** (твёрдый знак /tyórdiy znák/) after the consonant:

о**бъ**ём   /abyóm/

The letter **ъ** (твёрдый знак) is used in only this one situation: to indicate a plain consonant that is followed by the sound of /y/. The number of items in which it is necessary to write it is very small.²

The use of the твёрдый знак to represent plain consonants before /y/ parallels the use of the мягкий знак to represent palatalized consonants before /y/. We have then, in writing consonant plus vowel, a four-way combination in Russian:

---

¹ The letter **и** is exceptional in that it represents the vowel sound /i/ rather than /yi/ when it occurs at the beginning of a word. This spelling is possible because the other letter for the vowel sound /i/, **ы**, never occurs at the beginning of a word. (For some speakers of Russian the letter **и** does represent initial /yi/, but only in certain forms of the third person pronoun **йм, йх, йми**.)

² A small number of words are spelled in a manner that is inconsistent with the preceding statements. For example, the second word in *New York* is written **Йо́рк** /yórk/ although you would expect the letter **ё** in initial position, as in **ёлка** /yólka/ *fir tree*. Similarly, the word for *region* is written **райо́н** /rayón/ although you would expect the letter **ё** in this position, as in **мое́** /mayó/ *my*.

Plain consonant plus vowel

бо́ /bó/ : бо́мба /bómba/ *bomb*

Palatalized consonant plus vowel

бё /bo/ : гребём /gribóm/ *we row*

Palatalized consonant plus /y/ plus vowel

бьё /byo/ : убьём /ubyóm/ *we will kill*

Plain consonant plus /y/ plus vowel

бъё /byo/ : объём /abyóm/ *volume*

2. The Nominative Case

2.1 The Nominative Plural Forms of Nouns

The chart that follows gives a comparative picture of the endings of the nominative singular (studied in Grammar Unit One) and those of the nominative plural.

NOMINATIVE CASE ENDINGS: in terms of Basic Vowels				
	MASCULINE	NEUTER	FEMININE I	FEMININE II
SINGULAR	——	*-O*	*-A*	——
PLURAL	*-I (-A)*	*-A*	*-I*	*-I*

Depending upon the rules of spelling already established (that is, whether the consonant that precedes the ending is palatalized or plain, and whether or not a /y/ sound precedes it) the nominative plural endings are written as follows, whether stressed or unstressed:

$$-A = \text{а } or \text{ я}$$
$$-I = \text{ы } or \text{ и}$$

It should be noted, before we consider the nominative forms of all the nouns that we have thus far met, that the position of stress may change from the singular of a noun to the plural. This is illustrated in письмо́ > пи́сьма; сло́во > слова́; жена́ > жёны; сестра́ > сёстры; etc. This change of stress is not predictable and must be learned with individual nouns. However, while shift in stress occurs with high frequency in neuter nouns of two syllables, the great majority of Russian nouns show no shift in stress.

35

NOUNS SO FAR MET

Masculine: The nominative singular ends in a consonant.

(*a*) Masculine nouns with nominative plural in -*I*, written **ы** or **и**:

рестора́н	рестора́ны	*restaurant*
вокза́л	вокза́лы	*station*
Ива́н		*Ivan*
студе́нт	студе́нты	*student*
теа́тр	теа́тры	*theater*
Кре́мль		*Kremlin*
америка́нец	америка́нцы[1]	*American*
граждани́н	гра́ждане[2]	*Mr.*

(*b*) Masculine nouns with nominative plural in -*A*, written **a** or **я**:

учи́тель	учителя́	*teacher*
го́род	города́	*city*
господи́н	господа́	*Mr.*

The number of masculine nouns with nominative plural in -*A* is small. The first two nouns show shift in stress. The third, **господи́н**, has an irregular plural in which the **-ин** of the singular has been lost.

Neuter: The nominative singular ends in the Basic Vowel -*O*, written **o**, **e**, or **ё**. The nominative plural ends in the Basic Vowel -*A*, written **a** or **я**.

зда́ние зда́ния *building*

NEUTER nouns with shift in stress:

письмо́	пи́сьма	*letter*
сло́во	слова́	*word*

BORROWED neuter noun, showing no change for case or number:

кафе́ кафе́ *cafe*

Feminine, Class I: The nominative singular ends in the Basic Vowel -*A*, written **a** or **я**. The nominative plural ends in the Basic Vowel -*I*, written **ы** or **и**.

гости́ница	гости́ницы	*hotel*
кни́га	кни́ги	*book*
фра́за	фра́зы	*sentence*
учи́тельница	учи́тельницы	*teacher*
гражда́нка	гражда́нки	*Miss, Mrs.*
студе́нтка	студе́нтки	*student*

---

[1] This noun shows a consistent change in its stem which will be discussed in later units.
[2] Note that the plural of this noun is irregular.

у́лица	у́лицы	*street*
америка́нка	америка́нки	*American*
перево́дчица	перево́дчицы	*interpreter*
госпожа́	госпожи́	*Miss, Mrs.*
О́льга		*Olga*
де́вушка	де́вушки	*girl*
по́чта		*post office*

Feminine I nouns with shift in stress:

жена́	жёны	*wife*
сестра́	сёстры	*sister*[1]

2.2 The nominative case forms of "Special Adjectives"

There is a small group of words in Russian which we may call "Special Adjectives" which follow a particular inflectional pattern. Of these "Special Adjectives" we have met:

э́тот /état/ *this, that*
мо́й /móy/ *my*

"Special Adjectives", like adjectives in general, in Russian, agree in gender, case and number with the noun they modify or refer to. For example, if a noun is nominative singular and feminine the adjective meaning "my" has the form **моя́**: моя́ жена́ *my wife*. If the noun is nominative, singular, but masculine this adjective must then have the form **мо́й**: **мо́й учи́тель** *my teacher*.

The adjective is thus said to "agree" with the noun.

The following chart shows the endings of the "Special Adjectives" in the nominative singular and plural and gives, as examples, these forms of the adjectives **э́тот** and **мо́й**.

NOMINATIVE CASE ENDINGS: Special Adjectives			
SINGULAR			PLURAL
MASCULINE	NEUTER	FEMININE	ALL GENDERS
— (Consonant)	-*O*	-*A*	-*I*
э́тот /état/ мо́й /móy/	э́то /éta/ моё /mayó/	э́та /éta/ моя́ /mayá/	э́ти /éṭi/ мои́ /mayí/

---

[1] The words **ру́сский** and **ру́сская,** although used as nouns have the forms of ordinary adjectives and will not be discussed until the treatment of ordinary adjectives in *Grammar Unit Five.*

Regarding the ENDINGS: (1) The nominative singular endings of masculine and neuter Special Adjectives are the same as the nominative singular endings of masculine and neuter nouns. (2) The feminine singular Special Adjective has only one ending, -*A*, whether the noun which it modifies be of Class I or Class II. (3) The nominative plural Special Adjective has only one ending, -*I*, whether the noun which it modifies be masculine, feminine or neuter.

Regarding the examples **э́тот** and **мо́й**: (1) The stem of **э́тот** is **эт-**: but the nominative singular masculine has the irregular form **э́тот**. (2) The stress remains constant on the stem of the special adjective **э́тот** in all forms of the nominative case, but in **мо́й** the stress shifts to the ending in all but the nominative singular masculine form. (3) The stem of the word **мо́й** is /moy-/. The stem ends in the consonant sound /y/ to which the regular endings are added, producing /may-á/, /may-ó/, /may-í/. Due to the two methods of writing the consonant sound /y/ in Russian, the Russian writing system does not show the endings (consonant, -*A*, -*O*, -*I*) as clearly as does the transcription. (4) It is a peculiarity of all special adjectives that the final consonant of the stem will be palatalized in the plural if possible, as in **э́ти** /éṭi/. This accounts for the spelling **и** for the plural ending *I* rather than the spelling **ы**.

Study and pronounce aloud the following examples:

э́тот студе́нт	*this student*	э́ти студе́нты	*these students*
мо́й студе́нт	*my student*	мои́ студе́нты	*my students*
э́то зда́ние	*this building*	э́ти зда́ния	*these buildings*
моё зда́ние	*my building*	мои́ зда́ния	*my buildings*
э́та кни́га	*this book*	э́ти кни́ги	*these books*
моя́ кни́га	*my book*	мои́ кни́ги	*my books*

2.2.1   Special Use of the Neuter Form **э́то**.

Э́то, the neuter form of the adjective **э́тот**, **э́та**, **э́то**, **э́ти**, is used with no variation for gender or number to mean *this is, that is, these are, those are:*

Э́то мо́й студе́нт.	*This is my student. (Or: That is...)*
Э́то мои́ студе́нты.	*These are my students. (Or: Those are...)*
Э́то моё зда́ние.	*This is my building. (Or: That is...)*
Э́то мои́ зда́ния.	*These are my buildings. (Or: Those are...)*
Э́то моя́ кни́га.	*This is my book. (Or: That is...)*
Э́то мои́ кни́ги.	*These are my books. (Or: Those are...)*

Now, compare:

э́тот рестора́н	/état.../	*this restaurant*
Э́то — рестора́н.	/éta.../	*This is a restaurant.*
э́та гости́ница	/éta.../	*this hotel*
Э́то — гости́ница.	/éta.../	*This is a hotel.*
Э́то — мои́ кни́ги.	/éta.../	*These are my books.*

Э́то, meaning *this is, that is, these are, those are*, is quite different in sound and spelling from the masculine singular and plural forms of the special adjective: **э́тот** /état/; **э́ти** /éṭi/. However, compare both sound and spelling with the feminine and neuter forms of the special adjective:

э́то /éta/ *this is, that is, these are, those are*

DIFFERENT IN SPELLING BUT IDENTICAL IN PRONUNCIATION

э́та /éta/ (Feminine singular) *this, that*

IDENTICAL IN SPELLING AND IDENTICAL IN PRONUNCIATION

э́то /éta/ (Neuter singular) *this, that*

However, in spoken Russian there is no confusion. The words **э́то письмо́** are spoken as a single phrase with a single primary stress, whereas **Э́то—письмо́** is spoken as two phrases with two primary stresses (cf. *Pronunciation Section* **5**). Moreover, in the writing system it is permissible, but not necessary, to distinguish these two types of expressions by writing a dash after **э́то** meaning *this is* (*that is, these are, those are*). The dash should also be used in equational sentences composed of two nouns, e.g.

Ива́н — тури́ст.   Ivan is a tourist.
Э́то зда́ние — Большо́й теа́тр.   That building is the Bolshoy Theater.

2.3 Nominative Case Forms of the Personal Pronouns

Pronouns have the following forms in the nominative case:

	SINGULAR			PLURAL		
FIRST PERSON	**я**	/yá/	I	**мы**	/mí/	we
SECOND PERSON	**ты**	/ṭí/[1]	you	**вы**	/ví/	you
THIRD PERSON	**он**	/ón/	he, it	**они́**	/aṇí/	they
	она́	/aná/	she, it			
	оно́	/anó/	it			

The third person pronoun has endings identical with those of the special adjectives: **óн** /ón/ *he, it,* **онó** /anó/ *it;* **онá** /aná/ *she, it,* and **они́** /aṇí/ *they.*

---

[1] The pronoun **ты** /ṭí/, *you,* in the above paradigm will not be needed by the beginning student since it is used only in very special circumstances, i.e., with children, intimate friends, relatives and pets.

☯ 3.   The Non-Past Tense Form of Verbs

Verbs like **живу́т** /živút/ *they live* are frequently said to be in "the present tense", while others like **бу́дут** /búdut/, equivalent to *will be*, are said to be in the "future". In Russian, the endings of both types of verbs are the same and the term *"non-past"* is used in this book to describe them. The meaning of all the verbs treated in this unit except **бу́дут** is, however, present time, equivalent to the English verb forms *speak, am speaking, do speak*.

3.1   The Forms of the Non-Past Tense

The non-past tense in Russian is inflected for person and number. There are six forms: first, second and third person singular and first, second and third person plural.

All Russian verbs except four (*see* Appendix), have one of two types of endings hereafter referred to as Type I and Type II.

3.1.1   The Non-Past Tense: Verbs with Type I Endings

NON-PAST TENSE: Type I Verbs		
PERSON	SINGULAR	PLURAL
1st	-*U*	-*O*m
2nd	-*O*š	-*O*ţi
3rd	-*O*t	-*U*t

The spelling of the vowel in the first person singular is identical to that of the third plural for Type I verbs. If the letter preceding the ending is a vowel letter, the third plural is always **-ют**; if a consonant, usually **-ут**, rarely **-ют**. This is in accordance with the usual rules of spelling, since the stem final consonant of most Type I verbs is plain and the stem final consonant of very few Type I verbs is palatalized.

In all the other endings, a consonant preceding the ending (if there is a preceding consonant) will be palatalized where possible. Hence the endings /-Oš/, /-Ot/, /-Om/ and /-Oţi/ will always be written with the letters **ё** when stressed, and **e** when unstressed.

Examples of Type I Verbs:

STRESSED ENDINGS

я	живу́	/živú/	*I live*
ты́	живёшь	/žiγóš/	*you live*
о́н			*he lives*
она́	живёт	/žiγót/	*she lives*
оно́			*it lives*
мы́	живём	/žiγóm/	*we live*
вы́	живёте	/žiγóṭi/	*you live*
они́	живу́т	/živút/	*they live*

UNSTRESSED ENDINGS

я	зна́ю	/znáyu/	*I know*
ты́	зна́ешь	/znáyiš/	*you know*
о́н			*he knows*
она́	зна́ет	/znáyit/	*she knows*
оно́			*it knows*
мы́	зна́ем	/znáyim/	*we know*
вы́	зна́ете	/znáyiṭi/	*you know*
они́	зна́ют	/znáyut/	*they know*

Other Type I verbs you have had so far are:

бу́дут	(3rd pl.) *will be*
зову́т	(3rd pl.) *call*
понима́ют	(3rd pl.) *understand*

3.1.2 The Non-Past Tense: Type II Verbs

<table>
<tr><th colspan="3">NON-PAST TENSE: Type II Verbs</th></tr>
<tr><th>PERSON</th><th>SINGULAR</th><th>PLURAL</th></tr>
<tr><td>1st</td><td>-U</td><td>-Im</td></tr>
<tr><td>2nd</td><td>-Iš</td><td>-Iṭi</td></tr>
<tr><td>3rd</td><td>-It</td><td>-At</td></tr>
</table>

The consonant preceding these endings (if a consonant does precede the ending) will always be palatalized if possible. Thus, the ending -U of the first singular and the ending -At of the third plural will be written **-у** and **-ат** after the consonants **ш, ж, ч, щ,** and will be written **-ю** and **-ят** respectively

41

under all other conditions. The Basic Vowel -I- of the other four forms will always be written with the letter **и**.

EXAMPLES OF TYPE II VERBS:

STRESSED ENDINGS

я	говорю́	/gavarú/	*I speak*
ты́	говори́шь	/gavaríš/	*you speak*
о́н			*he speaks*
она́	говори́т	/gavarít/	*she speaks*
оно́			*it speaks*
мы́	говори́м	/gavarím/	*we speak*
вы́	говори́те	/gavaríti/	*you speak*
они́	говоря́т	/gavarát/	*they speak*

UNSTRESSED ENDINGS

я	ви́жу	/yížu/	*I see*
ты́	ви́дишь	/yídiš/	*you see*
о́н			*he sees*
она́	ви́дит	/yídit/	*she sees*
оно́			*it sees*
мы́	ви́дим	/yídim/	*we see*
вы́	ви́дите	/yíditi/	*you see*
они́	ви́дят	/yídit/	*they see*

The second singular of verbs of both Type I and Type II is written with the letter **ь** after the **ш**. The letter **ш** always represents a plain consonant, so that **ь** here is completely meaningless. But it is the conventional spelling and must be written.

3.1.3 Stress in the Non-Past Tense

The position in which stress may occur in Non-Past forms of verbs is one of the following:

(1) on the stem for all six forms,

(2) on the ending for all six forms,

(3) on the ending in the first person singular, and on the stem of the other five forms.

These are the only three possibilities for position of stress in Russian verbs (except for the four irregular verbs not of Type I or of Type II mentioned at the beginning of this section.)

3.1.4 Predicting the Forms of the Non-Past Tense

From the third person plural of the verb you can determine whether the verb is of Type I or of Type II; you can further predict the other Non-Past forms, although you cannot always predict the position of stress in the first person singular. You should, therefore, learn the third person plural Non-Past form on first meeting any verb. This is the form that will be given to you as you meet new verbs in succeeding conversations in this book. In addition you will also be given the first person singular form of those verbs which have the stress on the ending in that person but on the stem in the other five forms of the Non-Past tense. Some verbs of Type II have a stem in the first person singular which is different from that of the other five forms; thus **ви́жу**, **ви́дишь**, etc. For all such verbs you will also be given the first person singular form (cf. *Appendix*).

In answering a question it is customary, although not necessary, to repeat the verb form without an accompanying pronoun. In addition, instead of answering a question by a simple **да** or **нет**, one often adds something, such as a repetition of the verb, just as in English we say "*Yes, I do*," or "*No, I don't*". For example:

— Вы́ ви́дите э́то зда́ние?   — Do you see that building?
— Да́, **ви́жу**.   — Yes, *I do.* [*I see*].

— Вы́ понима́ете по-ру́сски?   — Do you understand Russian?
— Не́т, **не понима́ю**,   — No, *I don't.* [I don't understand]

4. The Negative Particle не

This particle (stressed form /ńé/, but usually occurring unstressed, /ńi/) negates the immediately following word, whether a verb or some other part of speech.

Óн **не** говори́т по-ру́сски.   He doesn't speak Russian.
Э́то **не** рестора́н.   That's *not* a restaurant.

УПРАЖНÉНИЯ

A. Read all of *Pronounciation Section* **5** and perform *Drills* **33** through **35** and also **21**.

B. Transform orally from singular to plural according to the model:

MODEL: Э́то рестора́н.   **Э́то рестора́ны.**

¹ письмо́	⁶ у́лица	¹¹ учи́тельница
² тури́ст	⁷ учи́тель	¹² студе́нт
³ кни́га	⁸ гости́ница	¹³ зда́ние
⁴ вокза́л	⁹ студе́нтка	¹⁴ го́род
⁵ америка́нец	¹⁰ теа́тр	¹⁵ перево́дчица

43

C. Transform orally from singular to plural according to the model:

MODEL: Рестора́н напро́тив. **Рестора́ны напро́тив.**

¹ Где́ гости́ница?
² Учи́тель—америка́нец.
³ Учи́тельница—америка́нка.
⁴ Студе́нт—тури́ст.

⁵ Тури́ст—америка́нец.
⁶ Теа́тр здесь.
⁷ Письмо́ то́же здесь.
⁸ Где́ кни́га?

D. Substitute orally **мо́й, моя́, моё, мои́:**

MODEL: Где́ . . . кни́га? **Где́ моя́ кни́га?**

¹ учи́тель?
² гости́ница?
³ пи́сьма?
⁴ учи́тельница?

⁵ кни́ги?
⁶ жена́?
⁷ студе́нты?

⁸ письмо́?
⁹ сёстры?
¹⁰ перево́дчица?

E. (1) Listen to each of the following sentences and transform to first person singular (**Я** . . . . .).
(2) Now repeat the exercise, transforming to third person singular (**Он** . . . . .). Then transform to first plural **Мы** . . .) and second plural (**Вы** . . . .).

MODEL: Они́ говоря́т по-ру́сски. **Я́ говорю́ по-ру́сски.**

¹ Они́ понима́ют по-ру́сски.
² Они́ ви́дят э́то зда́ние.
³ Они́ не зна́ют.

⁴ Они́ живу́т здесь.
⁵ Они́ бу́дут та́м.

F. READING EXERCISE

Listen to each of the following words and mimic its pronunciation. Then read the words aloud. (Note that the letters **o** and **a** are pronounced the same when unstressed.)

вода́	water		города́	cities
сама́	she herself		табака́	of tobacco
гора́	hill		пи́во	beer
дала́	she gave		да́ма	lady
дома́	houses		сло́во	word
даду́т	will give		бра́та	of brother
молоко́	milk		э́том	this, that
каранда́ш	pencil		жёнам	to wives

In the following forms note the weakening of vowels as the stress shifts.

во́ду	*water*	сло́во	*word*	са́м	*self*
вода́	*water*	слова́	*words*	сама́	*self*
до́м	*house*	хоро́ш	*good*	да́л	*he gave*
дома́	*houses*	хорошо́	*well*	дала́	*she gave*
го́род	*city*	хо́лод	*cold*	бра́л	*he took*
города́	*cities*	холо́дный	*cold*	брала́	*she took*
		холода́	*cold spells*		

G. READING EXERCISE

Perform as you performed the preceding exercise. Note that the letters **е, я** and **и** in unstressed position do not differ from each other in pronunciation in normal conversational style.

нести́	*carry*	ещё	*still*
пяти́	*of five*	язы́к	*language*
пишу́	*I write*	сиде́ть	*sit*
сестра́	*sister*	земля́	*land*
тяну́ть	*pull*	взяла́	*she took*
никто́	*no one*	мила́	*nice*

In the following forms note the weakening of vowels as the stress shifts.

пя́ть	*five*	жёны	*wives*
пяти́	*of five*	жена́	*wife*
взя́л	*he took*	сёстры	*sisters*
взяла́	*she took*	сестра́	*sister*
тя́нет	*pulls*	Пётр	*Peter*
тяну́	*I pull*	Петра́	*Peter's*
де́ти	*children*	пи́шет	*writes*
детей	*children's*	пишу́	*I write*
де́ло	*affair*	ми́ло	*nice*
дела́	*affairs*	мила́	*nice*
всё	*all*		
всегда́	*always*		

45

REVIEW LESSON ONE

A. FLUENCY DRILL

1. Where is the theater? 2. Is that building the Bolshoy theater? 3. No, that's a hotel. 4. The theater's over there on the left. 5. The Kremlin's on the right. 6. Do you see that building? 7. That's the station. 8. I'm a tourist. 9. My name's John. 10. What's your name?

11. My name is Olga. 12. I'm an interpreter. 13. That girl's an interpreter. 14. This girl's a student. 15. My sister's a teacher. 16. Ivan's a Russian. 17. He's a student. 18. He speaks English but not Russian. 19. My wife speaks English well. 20. The interpreter speaks Russian fluently.

21. These interpreters speak English fluently. 22. These tourists speak Russian fluently. 23. My sisters live there. 24. Where are my teachers? 25. Where are those cities? 26. Where are the girls? 27. Where are the tourists? 28. Where are my books? 29. Where are the Americans? 30. Where are my letters?

B. CONVERSATION TOPICS

(To derive as great a benefit as possible from conversational practice the student should try to speak as fluently as possible and use only the material learned so far. Avoid trying to say things that involve vocabulary or grammatical constructions that have not yet been presented.)

(1) A, an American tourist in Moscow, stops B on the street and asks where various things are (the hotel, the station, the Kremlin, etc.). A explains that he doesn't speak Russian fluently and he frequently asks B to repeat.

(2) An American tourist gets acquainted with nis Intourist guide. They tell each other their names and nationalities. The guide notices that the tourist speaks Russian well and the tourist mentions that his wife also speaks Russian, although not very fluently. The guide asks whether he is here for the first time; he says he is and they decide to take a trip around the city.

(3) Two people discuss their acquaintances (student, guide, teacher, etc.) and relatives (wife, sister): their nationality and what languages they speak.

CONVERSATION 5

Where do you work?

John and his friend Boris Semenov are walking on Red Square after supper at Boris' home.

CONVERSATION UNIT FIVE ————————————

JOHN	[1] What does your brother do?
BORIS	[2] He's an engineer. [3] We work together in the factory.
JOHN	[4] And does his wife Vera also work?
BORIS	[5] Yes. She does.
JOHN	[6] They say women in your country often work.
BORIS	[7] Of course. And in your country?
JOHN	[8] Yes, but less. [9] My sister works. [10] She's a teacher.
BORIS	[11] Does she live in New York?
JOHN	[12] No, she and her husband live in Boston. [13] They always talk about Boston.
BORIS	[14] Then she's married!
JOHN	[15] Yes. Her husband is a professor of Russian.
BORIS	[16] Is he Russian?
JOHN	[17] No, he's an American.

NOTES

1 **Кéм рабóтает** means literally *As whom does he work*

6 **у вác** means literally *at you.*

7 Pronounced /kaṇéšna/.

14 **знáчит**, literally, *it means.*
зáмужем *married*, is used only of women. Note the root -**муж**- *husband*, in this word.

15 **профéссор рýсского языкá** means Russian professor only in the sense of professor of the Russian language. "Russian professor" in the sense of a professor from Russia is **рýсский профéссор**. Note the pronunciation /v/ for the letter **г** in **рýсского**.

ADDITIONAL VOCABULARY:

нáш *our*

_____ Где вы работаете?

ДЖО́Н ¹ Ке́м рабо́тает ва́ш бра́т?

БОРИ́С ² О́н инжене́р. ³ Мы́ рабо́таем вме́сте на фа́брике.

ДЖО́Н ⁴ И его́ жена́ Ве́ра то́же рабо́тает? _его́ → pronounced /ево́/_

БОРИ́С ⁵ Да́. Она́ рабо́тает.

ДЖО́Н ⁶ Говоря́т, что же́нщины у вас ча́сто рабо́тают.

БОРИ́С ⁷ Коне́чно. А у ва́с?

ДЖО́Н ⁸ Да́, но́ ме́ньше. ⁹ Моя́ сестра́ рабо́тает. ¹⁰ Она́ учи-
тельни́ца.

БОРИ́С ¹¹ Она́ живёт в Нью-Йо́рке?

ДЖО́Н ¹² Не́т, она́ и её му́ж живу́т в Босто́не. ¹³ Они́ всегда́
говоря́т о Босто́не.

БОРИ́С ¹⁴ Зна́чит, она́ за́мужем!

ДЖО́Н ¹⁵ Да́. Её му́ж профе́ссор-ру́сского-языка́.

БОРИ́С ¹⁶ О́н ру́сский?

ДЖО́Н ¹⁷ Не́т, о́н америка́нец.

NEW SPECIAL ADJECTIVES

ва́ш, **на́ш** are two more special adjectives (cf. *Grammar Unit* **2**:**2.2**) and have the regular forms ва́ш, ва́ша, ва́ше, ва́ши; на́ш, на́ша, на́ше, на́ши.

The forms **его́** *his*, **её** *her*, and **и́х** *their*, although semantically parallel to the special adjectives **мо́й** *my*, **ва́ш** *your*, **на́ш** *our*, are not special adjectives since they do not agree in gender and number with the following noun, e.g. его́ бра́т, его́ сестра́, его́ сёстры. Note the pronunciation /v/ for the letter **г** in **его́**.

NEW VERBS

рабо́тают   they work

The letter **ю** in this third plural form marks this verb as Type I.

NEW NOUNS

MASCULINE

Singular	Plural	
Бори́с		Boris
инжене́р	инжене́ры	engineer
язы́к	языки́	language
профе́ссор	профессора́	professor
му́ж	мужья́	husband
бра́т	бра́тья	brother

FEMININE I

фа́брика	фа́брики	factory
же́нщина	же́нщины	woman
Ве́ра		Vera

The irregular plural **профессора́** is like **учителя́** and **города́** (*Grammar Unit* **2**:**2.1.**) **Му́ж** and **бра́т** have completely irregular plural forms.

УПРАЖНЕ́НИЯ

A. Perform *Pronunciation Drills* **5** and **13.** Then perform *Drill* **12.**

B. Say in Russian:

1. What does your brother do?   2. He's an engineer.   3. We work together in the factory.   4. And does his wife Vera also work?   5. Yes. 6. They say women in your country often work.   7. Of course.   8. And

in your country? 9. Yes, but less. 10. My sister works. 11. She's a teacher. 12. Does she live in New York? 13. No, she and her husband live in Boston. 14. They are always talking about Boston. 15. Then she's married! 16. Yes. Her husband is a professor of Russian. 17. Is he Russian? 18. No, he's an American.

C. Transform orally according to the model. Substitute the following pronouns: **он, мы, вы, они.**

MODEL: Я говорю́ по-ру́сски. **—Óн говори́т по-ру́сски.**

    1. Я живу́ в Нью-Йо́рке.
    2. Я рабо́таю на фа́брике.
    3. Я ви́жу э́то зда́ние.

D. Listen to the following questions and answer them according to the model:

MODEL: Э́то ва́ша сестра́? **— Да́, э́то моя́ сестра́.**

    1. Э́то ваш профе́ссор?   5. Э́то ва́ше письмо́?
    2. Э́то ваш бра́т?   6. Э́то ва́ша кни́га?
    3. Э́то ваш учи́тель?   7. Э́то ва́ша жена́?
    4. Э́то ва́ша учи́тельница?   8. Э́то ваш му́ж?

E. Repeat Exercise D but transform to plural: (Omit the last two items.)

    Э́то ва́ши сёстры?   — Да́, э́то мои́ сёстры.

F. Give the Russian equivalents:

1. This is my teacher (*m.*).   8. This is our teacher of Russian.
2. This is your teacher (*m.*).   9. These are your letters.
3. This is his wife.   10. These are our books.
4. This is your letter.   11. These are their books.
5. This is your hotel.   12. These are their wives.
6. This is her hotel.   13. These are our students.
7. This is their book.

G. Give the Russian equivalents:

1. What does his brother do? 2. What does his sister do? 3. They work at a factory. 4. We work at a factory. 5. He's a professor. 6. His wife

works, too.   7. My brothers work, too.   8. My brother's an engineer.   9. His brother's a teacher.   10. He lives in New York.

11. He and his wife live in New York.   12. Does your sister live in New York?   13. My sister's married.   14. Her husband's a professor.   15. Her husband's a Russian professor. (two ways)   16. The professor's an American. 17. The professors are Americans.

H. READING EXERCISE

Listen to each of the following words and imitate it. Next, read aloud the list of words in order to become familiar with their written form. Note the spelling of the /y/ sound.

эта	*this*		á	*and*
éду	*I am going*		я	*I*
éм	*I eat*		Ялта	*Yalta*
éст	*he eats*		мáя	*of May*
éсть	*to eat; is*		стóя	*standing*
Óльга	*Olga*		ýха	*ear's*
ёлка	*fir tree*		юга	*south's*
даёт	*gives*		даю́	*I give*
даём	*we give*		знáю	*I know*
приём	*reception*			
йх	*them; their*		польёт	*it will pour*
йга	*yoke's*		полёт	*flight*
стóит	*costs*			
			съéсть	*eat*
пьём	*we drink*		сéсть	*sit*
Пётр	*Peter*			
			съéл	*ate*
чьём	*whose*		сéл	*sat*
чём	*what*			
			объём	*volume*
чьегó	*whose*		убьём	*we'll kill*
чегó	*what*		гребём	*we row*

CONVERSATION 6

What do you do?

John, visiting the famous Hermitage in Leningrad has fallen into conversation with a young Russian who is much interested in life in America.

CONVERSATION UNIT SIX ⎯⎯⎯⎯⎯⎯⎯

ENGLISH EQUIVALENTS

PETER	[1] What do you do in America?
JOHN	[2] I'm a writer. [3] I write articles and books.
PETER	[4] My father likes to read English. [5] As for me, I can't.
JOHN	[6] And where does your father live? Here in Leningrad?
PETER	[7] No. He lives in Moscow, [8] but he used to live in Leningrad, too. [9] He's a chemist and my mother is a doctor.
JOHN	[10] Your mother? You say she's a doctor?
PETER	[11] Yes, she works in a hospital in Moscow.
JOHN	[12] My uncle is a doctor, too, [13] but he's always busy in the laboratory.
PETER	[14] Do you have only one uncle?
JOHN	[15] No, two. [16] The second one, [17] my mother's brother, works at the post office.
PETER	[18] Just like me?
JOHN	[19] Yes, but in a small city.

NOTES

1 Literally *what is your profession.*

5 **Я умéю** means *I can, I am able* only in the sense of having intellectual (as against physical) capability. For example, in the sentence "I can go to Moscow tomorrow", It would be impossible to use this verb.

   Cáм means literally *myself.*

10 **Онá дóктор.** Note that the word for *doctor* does not have a special form for the feminine. Cf. студéнт — студéнтка.

54

Какая ваша профессия?

ПЁТР	[1] Какая ваша профессия в Америке?
ДЖОН	[2] Я писатель. [3] Пишу статьи и книги.
ПЁТР	[4] Мой отец любит читать по-английски. [5] Сам я не умею.
ДЖОН	[6] А где живёт ваш отец? Здесь в Ленинграде?
ПЁТР	[7] Нет. Он живёт в Москве, [8] но он жил и в Ленинграде. [9] Он химик, а моя мать доктор.
ДЖОН	[10] Ваша мать? Вы говорите, что она доктор?
ПЁТР	[11] Да, она работает в больнице в Москве.
ДЖОН	[12] Мой дядя тоже доктор, [13] но он всегда занят в лаборатории.
ПЁТР	[14] У вас только один дядя?
ДЖОН	[15] Нет, два. [16] Второй, [17] брат моей матери, работает на почте.
ПЁТР	[18] Так же как и я?
ДЖОН	[19] Да, но в маленьком городе.

NEW VERBS

TYPE I

пи́шут, пишу́	write
чита́ют	read
уме́ют	can, are able

TYPE II

лю́бят, люблю́	love, like

The verb **лю́бят, люблю́** *love, like* is another example of the regular consonant alternation in the first singular of Type II verbs. Cf. **ви́дят, ви́жу** *see* and the *Appendix*.

NEW NOUNS

MASCULINE

Singular	*Plural*	
Пётр		Peter
Ленингра́д		Leningrad
хи́мик	хи́мики	chemist
писа́тель	писа́тели	writer
оте́ц	отцы́	father
до́ктор	доктора́	doctor
дя́дя	дя́ди	uncle

FEMININE I

Singular	*Plural*	
Аме́рика		America
статья́	статьи́	article
больни́ца	больни́цы	hospital
лаборато́рия	лаборато́рии	laboratory
Москва́		Moscow
профе́ссия	профе́ссии	profession

FEMININE II

Singular	*Plural*	
ма́ть	ма́тери	mother

The noun **оте́ц** shows a stem change comparable to that of **америка́нец, америка́нцы.**

There is one more masculine noun in this list with the nominative plural ending in -A: **до́ктор.**

The noun **дя́дя** has the agreement of a masculine noun (**мо́й дя́дя**) but the forms of a feminine noun.

Ма́ть has an irregular stem **матер-** in the plural.

The form **оди́н** *one, only, alone,* is a special adjective with the regular endings оди́н, одно́, одна́, одни́. Note that in all forms except оди́н the stem is **одн-**.

УПРАЖНЕ́НИЯ

A. Perform *Pronunciation Drill* **16.**

B. Say in Russian:

1. What do you do in America? 2. I'm a writer. 3. I write articles and books. 4. My father likes to read English. 5. As for me, I can't. 6. And where does your father live? 7. Here in Leningrad? 8. No. He lives in Moscow, but he used to live in Leningrad. 9. He's a chemist. 10. And your mother? 11. You say she's a doctor? 12. Yes, she works in a hospital in Moscow. 13. My uncle is a doctor, too, but he's always busy in the laboratory. 14. Do you have only one uncle? 15. No, two. The second one, my mother's brother, works at the post office. 16. Just like me? 17. Yes, but in a small city.

C. Transform orally according to the model.

MODEL: Они́ рабо́тают в лаборато́рии.
Мы́ рабо́таем в лаборато́рии.

1. Они́ пи́шут статьи́.
2. Они́ чита́ют по-англи́йски.
3. Они́ говоря́т по-ру́сски.
4. Они́ понима́ют.
5. Они́ уме́ют говори́ть по-ру́сски.

D. Repeat Exercise C according to the following model:

Они́ рабо́тают в лаборато́рии.
О́н рабо́тает в лаборато́рии.

E. Make the following substitutions orally:

Э́то . . . . **мой брат**

¹ an engineer	⁵ a writer	⁹ his mother	¹³ our laboratory
² your sister	⁶ his sisters	¹⁰ his father	¹⁴ my letters
³ her husband	⁷ her mother	¹¹ our doctor	¹⁵ our city
⁴ our professor	⁸ her father	¹² my uncle	¹⁶ our theater

F. Make the following substitutions orally:

Они . . . . рабо́тают вме́сте на фа́брике.

[1] my brothers	[7] my mother and my father
[2] Peter and Ivan	[8] these women
[3] his sisters	[9] those Americans
[4] the engineers	[10] those students
[5] the chemists	[11] Peter and Vera
[6] her uncles	[12] Olga and Vera

G. Give the Russian equivalents:

1. I'm a writer. 2. I write articles. 3. My father is also a writer. 4. He writes books. 5. I like to read. 6. Do you like to read? 7. My wife likes to read English. 8. She can't read Russian. 9. Where does your father live? 10. My father lives in Moscow. 11. He's a doctor. 12. My mother's an engineer. 13. She works in Moscow too. 14. What does your father do? 15. My father works in the lab. 16. He's a chemist. 17. Just like me! 18. That's right.

GRAMMAR UNIT THREE

🌑 1.   The Russian Consonants

1.1   Voiced and Voiceless Consonants

In Russian as in English there are voiced and voiceless consonants. Most of the voiced consonants have voiceless counterparts.

VOICED: **б д г в з ж**
                      /b d g v z ž/

VOICELESS PARTNER: **п т к ф с ш**
                      /p t k f s š/

At normal conversational speed in Russian, the above voiced consonant letters are pronounced voiceless when they occur at the end of a phrase.

Это мой му**ж**. /múš/	*That's my husband.*
Ресторан напроти**в**. /naprótif/	*The restaurant is across the way.*
Вот наш горо**д**. /górat/	*Here's our city.*
Вот Ленингра**д**. /liningrát/	*Here's Leningrad.*

The following consonants are also voiced, but they have no voiceless counterparts: **м н л р**
                      /m n l r/

Generally, when one consonant immediately follows another within a phrase or a word, the pronunciation of the first consonant is assimilated to that of the second, i.e., the second consonant influences the pronunciation of the preceding one. Details vary depending on the type of consonant involved. Thus, with prepositions that end in a voiced consonant, this consonant is pronounced voiceless when the next word begins with a voiceless consonant. (Cf. also *Pronunciation Section* **5.2**). For example:

в Ленинграде	/v liningrádi/	*in Leningrad*
в Москве	/v maskvé/	*in Moscow*
в ресторане	/v ristaráni/	*in the restaurant*
в Бостоне	/v bastóni/	*in Boston*

But:

в книге	/f knígi/	*in the book*
в театре	/f tiátri/	*in the theater*
в Киеве	/f kíyiyi/	*in Kiev*

59

Within a word a similar type of assimilation takes place, usually involving the consonants listed at the beginning of this section. That is, a voiceless letter may be pronounced voiced, or a voiced letter may be pronounced voiceless, depending upon the following consonant.

во**кз**а́л	/vagzál/	*station*
перево́**дч**ица	/piṛivótčica/	*interpreter*
второ́й	/ftaróy/	*second*

There is one consistent exception to this rule, namely, when the second consonant is the voiced consonant **в** /v/, a preceding voiceless consonant remains voiceless. For example:

твёрдый зна́к /ṭyórday znák/ *hard sign*

1.2 The Writing of the Basic Vowel *O*

The basic vowel *O* after the consonants **ш, ж, ц, щ, ч** is sometimes written with **о**, sometimes with **e** and sometimes with **ё**. The distribution of these letters is generally as follows:

ш, ж, ц, щ, ч + *O*	NOUN AND ADJECTIVE ENDINGS	ELSEWHERE
STRESSED	**о**	**ё**
UNSTRESSED	**e**	**e**

For example, хоро**шо́** *good*, and на́**ше** *our*, both end in the basic vowel -*O*, which is a neuter adjective ending. But **жё**ны *wives*, and **же**на́ *wife*, have a STEM with the basic vowel -*O*- and те**чёт** *flows*, and пи́**шет** *writes*, have the Type I VERB ENDING /-Ot/.

❷ 2. The Locative Case

2.1 Locative Case Forms of Nouns

You are already acquainted with the use of the locative case in the sentences which follow:

О́н живёт **в Москве́**.	He lives *in Moscow*.
Она́ рабо́тает **в больни́це**.	She works *in a hospital*.
О́н рабо́тает **на по́чте**.	He works *at the post office*.

Now, note the endings:

LOCATIVE CASE ENDINGS: in terms of Basic Vowels				
	MASCULINE	NEUTER	FEMININE I	FEMININE II
SINGULAR	-E	-E (-I)	-E (-I)	-I
PLURAL	-Ax			

SUMMARY: The locative singular form of neuter nouns which have a nominative in **-ие** and of feminine Class I nouns which have a nominative in **-ия** is written **-ии**. The locative singular ending of all feminine Class II nouns is -I, written **-и**. The locative singular ending of all other nouns is -E. Since the final consonant of the stem is always palatalized (where possible) before this ending, the ending is always written with the letter **-е**. The locative plural ending of all nouns is -Ax, written **-ах** or **-ях**.

Finally, compare the nominative and locative forms of nouns with which you are already familiar:

MASCULINE NOUNS: The locative singular ends in -E, written **-е**. The locative plural ends in -Ax, written **-ах** or **-ях**.

		SINGULAR		PLURAL
Nom.	ресторáн	/ṛistarán/	рестораны	/ṛistarány/
Loc.	ресторáн**е**	/ṛistaráṇi/	рестораáн**ах**	/ṛistaránax/
Nom.	брáт	/brát/	брáтья	/bráṭya/
Loc.	брáт**е**	/bráṭi/	брáть**ях**	/bráṭyix/
Nom.	гóрод	/górat/	городá	/garadá/
Loc.	гóрод**е**	/góraḍi/	городáх	/garadáx/
Nom.	мýж	/múš/	мужья́	/mužyá/
Loc.	мýж**е**	/múži/	мужь**ях**	/mužyáx/
Nom.	отéц	/aṭéc/	отцы́	/atcí/
Loc.	отц**é**	/atcé/	отцáх	/atcáx/

Masculine nouns of the type **отéц** and **америкáнец**, which lose the final vowel of the stem in the nominative plural, lose this vowel also in the locative as well as in all forms other than the masculine singular.

Nom.	учи́тель	/učíṭiḷ/	учителя́	/učiṭiḷá/
Loc.	учи́теле	/učíṭiḷi/	учителя́х	/učiṭiḷáx/

61

Masculine nouns ending in the letter **ь** and all feminine Class II nouns, according to the regular rules of writing, drop the **ь** when endings are added.

NEUTER NOUNS: If the nominative singular ends in **-ие**, the locative singular ends in *-I*, spelled **-и.**

Nom.	зда́ние	/zdániya/	зда́ния	/zdániya/
Loc.	зда́нии	/zdániyi/	зда́ниях	/zdániyix/

The locative singular of all other neuter nouns ends in *-E*, spelled **e.** The locative plural ends in *-Ax*, spelled **-ах** or **-ях.**

Nom.	письмо́	/piṣmó/	пи́сьма	/píṣma/
Loc.	письме́	/piṣmé/	пи́сьмах	/píṣmax/
Nom.	сло́во	/slóva/	слова́	/slavá/
Loc.	сло́ве	/slóyi/	слова́х	/slaváx/

FEMININE: CLASS I. If the nominative ends in **-ия** the locative singular ends in *-I*, spelled *-й.*

Nom.	лаборато́рия	/laboratóriya/	лаборато́рии	/laboratóriyi/
Loc.	лаборато́рии	/laboratóriyi/	лаборато́риях	/laboratóriyix/

The locative singular of all other feminine nouns of Class I ends in *-E*, spelled **-e.** The locative plural ends in *-Ax*, spelled **-ах** or **-ях.**

Nom.	у́лица	/úḷica/	у́лицы	/úḷici/
Loc.	у́лице	/úḷici/	у́лицах	/úḷicax/
Nom.	жена́	/žiná/	жёны	/žóni/
Loc.	жене́	/žiṇé/	жёнах	/žónax/
Nom.	сестра́	/ṣistrá/	сёстры	/ṣóstri/
Loc.	сестре́	/ṣiṣṭré/	сёстрах	/ṣóstrax/

FEMININE: CLASS II. The locative singular ends in *-I*, written **и.** The locative plural ends in *-Ax*, written **-ах** or **-ях.**

Nom.	ма́ть	/máṭ/	ма́тери	/máṭiṛi/
Loc.	ма́тери	/máṭiṛi/	матеря́х	/maṭiṛáx/

In all forms except the nominative and accusative singular, this noun has the irregular stem **матер-.**

2.2 Stress in Noun Forms

In the singular: The position of stress indicated in the nominative singular of most Russian nouns is maintained throughout all cases in the singular. There is one major exception: those masculine nouns in which the stress occurs on the last syllable of the nominative singular. In such nouns the position of stress in the other cases of the singular cannot be predicted. It may occur on the same syllable as in the nominative, or it may occur on the ending.

	Nom. Sing. инжене́р *engineer*	Loc. Sing. инжене́ре
BUT:	Nom. Sing. язы́к *language*	Loc. Sing. языке́

Other masculine nouns we have met in which the stress occurs on the last syllable of the nominative singular, and which show a shift of stress in other endings of the singular are:

Кре́мль	/kŗémļ/	Кремле́	/kŗimļé/	*Kremlin*
пётр	/pótr/	Петре́	/piţré/	*Peter*
оте́ц	/aţéc/	отце́	/atcé/	*father*

If the stress on the nominative singular of a masculine noun falls on any syllable other than the last syllable, the stress will remain on the same syllable throughout the singular just as with most other Russian nouns, e.g. профе́ссор, профе́ссоре, *professor;* писа́тель, писа́теле *writer.*

Exceptions to this principle involve a relatively small number of nouns, and the forms of these nouns will be given as you meet them.

In the plural: While most Russian nouns have the same position of stress in the plural that they have in the singular, some do show an unpredictable shift. Usually, when they do show a shift in the position of stress, this shift is evidenced in the nominative plural form and the same position of stress is maintained throughout all of the cases in the plural.

Most Russian dictionaries and grammars offer little help in determining what nouns show a shift in the position of stress from singular to plural, for they cite the noun only in its nominative singular form. Therefore, when you first encounter a noun in which the position of stress shifts from the singular to the plural, you should learn both the nominative singular and the nominative plural forms of that noun. E.g.

го́род	*Nom. pl.* города́	жена́	*Nom. pl.* жёны
письмо́	*Nom. pl.* пи́сьма	сестра́	*Nom. pl.* сёстры

2.3   Locative Case Forms of Special Adjectives

LOCATIVE SINGULAR:

Masculine and *Neuter:* Basic ending -*O*m.

Feminine: Basic ending -*O*y; except for **мо́й** which has Basic ending -*E*y.

SPELLING: According to the rules. See *Grammar Units* 1:1; 3:1.2.

LOCATIVE PLURAL: Basic ending -*I*x.

SPELLING: **-их** (the plural stem is always palatalized).

63

Compare the nominative and locative forms:

			SINGULAR		PLURAL	
		NOM.	LOCATIVE		NOM.	LOCATIVE
э́тот	M	э́тот	э́том	/étam/		
	N	э́то			э́ти	э́тих /éțix/
	F	э́та	э́той	/étay/		
оди́н	M	оди́н	одно́м	/adnóm/		
	N	одно́			одни́	одни́х /adņíx/
	F	одна́	одно́й	/adnóy/		
мой	M	мой	моём	/mayóm/		
	N	моё			мои́	мои́х /mayíx/
	F	моя́	мое́й	/mayéy/		
ваш	M	ва́ш	ва́шем	/vášim/		
	N	ва́ше			ва́ши	ва́ших /vášix/
	F	ва́ша	ва́шей	/vášiy/		
наш	M	на́ш	на́шем	/nášim/		
	N	на́ше			на́ши	на́ших /nášix/
	F	на́ша	на́шей	/nášiy/		

2.4   Locative case forms of pronouns

The locative of the first and second person pronominal forms is irregular and should be memorized. The locative endings of the third person pronoun and of **что** are similar to those of special adjectives.

PERSONAL PRONOUNS

	SINGULAR			PLURAL	
1.	*Nom.*	(*I, me*) **я**	1.	*Nom.*	(*we, us*) **мы́**
	Loc.	**мне́** /mn̦é/		*Loc.*	**нас** /nás/
2.	*Nom.*	(*you*) **ты́**	2.	*Nom.*	(*you*) **вы́**
	Loc.	**тебе́** /țib̦é/		*Loc.*	**вас** /vás/
3.	*Nom.*	(*he, him*) **о́н**	3.		
	Loc.	**нём** /n̦óm/			
	Nom.	(*it*) **оно́**		*Nom.*	(*they, them*) **они́**
	Loc.	**нём** /n̦óm/		*Loc.*	**ни́х** /n̦íx/
	Nom.	(*she, her*) **она́**			
	Loc.	**не́й** /n̦éy/			

INTERROGATIVE PRONOUN

	(what)	
Nom.	**что́**	
Loc.	**чём**	(čóm)

2.5 The Uses of the Locative Case

(1) The locative case is used after the preposition **о, об, обо** *about, concerning*.

Они́ всегда́ говоря́т **о Босто́не**.	They are always talking *about Boston*.
О́н говори́т **об э́том го́роде**.	He is talking *about that city*.
О́н чита́ет **об э́той кни́ге**.	He is reading *about that book*.
О́н пи́шет **о фа́брике**.	He is writing *about the factory*.
О́н зна́ет **о мое́й лаборато́рии**.	He knows *about my laboratory*.
О́н зна́ет **о на́шем письме́**.	He knows *about our letter*.
Ива́н говори́т **обо мне́**.	Ivan is talking *about me*.
Они́ говоря́т **о его́ сестре́**.	They are talking *about his sister*.
Моя́ жена́ пи́шет **о тури́стах**.	My wife writes *about tourists*.
Профе́ссор говори́т **о на́с**.	The professor is talking *about us*.
О чём вы́ говори́те?	*What* are you talking *about*?

65

The preposition **об** has the form **обо** only when used before the pronoun **мне́**. It has the form **о** when used before a consonant (including the consonant /y/, as in **о его́ сестре́** /a yivó șișțré/. It has the form **об** elsewhere.

(2) The locative case is also used after the preposition **в** *in, at* and **на** *in, at* when these prepositions specify location. The preposition **в** sometimes has the alternative spelling **во** when the following word begins with two or more consonants.

Мы́ рабо́таем **на фа́брике**.	We work *at the factory.*
Она́ живёт **в Нью-Йо́рке**.	She lives *in New York.*
Она́ рабо́тает **в больни́це**.	She works *in the hospital.*
Он всегда́ за́нят **в лаборато́рии**.	He's always busy *in the laboratory.*
Бра́т мое́й ма́тери рабо́тает **на по́чте**.	My mother's brother works *at the post office.*
Он живёт **в ма́леньком го́роде**.	He lives *in a small town.*
Что́ он де́лает **в Москве́**?	What does he do *in Moscow?*
Моя́ жена́ **на вокза́ле**.	My wife is *at the station.*
Его́ сестра́ живёт **на э́той у́лице**.	His sister lives *on that street.*

The prepositions **в** and **на** both mean *in, at.* In this meaning the preposition **в** is used with some nouns, by far the majority, and the preposition **на** is used with a relatively small number of nouns. You should learn the nouns that are used with **на** as you meet them; all others will be used with **в**.

The nouns used with **на** that you have had so far are:

на вокза́ле	*in (at) the station*
на фа́брике	*in (at) the factory*
на по́чте	*in (at) the post office*
на у́лице	*in (on) the street*

🌑 3. The conjunctions **и, а, но**

The conjunction **и** means that additional information is being provided (English *and*).

The conjunction **а** means that a contrast or comparison is involved (English *and* or *but*).

The conjunction **но** means that the statement following **но** is in some way not expected on the basis of the information preceding **но**. (English *but*).

Он хи́мик, **и** рабо́тает в лаборато́рии.	He's a chemist *and* [in addition] works in the lab.
Он хи́мик, **а** она́ до́ктор.	He's a chemist *and* [but] she's a doctor.
Он хи́мик, **но** не рабо́тает.	He's a chemist *but* [strange though it be] doesn't work.
Я хи́мик, **и** он хи́мик.	I'm a chemist *and* [also] he's a chemist.
Я хи́мик, **а** он до́ктор.	I'm a chemist *and* [but] he's a doctor.

66

Я рабо́таю в рестора́не, **и** о́н рабо́тает в рестора́не.	I work in a restaurant *and* [also] he works in a restaurant.
Я рабо́таю в Ленингра́де, **а** о́н рабо́тает в Москве́.	I work in Leningrad *and* [but] he works in Moscow.
Я рабо́таю в Ленингра́де, **но** живу́ в Москве́.	I work in Leningrad, *but* [it would surprise you to know] I live in Moscow.

The word **и** is also equivalent to *also, too:*

Но́ о́н жи́л **и́** в Ленингра́де.	But he used to live in Leningrad, *too.*
Та́к же ка́к **и** я́.	Just like me (*too*).

◑ 4. по- with language names

Just as you can say **Я́ говорю́ по-ру́сски (по-англи́йски)** *I speak Russian (English)* you can also say **понима́ю (пишу́, чита́ю) по-ру́сски,** *I understand (write, read) Russian.* These are the only verbs you should try to use with this expression.

◑ 5. *"They say":* Говоря́т

Говоря́т, что же́нщины у ва́с ча́сто рабо́тают.	*They say* that women in your country often work.
	It is said that...
	People say that...

In constructions such as this, where the subject is indefinite, Russian uses the verb in the third person plural without any subject.

УПРАЖНЕ́НИЯ

A. Perform *Pronunciation Drill* **36.**

B. Make the following substitutions orally.

Он живёт . . . .

¹ in the hotel	⁵ in Moscow
² in New York	⁶ on this street
³ in Leningrad	⁷ on my street
⁴ in Boston	

C. Make the following substitutions orally:

Они́ рабо́тают . . . .

¹ in the restaurant	⁷ in New York
² in the theater	⁸ in the hospital
³ in the station	⁹ in America
⁴ in the cafe	¹⁰ in Leningrad
⁵ in the hotel	¹¹ in the laboratory
⁶ in the factory	¹² in the post office

D. Substitute orally, using the proper forms of the words listed:

Óн говори́т о (об) . . . .

¹ моё письмо́	¹² мо́й профе́ссор
² э́то письмо́	¹³ ва́ш профе́ссор
³ э́то зда́ние	¹⁴ э́тот писа́тель
⁴ э́то сло́во	¹⁵ э́та гости́ница
⁵ э́тот рестора́н	¹⁶ моя́ гости́ница
⁶ э́тот студе́нт	¹⁷ ва́ша учи́тельница
⁷ мо́й учи́тель	¹⁸ ва́ша жена́
⁸ на́ш учи́тель	¹⁹ на́ша сестра́
⁹ на́ш оте́ц	²⁰ моя́ статья́
¹⁰ на́ш бра́т	²¹ моя́ учи́тельница
¹¹ мо́й студе́нт	

E. Repeat *Exercise D*, transforming to plural:

Óн говори́т **о мои́х пи́сьмах.**

F. Listen to the following questions and answer them according to the model, substituting the appropriate pronoun:

MODEL: Óн зна́ет об э́том рестора́не?
Да́, о́н зна́ет о нём.

1. Они́ говоря́т об э́тих же́нщинах?
2. Она́ пи́шет об э́тих тури́стах?
3. Óн зна́ет о моём отце́?
4. Она́ чита́ет о на́шем го́роде?
5. Они́ говоря́т о мое́й кни́ге?
6. Они́ пи́шут о студе́нтах?
7. Она́ чита́ет об америка́нке?
8. Они́ зна́ют о мои́х бра́тьях?
9. Она́ зна́ет об э́том сло́ве?

G. Make the following substitutions orally:

Они́ чита́ют о (об) . . . .

¹ Moscow
² this city
³ our mother
⁴ doctors
⁵ this lab
⁶ my article
⁷ a chemist

⁸ America
⁹ our language
¹⁰ my husband
¹¹ his sisters
¹² your factory
¹³ Peter
¹⁴ him
¹⁵ the Kremlin

¹⁶ our books
¹⁷ her
¹⁸ the hotels in Moscow
¹⁹ the restaurants in New York
²⁰ them
²¹ Vera
²² Ivan

REVIEW EXERCISES

H. Make the following substitutions orally:

Э́то . . . .

¹ my restaurant
² his book
³ her letter
⁴ my letter
⁵ our teacher (*m.*)
⁶ their teachers (*m.*)
⁷ his wife

⁸ their brother
⁹ his brothers
¹⁰ your sister
¹¹ his sisters
¹² her husband
¹³ my student
¹⁴ our books

¹⁵ his professors
¹⁶ their husbands
¹⁷ their wives
¹⁸ our father
¹⁹ my lab
²⁰ our doctors
²¹ our uncles

I. Listen to the following questions and answer them according to the model:

MODEL: Вы́ понима́ете по-ру́сски?
Да́, я́ понима́ю по-ру́сски.

1. Вы́ рабо́таете на фа́брике?
2. Вы́ говори́те по-англи́йски?
3. Вы́ живёте в Босто́не?

4. Вы́ ви́дите э́то зда́ние?
5. Вы́ та́м бу́дете?
6. Вы́ лю́бите чита́ть?

J. Transform orally from third person singular to third person plural negative according to the model:

MODEL: О́н понима́ет по-ру́сски.
Они́ не понима́ют по-ру́сски.

1. О́н рабо́тает в Босто́не.
2. О́н говори́т по-англи́йски.
3. О́н хорошо́ живёт.

4. О́н пи́шет.
5. О́н уме́ет чита́ть по-ру́сски.

CONVERSATION 7

Let's talk about the family

Tired by the visit to the Petrodvorets John sits on a bench in Kirov Park. He has a chance to rest and to practice his Russian with the good-natured worker enjoying his lunch hour.

CONVERSATION UNIT SEVEN _____

ENGLISH EQUIVALENTS

JOHN	[1] Do you have a large family?
AKIMOV	[2] No, only a wife and daughter. [3] Here's [here I have] a picture of them.
JOHN	[4] [What] a fine child! And who's that?
AKIMOV	[5] That's my wife's sister. [6] And this is me.
JOHN	[7] Do you want to look at pictures of my relatives?
AKIMOV	[8] I'd be glad to. [With pleasure]. [9] Is that your house?
JOHN	[10] Yes, and there sit my children, a son and two daughters. [11] This is my son's friend [comrade].
AKIMOV	[12] What does he have in his hands?
JOHN	[13] Who [has?]
AKIMOV	[14] Your son [has].
JOHN	[15] I don't know what [how] that's called. [16] How do you say "model" in Russian?
AKIMOV	[17] Model.
JOHN	[18] That's a model of an airplane.
AKIMOV	[19] So that's what it is! [20] Did he build it himself?
JOHN	[21] Yes. His friends also make models. [22] They have a lot of planes like that [such].
AKIMOV	[23] Good for them!

NOTES

2 **Акимов** is a family name.

16 Literally, "how to say *model* in Russian?"

17 Pronounced /madél/ with a plain rather than palatalized /d/.

23 **Молодéц** *good for you!* has the literal meaning *fine fellow.* It is used with reference to both men and women, though a masculine noun in form.

ADDITIONAL VOCABULARY

раз[1]	*one*	**четы́ре**	*four*
два́	*two*	**пя́ть**	*five*
три́	*three*	**ше́сть**	*six*

[1] (used instead of **оди́н** in counting).

Поговорим о семье

ДЖОН	¹ У вас большая семья?
АКИМОВ	² Нет, только жена и дочка. ³ Вот у меня их фотография.
ДЖОН	⁴ Хороший ребёнок! А это кто?
АКИМОВ	⁵ Это сестра моей жены. ⁶ А вот и я.
ДЖОН	⁷ Хотите посмотреть фотографии моих родных?
АКИМОВ	⁸ С удовольствием. ⁹ Это ваш дом?
ДЖОН	¹⁰ Да, а вот сидят мои дети, сын и две дочки. ¹¹ Вот это товарищ моего сына.
АКИМОВ	¹² Что у него в руках?
ДЖОН	¹³ У кого?
АКИМОВ	¹⁴ У вашего сына.
ДЖОН	¹⁵ Я не знаю, как это называется. ¹⁶ Как сказать « model » по-русски?
АКИМОВ	¹⁷ Модель.
ДЖОН	¹⁸ Это модель самолёта.
АКИМОВ	¹⁹ Вот как! ²⁰ Он сам её построил?
ДЖОН	²¹ Да. Его товарищи также делают модели. ²² У них много таких самолётов.
АКИМОВ	²³ Молодцы!

NEW VERBS

Type i

де́лают	do, make
называ́ется	is called
называ́ются	are called

This verb occurs most frequently in the third singular and third plural forms, as cited above.

Type ii

сидя́т, сижу́	are sitting, sit
постро́ят	will build
посмо́трят, посмотрю́	will look

The verb **сидя́т, сижу́** *sit*, shows the alternation of **ж** in the first singular with **д** in the other non-past forms. (Cf. *Grammar Unit* **2:3.1** and *Appendix*.)

Irregular

хочу́	хоти́м	
хо́чешь	хоти́те	want
хо́чет	хотя́т	

The verb *want* is one of the four Russian verbs that have irregular endings in the non-past. The singular endings of this verb are those of *Type I*, but the plural endings are those of *Type II*.

NEW NOUNS

Masculine

NOMINATIVE SINGULAR	LOCATIVE SINGULAR	NOMINATIVE PLURAL	LOCATIVE PLURAL	
самолёт	самолёте	самолёты	самолётах	airplane
това́рищ	това́рище	това́рищи	това́рищах	comrade, friend
ребёнок	ребёнке			child
молоде́ц	молодце́	молодцы́	молодца́х	fine fellow
до́м	до́ме	дома́	дома́х	house
сы́н	сы́не	сыновья́	сыновья́х	son

Neuter

удово́льствие	удово́льствии			pleasure

Feminine I

до́чка	до́чке	до́чки	до́чках	daughter
рука́	руке́	ру́ки	рука́х	hand, arm
семья́	семье́	се́мьи	се́мьях	family
фотогра́фия	фотогра́фии	фотогра́фии	фотогра́фиях	photograph

Feminine II

| моде́ль | моде́ли | моде́ли | моде́лях | model |

Plural only

| | | де́ти | де́тях | children |

The noun **ребёнок** in the meaning *child* is used almost exclusively in the singular.

The nouns **ребёнок** and **молоде́ц** lose their last vowel when an ending is added to the stem.

The noun **сы́н** has an irregular stem throughout the plural, as illustrated above.

The form **родны́е** though used as a noun, has the form of an ordinary adjective (Cf. *Grammar Unit* 5:3).

NEW PRONOUNS

NOMINATIVE	LOCATIVE	
кто́	ко́м	*who*

УПРАЖНЕ́НИЯ

A. Transform orally from singular to plural according to the model:

MODEL: Во́т его́ моде́ль.
Во́т его́ моде́ли.

1. Во́т его́ до́м.
2. Во́т его́ самолёт.
3. Во́т его́ фотогра́фия.
4. Во́т его́ до́чка.
5. Во́т его́ сестра́.
6. Во́т его́ бра́т.

B. Listen to the following questions and answer them according to the model:

MODEL: Вы́ хоти́те посмотре́ть фотогра́фии?
Да́, я́ хочу́ посмотре́ть фотогра́фии.

1. Вы́ сиди́те здесь?
2. Вы́ рабо́таете на по́чте?
3. Вы́ пи́шете кни́ги?
4. Вы́ говори́те о нём?
5. Вы́ живёте в Москве́?
6. Вы́ бу́дете в рестора́не?

75

C. Make the following substitutions orally:

Я живу́ . . . .

¹ in this hotel	⁴ on that street
² in that building	⁵ in Moscow
³ in this house	⁶ in this city

D. Make the following substitutions orally:

Óн пи́шет о (об) . . . .

¹ us	⁷ my comrades	¹⁴ those children
² Americans	⁸ my mother	¹⁵ their daughters
³ airplanes	⁹ the interpreter	¹⁶ Leningrad
⁴ our comrades	¹⁰ that girl	¹⁷ Vera
⁵ my family	¹¹ doctors	¹⁸ Peter
⁶ these houses	¹² chemists	¹⁹ Boris
	¹³ my son	

E. Give the Russian equivalents:

1. Do you have a large family? 2. No, only a wife and daughter. 3. No, only a wife and son. 4. My son lives in Moscow. 5. My daughter and her husband live in Leningrad. 6. They are doctors. 7. They work in a hospital in Leningrad. 8. Do they work in the laboratory? 9. Yes, but not always. 10. Is this your house? 11. No, it's not my house. 12. My friend lives in this house. 13. He's a writer. 14. He writes about airplanes. 15. I like to read about airplanes. 16. I like to read about America.

CONVERSATION 8

Where are you from?

Two weeks later, and John is off on another trip. At the Moscow station he politely gives information to a middle aged woman and doing so awakes her interest by his foreign accent.

CONVERSATION UNIT EIGHT ─────────────

ENGLISH EQUIVALENTS

OLGA   [1] Where are you from? [2] I see that Russian isn't your native language [native for you].

JOHN   [3] I'm American and I've come to the Soviet Union just recently.

OLGA   [4] Oh! Now I understand! [5] Where do you live in America?

JOHN   [6] I'm from Detroit. [7] And where are you from?

OLGA   [8] I was born in Kiev.

JOHN   [9] That's a very old city, isn't it [the truth]?

OLGA   [10] Yes, it's an old city in the Ukraine. [11] Now I live in Smolensk.

JOHN   [12] Where is Smolensk located? In the east?

OLGA   [13] No, it's to the west of Moscow.

JOHN   [14] Have you been in Moscow long?

OLGA   [15] Only a month. I'm here for the first time.

JOHN   [16] Are you alone?

OLGA   [17] No. That young man there is my son Misha. [18] Do you have any children?

JOHN   [19] Yes. I have two girls. [20] They're in Detroit.

OLGA   [21] Excuse me, here's my train. [22] Are you staying here?

JOHN   [23] Yes, my train isn't here yet. [24] Good luck!

OLGA   [25] Good-bye!

NOTES

3   In English it is customary to use either *Russia* or the *Soviet Union* as the name of the country. In Russian the customary term is **Советский Союз**. The term **Россия** *Russia*, is used for the most part in historical contexts.

8   **Родилась** is the form used when the subject is feminine; **родился** is used when the subject is masculine.

9   **Правда**, literally *truth*. Also the name of a newspaper.

14   **Давно** means *a long time ago* or *for a long time.*

16   **Одна** is an example of the word **один** used in the meaning *alone.*

18   **у вас есть** literally *are there at you* is the equivalent of English "do you have".

19   **Девочка** refers to a girl in her early teens or less and **девушка** to an older girl.

21   **Простите** means *pardon me* or *excuse me* in situations where you are asking pardon for something you have done or are excusing yourself. In English we say *pardon me* or *excuse me* to attract somebody's attention, but Russians say **Скажите мне, пожалуйста** in this situation (cf. *Conversation* I).

24   **Бсего хорошего** literally *all good.*

Откуда вы?

ОЛЬГА   ¹ Откуда вы? ² Я вижу, что русский язык не родной для вас.

ДЖОН   ³ Я — американец, и приехал в Советский Союз недавно.

ОЛЬГА   ⁴ А, теперь понимаю! ⁵ Где вы живёте в Америке?

ДЖОН   ⁶ Я из Детройта. ⁷ А вы откуда?

ОЛЬГА   ⁸ Я родилась в Киеве.

ДЖОН   ⁹ Это очень старый город, не правда ли?

ОЛЬГА   ¹⁰ Да, старый город на Украине. ¹¹ Теперь я живу в Смоленске.

ДЖОН   ¹² Где находится Смоленск? На востоке?

ОЛЬГА   ¹³ Нет, он к западу от Москвы.

ДЖОН   ¹⁴ Давно вы в Москве?

ОЛЬГА   ¹⁵ Только месяц. Я здесь в первый раз.

ДЖОН   ¹⁶ Вы одна?

ОЛЬГА   ¹⁷ Нет. Вот этот молодой человек—мой сын Миша. ¹⁸ А у вас есть дети?

ДЖОН   ¹⁹ Да. У меня две девочки. ²⁰ Они в Детройте.

ОЛЬГА   ²¹ Простите, вот мой поезд. ²² Вы остаётесь?

ДЖОН   ²³ Да, моего поезда ещё нет. ²⁴ Всего хорошего!

ОЛЬГА   ²⁵ До свидания!

ADDITIONAL VOCABULARY

се́мь[1]	*seven*
во́семь[2]	*eight*
де́вять	*nine*
де́сять	*ten*
оди́надцать	*eleven*
двена́дцать	*twelve*

NEW VERBS

Type i

прие́дут	will come, arrive (by vehicle)
остаю́тся	remain

The verb you met in the form **остаётесь** has the following forms:

остаю́сь	остаёмся
остаёшься	остаётесь
остаётся	остаю́тся

These are perfectly regular endings for a verb of Type I with **-сь** added to the forms that end in a vowel (i.e., first singular and second plural) and **-ся** added to the others. Verbs which have this particle added are called *reflexive* verbs. (Cf. also the verb **называ́ются** *are called* in *Conversation* **VII**).

Type ii

нахо́дятся, нахожу́сь   *are located*

NEW NOUNS

Masculine

NOMINATIVE SINGULAR	LOCATIVE SINGULAR	NOMINATIVE PLURAL	LOCATIVE PLURAL	
Детро́йт	Детро́йте			Detroit
Ки́ев	Ки́еве			Kiev
Смоле́нск	Смоле́нске			Smolensk
восто́к	восто́ке			east
за́пад	за́паде			west
ме́сяц	ме́сяце	ме́сяцы	ме́сяцах	month
по́езд	по́езде	поезда́	поезда́х	train
челове́к	челове́ке	(*see* лю́ди)		man, person
Ми́ша	Ми́ше			Mike
сою́з	сою́зе	сою́зы	сою́зах	union

[1] Pronounced either /şem/ or /şem̦/.
[2] Pronounced either /voşim/ or /voşim̦/.

Feminine I

Росси́я	Росси́и			Russia
пра́вда	пра́вде			truth
Укра́ина	Укра́ине			Ukraine
де́вочка	де́вочке	де́вочки	де́вочках	young girl

Plural only

	лю́ди	лю́дях	people

The use of **челове́к** *man, person* and **лю́ди** *people* will be discussed in *Grammar Unit* **4:2.6**.

The noun **Ми́ша** diminutive of **Михаи́л** *Michael*, is like **дя́дя** in that it is masculine with respect to agreement (мо́й Ми́ша), but has the endings of a feminine I noun. All diminutives in **-а** derived from men's names act this way.

In this lesson you have met three more nouns which use the preposition **на** to express location: восто́к, за́пад, Укра́ина.

Ки́ев — ста́рый го́род **на Укра́ине**.
Смоле́нск нахо́дится не **на восто́ке**, а́ **на за́паде**.

Давно́ вы́ в Москве́? *Have you been* in Moscow long? is literally *Are* you in Moscow for a long time? Note that Russian, unlike English, does not use a past tense in this construction.

Я́ зде́сь то́лько ме́сяц.   I *have been* here only (for) a month.
                          Literally: I *am* here only a month.

УПРАЖНЕ́НИЯ

A. Transform orally from nominative singular to nominative plural according to the model:

MODEL: **Мо́й сы́н** живёт зде́сь.
       Мои́ сыновья́ живу́т зде́сь.

1. **Э́та де́вушка** рабо́тает на фа́брике.
2. **Ва́ш бра́т** живёт в Аме́рике?
3. Во́т **по́езд**.
4. Её **сы́н** свобо́дно говори́т по-ру́сски.
5. **Э́тот до́ктор** рабо́тает в лаборато́рии.
6. **Мой учи́тель** живёт на восто́ке.
7. **Э́тот америка́нец** понима́ет по-ру́сски.
8. **На́ш това́рищ** остаётся зде́сь.

B. Make the following substitutions orally:

Они́ рабо́тают . . . .

¹ in this city	⁸ in the Ukraine
² in Kiev	⁹ in the West
³ in Moscow	¹⁰ in this house
⁴ in the east	¹¹ in this building
⁵ in the lab	¹² on this street
⁶ in the post office	¹³ in America
⁷ in Leningrad	¹⁴ in the Kremlin

C. Transform orally from locative singular to locative plural according to the model:

Model: О́н говори́т об э́том го́роде.
  О́н говори́т об **э́тих города́х.**

1. О́н говори́т о перево́дчице.
2. О́н говори́т о по́езде.
3. О́н говори́т об э́той де́вушке.
4. О́н говори́т об э́том самолёте.
5. О́н говори́т о моём това́рище.
6. О́н говори́т о мое́й кни́ге.
7. Они́ пи́шут о теа́тре.
8. Они́ пи́шут о тури́сте.
9. Они́ пи́шут об америка́нке.
10. Они́ пи́шут о фа́брике в Москве́.
11. Они́ пи́шут о профе́ссоре.
12. Они́ пи́шут об э́том писа́теле.
13. Они́ пи́шут об и́х ма́тери.

D. Give the Russian equivalents:

1. Where do you live in America? 2. I live in Detroit. 3. I live in New York. 4. She lives in the west. 5. They live in the east. 6. New York is located in the east. 7. He lives in Moscow. 8. He works in Leningrad. 9. His friend lives in Smolensk. 10. Where is Smolensk located? 11. Smolensk is located to the west of Moscow. 12. Smolensk is located in the west.

13. Where are you from? 14. I was born in Kiev. 15. I live in Kiev. 16. Kiev is a very old city. 17. Kiev is a city in the Ukraine. 18. Kiev is located in the Ukraine. 19. Where is the Ukraine located?

20. Have you been in Moscow long? 21. I've been here a month. 22. I've only been here a month. 23. He's been in Moscow for a month. 24. Is he alone? 25. Is she alone? 26. Are they alone? 27. I'm alone.

28. Are you staying? 29. Are you staying here? 30. I'm staying here. 31. I'm staying here at the station. 32. Good luck!

GRAMMAR UNIT FOUR

1. The Genitive Case

1.1 Genitive Case Forms of Nouns

Notice the genitive case forms in these sentences with which you are already familiar:

Это сестра́ мое́й **жены́.**	That's my wife's sister.
Я из **Детро́йта.**	I'm from Detroit.

GENITIVE CASE ENDINGS in terms of Basic Vowels				
	MASCULINE	NEUTER	FEMININE I	FEMININE II
SINGULAR	-A		*a-я* -I	*я-ь*
PLURAL	-Of, -Ey	—, Ey	—	-Ey

SUMMARY: The genitive singular ending of masculine and neuter nouns is -*A*, written **-а** or **-я**.

The genitive singular ending of feminine Class I nouns is -*I*, written **-ы** or **-и**.

The genitive singular ending of feminine Class II nouns is -*I*, always written **-и**.

The genitive plural ending of masculine and neuter nouns which have a stem ending in /-y/ or in a plain consonant excluding **ш, ж** is -*Of* for masculines, written **-ов, ёв,** or **-ев** and no ending for neuters. Other masculine and neuter nouns have the ending -*Ey*, always written **-ей**.

Feminine Class I nouns have no ending in the genitive plural.

The genitive plural ending for feminine Class II nouns is -*Ey*, always written **-ей**.

MASCULINE NOUNS

SINGULAR	PLURAL
All masculine nouns have the genitive singular ending -*A*, written **-а** or **-я**.	(1) Masculine nouns with stem final /y/, or *plain consonant* (excluding **ш, ж**)/ have the genitive plural ending -*Of*, written **-ов, ёв, ев**.

Nom.	брат	бра́тья[1]
Gen.	бра́та	бра́тьев
Loc.	бра́те	бра́тьях

---

[1] The plural stem as shown in the nominative, and in other case forms, is /braty-/, ending in the consonant sound /y/.

	SINGULAR		PLURAL	
Nom.	отéц[1]		отцы́	
Gen.	отцá		отцо́в	
Loc.	отцé		отцáх	
Nom.	турúст		турúсты	
Gen.	турúста		турúстов	
Loc.	турúсте		турúстах	

(2) Other masculine nouns have the genitive plural ending *-Ey*, written **-ей**.

Nom.	товáрищ[2]	товáрищи	
Gen.	товáрища	товáрищей	
Loc.	товáрище	товáрищах	

NEUTER NOUNS

All neuter nouns have the genitive singular ending *-A*, written **а** or **я**.

The neuter nouns which we have so far met have no ending in the genitive plural.

Nom.	слóво	письмó	словá	пúсьма
Gen.	слóва	письмá	слóв	пúсем
Loc.	слóве	письмé	словáх	пúсьмах
Nom.	здáние		здáния	
Gen.	здáния		здáний[3]	
Loc.	здáнии		здáниях	

FEMININE NOUNS: CLASS I

Feminine nouns of Class I have the genitive singular ending *-I*, written **ы** or **и**.

Feminine nouns of Class I have no ending in the genitive plural.

Nom.	кнúга	кнúги
Gen.	кнúги	**кнúг**
Loc.	кнúге	кнúгах

---

[1] Remember: the non-paired consonant **ц** is always plain.

[2] Remember: the non-paired consonants **ч** and **щ** are always palatalized.

[3] The fact that the genitive plural of the word for *building* has no ending shows up more clearly in transcription (Nominative Singular /zdáṇiya/, Genitive Plural /zdáṇiy/) than in Cyrillic, where it is obscured because of the principles of spelling the sound /y/. (See *Grammar Unit 2:1.2.*)

Nom.	сестра́	сёстры
Gen.	сестры́	**сестёр**
Loc.	сестре́	сёстрах

FEMININE NOUNS: CLASS II

Feminine nouns of Class II have the genitive singular ending -*I*, written **и** in all cases, since the stems of Class II feminine nouns always end in a palatalized consonant.

Feminine nouns of Class II have the genitive plural ending -*Ey*, written **ей**.

Nom.	ма́ть	ма́тери
Gen.	ма́тери	матер**е́й**
Loc.	ма́тери	матеря́х

Nom.	моде́ль	моде́ли
Gen.	моде́ли	моде́л**ей**
Loc.	моде́ли	моде́лях

All the genitive endings are written according to the regular rules of spelling as discussed in *Grammar Units* **1** to **3**.

1.2 The inserted vowel e, o.

Compare the basic stem of each of the following nouns with that form of the noun to which no endings are added:

BASIC STEM	NOM. SINGULAR	LOC. SING.	GEN. SING.	NOM. PLUR.	LOC. PLUR.	GEN. PLURAL
(*Masculine Nouns*)						
американц-	америка́нец	-е	-а	-ы	-ах	-ев
отц-	оте́ц	-е	-а	-ы	-ах	-ов
ребёнк-	ребёнок	-е	-а	—	—	—
(*Neuter Nouns*)						
письм-	-о	-е	-а	-а	-ах	**писем**
(*Feminine Nouns*)						
американк-	-а	-е	-и	-и	-ах	**америка́нок**
дочк-	-а	-е	-и	-и	-ах	**до́чек**
сестр-	-а	-е	-ы	-ы	-ах	**сестёр**

85

The forms **отéц**, **пи́сем**, and **дóчек** etc. involve a general principle of wide application throughout the noun system, affecting the nominative singular of masculine nouns and the genitive plural of neuter and feminine nouns of Class I—that is those forms of nouns which have no ending. When these forms end in two or more consonants, one of the vowels **o**, **ё** or **e** is inserted between the last two consonants, as shown in the list above.

This is not true of *all* nouns with a basic stem ending in two or more consonants, e.g., тури́ст, Кре́мль, Пётр, but it is true of a sufficiently large number of forms that it deserves mention as a principle feature of the language.

We will call this feature *Vowel insertion* and use the words *inserted vowel* as a cover term for the three vowels **o**, **ё**, **e**. Unfortunately for the beginner there is no sure way, as has just been illustrated, of telling whether a vowel will be inserted; nor is there any sure way of telling which of the three vowels will be inserted for a specific noun. This must simply be learned along with the noun.

In citing new nouns in future lessons, if the noun has an inserted vowel, then the particular vowel will be written in parentheses after the noun, e.g.,

ребёнок (о)

до́чка (е)

This means for a masculine noun like **ребёнок** that the vowel occurs only in this form, hence the genitive singular would be **ребёнка**. For a neuter or feminine I noun it means that the vowel would be inserted only in the genitive plural, e.g., **дóчек**. So far you have had the following forms with an inserted vowel:

MASCULINE	NEUTER	FEMININE I
америка́нец (е)	письмо́ (е)	студе́нтка (о)
отéц (е)		америка́нка (о)
ребёнок (о)		до́чка (е)
молоде́ц (е)		де́вушка (е)
		сестра́ (ё)
		статья́ (е)
		семья́ (е)
		де́вочка (е)

Compare the genitive plural of the Feminine Class I nouns **статья́** and **семья́** with that of **дóчка**, which we studied at the beginning of this paragraph:

BASIC STEM		NOMINATIVE SINGULAR		GENITIVE PLURAL	
дочк-	/dóčk-/	-а	/dóčk-a/	до́чек	/dóčik/
стать-	/staṭy-/	-я	/staṭy-á/	стате́й	/staṭéy/
семь-	/ṣeṃy-/	-я	/ṣiṃy-á/	семе́й	/ṣiṃéy/

The insertion of the vowel in стате́й and семе́й is exactly parallel to its insertion in до́чек, but this parallelism is not as obvious from the writing system as it is from the transcription. In all forms of the noun the stem ends in the sound /y/. In the plural the forms are /staṭéy/, /ṣiṃéy/, with the inserted vowel /e/ added before the /y/. It is coincidental that these nouns have the last two letters **ей** and that there is a genitive plural *ending* **-ей**. In the form статéй, **ей** is a part of the stem, and no ending follows, just as the genitive plural дóчек has no ending; it is different from the **-ей** of the genitive plural товáрищей, where **-ей** is the genitive plural added to the stem.

1.3   Citing Russian nouns

In citing a new noun in conversation lessons we will give a sufficient number of forms so that all the forms of that noun can be derived. For most of the nouns of Russian the nominative singular is sufficient.

There are three types of irregularity in Russian nouns: the position of stress, the form of the stem, and the form of the ending.

STRESS

(1) For masculine nouns with the stress on the last oyllable of the stem the position of stress in the other forms of the singular is not predictable from the nominative. If the stress occurs on the ending in these other forms, then for these nouns the genitive singular will be cited. Thus, **Пётр, Петрá**. (Cf. *Grammar Unit* **3:2.2.**).

(2) For some nouns the stress does not occur on the same syllable in both the singular and the plural. When it occurs on a different syllable in the plural, the nominative plural form will be cited. Thus, **женá, жёны; гóрод, городá**.

STEMS

Some nouns have a stem form in the plural which is different from the stem of the singular. When this is so, the nominative plural will be cited. Thus, **брáт, брáтья**.

ENDINGS

(1) Nouns which do not have the nominative plural endings listed in *Grammar Unit* **2** (masculine and feminine *-I*, neuter *-A*) are considered to be irregular. Most irregularities of this type are masculines having the nominative plural in *-A*. All irregular nominative plurals will be cited. Thus, **дóм, домá; брáт, брáтья**.

(2) Any nouns which do not have the genitive plural endings listed in section 1.1 of this unit (masculine -*Of*/-*Ey*, neuter —/-*Ey*, feminine I —, feminine II -*Ey*) are considered to be irregular. For such nouns the genitive plural will be cited, e.g., **мýж**, Nominative Plural **мужья́**, Genitive Plural **мужéй** (where -*Of* is expected, as in брáтьев.)

There are other irregularities, both of stress and of form, which are not included in the above statements, but they are rather rare. When these do occur they will be cited along with the nouns, so that for any noun cited in this book all the case forms can be predicted.

From the irregularities listed above it can be seen that generally speaking a maximum of three different forms besides the nominative singular must be cited (nominative plural and the genitive forms), but even for most irregular nouns all of these forms would not be irregular.

1.4   Irregular genitive forms

In this section all of the nouns you have had that have irregular genitives, either singular or plural or both, are cited along with the irregular forms.

Irregular stress

The following masculine nouns have stress on the genitive singular (as well as on all other case forms in the singular), which is not predictable from the nominative singular. (From this point on we will present the forms in the traditional order: nominative... genitive... etc.)

SINGULAR			PLURAL		
NOMIN.	GENITIVE	LOCATIVE	NOMIN.	GENITIVE	LOCATIVE
Кре́мль	Кремля́	Кремле́	—	—	—
Пётр	Петра́	Петре́	—	—	—
язы́к	языка́	языке́	языки́	языко́в	языка́х
оте́ц	отца́	отце́	отцы́	отцо́в	отца́х
молоде́ц	молодца́	молодце́	молодцы́	молодцо́в	молодца́х

If the position of stress in the nominative plural changes from that of the case forms in the singular the stress of the nominative plural is normally retained throughout the plural:

SINGULAR			PLURAL		
го́род,	го́рода	го́роде	города́	городо́в	города́х

This is not the case with four nouns which we have met, which exemplify a rare type of irregular stress in the genitive plural. In them the position of stress in the genitive plural cannot be predicted from the nominative plural form:

SINGULAR			PLURAL		
NOMINATIVE	GENITIVE	LOCATIVE	NOMIN.	GENITIVE	LOCATIVE
сестра́	сестры́	сестре́	сёстры	сестёр	сёстрах
семья́	семьи́	семье́	се́мьи	семе́й	се́мьях
---	---	---	де́ти	дете́й	де́тях
---	---	---	лю́ди	люде́й	лю́дях

IRREGULARITIES IN FORM

The only other irregularities in the genitive that you have met so far are:

SINGULAR			PLURAL		
NOMIN.	GENITIVE	LOCATIVE	NOMIN.	GEN.	LOCATIVE
му́ж	му́жа	му́же	мужья́	муже́й	мужья́х
сы́н	сы́на	сы́не	сыновья́	сынове́й	сыновья́х
ра́з	ра́за	ра́зе	ра́зы	ра́з	ра́зах
челове́к	челове́ка	челове́ке	—	челове́к	—
граждани́н	граждани́на	граждани́не	гра́ждане	гра́ждан	гра́жданах
господи́н	господи́на	господи́не	господа́	госпо́д	господа́х
дя́дя	дя́ди	дя́де	дя́ди	дя́дей	дя́дях

The first six·nouns have no ending in the genitive plural, which is irregular for masculine nouns. Note that the **-ей** of the genitive plural of the first two nouns is an inserted vowel plus the /y/ of the stem, not the genitive plural ending -Еy.

89

The noun **дя́дя** although masculine in agreement (**мо́й** дя́дя), has the forms of a feminine I noun and hence it would be expected to have no ending in the genitive plural, but instead it has the genitive plural ending -*E*y, **дя́дей**.

1.5   Genitive forms of Special Adjectives

In terms of the basic vowels, special adjectives have the following endings in the genitive case:

	MASCULINE	NEUTER	FEMININE
GENITIVE SINGULAR	-*OvO*		-*O*y
GENITIVE PLURAL	-*I*x		

With one exception these endings are spelled according to the spelling rules previously discussed. The exception is that the /v/ of the genitive singular masculine and neuter is spelled with the letter **r**. The genitive singular of all adjectives and pronouns is spelled with this letter and pronounced /v/, but these are the only forms in the language with this irregular spelling.

The genitive forms of the special adjectives are as follows:

		SINGULAR			PLURAL	
	NOMINATIVE	GENITIVE	LOCATIVE	NOMIN.	GENITIVE	LOCATIVE
M	э́тот	э́того	э́том			
N	э́то			э́ти	э́тих	э́тих
F	э́та	э́той	э́той			
M	оди́н	одного́	одно́м			
N	одно́			одни́	одни́х	одни́х
F	одна́	одно́й	одно́й			
M	мо́й	моего́	моём			
N	моё			мои́	мои́х	мои́х
F	моя́	мое́й	мое́й			

M	ваш	вáшего	вáшем			
N	вáше			вáши	вáших	вáших
F	вáша	вáшей	вáшей			
M	наш	нáшего	нáшем			
N	нáше			нáши	нáших	нáших
F	нáша	нáшей	нáшей			

Note that the genitive singular feminine and the genitive plural forms have the same ending as the locative (cf. *Grammar Unit* **3:2.3**) and hence the same irregularity appears, namely **моéй**, with the stressed ending -*Ey* instead of -*Oy*.

1.6 Genitive forms of pronouns.

PERSONAL PRONOUNS					
SINGULAR			PLURAL		
1.		(*I, me*)	1.		(*we, us*)
	Nom.	я		*Nom.*	мы́
	Gen.	меня́		*Gen.*	нáс
	Loc.	мнé		*Loc.*	нáс
2.		(*you*)	2.		(*you*)
	Nom.	ты́		*Nom.*	вы́
	Gen.	тебя́		*Gen.*	вáс
	Loc.	тебé		*Loc.*	вáс
3.		(*he, him*)			
	Nom.	óн			
	Gen.	(н)егó			
	Loc.	нём			
		(*it*)	3.		(*they, them*)
	Nom.	онó		*Nom.*	они́
	Gen.	(н)егó		*Gen.*	(н)и́х
	Loc.	нём		*Loc.*	ни́х
		(*she, her*)			
	Nom.	онá			
	Gen.	(н)её			
	Loc.	ней			

INTERROGATIVE PRONOUNS		
	(who, whom)	*(what)*
Nom.	ктó	чтó
Gen.	когó	чегó
Loc.	кóм	чём

The first and second person singular and plural forms are irregular and the others, except for **её** have genitive endings like special adjectives. The genitive singular of the masculine and neuter forms are all spelled with **-г-** pronounced /v/, as mentioned in the preceding section.

The occurrence of **егó, её, йх** as against **негó, неё, нйх**, will be treated in section 2.2, which follows.

❷ 2. Uses of the Genitive case

2.1 Possession

(1) The possessive construction with nouns

The genitive in Russian is equivalent to the English possessive construction with *'s* or *of*. The order of the words in Russian is that of the words in English with the *"of"* construction:

Óн профéссор **рýсского языкá**.	He is a professor *of the Russian language*.
Брáт **инженéра** рабóтает на пóчте.	The *engineer's* brother works at the post office.
Э́то — модéль **самолёта**.	This is a model *of an airplane*.
Э́то — дóм **дóктора**.	This is the *doctor's* house.

(2) The possessive adjectives

The Russian equivalents of *my, your, our* **мóй, твóй, вáш, нáш** are special adjectives which agree in gender, number and case with the nouns with which they are used. The Russian equivalents of *his, her, their*, however, are the genitive forms of the personal pronouns **егó, её, их**, (literally *of him, of her, of them*) and these three forms do not vary or change in any way in the meaning *his, her, their*. Compare:

				мои брáтья, сёстры, пйсьма
(my)	мóй брáт	моё письмó	моя сестрá	
(your, familiar)	твóй "[1]	твоё "	твоя "	твои "
(your)	ваш "	вáше "	вáша "	вáши "
(our)	наш "	наше "	нáша "	нáши "

[1] For the use of the familiar pronoun and possessive adjective see *Grammar Unit* **2:2.3**.

BUT: (his)	егó	"	егó	"	егó	"	егó	"
(her)	её	"	её	"	её	"	её	"
(their)	их	"	их	"	их	"	их	"

(my) (your) (our)	Э́то дéти моегó брáта. вáшего нáшего		Э́то дéти мои́х сестёр. вáших нáших
BUT:	(his) (her) (their)	егó её их	егó её их

2.2 The use of the genitive after certain prepositions

Most prepositions in Russian require that the noun or pronoun that follows be in the genitive case. So far you have met only four such prepositions:

от *from*, из *from, out of*
у *at* для *for, for the benefit of*

2.2.1 The preposition от *from*[1]

The preposition от *from*, should at this stage of learning Russian be used only with nouns and pronouns referring to persons.

Гдé письмó **от Ивáна**?	Where's the letter *from Ivan?*
Гдé письмó **от негó**?	Where's the letter *from him?*
Гдé письмó **от егó брáта**?	Where's the letter *from his brother?*
Э́то письмó **от моегó сы́на**.	This letter is *from my son.*

The pronouns in the third person genitive, **егó, её, их**, when used after prepositions and having the meaning *him*, etc. (but not *his*, etc.) add the prefix **н-: негó, неё, ни́х**. Recall that when you learned the locative case forms of the third person pronouns they were given only in the forms нём, нéй, ни́х, with the prefix **н-**, since the locative case occurs only after prepositions.

2.2.2 The preposition из *from* (a place)

The prepósition **из** is used to mean *from* (*a place*) with those nouns which use **в** to mean *at* (*a place*). (See **в** with the locative case, *Grammar Unit* **3:2.5.**)

---

[1] The preposition **от** in the meaning *away from*, will be discussed later: **Óн к зáпаду от Москвы́.** It is to the west of (*away from*) *Moscow.*

Óн живёт в Ки́еве.	He lives in Kiev.
Я из Ки́ева.	I'm *from Kiev.*
Óн в Москвé.	He is in Moscow.
Óн из Москвы́.	He is *from Moscow.*

2.2.3 The preposition **y**

The object of the preposition **y** is in the genitive case. Two important uses are:

(1) **y** *at* (the place of).

y plus a noun or pronoun referring to persons can refer to the person's home, place of work, country, or any place normally associated with him, provided the context makes it clear.

Мóй брáт **y дóктора.**	My brother is *at the doctor's* (office or home, depending on context).
Я живý **y брáта.**	I live *at my brother's* (place).
Жéнщины **y вáс** в Амéрике чáсто рабóтают?	Do women *in (your country)* America often work?

The sentence containing **y вáс** which you had in Conversation Lesson 5 did not have the phrases в Амéрике in it. In that context it was clear that **y вáс** meant *in your country*. This sentence out of context could mean *in your home, factory, country,* etc., but the addition of the phrase **в Амéрике** makes clear what is meant.

(2) **y** plus (person) noun or pronoun equals (*person*) *has,* (*persons*) *have.* Compare the Russian and its English equivalent:

<blockquote>

У меня́ кни́га.   *I have the book.*

</blockquote>

Literally, the Russian sentence would be rendered: "*At* (*to, by*) *me* (*is a, is the*) *book,*" though it is simply the equivalent of "*I have a book.*"
Compare the following examples:

У меня́ кни́ги.⎫	*I have the books.*
У меня́ éсть кни́ги.⎭	
У когó мои́ кни́ги?	*Who has* my books?
Эти кни́ги **y вáшего сы́на.**	*Your son has* these books.
Чтó **y негó** в рукáх?	*What does he have* in (his) hands?
Чтó **y егó сестры́** в рукáх?	*What does his sister have* in (her) hands?
У моéй жены́ тóлько оди́н брáт.	*My wife has* only one brother.

In these sentences it is permissible to use the form **éсть** *there is, there are.* Some speakers use it with fairly high frequency but others rarely use it in this context.

Finally, note the contrast in the use of **y** to render *at one's place,* etc. and *to have.* The word order is frequently but not always significant.

Ивáн **y меня́.**	Ivan is *at my place.*	**У меня́** кни́га.	*I have a book.*

2.3 The use of the Genitive with numerals

With the numerals **двá**, **двé** *two*, **три** *three* and **четы́ре** *four* an accompanying noun is in the genitive singular case. Further, the numeral *two*, but only that numeral, agrees with the accompanying noun in that the form **двá** is used if the noun is masculine or neuter and **двé** is used if the noun is feminine.

With the numerals five through nineteen (and also the even tens) the accompanying noun must be in the genitive plural case.

двá студéнта	двé кни́ги
три студéнта	три кни́ги
четы́ре студéнта	четы́ре кни́ги
пя́ть студéнтов	пя́ть кни́г
шéсть студéнтов	шéсть кни́г

The form **рáз** in the meaning *one* is used only in counting.

The form **оди́н** *one*, is a special adjective and agrees with the following noun.

2.4 The use of the Genitive with quantity words

After a number of words specifying quantity,

мнóго	*much, many, a lot*
мáло	*little, few, not much, not many*
скóлько	*how much, how many*

the following noun must be in the genitive.

If the noun is countable it is in the genitive plural; if not, it is in the genitive singular. This is like English, where the plural is used with countable nouns (a lot *of airplanes*) and the singular with others (a lot *of sugar*). Of the above quantity words you have had only **мнóго** so far.

Тáм **мнóго таки́х самолётов**. There are *many such airplanes* there.
В Москвé **мнóго гости́ниц**. In Moscow there are *many hotels*.

2.5 The use of the Genitive in **нéт** constructions

In positive statements with **у** meaning *have*, the thing possessed is in the nominative case. In the corresponding negative statements the thing possessed is transformed to the genitive. The negative always has the form **нéт** *there isn't any, there aren't any*. If the positive has **éсть**, **нéт** replaces it.

У вáс éсть дéти?	Do you have children?
У меня́ **нéт детéй**.	I *don't have any children.*
У моегó брáта кни́ги.	My brother has the books.
У моегó брáта **нéт кни́г**.	My brother *doesn't have any books.*

95

У меня́ есть сестра́.   ) I have a sister.
У меня́ **нет сестры́**.   ) I *don't have a sister.*

In stating the location of something or someone: (1) if the statement is positive, the thing or person referred to is in the nominative case; (2) if the statement is negative, the thing or person referred to is in the genitive case. As in the previous type of sentence the negative always has the form **нет**. If **есть** occurs in the positive, **нет** replaces it in the negative.

В э́той гости́нице есть рестора́н.   ) There is a restaurant in this hotel.
В э́той гости́нице **нет рестора́на**.   ) There *isn't any restaurant* in this hotel.

В э́том го́роде есть гости́ницы.   ) There are hotels in this city.
В э́том го́роде **нет гости́ниц**.   ) There *aren't any hotels* in this city.

О́н та́м.   ) He's there.
Его́ та́м **нет**.   ) *He's not* there.

Мо́й по́езд здесь.   ) My train is here.
Моего́ по́езда здесь **нет**.   ) *My train isn't* here.

2.6   Челове́к, лю́ди

The noun **челове́к** *man, person* does not have any plural forms other than the genitive plural **челове́к**, which is used after the numerals five and above. In all other situations **лю́ди** *people* functions as the plural of челове́к.

Та́м **пя́ть челове́к**.   There are *five people* there.
But: Та́м **мно́го люде́й**.   There are *many people* there.

3.   До́ма, *at home*

There is a contrast in Russian between the meaning *at home* and *in the house.* The meaning *at home* is rendered by the special form **до́ма**. *In the house* has the expected form **в до́ме**.

Ива́н в рестора́не.   Ivan is in the restaurant.
Ива́н в до́ме.   Ivan is in the house.
Ива́н **до́ма**.   Ivan is *at home.*

УПРАЖНЕ́НИЯ

A. Make the following substitutions orally:

Где́ письмо́ от . . . .?

¹ Ива́н	⁸ учи́тельница	¹⁵ мо́й му́ж
² инжене́р	⁹ мо́й това́рищ	¹⁶ на́ш профе́ссор
³ хи́мик	¹⁰ О́льга	¹⁷ на́ша ма́ть
⁴ до́ктор	¹¹ э́тот тури́ст	¹⁸ мо́й дя́дя
⁵ Пётр	¹² америка́нец	¹⁹ Ве́ра
⁶ жена́	¹³ ва́ш бра́т	²⁰ э́тот челове́к
⁷ сестра́	¹⁴ э́та де́вушка	

B. Transform orally according to the model:

MODEL: Та́м самолёты.
  Та́м мно́го самолётов.

¹ Та́м фотогра́фии.	⁷ Та́м америка́нцы.	¹⁴ Та́м гости́ницы.
² Та́м города́.	⁸ Та́м америка́нки.	¹⁵ Та́м студе́нты.
³ Та́м больни́цы.	⁹ Та́м у́лицы.	¹⁶ Та́м студе́нтки.
⁴ Та́м статьи́.	¹⁰ Та́м зда́ния.	¹⁷ Та́м кни́ги.
⁵ Та́м писа́тели.	¹¹ Та́м теа́тры.	¹⁸ Та́м поезда́.
⁶ Та́м инжене́ры.	¹² Та́м пи́сьма.	¹⁹ Та́м перево́дчицы.
	¹³ Та́м рестора́ны.	

C. Make the following substitutions orally:

У . . . . мно́го таки́х кни́г.

¹ he has	¹³ that doctor has
² his comrade has	¹⁴ my uncle has
³ his daughter has	¹⁵ those engineers have
⁴ his comrades have	¹⁶ her husband has
⁵ she has	¹⁷ Ivan has
⁶ her sister has	¹⁸ who has . . .?
⁷ her son has	¹⁹ those professors have
⁸ they have	²⁰ that writer has
⁹ their children have	²¹ those writers have
¹⁰ their sisters have	²² my mother has
¹¹ Misha has	²³ Vera has
¹² Olga has	²⁴ that man has

D. Make the following substitutions orally:

Брáт . . . . рабóтает на пóчте.

¹ of my friend	⁶ of this chemist	¹¹ of those women
² of his friend	⁷ of our father	¹² of the engineer
³ of those children	⁸ of that writer	¹³ of Peter
⁴ of that doctor	⁹ of our teacher	¹⁴ of Vera
⁵ of my uncle	¹⁰ of my wife	¹⁵ of my interpreter

E. Make the following substitutions orally. Then repeat, transforming to plural:

. . . . живёт в Нью-Йóрке.

¹ his brother	⁵ the doctor	⁹ our brother
² her son	⁶ that chemist	¹⁰ our child
³ their comrade	⁷ my professor of Russian	¹¹ that girl
⁴ your uncle	⁸ his sister	

F. Transform orally from third person singular to third person plural according to the model:

MODEL: Óн рабóтает в э́том дóме?
Нéт, нó **онú** рабóта**ют** в э́том дóме.

1. Óн читáет о самолётах?
2. Óн умéет читáть по-англи́йски?
3. Óн сиди́т в ресторáне?
4. Óн говори́т о её товáрище?
5. Óн хóчет посмотрéть э́ти фотогрáфии?

REVIEW LESSON TWO

A. FLUENCY DRILL

1. What do your brothers do? 2. They are engineers. 3. They work in a factory in Moscow. 4. My father's also an engineer. 5. He lives in Leningrad and works in a lab there. 6. He works a lot. 7. He's always in the lab.

8. Doctors work in hospitals. 9. Chemists work in laboratories. 10. Engineers often work in factories. 11. Tourists live in hotels. 12. Americans live in cities. 13. My daughters live in New York. 14. Our sons work in Moscow. 15. Writers often work at home.

16. What's he talking about? 17. I don't know what he's talking about. 18. Where does the professor live? 19. Do you know where the professor lives? 20. Where is Moscow located? 21. Do you know that Kiev is located in the Ukraine?

22. What are they saying? 23. I don't know what they are saying. 24. He doesn't know what you're talking about. 25. I don't know who you're talking about. 26. I know who that letter is from. 27. They say that engineers work a lot. 28. It is said that students read a lot. 29. They say he works in a laboratory. 30. They say that there are many tourists in the Soviet Union. 31. People say that he's from Boston.

B. Conversation topics

(1) An American meets his Russian guide. They talk about where they are from and what the American wants to see in the Soviet Union.

(2) A and B discuss their immediate relatives, where they live and work.

(3) An American and a Russian show each other photographs of their relatives and friends and discuss them.

Moscow.
View of Kremlin
from the Sophysky Embankment

СССР

СССР[1] (Сою́з Сове́тских Социалисти́ческих Респу́блик) состои́т из[2] пятна́дцати[3] респу́блик. К ю́гу[4] от Кавка́за[5] нахо́дятся Азербайджа́нская Сове́тская Социалисти́ческая Респу́блика, Армя́нская ССР и Грузи́нская[6] ССР. В Сре́дней[7] А́зии — Каза́хская, Туркме́нская, Узбе́кская, Таджи́кская и Кирги́зская Респу́блики. В Европе́йской ча́сти[8] СССР нахо́дятся сле́дующие[9] респу́блики: Латви́йская, Лито́вская,[10] Эсто́нская, Молда́вская, Украи́нская и Белору́сская. Са́мая больша́я[11] респу́блика, э́то РСФСР[12] (Росси́йская Сове́тская Федерати́вная Социалисти́ческая Респу́блика), кото́рая[13] простира́ется[14] от Балти́йского мо́ря[15] до Ти́хого[16] океа́на.

Три́ сове́тские респу́блики посыла́ют[17] представи́телей[18] в Организа́цию Объединённых[19] На́ций (ООН): РСФСР, Украи́нская ССР и Белору́сская ССР.

В Сове́тском Сою́зе мно́го больши́х городо́в. Населе́ние[20] Москвы́, столи́цы[21] Сове́тского Сою́за, — пять миллио́нов. Населе́ние Ленингра́да, кото́рый был столи́цей Росси́и до револю́ции, — приме́рно[22] три миллио́на. Други́е[23] больши́е города́ Сове́тского Сою́за — Ки́ев, Ха́рьков, Баку́, Го́рький и Оде́сса.

1 pronounced /èsèsèsér/
2 consists of
3 fifteen
4 south
5 Caucasus
6 Georgian
7 central

8 part
9 following
10 Lithuanian
11 largest
12 pronounced /èrèsèfèsér/
13 which
14 extends
15 sea
16 pacific, quiet
17 send
18 representatives
19 united

20 population
21 capital
22 approximately
23 other

CONVERSATION 9

Buying cigarettes

John is still having trouble with making change in Russian; he should look closer at the money he spends.

CONVERSATION UNIT NINE ━━━━━━━━━━━━━━━

ENGLISH EQUIVALENTS

JOHN	[1] Hello! [2] Don't you have any filter cigarettes?
SALESMAN	[3] Of course! [4] We have them [there are] with filter and without filter, both Laika and Friend.
JOHN	[5] Are your cigarettes expensive?
SALESMAN	[6] No, these, for example, are cheaper than Kazbek papirosas.
JOHN	[7] How much do they cost?
SALESMAN	[8] Twenty kopecks a pack.
JOHN	[9] And those over there?
SALESMAN	[10] Kazbek? Thirty kopecks. Which ones do you want?
JOHN	[11] I want just one pack of Laikas, please. [12] Here's three rubles.
SALESMAN	[13] No, you're mistaken. [14] You've given me five rubles.
JOHN	[15] Really! Thanks a lot!
SALESMAN	[16] Here's your [for you] change. Come again!
JOHN	[17] I'll come [again]. [18] Do you have many customers here?
SALESMAN	[19] So-so. Not too many.
JOHN	[20] Good-bye! But I'll come back again.
SALESMAN	[21] Good-bye!

NOTES

4 Brand names of cigarettes:
 Ла́йка *Eskimo dog* is the name of the dog sent aloft in the second Soviet earth satellite.
 Дру́г literally, *friend*
 Казбе́к one of the highest mountains in the Caucasus.

6 **папиро́са** a cigarette with a hollow cardboard mouthpiece which may be as much as several inches long. A **сигаре́та** is like an American cigarette.

8 There are 100 kopecks in a ruble.

10 **ва́м** *to you* or *for you.*

11 **мне́** *to me* or *for me.*

14 A five ruble note is the same size as a three, but in general the larger the denomination, the larger the size of the note.

Покупка папирос

ДЖОН   ¹ Здравствуйте! ² Нет ли у вас сигарет с фильтром?

ПРОДАВЕЦ   ³ Конечно! ⁴ Есть и с фильтром и без фильтра, и « Лайка » и « Друг ».

ДЖОН   ⁵ Дорогие у вас сигареты?

ПРОДАВЕЦ   ⁶ Нет. Эти, например, дешевле, чем папиросы « Казбек ».

ДЖОН   ⁷ Сколько они стоят?

ПРОДАВЕЦ   ⁸ Двадцать копеек пачка.

ДЖОН   ⁹ А вон те?

ПРОДАВЕЦ   ¹⁰ « Казбек »? Тридцать копеек. Каких вам?

ДЖОН   ¹¹ Мне только одну пачку « Лайки », пожалуйста. ¹² Вот три рубля.

ПРОДАВЕЦ   ¹³ Нет, вы ошибаетесь. ¹⁴ Вы мне дали пять рублей.

ДЖОН   ¹⁵ Действительно! Большое спасибо!

ПРОДАВЕЦ   ¹⁶ Вот вам сдача. Приходите ещё!

ДЖОН   ¹⁷ Приду. ¹⁸ У вас много здесь покупателей?

ПРОДАВЕЦ   ¹⁹ Так себе. Не очень.

ДЖОН   ²⁰ До свидания! Но я ещё приду.

ПРОДАВЕЦ   ²¹ До свидания!

ADDITIONAL VOCABULARY

два́дцать	*twenty*
три́дцать	*thirty*
со́рок	*forty*
пятьдеся́т	*fifty*
шестьдеся́т	*sixty*
се́мьдесят	*seventy*
во́семьдесят	*eighty*
девяно́сто	*ninety*

NEW VERBS

TYPE I

приду́т	will come, will arrive
ошиба́ются	are mistaken

(See *Conversation 8 New Verbs* for the reflexive ₁ particle.)

TYPE II

сто́ят	cost
прихо́дят, прихожу́	come, arrive

The verb form **прихо́дят** *they come, are coming* has present meaning and the form **приду́т** has future meaning (Cf. *Grammar Unit* **2:3.2**). Note that the form you met in the text, **приходи́те** is an imperative form, which will be discussed later. Do not confuse **приходи́те** *come!* with the second plural non-past, **прихо́дите** *you come, are coming* which has the stress on the stem.

NEW NOUNS

Masculine

NOMINATIVE SINGULAR	GENITIVE SINGULAR	NOMINATIVE PLURAL	GENITIVE PLURAL	
Казбе́к				Kazbek
покупа́тель				customer
фи́льтр				filter
приме́р				example
продаве́ц (е)	продавца́	продавцы́		salesman
ру́бль	рубля́	рубли́		ruble
дру́г		друзья́	друзе́й	friend

Feminine I

Ла́йка	Laika
сигаре́та	cigarette
папиро́са	papirosa
па́чка (е)	pack
сда́ча	change
копе́йка (е)	kopeck

NUMERALS

Note that the numerals **два́дцать** *twenty* and **три́дцать** *thirty* end in a palatalized consonant, whereas the other tens do not.

With a numeral that is an *even ten* (20, 30, 40 etc.) the noun is in the genitive plural (cf. *Grammar Unit* **4:2.3**).

УПРАЖНЕ́НИЯ

A. Make the following substitutions orally:

У него́ то́лько . . . .

1 ruble	1 letter	1 kopeck
2 rubles	2 letters	2 kopecks
3 rubles	3 letters	3 kopecks
4 rubles	4 letters	4 kopecks
5 rubles	5 letters	5 kopecks
6 rubles	6 letters	6 kopecks

B. Transform orally from the singular to the numeral *two* according to the model:

MODEL: У меня́ ру́бль. **У меня́ два́ рубля́.**

1. У меня́ сигаре́та.
2. У моего́ бра́та то́лько рубль.
3. У неё кни́га.
4. У Ива́на до́чка.
5. У Петра́ бра́т.
6. У моего́ му́жа самолёт.
7. У Ве́ры сестра́.

C. Repeat exercise B, transforming to **У меня́ пя́ть** . . . .

D. Give the Russian equivalents:

1. Do you have filter cigarettes? 2. Certainly we have filter cigarettes. 3. We also have cigarettes without a filter. 4. What's that? 5. That's a papirosa. 6. We don't have that kind of (such) cigarettes in America.

105

7. How much do they cost? 8. These cigarettes are cheaper than papirosas. 9. These cigarettes cost twenty kopecks a pack. 10. These cigarettes cost fifty kopecks a pack. 11. These papirosas cost thirty kopecks a pack.

12. Do you have a cigarette? 13. Who has a cigarette? 14. Who has a ruble? 15. I don't have a ruble. 16. I have four rubles. 17. I have six rubles.

18. This is my wife's sister. 19. This is my sister's son. 20. This is my brother's friend. 21. This is my friend's brother. 22. This is my husband's sister. 23. This is my sister's husband. 24. This is Vera's daughter. 25. This is Peter's father.

CONVERSATION 10

Where are you going?

John, who misses an appointment with a friend, winds up directing Boris to a kiosk.

CONVERSATION UNIT TEN ───────────

ENGLISH EQUIVALENTS

JOHN	[1] Hello, Boris.
BORIS	[2] Hello, John. Where are you going [on foot]?
JOHN	[3] I'm going [on foot] to the railroad station.
BORIS	[4] You're [going] to the station too? [5] Where are you going [by vehicle]?
JOHN	[6] Nowhere. I have to meet my friend there. And you?
BORIS	[7] I'm going [by vehicle] to the country. [8] I have a vacation.
JOHN	[9] That's fine! Write me.
BORIS	[10] Of course I'll write. [11] Well, here we are at the station. [12] But where is your friend?
JOHN	[13] I don't know. I always meet him here when he is free.
BORIS	[14] At what time do you meet him?
JOHN	[15] At five o'clock. [16] And what time is it now?
BORIS	[17] [It's] already five.
JOHN	[18] He's not here yet. [19] He's probably busy and won't come.
BORIS	[20] In that case we can go to the restaurant. [21] I still have time.
JOHN	[22] That's a fine idea! [23] Let's go!
BORIS	[24] But first I have to buy some cigarettes.
JOHN	[25] I saw a kiosk at the entrance. [26] You can buy them there.

NOTES

2, 3 These verbs mean *go* under one's own steam. They are used of a person going on foot, of time passing, of machines running, etc.

5, 7 This verb means *go* by some means of locomotion other than one's own power, e.g., by car, train, horse, etc.

6 **Мне́ на́до** literally, *for me it is necessary.*

7 **Дере́вня** means *country* as opposed to city and also means *small village.* **Óтпуск** is the equivalent of English *leave* for military and government personnel and of *vacation* from a job (but not vacation from school).

25 **Кио́ск** is a small booth the size of a newsstand frequently seen on the sidewalks in the Soviet Union. A particular kiosk specializes in a particular commodity, e.g., cigarettes, books, newspapers, small gifts, etc.

26 **Мóжете** *you can* means you have the physical capacity or opportunity of doing something. Contrast this with **умéете** *have the intellectual capacity.* Cf. *Conversation* **6.**

Куда вы идёте?

ДЖОН	¹ Здра́вствуйте, Бори́с.
БОРИ́С	² Здра́вствуйте, Джон. Куда́ вы́ идёте?
ДЖОН	³ Я́ иду́ на вокза́л.
БОРИ́С	⁴ Вы́ то́же на вокза́л? ⁵ Куда́ же вы́ е́дете?
ДЖОН	⁶ Никуда́. Мне́ на́до та́м встре́тить моего́ дру́га. А вы́?
БОРИ́С	⁷ Я́ е́ду в дере́вню. ⁸ У меня́ о́тпуск.
ДЖОН	⁹ Э́то хорошо́! Пиши́те мне́.
БОРИ́С	¹⁰ Коне́чно, напишу́. ¹¹ Ну́, во́т мы́ и на вокза́ле. ¹² Где́ же ва́ш дру́г?
ДЖОН	¹³ Не зна́ю. Я́ всегда́ его́ зде́сь встреча́ю, когда́ о́н свобо́ден.
БОРИ́С	¹⁴ В кото́ром часу́ вы́ его́ встреча́ете?
ДЖОН	¹⁵ В пя́ть часо́в. ¹⁶ А кото́рый сейча́с ча́с?
БОРИ́С	¹⁷ Уже́ пя́ть.
ДЖОН	¹⁸ Его́ ещё зде́сь не́т. ¹⁹ Наве́рно о́н за́нят и не придёт.
БОРИ́С	²⁰ В тако́м слу́чае мы́ мо́жем пойти́ в рестора́н. ²¹ У меня́ ещё е́сть вре́мя.
ДЖОН	²² Во́т и прекра́сно! ²³ Пойдём!
БОРИ́С	²⁴ Но́ сперва́ мне́ на́до купи́ть сигаре́ты.
ДЖОН	²⁵ Я́ ви́дел кио́ск у вхо́да, ²⁶ вы́ мо́жете и́х купи́ть та́м.

ADDITIONAL VOCABULARY

трина́дцать	thirteen	семна́дцать	seventeen
четы́рнадцать	fourteen	восемна́дцать	eighteen
пятна́дцать	fifteen	девятна́дцать	nineteen
шестна́дцать	sixteen		

NEW VERBS

TYPE I

иду́т	are going (not by vehicle)
пойду́т	will go (not by vehicle)
е́дут	are going (by vehicle)
напи́шут, напишу́	will write
встреча́ют	meet

TYPE II

встре́тят, встре́чу	will meet
ку́пят, куплю́	will buy

Note that **пиши́те** *write!* is an imperative form, which will be discussed later. Do not confuse with the non-past second plural form **пи́шете** *you write, are writing.*

NEW NOUNS

Masculine

NOMINATIVE SINGULAR	GENITIVE SINGULAR	NOMINATIVE PLURAL	
слу́чай			case, occurrence
о́тпуск		отпуска́	vacation, leave
ча́с	часа́	часы́	hour
вхо́д			entrance
кио́ск			kiosk

Feminine I

дере́вня	country (as opposed to city)

NUMERALS

A noun accompanying the numerals *five* through *nineteen* is in the genitive plural (cf. *Grammar Unit* **4:2.3**).

110

УПРАЖНÉНИЯ

A. Transform orally from second person plural to first person singular according to the model.

MODEL : Вы́ идёте на вокзáл? **Я́ иду́ на вокзáл.**

1. Вы́ éдете в дерéвню?
2. Вы́ мнé напи́шете?
3. Вы́ придёте?
4. Вы́ чáсто ошибáетесь?
5. Вы́ живёте в Нью-Йóрке?
6. Вы́ рабóтаете на пóчте?
7. Вы́ бýдете тáм?
8. Вы́ умéете читáть по-рýсски?

B. Make the following substitutions orally:

Мóй брáт живёт в .....

¹ дерéвня
² э́тот дóм
³ Москвá
⁴ Ленингрáд
⁵ Амéрика
⁶ э́та гости́ница
⁷ э́то здáние
⁸ э́тот гóрод
⁹ Смолéнск

C. Make the following substitutions orally:

. . . . здéсь нéт.

¹ the entrance
² the kiosks
³ the papirosas
⁴ your pack of cigarettes
⁵ the cigarettes
⁶ our friends
⁷ my wife
⁸ the post office
⁹ the chemists
¹⁰ his sister
¹¹ the tourists
¹² my letter
¹³ his hotel
¹⁴ the girls

D. Make the following substitutions orally:

В э́том гóроде мнóго . . . .

¹ restaurants
² hotels
³ engineers
⁴ professors
⁵ buildings
⁶ houses
⁷ tourists
⁸ factories
⁹ writers
¹⁰ kiosks
¹¹ teachers (*m.*)
¹² teachers (*f.*)
¹³ Americans
¹⁴ interpreters

E. Give the Russian equivalents:

1. Where are you going? (vehicle) 2. I'm going to the country. (vehicle) 3. Where are you going? (foot) 4. I'm going to the station. (foot)

5. I have to meet my friend there. 6. I have to meet my friend at the station. 7. I have to meet my friend at my hotel. 8. I often meet him at the restaurant.

111

9. At what time do you meet him? 10. I always meet my friend at 7 o'clock. 11. I always meet him at 3 o'clock. 12. Do you always meet him here? 13. No, not always. 14. What time is it now? 15. What time is it? 16. It's 9 o'clock. 17. It's 9. 18. It's now 9 o'clock.

19. Where's your friend? 20. He isn't here. 21. He isn't here yet. 22. My friend isn't here. 23. He's busy. 24. He's probably busy. 25. He's always busy at the factory. 26. He works at the factory. 27. Does he work hard [much]? 28. That's fine! 29. Good for him!

30. I have to buy some cigarettes. 31. Where's a kiosk? 32. Is there a kiosk at the entrance? 33. I saw a kiosk at the entrance. 34. There is no kiosk at the entrance. 35. Yes, there is. 36. There are two kiosks there. 37. Well what do you know about that! [what do you say] 38. How much do these cigarettes cost? 39. These cigarettes cost forty kopecks a pack. 40. One pack costs thirty kopecks. 41. Two packs cost sixty kopecks.

GRAMMAR UNIT FIVE

⟳ 1. The Accusative Case

Notice the use of the accusative case in these sentences with which you are already familiar:

Мне́ на́до там встре́тить **моего́ дру́га**.   I have to meet *my friend* here.
Мне́ на́до купи́ть **сигаре́ты**.   I have to buy *cigarettes*.

Only the singular of feminine I nouns has an ending in the accusative that is different from the endings you have already learned. These nouns have an accusative singular ending in the basic vowel -*U*, written **у** or **ю**.

Thus:

NOMINATIVE SINGULAR	ACCUSATIVE SINGULAR
сестра́	сестру́
Ве́ра	Ве́ру
гости́ница	гости́ницу

The singular of feminine II nouns has an accusative case form that is identical with the nominative singular.

Thus:

NOMINATIVE SINGULAR	ACCUSATIVE SINGULAR
ма́ть	**ма́ть**
моде́ль	**моде́ль**

All other nouns, that is, masculine nouns (singular and plural), neuter nouns (singular and plural) and the plural of all feminine nouns have an accusative form that is identical with the nominative if the noun refers to an inanimate object; they have an accusative that is identical with the genitive if the noun refers to an animate object.
Some examples of nouns that refer to inanimate objects are:

NOMINATIVE	GENITIVE	ACCUSATIVE (like *Nom.*)
рестора́н	рестора́на	рестора́н
рестора́ны	рестора́нов	рестора́ны
письмо́	письма́	письмо́

113

пи́сь**ма**	пи́сем	пи́сь**ма**
гости́ниц**ы**	гости́ниц	гости́ниц**ы**
моде́л**и**	моде́лей	моде́л**и**

Some examples of nouns referring to animate objects are:

NOMINATIVE	GENITIVE	ACCUSATIVE (like *Gen.*)
инжене́р	инжене́р**а**	инжене́р**а**
инжене́ры	инжене́р**ов**	инжене́р**ов**
Ива́н	Ива́н**а**	Ива́н**а**
бра́т	бра́т**а**	бра́т**а**
бра́тья	бра́ть**ев**	бра́ть**ев**
жёны	жён	жён
ма́тери	матер**е́й**	матер**е́й**

A very small number of feminine I nouns with stress on the ending in the nominative singular have a shift of stress to the stem in the accusative singular. So far you have had only two such nouns:

NOMINATIVE SINGULAR	ACCUSATIVE SINGULAR
рук**а́**	ру́ку
гор**а́**	го́ру

For these nouns the accusative singular will be cited along with the nominative.

1.2 Accusative forms of special adjectives

Only the feminine singular of special adjectives has an accusative form different from those you have already learned, namely, the same ending -*U* of feminine I nouns.

Thus: э́т**у** до́чку
           э́т**у** ма́ть

All other forms of the special adjectives have a form identical with the nominative when agreeing with an inanimate noun and identical with the genitive when agreeing with an animate noun.

Examples of inanimates are:

NOMINATIVE	GENITIVE	ACCUSATIVE (like *Nom.*)
э́то**т** теа́тр	э́того теа́тра	э́то**т** теа́тр
э́т**и** самолёты	э́тих самолётов	э́т**и** самолёты
э́т**о** сло́во	э́того сло́ва	э́т**о** сло́во
э́т**и** зда́ния	э́тих зда́ний	э́т**и** зда́ния
э́т**и** моде́ли	э́тих моде́лей	э́т**и** моде́ли

Examples of animates are:

114

NOMINATIVE	GENITIVE	ACCUSATIVE (like *Gen.*)
мо́й сы́н	моего́ сы́на	моего́ сы́на
на́ши това́рищи	на́ших това́рищей	на́ших това́рищей
ва́ши сёстры	ва́ших сестёр	ва́ших сестёр

The complete list of the feminine singular forms of the special adjectives you have had so far is:

э́ту   мою́   ва́шу   на́шу   одну́

1.3 Accusative case forms of pronouns

The personal pronouns **я**, **ты́**, **мы́**, **вы́** always refer to animate beings while **о́н**, **оно́**, **она́**, and **они́** sometimes refer to persons, sometimes to things. Nonetheless, the accusative case of all the personal pronouns is identical to the genitive, as if the reference were always to animate beings.

The relative and interrogative pronoun **кто́** *who* always refers to an animate object; therefore the accusative is identical to the genitive.

The relative and interrogative pronoun **что́** *what* always refers to an inanimate object; therefore the accusative is identical to the nominative:

ACCUSATIVE CASE FORMS OF PRONOUNS

(1) The accusative case is identical to the genitive.

NOMINATIVE	GENITIVE = ACCUSATIVE
я	меня́
ты́	тебя́
мы́	на́с
вы́	ва́с
о́н	(н)его́
оно́	(н)его́
она́	(н)её
они́	(н)и́х
кто́	кого́

(2) The accusative case is identical to the nominative.

NOMINATIVE = ACCUSATIVE	GENITIVE
что́	чего́

1.4 The uses of the accusative case

1.41   Accusative with direct objects of verbs not in the negative

The accusative case is used as the direct object of most verbs. (The direct object of negated verbs is treated in *section* **2.**, below.)

Вы ви́дите **э́то зда́ние**?	Do you see *that building?*
Я пишу́ **статьи́ и кни́ги**.	I write *articles and books.*
Повтори́те за мно́й **э́ту фра́зу**.	Repeat *this sentence* after me.
Его́ това́рищи де́лают **моде́ли**.	His comrades make *models.*
Я хочу́ та́м встре́тить **моего́ дру́га**.	I want to meet *my friend* there.
В кото́ром часу́ вы́ **его́** встреча́ете?	At what time do you meet *him?*
Вы́ мо́жете **и́х** купи́ть та́м.	You can buy *them* there.
Кого́ вы́ встреча́ете?	*Whom* are you meeting?

The most frequently employed word order, which is illustrated above, puts the direct object after the verb if it is a noun and before the verb if a pronoun.

1.42   Accusative after certain prepositions

(1) Indicating motion to a place.

The accusative case is used after the prepositions **в** *to* and **на** *to*, indicating motion to a place.

Я иду́ **на вокза́л**.	I'm going *to the station.*
Я е́ду **в дере́вню**.	I'am going *to the country.*
Мы́ мо́жем пойти́ **в рестора́н**.	We can go *to the restaurant.*
Óн е́дет **в Москву́**.	He's going *to Moscow.*
Вы́ то́же **на вокза́л**?	Are you (going) *to the station* too?

As indicated in the last example, the verb is not necessary if the context is clear without it.

Any noun that is used with **в** *at, in* with the locative case to express location will be used with **в** *to, into* plus the accusative case to express motion to a place.

Any noun that is used with **на** *at, in* with the locative case to express location will be used with **на** *to, into* plus the accusative case to express motion to a place (cf. *Grammar Unit* **3:2.5**).

Óн **в рестора́не**.	He is *in the restaurant.*
Óн идёт **в рестора́н**.	He's going *to the restaurant.*
Они́ **в Москве́**.	They are *in Moscow.*
Они́ е́дут **в Москву́**.	They are going *to Moscow.*
Óн рабо́тает **на фа́брике**.	He works *in the factory.*
Óн идёт **на фа́брику**	He's going *to the factory.*

A number of adverbial forms occur in pairs, one form indicating location and the other form indicating motion under the same conditions as **в** and **на** *to, in, at* above.

Куда́ он идёт?	*Where* is he going?
Где́ он?	*Where* is he?
Он идёт **домо́й**.	He's going *home*.
Он **до́ма**.	He's *at home*.
Он е́дет **туда́**.	He's going *there*.
Он живёт **та́м**.	He lives *there*.
Он придёт **сюда́**.	He'll come *here*.
Он рабо́тает **здесь**.	He works *here*.

The following is a summary of the contrast between location and motion.

LOCATION:	где́?	здесь	та́м	до́ма	**в, на** plus Loc.
	in what place?	*in this place*	*in that place*	*at home*	*in, at*
MOTION:	куда?	сюда́	туда́	домо́й	**в, на** plus Acc.
	to what place?	*to this place*	*to that place*	*home(-ward)*	*into, to*

Сюда́ *to this place* is pronounced either /ṣudá/ or /sudá/.

(2) The accusative indicating *"for, in return for."*

The preposition **за** has several meanings, depending upon the case form of the following noun. When followed by the accusative, **за** means *for*, but only in the sense of "something *in return for* something." This usage is most frequent when money is given in return for a certain article. For example:

Вы́ мне́ да́ли пя́ть рубле́й	You've given me 5 rubles
за э́ти сигаре́ты.	*for these cigarettes.*

1.43 The Use of the Accusative case, without a verb, in ordering

It is customary, when ordering things, to state the thing ordered in the accusative caśe without any verb form:

Мне́ то́лько **одну́ па́чку**.	I want (For me) only *one pack.*

This kind of expression is used with high frequency when ordering a meal at a restaurant.

117

2. The Use of either the Accusative or the Genitive with direct objects of negated verbs

When a verb in the negative has a direct object some Russian speakers put the direct object in the accusative, some speakers put it in the genitive. Either case form is acceptable:

Я не зна́ю **э́ту де́вушку.**
Я не зна́ю **э́той де́вушки.** } I don't know *this girl.*

Я не зна́ю **э́тот рестора́н.**
Я не зна́ю **э́того рестора́на.** } I don't know *that restaurant.*

Since the genitive and accusative forms of masculine animate nouns in the singular, and of all animate nouns in the plural are identical, no problem of selection is involved with them.

Я не зна́ю **его́ бра́та.**   I don't know *his brother.*

Я не зна́ю **э́тих де́вушек.**   I don't know *these girls.*

Я не зна́ю **его́ бра́тьев.**   I don't know *his brothers.*

3. Ordinary Adjectives

Ordinary adjectives have the same endings as special adjectives except in the nominative (all forms) and the accusative feminine singular.

DISTINCTIVE CASE ENDINGS OF "ORDINARY" ADJECTIVES				
NOMINATIVE	MASC. SING.	NEUT. SING.	FEM. SING.	PLURAL
Basic Vowel	-*Oy*/-*Iy*	-*O*ya	-*A*ya	-*I*ya
Spelling	**-ой, -ый, -ий**	**-ое, -ее**	**-ая, -яя**	**-ые, -ие**
ACCUSATIVE				
Basic Vowel			-*UyU*	
Spelling			**-ую, -юю**	

In the nominative singular masculine the ending -*O*y is used when the ending is stressed; otherwise the ending -*I*y is used. (For some speakers of Russian the ending is -*O*y under all conditions, with the normal weakening to /-ay/ and /-iy/ when unstressed. Thus some speakers say /rúskay/, basic -*O*y, and some say /rúsk̦iy/, basic -*I*y.)

The nominative singular masculine·ending is always written **ой** when the ending is stressed, e.g.,

> втор**ой**   *second*
> больш**ой**   *big*

When the ending is not stressed the nominative singular masculine is written either **-ый** or **-ий** according to the rules of spelling.

> пе́рв**ый**   *first*
> ру́сск**ий**   *Russian*

In the endings which are peculiar to the ordinary adjective, the first letter is spelled according to the usual rules of spelling and the second letter is constant for any particular form. It should also be noted that aside from stems ending in **к, г, х, ч, ж, ш, щ, ц,** where special spelling rules apply, the first letter of any case ending is one of the set **ы, а, о, у** for almost all adjectives. A very small number of adjectives have a stem ending in a palatalized consonant, which requires the ending to be spelled with the letters **и, я, е, ю.** So far you have had none of the latter type.

второ́й	second	пе́рвый	first
како́й	which, what	ста́рый	old
тако́й	such	ру́сский	Russian
дорого́й	dear, expensive	ма́ленький	little, small
родно́й	native	хоро́ший	good
большо́й	big, large	сове́тский	Soviet
молодо́й	young	англи́йский	English
кото́рый	which, what		

You have also met a number of words that are used as nouns but are inflected with adjective endings. Thus:

> ру́сский   (masculine)   *a Russian*
> ру́сская   (feminine)   *a Russian*
> родны́е   (plural)   *relatives*

Now, practice reading the following sentences and compare the endings of special adjectives, ordinary adjectives and nouns: (M = Masculine; A = Animate; I = Inanimate; N = Neuter; F = Feminine).

119

(1) Вот... + NOMINATIVE CASE.

(There is that big...)   *(There are those big...)*

M-A	этот большо́й ма́льчик.	эти больши́е[1] ма́льчики.
M-I	этот большо́й теа́тр.	эти больши́е теа́тры.
N	Вот... это большо́е зда́ние.	эти больши́е зда́ния.
F-A	эта больша́я же́нщина.	эти больши́е же́нщины.
F-I	эта больша́я кни́га.	эти больши́е кни́ги.

(2) Это фотогра́фия... + GENITIVE CASE.

(That's a photograph of that big...)   *(That's a photograph of those big...)*

M-A	этого большо́го ма́льчика.	этих больши́х ма́льчиков.
M-I	этого большо́го теа́тра.	этих больши́х теа́тров.
N	Это фото-гра́фия... этого большо́го зда́ния.	этих больши́х зда́ний.
F-A	этой большо́й же́нщины.	этих бо́льших же́нщин.
F-I	этой большо́й кни́ги.	этих больши́х кни́г.

(3) Вы зна́ете...? + ACCUSATIVE CASE.

(Do you know that big...?)   *(Do you know those big...?)*

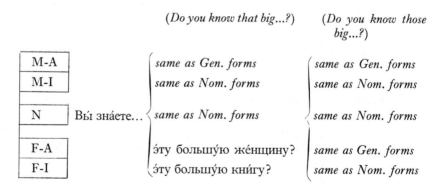

M-A	*same as Gen. forms*	*same as Gen. forms*
M-I	*same as Nom. forms*	*same as Nom. forms*
N	Вы зна́ете... *same as Nom. forms*	*same as Nom. forms*
F-A	эту большу́ю же́нщину?	*same as Gen. forms*
F-I	эту большу́ю кни́гу?	*same as Nom. forms*

[1] The basic vowel *I* in the ordinary adjective большо́й ın these examples (больши́е, больши́х, etc.) is spelled **и** rather than **ы** because of the stem final **ш** (cf. *spelling rule*).

(4) Она говорит об ... + LOCATIVE CASE.

		(*She's talking about that big...*)	(*She's talking about those big...*)
M-A		этом большóм мáльчике.	этих больши́х мáльчиках.
M-I		этом большóм теáтре.	этих больши́х теáтрах.
N	Онá говори́т об...	этом большóм здáнии.	этих больши́х здáниях.
F-A		этой большóй жéнщине.	этих больши́х жéнщинах.
F-I		этой большóй кни́ге.	этих больши́х кни́гах.

● 4. Telling time

Asking and telling "what time it is" is expressed as follows:

Котóрый чáс?	What time is it?
Чáс.	It is one o'clock.
Двá (три́, четы́ре) часá.	It is two (three, four) o'clock.
Ужé пя́ть (шéсть, сéмь...) часóв.	It is already five (six, seven, ...) o'clock.

Asking and telling "at what time *something happens* or *happened*" is expressed as follows:

В котóром часý вы́ егó встречáете?	At what time do you meet him?
В чáс.	At one.
В двá (три́, четы́ре) часá.	At two (three, four) o'clock.
В пя́ть (шéсть, сéмь...) часóв.	At five (six, seven...) o'clock.

In conversational Russian it is common to use **скóлько** *how much, how many* in such expressions. For example:

Скóлько врéмени?	What time is it?
Сейчáс скóлько?	What time is it now?
Во скóлько вы́ егó встречáете?	At what time do you meet him?

● 5. The special adjective тóт

The special adjective **тóт** *that*, has the following forms:

121

Special Adjective тóт	MASCULINE	NEUTER	FEMININE	PLURAL
Nominative	тóт	тó	тá	тé
Genitive	тогó	тогó	тóй	тéх
Accusative	N/G	N/G	тý	N/G
Locative	тóм	тóм	тóй	тéх

The special adjective **тóт** has the same endings as **э́тот** with one exception: wherever э́тот has **-и-** in the ending (э́ти, э́тих, etc.) тот has **-е-** (тé, тéх, etc.).

You have learned that the special adjective **э́тот** means both *this* and *that*. The special adjective **тóт** *that*, is used instead of э́тот when there is a contrast between *this* and *that*.

Э́та кни́га моя́, á тá кни́га вáша.	*This* book is mine and *that* book is yours.
Э́ти деше́вле чéм папирóсы "Казбéк".	*These* are cheaper than Kazbek papirosas (cigarettes).
Á вóн тé?	And *those* over there?

◑ 6. The particle **ли**

In both English and Russian, questions without an interrogative word may be, and in Russian most frequently are, identical in form with a statement, but with a different intonation.

Вáш отéц живёт в Ленингрáде.	Your father lives in Leningrad.
Вáш отéц живёт в Ленингрáде?	Does your father live here in Leningrad?
Éсть сигарéты с фи́льтром.	We have (There are) filter cigarettes.
Éсть сигарéты с фи́льтром?	Do you have (Are there) filter cigarettes?
У вáс нéт сигарéт с фи́льтром.	You don't have any filter cigarettes.
У вáс нéт сигарéт с фи́льтром?	Don't you have any filter cigarettes?
Прáвда.	That's right.
Прáвда?	Is that right?

Such questions may usually be stated in an alternative form. The "key" word or phrase—that of most importance in the mind of the questioner—is put in first position in the sentence. This "key" word is then immediately followed by the question word **ли**.

Живёт *ли* ваш отец здесь в Ленинграде?	Does your father live here in Leningrad?
Есть *ли* сигареты с фильтром?	Do you have filter cigarettes?
Нет *ли* у вас сигарет с фильтром?	Don't you have any filter cigarettes?
Не правда *ли*?	Isn't that right?

In these sentences **ли** is not translatable, but is simply an indication that this is a question. Generally, questions with **ли** are not used in spoken Russian with very high frequency.

● 7. и . . . . и, *both . . . and*; ни . . . . ни, *neither . . . nor*

The Russian **и...и** is the equivalent of English *both...and*, and **ни...ни** is the equivalent of *neither...nor*.

Есть **и** с фильтром **и** без фильтра.	We have them *both* with *and* without filter.

Ни он **ни** его брат **не** придёт.	*Neither* he *nor* his brother will come.

From the last example you will notice that the verb must have the negative particle **не**.

● 8. время, *time*

The word **время** belongs to a very small class of neuter nouns that have forms different from those previously discussed.

	SINGULAR	PLURAL
Nominative	время	времена
Genitive	времени	времён
Accusative	время	времена
Locative	времени	временах

● 9. ещё один; другой: *another*

The English word *another* is used in two contexts for which Russian uses two different expressions. *Another* may mean "an additional one", in which case Russian uses **ещё один**; or *another* may mean "a different one", in which case Russian uses **другой**. **Ещё** implies something additional and **другой** implies something different.

Я хочу **ещё один** дом.	I want *another* house (in addition to the one I have.)
Я хочу **другой** дом.	I want *another* house (instead of the one I have.)

123

Я хочу́ **ещё** папиро́сы.   I want *some more* cigarettes.
Я хочу́ **други́е** папиро́сы.   I want *other* cigarettes.

Ещё is also used in the meaning *still*.

Óн **ещё** рабо́тает.   He's *still* working.

УПРАЖНЕ́НИЯ

A. Listen to the following questions and answer them according to the model:

MODEL: Вы́ ви́дите э́то письмо́?   — **Да́, я его́ ви́жу.**

1. Вы́ ви́дите моего́ дру́га?
2. Вы́ ви́дитс э́тот кио́ск?
3. Вы́ ви́дите его́ сестру́?
4. Вы́ ви́дите э́ти дома́?
5. Вы́ ви́дитс э́ту у́лицу?
6. Вы́ ви́дите э́тих учи́тельниц?

B. Make the following substitutions orally, using the proper word order:

Óн зна́ет . . . .

¹ that doctor	¹⁰ us	¹⁹ those engineers
² me	¹¹ my sister	²⁰ this chemist
³ him	¹² you	²¹ this language
⁴ my daughter	¹³ those tourists	²² these chemists
⁵ our teacher (m.)	¹⁴ those students (m.)	²³ these languages
⁶ our teacher (f.)	¹⁵ those students (f.)	²⁴ who?
⁷ them	¹⁶ my children	²⁵ my mother
⁸ his wife	¹⁷ his comrades	²⁶ Olga
⁹ her	¹⁸ her sons	²⁷ Misha

C. Make the following substitutions orally:

Они́ иду́т . . . .

¹ to the restaurant	⁴ to the theater
² to the station	⁵ to the Kremlin
³ to the hotel	⁶ to the factory

Они́ е́дут . . . .

¹ to Moscow	⁶ to the post office	¹⁰ to the west
² to Leningrad	⁷ to America	¹¹ to the east
³ to the lab	⁸ to the country	¹² to the Ukraine
⁴ to the city	⁹ to the lab in	¹³ to the Soviet Union
⁵ to New York	that building	¹⁴ to Kiev

D. Make the following substitutions orally:

Óн мнé дáл пятьдеся́т копéек за . . . .

> ¹ this pack of cigarettes
> ² this book
> ³ the cigarettes
> ⁴ the papirosas
> ⁵ these books

E. Make the following substitutions orally:

Э́то . . . .

¹ a big restaurant	¹¹ another (different) word
² a big hotel	¹² another (different) entrance
³ a big building	¹³ an old building
⁴ big airplanes	¹⁴ a young girl
⁵ a small building	¹⁵ my native language
⁶ a small factory	¹⁶ my home (native) town
⁷ a small town (city)	¹⁷ an old lab
⁸ an expensive restaurant	¹⁸ a good hospital
⁹ a Russian chemist	¹⁹ the young American
¹⁰ expensive cigarettes	²⁰ the first word

F. Transform orally according to the model:

MODEL: У Ивáна самолёт. **У Ивáна нéт самолёта.**

1. У моегó дрýга брáт.	7. В э́том гóроде éсть ресторáны.
2. У Вéры письмó.	8. В Бостóне éсть теáтры.
3. У студéнта кни́ги.	9. В Амéрике éсть писáтели.
4. У дóктора женá.	10. У негó éсть врéмя.
5. В э́том гóроде éсть гости́ница.	11. Óн здéсь.
6. В э́том гóроде éсть ресторáн.	12. На э́той ýлице éсть киóск.

G. Make the following substitutions orally:

Они́ говоря́т о (об, обо) . . . .

¹ me	⁷ their comrades	¹³ the Soviet Union
² this kiosk	⁸ us	¹⁴ you
³ his vacation	⁹ my wife's brother	¹⁵ Misha
⁴ him	¹⁰ the doctor's friend	¹⁶ trains
⁵ her	¹¹ the tourists in America	¹⁷ the Ukraine
⁶ papirosas	¹² the tourists in the Soviet Union	

125

CONVERSATION 11

Where were you yesterday?

Natasha is a young librarian. While on vacation she telephones her American friend Mary.

CONVERSATION UNIT ELEVEN ⸻

ENGLISH EQUIVALENTS

NATASHA   [1] Where were you yesterday? [2] I called several times, but you weren't at home.

MARY   [3] I was looking over the Kremlin. [4] Somehow I wasn't able to go there earlier, [5] but yesterday I made it [succeeded in going].

NATASHA   [6] Did you like the Kremlin?

MARY   [7] Very much! I liked it so much that I'm going there again tomorrow.

NATASHA   [8] Did you see the Uspensky cathedral?

MARY   [9] Yes, I saw it. And I saw the museum, too. [10] The architecture of the cathedral is not at all like western [architecture].

NATASHA   [11] And what do you intend to do today?

MARY   [12] I don't know. Are you still on [Do you still have] vacation?

NATASHA   [13] Yes. Maybe you'd like to go to the Lenin Hills.

MARY   [14] Wonderful! [15] What a fine day it is today!

NATASHA   [16] When will you be ready?

MARY   [17] I'm almost ready. [18] I'll come by for you in ten minutes. [19] OK?

NATASHA   [20] Fine!

NOTES

6 Literally. Did the Kremlin please you?

13 Ле́нинские го́ры are low hills in the southern part of the city of Moscow on which the University is located.

ADDITIONAL VOCABULARY

два́дцать оди́н	*twenty-one*
два́дцать два́	*twenty-two*
два́дцать три́	*twenty-three*
два́дцать четы́ре	*twenty-four*
два́дцать пя́ть	*twenty-five*
два́дцать ше́сть	*twenty-six*
два́дцать се́мь	*twenty-seven*
два́дцать во́семь	*twenty-eight*
два́дцать де́вять	*twenty-nine*

128

_____ Где вы были вчера?

НАТА́ША [1] Где́ вы́ бы́ли вчера́? [2] Я́ вам не́сколько ра́з звони́ла, а ва́с не́ было до́ма.

МЭ́РИ [3] Я́ осма́тривала Кре́мль. [4] Ра́ньше я́ ка́к-то не могла́ туда́ пойти́, [5] но́ вчера́ мне́ удало́сь.

НАТА́ША [6] Ва́м понра́вился Кре́мль?

МЭ́РИ [7] О́чень! Та́к понра́вился, что я́ за́втра пойду́ опя́ть.

НАТА́ША [8] Вы́ ви́дели Успе́нский собо́р?

МЭ́РИ [9] Да́, ви́дела. И музе́й то́же ви́дела. [10] Архитекту́ра собо́ра совсе́м не похо́жа на за́падную.

НАТА́ША [11] А что́ вы́ собира́етесь де́лать сего́дня?

МЭ́РИ [12] Не зна́ю. У ва́с всё ещё о́тпуск?

НАТА́ША [13] Да́. Мо́жет бы́ть вы́ хоти́те пое́хать на Ле́нинские го́ры?

МЭ́РИ [14] Прекра́сно! [15] Како́й сего́дня хоро́ший де́нь!

НАТА́ША [16] Когда́ вы́ бу́дете гото́вы?

МЭ́РИ [17] Я́ почти́ гото́ва. [18] Че́рез де́сять мину́т я́ зайду́ за ва́ми. [19] Хорошо́?

НАТА́ША [20] Прекра́сно!

NEW VERBS

Type I

поéдут	will go (by vehicle)
осмáтривают	are looking over
зайдýт	will come by for
собирáются	intend

Type II

звоня́т	phone
понрáвятся, понрáвлюсь	will be pleasing to

NEW NOUNS

	NOMINATIVE SINGULAR	GENITIVE SINGULAR	NOMINATIVE PLURAL	
Masculine				
	музéй			museum
	собóр			cathedral
	дéнь (е)	дня́	дни́	day
Feminine I				
	Натáша			Natasha
	архитектýра			architecture
	минýта			minute
	горá			hill, mountain

Горá has the same type of unusual stress pattern as the noun **рукá** *hand* (cf. *Conversation* **7**):

	SINGULAR	PLURAL
Nominative	горá	гóры
Genitive	горы́	гóр
Accusative	гóру	гóры
Locative	горé	горáх

Сегóдня

It was pointed out previously that the letter **г** represents the sound /v/ only in the genitive endings of adjectives and pronouns (cf. *Grammar Unit* **4:1.5**). The word **сегóдня** consists of the genitive singular **сегó** *of this*, a seldom used special adjective, plus **дня**, genitive singular of **день** *day*, and is pronounced /ṣivódṇa/.

Не́сколько is another one of the expressions of quantity which take the genitive case (cf. *Grammar Unit* **4:2.4**).

УПРАЖНЕ́НИЯ

A. Make the following substitutions orally:

За́втра я́ куплю́ . . . .

¹ an airplane	⁸ a book
² a small airplane	⁹ a Russian book
³ a model of an airplaine	¹⁰ Russian books
⁴ a big model of an airplane	¹¹ other (different) books
⁵ a house	¹² Russian cigarettes
⁶ a small house	¹³ other (different) cigarettes
⁷ a big house	

B. Make the following substitutions orally:

О́н встре́тит . . . . на вокза́ле.

¹ Ivan	⁵ their sons	⁹ the chemist
² Vera	⁶ our children	¹⁰ your father
³ my sister	⁷ your friend	¹¹ the doctor
⁴ our comrades	⁸ her daughter	¹² Peter

C. Make the following substitutions orally:

Мы́ рабо́таем . . . .

¹ in this restaurant	⁷ in the museum
² in this small restaurant	⁸ in the Russian museum
³ in this hotel	⁹ in a lab
⁴ in this big hotel	¹⁰ in a small lab
⁵ in such a hotel	¹¹ in the Soviet Union
⁶ in such hotels	

D. Transform orally from **они́** to **я́** according to the model. Then repeat the exercise, substituting **о́н**. Note that in the first group of sentence the verbs all have future meaning.

MODEL: За́втра они́ зайду́т за ва́ми.
   За́втра я́ зайду́ за ва́ми.

   1. Они́ бу́дут в э́том ма́леньком рестора́не.
   2. Они́ ку́пят ру́сские сигаре́ты.
   3. Они́ за́втра пое́дут на Ле́нинские го́ры.

131

4. Они́ пойду́т в ру́сский музе́й.
5. Они́ встре́тят э́ту де́вушку в рестора́не.
6. Они́ напи́шут кни́гу об Аме́рике.

7. Они́ всегда́ звоня́т в час.
8. Они́ тепе́рь осма́тривают э́тот ма́ленький го́род.
9. В тако́м слу́чае они́ мо́гут встре́тить ва́шу жену́.
10. Они́ всегда́ встреча́ют её бра́та.
11. Они́ ча́сто прихо́дят сюда́.
12. Они́ сего́дня е́дут в Москву́.
13. Тепе́рь они́ иду́т домо́й.
14. Они́ ча́сто ошиба́ются.
15. Они́ туда́ иду́т че́рез пять мину́т.
16. Они́ всегда́ сидя́т у вхо́да.
17. Они́ говоря́т об архитекту́ре.

E. Give the Russian equivalents:

1. I'll come by for you in ten minutes. 2. I'll come by for you at three o'clock. 3. I'll come by for you at eight o'clock. 4. When will you be ready? 5. Will you be ready at six o'clock? 6. Will you be ready in five minutes? 7. I'll be at home at four o'clock. 8. I'm going (on foot) home at seven o'clock. 9. What do you intend to do today? 10. What are you doing today? 11. I'm going (by vehicle) to the Kremlin. 12. I'm looking over the Kremlin. 13. I'm going (on foot) to the museum. 14. I'm on [I have] vacation. 15. Are you still on vacation? 16. I don't have a vacation.

In the following sentences translate *come* and *go* by the verbs meaning *on foot*.

17. When will he come home? 18. When will he come here? 19. He'll come here tomorrow. 20. He often comes here. 21. She's here now. 22. She'll go there tomorrow. 23. Is she there? 24. No, she's at the post office. 25. Where are they going? 26. Where will they go tomorrow? 27. Where are they now? 28. They're at home.

CONVERSATION 12

A trip to the Lenin Hills

Getting out of the subway Mary and Natasha find themselves near Moscow University.

CONVERSATION UNIT TWELVE ───────────

ENGLISH EQUIVALENTS

NATASHA	[1] Well, here we are [have arrived]! [2] How did you like the subway?
MARY	[3] To tell the truth [4] I thought we'd have to go on a bus or streetcar, and I had hoped to look out the window.
NATASHA	[5] However, we got here sooner. [6] Let's go! [7] From the Lenin Hills there's a wonderful view of the city.
MARY	[8] Yes, it's high here. [9] And what building is that?
NATASHA	[10] That's the Moscow State University. [11] I studied here.
MARY	[12] What an enormous building! [13] How many stories does it have?
NATASHA	[14] About thirty stories.
MARY	[15] American universities aren't so high.
NATASHA	[16] Where did you study?
MARY	[17] At Cornell University. [18] It's located in Ithaca.
NATASHA	[19] Where is Ithaca?
MARY	[20] To the west of New York in the same state.
NATASHA	[21] Is Ithaca a big city?
MARY	[22] No, not very big, but nevertheless quite pretty.

NOTES

3 Literally, *honorably speaking.*

10 Frequently referred to as **МГУ** /ém gé ú/.

14 The university has 32 stories.

NEW VERBS

TYPE I

ду́мают	think
наде́ются	hope

TYPE II

смо́трят, смотрю́	look
у́чатся, учу́сь	study

Поездка на Ленинские Горы

НАТÁША	[1] Вóт мы́ и приéхали! [2] Кáк вáм понрáвилось метрó?
МЭ́РИ	[3] Чéстно говоря́, [4] я́ дýмала, что нáдо бýдет éхать на автóбусе и́ли на трамвáе, и надéялась смотрéть в окнó.
НАТÁША	[5] Затó, мы́ приéхали скорéе. [6] Пойдёмте! [7] С Лéнинских гóр чудéсный ви́д на гóрод.
МЭ́РИ	[8] Дá, здéсь высокó. [9] А что́ э́то за здáние?
НАТÁША	[10] Э́то Москóвский госудáрственный университéт. [11] Я́ здéсь учи́лась.
МЭ́РИ	[12] Какóе огрóмное здáние! [13] Скóлько в нём этажéй?
НАТÁША	[14] Этажéй три́дцать.
МЭ́РИ	[15] Америкáнские университéты не таки́е высóкие.
НАТÁША	[16] Гдé вы́ учи́лись?
МЭ́РИ	[17] В Корнéльском университéте. [18] Óн нахóдится в Итáке.
НАТÁША	[19] А́ гдé Итáка?
МЭ́РИ	[20] К зáпаду от Нью-Йóрка в тóм же штáте.
НАТÁША	[21] Итáка большóй гóрод?
МЭ́РИ	[22] Не большóй, нó затó краси́вый.

NEW NOUNS

	NOMINATIVE SINGULAR	GENITIVE SINGULAR	NOMINATIVE PLURAL	
Masculine				
	автóбус			bus
	университéт			university
	вúд			view
	штáт			state
	трамвáй			streetcar
	этáж	этажá	этажú	story, floor
Neuter				
	окнó (о)		óкна	window
	метрó (*indeclinable*)			subway
Feminine I				
	Итáка			Ithaca

When a numeral is placed after a noun it indicates *approximately* that much.

трúдцать этажéй	30 stories
этажéй трúдцать	about 30 stories

УПРАЖНÉНИЯ

A. Make the following substitutions orally:

Мы́ тепéрь осмáтриваем . . . .

¹ the Kremlin
² a cathedral
³ the Uspensky cathedral
⁴ a museum
⁵ a Russian museum
⁶ the Russian museums

⁷ a big building
⁸ a factory
⁹ Leningrad
¹⁰ Moscow
¹¹ the Moscow University
¹² a beautiful hospital

B. Transform orally according to the model:

MODEL: Óн дóма.   **Óн éдет домóй.**

Моя́ сестрá в Совéтском Союзе.
Моя́ сестрá éдет в Совéтский Союз.

1. Я́ в музéе.
2. Мóй брáт в дерéвне.

3. Мы́ в большóм гóроде.
4. Óн в Москвé.

5. Они́ на по́чте.
6. Тури́ст в э́том ма́леньком зда́нии.
7. Ива́н на фа́брике.
8. Де́вушка в э́той большо́й гости́нице.

9. Э́тот молодо́й челове́к в Ки́еве.
10. До́ктор на Украи́не.
11. О́льга на восто́ке.
12. Ми́ша на за́паде.

C. Practice counting from 1 to 29.

D. Make the following substitutions orally:

Ско́лько в э́том го́роде . . . .

1 universities	8 streets	16 Russian chemists
2 factories	9 theaters	17 writers
3 big factories	10 good theaters	18 airplanes
4 museums	11 hotels	19 engineers
5 cathedrals	12 small hotels	20 tourists
6 old cathedrals	13 doctors	21 buildings
7 kiosks	14 young doctors	22 tall buildings
	15 chemists	

E. Give the Russian equivalents:

1. What kind of building is that? 2. That's the Moscow State University. 3. The university is in Moscow. 4. The university is an enormous building. 5. What an enormous building! 6. That's a beautiful building! 7. The university is on the Lenin Hills. 8. The university is an enormous building on the Lenin Hills. 9. This is a state university. 10. Where is the State University located? 11. The university is located in this city. 12. The university is located in this state. 13. I am studying at this university. 14. My wife is also studying at this university. 15. Where do you study?

16. He works in this factory. 17. She works in this factory too. 18. Both Ivan and Misha work in this factory. 19. When do they work? 20. Neither Olga nor Natasha work. 21. Are you working now? 22. She still works at the factory. 23. How many engineers work at this factory? 24. Several engineers work at this factory. 25. We often work in this factory.

GRAMMAR UNIT SIX

🌑 1. The Infinitive

In Russian the infinitive is identified by the endings **-ть, -ти,** or **-чь,** postfixed (that is added and attached) to the infinitive stem. E.g. **работать.** The overwhelming majority of Russian verbs have an infinitive ending in **-ть.** Only a very small number end in **-ти** or **-чь.** For a complete list of the infinitive forms of the verbs you have had so far, see *section* **4,** below.

1.2 The Use of the Infinitive

The Russian infinitive is used very much like the English infinitive (with or without the word *to*):

Мой отéц лю́бит читáть.	My father likes to read.
Я не умéю писáть по-рýсски.	I can't write in Russian.[1]
Я хочý встрéтить моегó дрýга.	I want to meet my friend.
Мнé нáдо купи́ть папирóсы.	I have to buy cigarettes.
Вы мóжете и́х купи́ть там.	You can buy them there.[1]

1.3 The Infinitive and the Non-Past Tense

In Russian the stem of the non-past tense is frequently different from the stem of the infinitive.

Notice:

	BUT:			
работать	*to work*	говори́ть	*to speak*	жи́ть	*to live*
рабóтают	*they work*	говоря́т	*they speak*	живýт	*they live*

Since in Russian the form of the infinitive is not predictable from the non-past stem, and vice versa, both the infinitive stem and the non-past stem must be learned in order to be able to make up the various possible forms of a Russian verb. Consequently, whenever a new verb is introduced in succeeding conversations, the infinitive of that verb will be cited along with the third person plural non-past, and, where necessary, the first person singular of the non-past as well. (See *Grammar Unit* **2:3.1.**).

While the stem of the infinitive is frequently different from that of the non-past tense, the infinitive does often indicate which type of conjugation (Type I or Type II) will be employed in the non-past tense:

I. Most verbs—but not all—with an infinitive ending in **-ать** will have a non-past inflection of Type I (**-ают**):

работать	*to work*
рабóтают	*they work*

---

[1] After words like "can", *to* of the infinitive is lost in English.

138

II. Most verbs—but not all—with an infinitive ending in **-ить** have a non-past inflection of Type II:

> говори́ть *to speak*
> говоря́т   *they speak*

For a complete list of infinitive and non-past stems and irregular forms see *section* **4**.

⏺ 2. The Past Tense

Almost all verbs with an infinitive ending in **-ть** form the past tense by replacing the **-ть** by the following endings:

-л   if the subject of the verb is masculine singular
-ла ” ”   ”   ” ” ” ” feminine singular
-ло ” ”   ”   ” ” ” ” neuter singular
-ли ” ”   ”   ” ” ” ” plural (any gender)

All of the verbs ending in **-ть** that you have met so far are of this type. For example:

INFINITIVE	PAST TENSE
писа́ть	писа́л
люби́ть	люби́л
хоте́ть	хоте́л
жи́ть	жи́л
е́хать	е́хал

The letter **-л-** is the distinctive suffix of the past tense. The endings added to it are like those of the nominative forms of special adjectives, including the palatalization of the consonant before the plural ending. Notice how the verb form agrees with the subject in gender and number in the following sentences:

Я писа́л.	*I was writing.* (Man speaking)
Я писа́ла.	*I was writing.* (Woman speaking)
Ты́ писа́л.	*You were writing.* (Man being spoken to)
Ты́ писа́ла.	*You were writing.* (Woman being spoken to)
Óн писа́л.	*He was writing.*
Она́ писа́ла.	*She was writing.*
Оно́ писа́ло.	*It was writing.*
Они́ (Вы́, Мы́) писа́ли.	*They* (*You,* polite; *We*) *were writing.*

2.1 Reflexive Verbs

Reflexive verbs have the same inflection as other verbs, but **-ся** is added to forms ending in a consonant and **-сь** to those ending in a vowel. E.g.

INFINITIVE		PAST TENSE
роди́ться	*to be born*	роди́лся, роди́лась

139

находи́ться	*to be located*	находи́лся, находи́лась
понра́виться	*to be pleasing to*	понра́вился, понра́вилась

3. Aspect in Verbs

The difference in meaning and use of English verb forms such as *he was writing* and *he wrote* is called VERBAL ASPECT, although this grammatical term is not usually used in textbooks on English grammar. Both forms refer to past time, but indicate a different type of action. While Russian verbs also show verbal aspect, the system is quite different from that of English.

In Russian most verbs appear in pairs: **писа́ть—написа́ть** both meaning *to write;* **встреча́ть—встре́тить**, both meaning *to meet*. One member of the pair (писа́ть, встреча́ть) is referred to as the *imperfective* member of the pair and the other member of the pair (написа́ть, встре́тить) is referred to as the *perfective* member.

A rough but workable statement of the distinction between perfective and imperfective aspect is the following:

PERFECTIVE

The verb specifies the completion of an event, usually of an event that takes place a single time:

Ве́ра **написа́ла** письмо́.   Vera *wrote a letter*. (She finished it.)

IMPERFECTIVE

The verb does not specify whether or not the event is completed, and therefore indicates (1) or (2):

(1) an event that is repeated a number of times:

О́н ча́сто мне́ **писа́л**.   He often *used to write* me.
He often *wrote* me.

(2) a continuous event that is taking place at the time under discussion:

Она́ **писа́ла** письмо́,   She *was writing* a letter
когда́ я пришёл.   when I arrived.

3.1 Aspect Pairs

So far we have had both members of the perfective-imperfective pair for the following verbs:

IMPERFECTIVE	PERFECTIVE	
смотре́ть	посмотре́ть	*to look*
приходи́ть	прийти́	*to come* (on foot)

писа́ть	написа́ть	*to write*
встреча́ть	встре́тить	*to meet*
итти́	пойти́	*to go* (on foot)
е́хать	пое́хать	*to go* (by vehicle)

3.2 Aspect and the Expression of Future Time

The idea of the future is expressed differently with imperfective and perfective verbs.

IMPERFECTIVE VERBS

Imperfective verbs express future time by combining a non-past form of **быть** *to be*, with the infinitive of the verb:

Я ча́сто ему́ **бу́ду писа́ть.** *I shall write him often.*

In English the present tense may sometimes have future implication. Likewise in Russian the non-past tense of some imperfective verbs, —usually verbs of motion—may also have future meaning with reference to an action firmly decided: За́втра я **е́ду** в Москву́. *I am going* (that is, *I shall go, I'll go*) *to Moscow tomorrow.*

PERFECTIVE VERBS

The non-past tense of perfective verbs is future in meaning.

Я ему́ за́втра **напишу́.** *I'll write* him tomorrow.

3.3 Aspect Forms of the Verb

EXAMPLE:

	IMPERFECTIVE (I)	PERFECTIVE (P)
INFINITIVE	писа́ть	написа́ть
PAST TIME	писа́л, etc.	написа́л, etc.
FUTURE TIME	бу́ду писа́ть, etc.	напишу́, etc.
PRESENT TIME	пишу́, etc.	(NONE)

> INFINITIVE писа́ть (I) написа́ть (P)

Aspect is significant in using the infinitive:

Imperfective:

Я хочу́ **писа́ть** письмо́. — I want *to write* a letter (no specification as to whether or not it is to be finished).

Perfective:

Я хочу́ **написа́ть** письмо́. — I want *to write* a letter. (I intend to finish it.)

> PAST TIME PAST TENSE: писа́л, etc. (I) PAST TENSE: написа́л, etc. (P)

Past time is expressed with the past tense of both imperfective and perfective verbs. Aspect is significant:

IMPERFECTIVE

Óн мнé писа́л...... — *He used to write me* (every day).
Óн мнé писа́л...... — *He wrote me* (that is, *he wrote me every day*).
Я ему́ писа́ла...... — *I was writing him* (when he telephoned).

PERFECTIVE

Я ему́ написа́ла...... — *I wrote him.*

Russian has only two past tense forms, the imperfective and the perfective. English has many forms referring to past time. The English forms *was writing* and *used to write* usually equate with Russian imperfective aspect, but the other English forms may equate with either imperfective or perfective aspect in Russian. Consider the following sentences:

I wrote her (frequently).
I have written her (a hundred times).
I had written her (more often than I had my own family). } Я éй писа́л...
I was writing her (when I received the announcement of her marriage).
I used to write her (every day).

I wrote her (as soon as I got the announcement).
I have written her (for the last time). } Я éй написа́л...
I had written her (when the announcement arrived).

> FUTURE TIME: бы́ть + INFINITIVE: Я бу́ду писа́ть, etc. (I)
>
> NON-PAST TENSE: напишу́ etc. (P)

142

Future time can be expressed with both imperfective and perfective verbs. As has been seen, imperfective verbs express the future by combining the appropriate form of the non-past tense of **быть** with the infinitive of the imperfective verb; perfective verbs express the future with their non-past tense. Aspect is, then, significant when referring to future events: if the future event is considered as repeated, continuing or unassured of completion, the imperfective verb is used; if the future event is considered as assured of completion the perfective verb is employed.

IMPERFECTIVE

Я часто **буду писать** письма.   *I'll write* letters often.

PERFECTIVE

Я напишу письмо.   *I'll write* a letter (and I intend to finish it).

PRESENT TIME NON-PAST TENSE: пишу, etc. (I)
No "Present Time" Meaning (P)

Present time is indicated by using the non-past tense of an imperfective verb. There is no form of a perfective verb that has present meaning. Aspect, therefore, has no significance when referring to an act in present time; the imperfective verb must always be used.

Я **пишу** письмо.   *I am writing* a letter.
Куда вы **идёте**?   Where *are you going*?

The non-past tense of the imperfective verb is also used (like the present tense in English) in situations where time is not specified. For instance, in the following sentence the action may have been going on for a long time in the past and may continue into the future, but the particular time is not important:

Я **работаю** в ресторане.   *I work* in a restaurant.

◐ 4.   Verbs thus far studied

TYPE I

INFINITIVE		3RD PLUR.	1ST SING.	*English*
IMPERFECTIVE	PERFECTIVE			*Equivalent*
1. встречать		встречают		meet
2. делать		делают		do, make
3. думать		думают		think
4. знать		знают		know
5. называться		называются		be called
6. осматривать		осматривают		look over

143

7. ошиба́ться		ошиба́ются		be mistaken
8. понима́ть		понима́ют		understand
9. рабо́тать		рабо́тают		work
10. собира́ться		собира́ются		intend
11. чита́ть		чита́ют		read
12.	написа́ть	напи́шут	напишу́	write
13. писа́ть		пи́шут	пишу́	write
14.	сказа́ть	ска́жут	скажу́	tell, say
15. жи́ть		живу́т		live
16. зва́ть		зову́т		call
17.*	бы́ть	бу́дут		be
18.* мо́чь		мо́гут	могу́	can, be able
19. наде́яться		наде́ются		hope
20. остава́ться		остаю́тся		remain, stay
21. уме́ть		уме́ют		be able
22.* итти́		иду́т		go (foot)
23.*	пойти́	пойду́т		go (foot)
24.*	зайти́	зайду́т		come by (foot)
25.*	прийти́	приду́т		come (foot)
26. е́хать		е́дут		go (veh.)
27.	пое́хать	пое́дут		go (veh.)
28.	прие́хать	прие́дут		come (veh.)

TYPE II

29.	встре́тить	встре́тят	встре́чу	meet
30. говори́ть		говоря́т		speak, talk, say
31. звони́ть		звоня́т		phone
32.	купи́ть	ку́пят	куплю́	buy
33. люби́ть		лю́бят	люблю́	love, like
34. находи́ться		нахо́дятся	нахожу́сь	be located
35. приходи́ть		прихо́дят	прихожу́	come (foot)
36.	понра́виться	понра́вятся	понра́влюсь	be pleasing to
37.	постро́ить	постро́ят		build
38.	роди́ться	родя́тся	рожу́сь	be born
39. сто́ить		сто́ят		cost
40. учи́ться		у́чатся	учу́сь	study
41. ви́деть		ви́дят	ви́жу	see
42.	посмотре́ть	посмо́трят	посмотрю́	look
43. смотре́ть		смо́трят	смотрю́	look
44. сиде́ть		сидя́т	сижу́	sit, be sitting
45.*	да́ть		(*irregular*)	give
46.*	уда́ться		(*irregular*)	turn out well, be successful
47.* хоте́ть			(*irregular*)	want

NOTES ON THE VERBS

No. 17. быть *to be.*

Note the irregularity of stress in the past tense: бы́л, ... бы́ло, бы́ли; but была́.

Also, in the negative, the stress falls on the negative particle rather than the verb except with the feminine: **не́** был, ... **не́** было, **не́** были; but не была́.

No. 18. мо́чь *can, to be able.*

In Conversation 10 you met the forms мо́жете, *you can,* and мо́жем, *we can.* While the non-past endings are perfectly regular Type I endings there is a consonant alternation characteristic of Type I verbs as follows: If the stem of a Type I verb in the 3rd person plural ends in **к** or **г**, this consonant will also appear in the first person singular of the verb, but will be replaced by **ч** or **ж** respectively, in the other four forms of the non-past tense. The non-past forms of мочь are as follows:

могу́	мо́жем
мо́жешь	мо́жете
мо́жет	мо́гут

In the past tense мочь has the past stem **мог-** and lacks the characteristic **-л-** in the masculine: мо́г, могла́, могло́, могли́.

No. 22-25. итти́ *to go on foot.*

The verb итти́ and all its prefixed forms such as пойти, *to go* (somewhere); зайти́, *to stop by for;* and прийти́, *come* has a completely irregular past stem: **шёл, шла́, шло́, шли́.**

No. 45. да́ть *to give.*

The non-past forms of this irregular verb are as follows: да́м, да́шь, да́ст, дади́м, дади́те, даду́т.

The verb да́ть is like the verb бы́ть in the past tense, in that the stress falls on the stem in all forms but the feminine singular, where it falls on the ending: да́л,... да́ло, да́ли, but дала́.

For some speakers in the negative form of the past tense, да́ть, again like бы́ть, carries the stress on the negative particle rather than the verb except with the feminine singular: **не́** дал, ... **не́** дало, **не́** дали; but не дала́.

No. 46. уда́ться *to turn out well.*

This reflexive, impersonal verb is composed of the prefix **у**, the verb **да́ть**, and the reflexive particle **-ся**. It is conjugated as is **да́ть**. It was first met in Conversation 11. Being used impersonally it has only one form, that of the third person singular, in the non-past, and one form in the past, that of the neuter.

Compare:

(Context)	I wasn't able to go there earlier...
...нó вчерá мнé удалóсь пойти.	..But yesterday I made it. (It turned out all right for me. I succeeded in going.)
...нó сегóдня мнé удáстся.	.But today I'll make it. (I'll succeed. It will turn out well for me).

No. 47. **хотéть** *to want.*

As you have already learned, the non-past forms of this verb are irregular:

хочý	хотим
хóчешь	хотите
хóчет	хотят

The past tense forms are regular: хотéл, etc.

🌀 5. Short Adjectives

A considerable number of Russian adjectives have both long and short forms. We have so far met four of these.

Compare:

	busy	*free, fluent*	*resembling, like*	*ready*
LONG FORM	зáнятый	свобóдный	похóжий	готóвый
SHORT FORM	зáнят	свобóден	похóж	готóв

5.1. Short Forms of the Adjective used as Adjectives

The short forms are used as adjectives only in predicate position, that is when no noun follows them. Being predicates they have only the nominative form, and while three forms indicate the gender and number in the singular, only one form indicates all three genders in the plural:

MASCULINE SINGULAR	зáнят	свобóден	похóж	готóв
FEMININE SINGULAR	занятá	свобóдна	похóжа	готóва
NEUTER SINGULAR	зáнято	свобóдно	похóже	готóво
PLURAL	зáняты	свобóдны	похóжи	готóвы

Compare:

Óн всегдá **зáнят** в лаборатóрии.	He's always *busy* in the lab.
Ивáн бы́л **готóв**.	Ivan was *ready*.
Я́ бы́л **готóв**.	I was *ready*. (Man speaking)
Я́ былá **готóва**.	I was *ready*. (Woman speaking)
Письмó **готóво**.	The letter is *ready*.
Ру́сская архитектýра совсéм не **похóжа** на нáшу.	Russian architecture is not at all *like* ours.

146

5.2. Short Forms of the Adjective used as Adverbs

The neuter singular short form of the adjective may be used as an adverb:

Óн **свобóдно** говори́т по-ру́сски.   He speaks Russian *fluently*.

You have met other short adjectives which have occurred only in the neuter short form. E.g. **хорошó** *well*.

Óн **хорошó** рабóтал в лаборатóрии.   He was working *well* in the laboratory.

5.3. Notes on the Short Forms of the Adjective

The endings of the short forms of the adjective are those already learned, and are written according to the regular rules of spelling. Just as the stress falls on the feminine ending in the past tense of certain verbs but on the stem in the other forms of the same verb, so a similar stress pattern occurs with the adjective за́нят; e.g. *Feminine Singular* занята́. Also, the **e** of свобóден is the same "inserted vowel" of отéц an дóчек. Thus, short adjectives have endings which are very similar to the nominative endings of nouns, special adjectives and the past endings of verbs.

⏺ 6. похóж на

The Russian equivalent of the English *similar to*, *like*, is the short adjective **похóж** plus the preposition **на** with an accusative case form.

Эта архитекту́ра не **похóжа на нáшу**.   That architecture is not *like ours*.
Óн **похóж на сестру́**.   He looks *like his sister*.

⏺ 7. вид на

The Russian equivalent of the English *view of* is **вид на** plus accusative case.

Вóт чудéсный **вид на гóрод**.   There is a wonderful *view of the city*.

⏺ 8. чéрез

The preposition **чéрез** is another preposition that is followed by the accusative case. It is used in time expressions as an equivalent of English *in*, meaning at the end of the time specified.

Я бу́ду готóв **чéрез чáс**.   I'll be ready *in an hour*.
Я пойду́ **чéрез мину́ту**.   I'll go *in a minute*.
Чéрез дéсять мину́т я зайду́ за вáми.   *In ten minutes* I'll come by for you.

In the last example note that the accusative form дéсять is determined by the preposition чéрез and that the genitive plural form мину́т is determined by the numeral дéсять.

147

9. с plus genitive

The preposition **с** *from*, is used with a following genitive case for those nouns that use **на** plus locative to indicate location and **на** plus accusative to indicate motion to.

С Ленинских гор чудесный вид на город.	There's a wonderful view of the city *from the Lenin Hills.*
На Ленинских горах находится МГУ.	The MGU is located *on the Lenin Hills.*
Хотите поехать **на Ленинские горы**?	Do you want to go *to the Lenin Hills?*
Он **с Украины**.	He's *from the Ukraine.*
Я еду **на Украину**.	I am going *to the Ukraine.*
Я живу **на Украине**.	I live *in the Ukraine.*

(Cf. the preposition **из** *from* in *Grammar Unit* **4:2.2.**).

10. чтó за

The Russian **чтó за** is an equivalent of English *what kind of* in expressions like the following:

Чтó это за фабрика? *What kind of* factory is that?

Note that in this type of expression the noun is in the nominative case. The phrase **чтó за** is unique in having a following dependent noun in the nominative case.

11. совсем

In Conversation 11 you met the word **совсем** used with **не** in the meaning *not at all.* When used without не, **совсем** means *completely, entirely.*

Архитектура собора **совсем не** похожа на нашу.	The architecture of the cathedral is *not at all* like ours.
Я **совсем не** знаю.	I *don't* know *at all.*
Он сегодня **совсем** свободен.	He's *completely* free today.

12. нé было, не будет

The past and future equivalents of **нет** *there is no, there are no* are **нé было** and **не будет**, respectively. Note that the construction itself does not change, that is, the thing of which there isn't any (or which isn't somewhere) is in the genitive. In constructions like these, where there is no noun or pronoun in the nominative case for the verb to agree with, a past form of the verb will be neuter singular (**нé было**) and a non-past will be third person singular (**не будет**).

У меня́ **не́т** папиро́с.	I *don't have* any cigarettes.
У меня́ **не́ бы́ло** папиро́с.	I *didn't have* any cigarettes.
У меня́ **не бу́дет** папиро́с.	I *won't have* any cigarettes.

Сего́дня его́ **не́т** до́ма.	He's *not* home today.
Вчера́ его́ **не́ бы́ло** до́ма.	He *wasn't* home yesterday.
За́втра его́ **не бу́дет** до́ма.	He *won't* be home tomorrow.

❷ 13. то́т же

The expression **то́т же** (with то́т inflected to agree with the following noun) is equivalent to English *the same*. The expression **то́т же... что́ и...** is equivalent to *the same... as...*

Ита́ка в **то́м же** шта́те, **что́ и** Нью-Йо́рк.	Ithaca is in *the same* state *as* the city of New York.
Та́ же фа́брика.	*The same* factory.
О́н написа́л **то́ же** письмо́.	He wrote *the same* letter.
О́н из **того́ же** го́рода, **что́ и** я́.	He's from *the same* town *as I.*

❷ 14. Numerals 20 to 100

Numerals between the even tens are formed in the same way as the numerals 21 through 29, which were given in Conversation Lesson 11.

три́дцать три́	thirty-three
со́рок четы́ре	forty-four
пятьдеся́т ше́сть	fifty-six
девяно́сто се́мь	ninety-seven

Like оди́н, numerals *ending* in оди́н agree with the noun they modify. Note that the noun is in the singular.

Э́то сто́ит три́дцать оди́н ру́бль.	That costs thirty-one rubles.
Во́т со́рок одна́ копе́йка.	Here's forty-one kopecks.
Вы́ мне́ да́ли два́дцать одну́ копе́йку.	You have given me twenty-one kopecks.

A noun with the numerals **два́**, **две́**, **три́** or **четы́ре** is in the genitive singular (cf. *Grammar Unit 4:2.3*). Likewise, with a compound numeral *ending* in **два́**, **две**, **три́**, **четыре**, the noun is in the genitive singular.

со́рок три́ копе́йки	forty-three kopecks
девяно́сто четы́ре рубля́	ninety-four rubles
со́рок два́ го́рода	forty-two cities

149

If the compound numeral ends in 5 to 9, the accompanying noun is in the genitive plural.

со́рок пя́ть копе́ек	forty-five kopecks
девяно́сто де́вять рубле́й	ninety-nine rubles

УПРАЖНЕ́НИЯ

A. Transform orally according to the model:

MODEL: О́н встре́тил мою́ жену́ на вокза́ле.
О́н хо́чет встре́тить мою́ жену́ на вокза́ле.

1. О́н купи́л папиро́сы в э́том кио́ске.
2. О́н пое́хал в Москву́.
3. О́н написа́л письмо́ по-ру́сски.
5. О́н постро́ил моде́ль самолёта.

B. Transform orally from (1) **о́н** to **она́** and then (2) from **о́н** to **они́**:

1. Вчера́ о́н бы́л в музе́е.
2. О́н осма́тривал го́род.
3. О́н зашёл за ва́ми в ча́с.
4. О́н ва́м звони́л три́ ра́за.
5. О́н не мо́г пойти́ в собо́р.
6. О́н встре́тил ва́шего дру́га у вхо́да.
7. О́н мне́ да́л ше́сть рубле́й.
8. О́н пошёл в больни́цу.
9. О́н пришёл сюда́ вчера́.
10. О́н написа́л статью́.
11. Вчера́ о́н прие́хал в Москву́.

C. Transform orally from non-past to past, according to the model. All the verbs in this exercise are imperfective verbs, so that the non-past tense has the meaning of present time.

MODEL: О́н о́чень хорошо́ чита́ет по-ру́сски.
О́н о́чень хорошо́ чита́л по-ру́сски.

1. Мы́ зна́ем ва́шего дру́га.
2. Что́ они́ де́лают?
3. Мо́й бра́т рабо́тает на фа́брике.
4. Кто́ живёт в э́том до́ме?
5. О ко́м вы́ говори́те?
6. О чём о́н пи́шет?
7. Кого́ она́ всегда́ встреча́ет на вокза́ле?
8. Куда́ они́ е́дут?
9. О́н лю́бит писа́ть по-англи́йски.
10. Мы́ уме́ем говори́ть по-ру́сски.
11. Ско́лько сто́ят э́ти кни́ги?
12. Они́ ча́сто ошиба́ются.
13. О́н всегда́ ошиба́ется.
14. Мы́ осма́триваем музе́й.
15. Они́ ва́м ча́сто звоня́т.
16. Мы́ живём зде́сь.
17. Мы́ наде́емся пое́хать в Москву́.
18. Э́тот го́род нахо́дится в на́шем шта́те.

D. Transform orally as in exercise C. All the verbs in this exercise are perfective verbs, so that the non-past tense has future meaning.

MODEL: Я встре́чу моего́ бра́та в рестора́не.
Я встре́тил моего́ бра́та в рестора́не.

1. Она́ пое́дет в Аме́рику.
2. Они́ ку́пят э́тот до́м.
4. Óн мне́ напи́шет письмо́.

4. Мóй сы́н постро́ит на́ш до́м.
5. Мы́ зайдём за ва́ми.
6. Они́ прие́дут в ча́с.

E. Transform orally according to the model:

У меня́ бы́ли папиро́сы. **У меня́ не́ было папиро́с.**

1. Она́ была́ до́ма.
2. У моего́ бра́та бы́ли ру́сские кни́ги.
3. В Москве́ бы́ли тури́сты.
4. Та́м бы́ли собо́ры.

5. У меня́ бы́ло вре́мя.
6. У до́ктора бы́ло тако́е письмо́.
7. В э́том го́роде бы́ли хоро́шие музе́и.

F. Transform orally according to the model:

Я́ пое́хал(а) в рестора́н.
Я́ прие́хал(а) сюда́ из рестора́на.

1. Я́ пое́хал(а) в Нью-Йо́рк.
2. Я́ пое́хал(а) в Ленингра́д.
3. Я́ пое́хал(а) в гости́ницу.
4. Я́ пое́хал(а) на вокза́л.
5. Я́ пое́хал(а) в Сове́тский Сою́з.
6. Я́ пое́хал(а) на Украи́ну.
7. Я́ пое́хал(а) в ру́сский музе́й.
8. Я́ пое́хал(а) на по́чту.
9. Я́ пое́хал(а) в Москву́.
10. Я́ пое́хал(а) на за́пад.
11. Я́ пое́хал(а) в дере́вню.
12. Я́ пое́хал(а) на Ле́нинские го́ры.
13. Я́ пое́хал(а) в Кре́мль.
14. Я́ пое́хал(а) на Восто́к.
15. Я́ пое́хал(а) на фа́брику.
16. Я́ пое́хал(а) в на́шу лаборато́рию.
17. Я́ пое́хал(а) в оди́н ма́ленький ру́сский го́род.

G. Transform orally from "э́тот" *this* to **то́т же** *the same,* according to the model:

О́н живёт в э́том шта́те.
О́н живёт в то́м же шта́те.

1. Э́ти де́вушки прие́хали вчера́.
2. Я́ ви́дел э́того студе́нта.
3. О́н прие́хал из э́той лаборато́рии.
4. О́н пое́дет на э́ту фа́брику.
5. Они́ прие́хали сюда́ с э́тих фа́брик.
6. О́н написа́л э́то письмо́ два́ ра́за.
7. Я́ осма́тривал э́ти собо́ры.

151

REVIEW LESSON THREE

A. FLUENCY DRILL

1. Do you want a cigarette? 2. What kind do you have? 3. These are Russian cigarettes. 4. I bought them in Moscow. 5. These cigarettes are called Kazbek. 6. Are cigarettes expensive in the Soviet Union? 7. No, they are cheaper in the Soviet Union than here. 8. How much do they cost? 9. Thirty kopecks a pack. 10. Do you want these cigarettes?

11. Yes, I like them very much. 12. I'll give you this pack. 13. I bought five packs in Moscow. 14. What time is it? 15. It's six o'clock. 16. In that case, I have to go. 17. Where are you going? 18. I have to meet Vera at the hotel. 19. Who's Vera? 20. She's an interpreter.

21. Where are you going? 22. We're going to the theater. 23. At what time are you meeting her? 24. At eight o'clock. 25. You have lots of time. 26. Yes, but first I have to go to the lab. 27. There's my bus. 28. Goodbye. 29. What do you intend to do today? 30. I don't know.

31. Maybe Natasha and I will go to the park. 32. Do you want to come? 33. I'd be glad to. 34. I'm still on vacation. 35. At what time are you going? 36. When will you be ready? 37. I'm ready. 38. In that case we'll go at three o'clock. 39. We'll meet you at the park. 40. I will stop by for you at two. 41. Fine. I'll meet you in an hour.

B. Conversation topics

(1) A and B discuss what they want to see in Moscow (the Kremlin, the University, a museum, a park, etc.) and whether they want to go there on the streetcar or subway. The conversation ends when A notices that it is five o'clock and remembers that he must meet Vera at six o'clock.

(2) A asks B where he was yesterday and what he was doing. A had called him several times since he wanted to go to the Lenin Hills with him. B says that he met his brother from Leningrad at the station and that they went to the Kremlin. B tells what they saw there. A asks B about his brother, what he does, where he works, etc.

(3) A, an American, meets his friend B, who has just returned from a trip to the Soviet Union. A asks his friend about the trip and B tells him the cities he visited, what he saw in Moscow, and tells him about his guide-interpreter and her family.

ПО МОСКВЕ́

Джо́н прие́хал в Москву́ на по́езде. С вокза́ла он пое́хал не метро́ в гости́ницу « Москва́ », где его́ встре́тила перево́дчица. Он ещё никогда́[1] не́ был в Москве́ и прие́хал сюда́ в пе́рвый ра́з. Он хоте́л хорошо́ осмотре́ть[2] столи́цу Сове́тского Сою́за. Одна́ко,[3] у него́ не́ было пла́на[4] го́рода Москвы́ и он пошёл в спра́вочное бюро́,[5] что́бы[6] спроси́ть,[7] где мо́жно[8] купи́ть тако́й пла́н. Ему́ сказа́ли, что кни́ги о Москве́ продаю́тся[9] в гости́нице.

Пото́м[10] Джо́н и его́ перево́дчица пошли́ в Кре́мль, кото́рый нахо́дится недалеко́[11] от гости́ницы « Москва́ ». Та́м они́ прове́ли[12] не́сколько часо́в в собо́рах и в музе́е. Музе́й э́тот называ́ется Оруже́йная пала́та,[13] и в нём нахо́дятся колле́кции ору́жия,[14] драгоце́нных камне́й,[15] сере́бряных[16] и золоты́х[17] изде́лий[18] и т. д.[19]

По́сле[20] осмо́тра Кремля́ они́ пое́хали в па́рк культу́ры (Центра́льный па́рк культу́ры и о́тдыха[21] и́мени Го́рького[22]), кото́рый нахо́дится на берегу́[23] Москва́-реки́.[24] В па́рке бы́ло о́чень мно́го люде́й. Одни́[25] сиде́ли[26] и чита́ли кни́ги, други́е гуля́ли.[27] Перево́дчица пока́зывала[28] Джо́ну Зелёный[29] теа́тр, кинотеа́тры, рестора́ны, стадио́ны, волейбо́льные и баскетбо́льные площа́дки, те́ннисные ко́рты, библиоте́ку, ша́хматный[30] клуб и не́которые[31] вы́ставки.[32] Э́тот па́рк о́чень понра́вился Джо́ну, и он реши́л[33] ещё ра́з прийти́.

[1] never
[2] look over
[3] however, only
[4] map, plan
[5] information office
[6] in order to
[7] ask
[8] it is possible, one can
[9] are sold
[10] then, next
[11] not far
[12] spent
[13] armory
[14] weapons
[15] precious stones
[16] silver
[17] gold
[18] articles
[19] abbreviation for **и та́к да́лее** *et cetera*
[20] after
[21] rest
[22] named after Gorky, i.e., Gorky Park
[23] bank
[24] Moscow river
[25] some
[26] were sitting
[27] were strolling
[28] showed
[29] green
[30] chess
[31] several
[32] exhibit, exhibition
[33] decided

CONVERSATION 13

Dinner in a restaurant

John and Boris are having a hearty meal at a restaurant.

CONVERSATION UNIT THIRTEEN —————

ENGLISH EQUIVALENTS

WAITER	[1] What would you like to order?
JOHN	[2] What [How] do you think, Boris? [3] What shall we order?
BORIS	[4] I'm very hungry [5] and I want to have a full meal. [6] Do you have a menu?
WAITER	[7] Here you are.
JOHN	[8] For the first course give me cabbage soup, [9] and for the second, sausages and potatoes.
WAITER	[10] And what will you have?
BORIS	[11] I'll have soup, please, and for the second course, mutton chops.
WAITER	[12] I'll bring it right away.
JOHN	[13] Are the prices high here?
BORIS	[14] The prices aren't high, but it's a good restaurant. [15] I often [am frequently] here.
WAITER	[16] Here you are. Here's your [for you] soup and cabbage soup.
BORIS	[17] You forgot to serve us any bread.
WAITER	[18] Pardon me, I'll serve it right away.
JOHN	[19] But we didn't order any bread.
BORIS	[20] In our country bread is usually on the table, both black and white bread.
JOHN	[21] In that case I want some butter, too.

NOTES

4 **Мне́ хо́чется** is roughly equivalent to **я хочу́**, but is often the equivalent of English *I feel like...* The expression **мне́ хо́чется е́сть** is the usual way of saying *I'm hungry.* **Пообе́дать** is literally *to have dinner* and **по-настоя́щему** is literally *really* (from the adjective настоя́щий, *real*).

8 **На пе́рвое** literally *for the first*, meaning for the first course.

9 **С гарни́ром** literally *garnished* and means with potatoes and possibly vegetables.

11 **Бара́ний** is a special adjective. Cf. section 1,2 of the Appendix.

15 **Быва́ть** means *to be somewhere frequently.*

Обед в ресторане

ОФИЦИА́НТ	¹ Что́ вы́ хоти́те заказа́ть?
ДЖО́Н	² Ка́к вы́ ду́маете, Бори́с? ³ Что́ нам заказа́ть?
БОРИ́С	⁴ Мне́ о́чень хо́чется е́сть, ⁵ и я́ хочу́ по-настоя́щему пообе́дать. ⁶ У ва́с есть меню́?
ОФИЦИА́НТ	⁷ Пожа́луйста.
ДЖО́Н	⁸ На пе́рвое да́йте мне́ щи́, ⁹ а на второ́е соси́ски с гарни́ром.
ОФИЦИА́НТ	¹⁰ А ва́м что́?
БОРИ́С	¹¹ Мне́, пожа́луйста, су́п, а на второ́е бара́ньи котле́ты.
ОФИЦИА́НТ	¹² Сейча́с принесу́.
ДЖО́Н	¹³ Здесь це́ны высо́кие?
БОРИ́С	¹⁴ Це́ны невысо́кие, но́ рестора́н хоро́ший. ¹⁵ Я́ здесь ча́сто быва́ю.
ОФИЦИА́НТ	¹⁶ Пожа́луйста, во́т ва́м су́п и щи́.
БОРИ́С	¹⁷ Вы́ забы́ли на́м пода́ть хле́ба.
ОФИЦИА́НТ	¹⁸ Прости́те, сейча́с пода́м.
ДЖО́Н	¹⁹ Но́ мы́ хле́ба не зака́зывали.
БОРИ́С	²⁰ У на́с хле́б обыкнове́нно стои́т на столе́, и чёрный и бе́лый.
ДЖО́Н	²¹ В тако́м слу́чае я́ та́кже хочу́ и ма́сла.

NEW VERBS

TYPE I

пообе́дать (P)	пообе́дают	to have dinner
быва́ть (I)	быва́ют	to be frequently
подава́ть (I)	подаю́т	to serve
зака́зывать (I)	зака́зывают	to order
заказа́ть (P)	зака́жут, закажу́	to order
принести́ (P)	принесу́т	to bring

принёс, принесла́,
принесло́, принесли́

забы́ть	забу́дут	to forget

Note that зака́зывать (I) and заказа́ть (P) form an aspect pair.

TYPE II

стоя́ть (I)	стоя́т	to stand

IRREGULAR

хоте́ться (I) occurs only in the forms хо́чется and хоте́лось.

е́сть (I) *to eat* is one of the four verbs in Russian which have irregular endings in the non-past. The forms are:

е́м	**еди́м**
е́шь	**еди́те**
е́ст	**едя́т**

Past: **е́л, е́ла, е́ло, е́ли**

The forms of the verb пода́ть *to serve* are like those of да́ть (cf. *Grammar Unit* **6:2** and **3**), but note the stress in the past tense: по́дал, подала́, по́дало, по́дали.

NEW NOUNS

	NOMINATIVE SINGULAR	GENITIVE SINGULAR	NOMINATIVE PLURAL	
Masculine				
	сто́л	стола́		table
	гарни́р			garnish
	су́п			soup
	хле́б			bread
	официа́нт			waiter

Neuter

ма́сло	butter
меню́ (*indeclinable*)	menu

Feminine I

соси́ска (о)		sausage
котле́та		chop
цена́	це́ны	price

Plural only

щи́	cabbage soup

THE PARTITIVE GENITIVE

Note the genitive form of the direct object in the sentence Вы забы́ли на́м пода́ть **хле́ба**. The contrast between genitive and accusative case in the direct object is frequently that of indefinite versus definite, respectively. This is referred to as the *partitive* use of the genitive. For example:

О́н на́м да́л **хле́ба**.	He gave us *some bread*.
О́н на́м да́л **хле́б**.	He gave us *the bread*.
Я́ хочу́ **ма́сла**.	I want *some butter*.
Я́ хочу́ **ма́сло**.	I want *the butter*.

Usage is not entirely consistent on this point, however.

УПРАЖНЕ́НИЯ

A. Transform orally according to the model. All the verbs in this exercise are perfective and will have future meaning with the non-past endings.

MODEL: Я́ хочу́ пообе́дать. **Я́ пообе́даю.**

1. О́н хо́чет ва́м принести́ котле́ты.
2. Мы́ хоти́м заказа́ть соси́ски.
3. О́н хо́чет зайти́ за ва́ми че́рез ча́с.
4. О́н хо́чет э́то забы́ть.
5. О́н хо́чет пода́ть щи́.
6. Я́ хочу́ постро́ить ма́ленький до́м.
7. Они́ хотя́т ва́м да́ть э́ту кни́гу.
8. О́н хо́чет сюда́ прие́хать в ча́с.

B. Transform orally according to the model:

MODEL: У на́с чёрный хле́б. У на́с **мно́го** чёрного хле́ба.

1. Во́т бе́лый хле́б.
2. Я́ е́м ру́сские щи́.
3. Они́ е́ли хоро́шие соси́ски.
4. Зде́сь подаду́т ма́сло.
5. О́н купи́л дороги́е кни́ги.
6. Она́ чита́ла ру́сские пи́сьма.

159

7. В Нью-Йóрке высóкие здáния.   университéты.
8. В Совéтском Сою́зе большúе   9. В Москвé стáрые собóры.

C. Make the following substitutions orally:

У нас нет . . . .

¹ black bread	⁶ other examples
² Russian chops	⁷ expensive cigarettes
³ butter	⁸ a good lab
⁴ such high prices	⁹ that kind of (such) bread
⁵ a good museum	¹⁰ cabbage soup

D. Repeat exercise C, but transform to past tense.

E. Give the Russian equivalents:

1. What shall we order? 2. I want to order chops. 3. I'll order white bread. 4. He'll order black bread. 5. The bread's standing on the table. 6. She ordered sausages. 7. She often eats sausages. 8. The waiter will bring the sausages. 9. I'll bring the sausages right away. 10. He brought the sausages and chops. 11. I'm very hungry. 12. I'm hungry. 13. I want to have dinner. 14. I want to have a full meal.

15. Today I'll have dinner at six o'clock. 16. Yesterday we had dinner at seven o'clock. 17. Do you have a menu? 18. Here you are. 19. For the first course give me cabbage soup. 20. For the second course give me chops. 21. For the second course I usually eat sausages. 22. Are sausages expensive? 23. No, prices in this restaurant are not very high. 24. Prices in the Soviet Union are not very high. 25. Prices in Russian restaurants are not very high.

(In the following group of sentences translate *come* by **бывáть**.)

26. I come here frequently. 27. My wife comes to this restaurant frequently. 28. He used to come to this restaurant frequently. 29. Do you often come here? 30. Yes, I do. 31. The prices aren't very high.

32. You forgot to serve us bread. 33. The waiter forgot to bring the bread. 34. He'll forget to bring us bread. 35. We didn't order bread. 36. We didn't order black bread. 37. This is good bread. 38. We ordered neither black nor white bread. 39. He didn't order butter. 40. The waiter didn't bring the sausages.

CONVERSATION 14

Wouldn't you like some dessert?

Mary is treating Natasha to a dinner at the Ukraine Hotel where
she is staying.

CONVERSATION UNIT FOURTEEN ─────────

WAITER	[1] Wouldn't you like some dessert?
NATASHA	[2] Yes, please, give me stewed fruit.
MARY	[3] I'll have [For me] ice cream with fruit. [4] Bring me some tea, too.
WAITER	[5] With sugar or with lemon?
MARY	[6] Just tea.
WAITER	[7] All right. Do you want [For you] tea, too?
NATASHA	[8] No, I'll drink coffee with milk.
WAITER	[9] Is that all?
NATASHA	[10] That's all.
MARY	[11] Is it customary in your country to drink tea with milk?
NATASHA	[12] No, not particularly. [13] And have you never eaten Russian dishes before
MARY	[14] In America, of course, I haven't eaten any. [15] But I like borsch and cabbage soup very much.
NATASHA	[16] Yes, cabbage is a good thing.
MARY	[17] Well, it's time to go.
NATASHA	[18] Yes, it's time for us to go. [19] Waiter! The check, please.

NOTE

19 Посчитáйте literally, *count*! (imperative)

NEW VERBS

TYPE I

посчитáть (P)	посчитáют	to count
пи́ть (I)	пью́т	to drink
пи́л, пила́, пи́ли		
вы́пить (P)	вы́пьют	to drink

Note that the last two verbs form an aspect pair.

TYPE II

нра́виться (I)	нра́вятся, нра́влюсь	to like

162

_____ Не хотите ли вы сладкого?

ОФИЦИА́НТ ¹ Не хоти́те ли вы́ сла́дкого?

НАТА́ША ² Да́, пожа́луйста, да́йте мне́ компо́т.

МЭ́РИ ³ А мне́, пожа́луйста, моро́женое с фру́ктами. ⁴ Принеси́те мне́ та́кже и ча́ю.

ОФИЦИА́НТ ⁵ С са́харом и́ли с лимо́ном?

МЭ́РИ ⁶ Про́сто ча́й.

ОФИЦИА́НТ ⁷ Хорошо́. Ва́м то́же ча́ю?

НАТА́ША ⁸ Не́т, я вы́пью ко́фе с молоко́м.

ОФИЦИА́НТ ⁹ Э́то всё?

НАТА́ША ¹⁰ Всё.

МЭ́РИ ¹¹ У ва́с при́нято пи́ть ча́й с молоко́м?

НАТА́ША ¹² Не́т, не о́чень. ¹³ А вы́ ра́ньше никогда́ не е́ли ру́сских блю́д?

МЭ́РИ ¹⁴ В Аме́рике, коне́чно, не е́ла. ¹⁵ Но́ мне́ о́чень нра́вится и бо́рщ и щи́.

НАТА́ША ¹⁶ Да́, капу́ста — ве́щь хоро́шая.

МЭ́РИ ¹⁷ Ну́, пора́ итти́.

НАТА́ША ¹⁸ Да́, на́м пора́. ¹⁹ Официа́нт! Посчита́йте, пожа́луйста.

NEW NOUNS

NOMINATIVE SINGULAR	GENITIVE SINGULAR	NOMINATIVE PLURAL	GENITIVE PLURAL	

Masculine

лимóн				lemon
компóт				stewed fruit
фрýкт				piece of fruit
чáй				tea
сáхар				sugar
кóфе (*indeclinable*)				coffee
бóрщ	борщá			borsch

Neuter

молокó				milk
блюдо				dish

Feminine I

капýста				cabbage
порá				time

Feminine II

вéщь		вéщи	вещéй	thing

Dative Plural: вещáм
Instrument. Pl.: вещáми
Locative Plural: вещáх

The final **-ь** of feminine II nouns ending in **-чь, жь, шь**, and **-щь** indicates only that the noun belongs to this class and it has no significance for the pronunciation of such words, e.g., **вéщь**. Compare masculine nouns such as **бóрщ** and **товáрищ**, where no **ь** is written.

The English noun *fruit* is a collective noun, but the Russian noun **фрýкт** is an ordinary noun just like **лимóн**. Thus, the singular **фрýкт** means *piece of fruit* just as **лимóн** means *a (single) lemon*, and the plural **фрýкты** is the equivalent of English *fruit* or *fruits*.

Э́то хорóший фрýкт.	This is a good piece of fruit.
Э́то хорóший лимóн.	This is a good lemon.
Э́то хорóшие фрýкты.	This is good fruit.

The nouns **чáй, сýп** and **сáхар**, in addition to the regular genitive forms чáя, сýпа, сáхара, have another genitive ending чáю, сýпу, сáхару, which is usually used in the indefinite meaning *some tea, some soup, some sugar*. This

164

second genitive form also occurs with **нёт** and **мно́го** as well, e.g., у на́с нёт ча́ю (су́пу, са́хару). Very few nouns have a second genitive form.

The noun **пора́** means *it is time* (to do something). If the context is clear, the verb need not be stated. Thus:

Пора́ итти́.	It's time to go.
Пора́.	It's time to go.

УПРАЖНЕ́НИЯ

A. Give the Russian equivalents:

1. I'm drinking.   2. He is drinking.   3. They are drinking.   4. They will drink.   5. We will drink.   6. I drank the milk.   7. She was drinking milk.

8. They are serving tea. 9. He served tea. 10. He forgot to bring the bread. 11. She forgot to bring the bread. 12. They will forget to bring the bread. 13. They brought the bread. 14. She brought the bread. 15. He brought the bread. 16. Did you bring the bread? 17. I will bring the bread. 18. We will bring the bread.

19. I had dinner at six o'clock. 20. She had dinner at six o'clock. 21. We will have dinner at six o'clock. 22. They will have dinner at six o'clock.

23. I am eating. 24. She is eating. 25. Are you eating? 26. They are eating. 27. They were eating sausages. 28. She was eating sausages.

29. I can work. 30. He can work. 31. We can work. 32. They can work. 33. He could work. 34. They could work. 35. She could work.

B. Listen to the following sentences and repeat them, substituting **она́** for о́н. Then do the exercise again, substituting **они́** for о́н.

1. О́н за́нят.
2. О́н похо́ж на отца́.
3. О́н почти́ гото́в.
4. О́н свобо́ден.

C. Complete the following sentences according to the model, using the proper form of **тот**. Say the entire sentence aloud:

MODEL: Я́ живу́ в э́том до́ме, а о́н **живёт в то́м до́ме.**

1. Я́ хочу́ э́ти папиро́сы, а о́н…
2. Я́ говорю́ об э́том блю́де, а о́н…
3. Я́ чита́ю э́ту статью́, а о́н…
4. Я́ иду́ в э́тот музе́й, а о́н…
5. Я́ пишу́ об э́тих профессора́х, а о́н…
6. Я́ рабо́таю на э́той фа́брике, а о́н…
7. Я́ бы́л у э́того вхо́да, а о́н…

D. Give the Russian equivalents:

1. I ordered tea. 2. I want to order some tea. 3. He wants some tea. 4. She wanted some tea. 5. Bring me some tea. 6. Do you want tea with sugar? 7. I always drink tea with milk. 8. She usually drinks tea with lemon. 9. Russians always drink tea without milk. 10. He was drinking black coffee. 11. In our country it is customary to drink coffee with milk. 12. I have never eaten Russian dishes. 13. In America they don't eat Russian dishes. 14. I like borsch and cabbage soup. 15. What do you want for the first course? 16. For the second course he wants sausages. 17. I want stewed fruit for dessert.

GRAMMAR UNIT SEVEN

1. The Dative Case

1.1 Dative Case forms of Nouns

DATIVE CASE ENDINGS OF NOUNS							
SINGULAR						PLURAL	
MASC. & NEUTER		FEMININE I		FEMININE II		M., N., & F.	
Sound	Spelling	Sound	Spelling	Sound	Spelling	Sound	Spelling
-U	у, ю	-E	е	-I	и	-Am	ам, ям

SPELLING: All endings are written according to the usual rules of spelling.

NOTE:

FEMININE I Nouns: Dative Singular Ending = Locative Singular Ending

FEMININE II Nouns: Dative Singular Ending = Genitive Singular Ending and Locative Singular Ending

The dative forms of the irregular neuter noun **врéмя** *time* are:

Singular **врéмени**

Plural **временáм**

1.2 Dative Case forms of Adjectives

DATIVE CASE ENDINGS OF ADJECTIVES					
SINGULAR				PLURAL	
MASC. & NEUTER		FEMININE		MASC., FEM. & NEUTER	
Sound	Spelling	Sound	Spelling	Sound	Spelling
-Omu	ому, ему	-Oy	ой, ей	-Im	ым, им

SPELLING: All endings are written according to the usual rules of spelling.

NOTE:

FEMININE Adjectives: Dative Singular Ending = Genitive and Locative
Singular Ending

1.3 Dative forms of special adjectives

The dative forms of the special adjectives are:

MASCULINE AND NEUTER SINGULAR	FEMININE SINGULAR	PLURAL
э́тому	э́той	э́тим
тому́	то́й	те́м
одному́	одно́й	одни́м
моему́	мое́й	мои́м
ва́шему	ва́шей	ва́шим
на́шему	на́шей	на́шим

With two exceptions, Special Adjectives have the same dative endings as regular adjectives:

(1) In the feminine the dative singular is identical with the genitive and locative. Thus мой has the same irregular stressed ending -Eу: мое́й, in the dative case as it has in the genitive and locative.

(2) According to the rule in *Grammar Unit 5:5* то́т has the vowel **-e-** where э́тот has **-и-**. *Dative plural* of э́тот = **э́тим**; of то́т = **те́м**.

In conversation 14 you met a new special adjective **ве́сь** *all*. The forms are:

	MASCULINE	NEUTER	FEMININE	PLURAL
Nominative	ве́сь	всё	вся́	все́
Genitive	всего́		все́й	все́х
Dative	всему́		все́й	все́м
Accusative	N/G		всю́	N/G
Locative	всём		все́й	все́х

SPELLING:

Since the stem /fş-/ ends in a palatalized consonant, the endings are all written with the vowel symbols which one would expect after a palatalized consonant.

Note:

This special adjective has an inserted **-e-** in the nominative singular masculine. It has the same ending -Eу as мо́й does in the genitive, locative and dative singular feminine. It is similar to то́т in having the vowel **-e-** in all endings in which э́тот has the vowel **-и-**. These two adjectives, **то́т** and **ве́сь** are the only ones in the language which have this peculiarity.

When used without a following noun, the neuter singular forms may have the meaning *everything;* and the plural forms may have the meaning *everybody.* For example:

Всё гото́во.	*Everything's* ready.
Все́ пришли́.	*Everybody* came.

1.4 Dative Case forms of Pronouns

PERSONAL PRONOUNS:

	SINGULAR		*PLURAL*
1 (я́)	мне́	(мы́)	на́м
2 (ты́)	тебе́	(вы́)	ва́м
3 (о́н)	(н)ему́		
(оно́)	(н)ему́	(они́)	(н)и́м
(она́)	(н)е́й		

INTERROGATIVE PRONOUNS:

(кто́)	кому́
(что́)	чему́

◑ 2. The uses of the Dative Case

2.1 The Indirect Object

The indirect object specifies the person *to whom* or *for whom* something was done.

English expresses the indirect object in what would be to a non-native speaker a very complex manner. Consider:

(1) The idea of "to whom" may sometimes be expressed either with or without the preposition "to":
I wrote a letter *to my brother.* OR: I wrote *my brother* a letter.

(2) However, with certain verbs the indirect object is expressed *only with* the preposition "to":
I spoke *to him.*

(3) And again, with other verbs the preposition "to" is never used in expressing the indirect object:
I phoned *him* this morning.
In Russian these difficulties do not exist. No preposition such as "for," or "to," is used. The indirect object is merely expressed in the dative case.

169

Compare:

Я написа́л моему́ бра́ту письмо́.	I wrote my brother a letter.
	or
	I wrote a letter to my brother.
Кому́ вы́ пи́шете?	Who are you writing (to)?
	or
	To whom are you writing?
Я ва́м не́сколько ра́з звони́ла.	I phoned you several times.
Вы́ мне́ да́ли пя́ть рубле́й.	You've given me five rubles.
	or
	You've given five rubles to me.

2.2   Object of "понра́виться"

The Russian verb **понра́виться** is an equivalent of the English verb *to like*. In Russian the person who likes something is in the dative case, the thing liked is the subject in the nominative case, and the verb agrees with it. Thus, in the sentence:

Понра́вился ва́м Кре́мль?   Did *you* like the Kremlin?

you is in the dative case, Кре́мль is the subject in the nominative case, and the verb agrees with it. This sentence could be literally translated "Did the Kremlin appeal to you," but is the normal equivalent of the English *Did you like the Kremlin?*

2.3   Impersonal constructions

Impersonal constructions are those which do not have an overt subject. They are usually expressed by an adverb, an infinitive, a verb in the third singular non-past, or a verb in the neuter singular past. In these impersonal constructions the dative is used to indicate the person involved.

Мне́ на́до купи́ть сигаре́ты.	*I* have to buy cigarettes.
Что́ **на́м** заказа́ть?	What shall *we* order?
Мне́ о́чень хо́чется е́сть.	*I'm* very hungry.
Ему́ хоте́лось е́сть.	*He* was hungry.
Моему́ бра́ту на́до бы́ло пое́хать в Москву́.	*My brother* had to go to Moscow.
Мое́й жене́ на́до бу́дет прийти́ сюда́.	*My wife* will have to come here.

The construction **мне́ на́до** can be literally rendered "It is necessary for me...," but **мне́ на́до** is the normal equivalent of English *I must, I have to.*

Impersonal constructions expressed by an adverb, such as **мне́ на́до**, form the past with the neuter singular form **бы́ло** and the future with the third singular form **бу́дет**. (Cf. the similar constructions with **не́т**, *Grammar Unit* **4:2.5**).

Examples of impersonal constructions without a verb or adverb for the dative case to depend on are the following:

Мне́ то́лько одну́ па́чку.	*I want (For me) only one pack.*
Мне́ су́п.	*I want (For me) soup.*
Во́т **ва́м** су́п.	*Here's the soup for you.*
На́м пора́.	*It's time for us (to go).*

2.4   With certain prepositions

The dative case is used with the preposition **по** *around, along* and **к(ко)** *to, towards.*

Мы́ мо́жем пое́хать **по го́роду**.	We can take a trip *around the city.*
Когда́ я шёл **по у́лице**, я встре́тил Ива́на.	As (When) I was walking *down (along) the street* I met Ivan.
Он пое́хал **по Сове́тскому Сою́зу**.	He took a trip *through (around) the Soviet Union.*
Смоле́нск нахо́дится **к за́паду** от Москвы́.	Smolensk is located *to (towards) the west* of Moscow.
Он идёт **к до́ктору**.	He's going *to the doctor's.*
Он придёт за́втра **ко мне́**.	He'll come *to my place* tomorrow.

Note that before the pronoun **мне** the preposition **к** has the form **ко**.

3.   The prepositions у, к, от

The prepositions **у** *at*, **к** *to* and **от** *from* form a series whose use is parallel to other prepositions you have met with the same meaning.

Location in, at:	**в** + Loc.	**на** + Loc.	**у** + Gen.
Motion to:	**в** + Acc.	**на** + Acc.	**к** + Dat.
Motion from:	**из** + Gen.	**с** + Gen.	**от** + Gen.

The prepositions **у, к, от** are most frequently used with persons to express *location in, motion to* and *motion from* their place, i.e., their house, their office, etc.:

Он **у до́ктора**.	He is *at the doctor's* (office).
Он пое́хал **к до́ктору**.	He went *to the doctor's.*
Он прие́хал **от до́ктора**.	He came *from the doctor's.*
Он **у Ива́на**.	He's *at Ivan's* (Ivan's house, place).
Он пое́хал **к Ива́ну**.	He went *to Ivan's* (house, place).
Он прие́хал **от Ива́на**.	He came *from Ivan's* (house, place).

The other two series are used with nouns referring to places, the series (**на, на, с**) being used with a very limited number of them, and the other series (**в, в, из**) with all the others.

Он **в Москве́**.	He is *in Moscow.*
Он пое́хал **в Москву́**.	He went *to Moscow.*

171

Óн приéхал **из Москвы́**.	He came *from Moscow.*
Óн **на Украи́не**.	He is *in the Ukraine.*
Óн поéхал **на Украи́ну**.	He went *to the Ukraine.*
Óн приéхал **с Украи́ны**.	He came *from the Ukraine.*

The above uses of these prepositions are very important but do not cover all of their uses (for example **к за́паду от Москвы́** *to the west of Moscow,* **у вхо́да** *at the entrance,* **вид на го́род** *a view of the city*). At this stage of learning these latter examples should be memorized simply as fixed expressions.

◐ 4. Negatives

The form **никогда́** *never* is made from the negative particle **ни-** plus the interrogative form **когда́** *when.* Similar negative expressions are:

Interrogative		*Negative*	
куда́	where to?	никуда́	nowhere
где	where at?	нигде́	nowhere
кто	who?	никто́	nobody
		никого́,	
		никому́,	etc.,
что	what?	ничто́,	nothing
		ничего́,	
		ничему́,	etc.

The form **ничего́** besides being used where a genitive is required, is also used where a nominative or accusative would be expected, and the form **ничто́** is very rarely used in Russian.

In Russian a verb form used with these negative words also has the particle **не**. (Two negatives do not a positive make. Cf. ни... ни in *Grammar Unit* **5:7**).

Examples:

Óн **никогда́** ра́ньше **не** éл ру́сских блюд.	He had *never* eaten Russian dishes before.
Óн **никуда́ не** éдет.	He's *not* going *anywhere.*
Никто́ не понима́ет.	*Nobody* understands.
Никого́ здесь **нéт**.	*Nobody's* here.
Я **никому́ никогда́ не** пишу́.	I *never* write *anybody.*
Это **ничего́**.	That's *nothing.*
Óн **ни о чём не** говори́т.	He's *not* talking about *anything.*
Óн **ни о ко́м не** говори́т.	He's *not* talking about *anyone.*

When these negative words are used with a preposition, the preposition occurs after the particle **ни** and before the rest of the forms (ни о чём, ни о ко́м).

⊙ 5. *To like*

In English, the one verb *to like* may be used with two quite different connotations. Compare:

A	B
I like borsch.	I like the borsch very much.
I like Russian students.	I like the Russian students better than the French here at school.

The sentences in A denote a more or less permanent feeling; those in B indicate an impression at a given moment.

In Russian the distinction in meaning is made by the use of two different verbs. The verb **любить** indicates a more or less permanent feeling. The verb **нравиться** (and its perfective partner **понравиться**) indicates an impression at a given moment. Compare:

Я о́чень **люблю́** бо́рщ.	I *like* borsch very much.
Ка́к ва́м **нра́вится** э́тот бо́рщ?	How do you *like* this borsch?
Ка́к ва́м **понра́вился** Кре́мль?	How did you *like* the Kremlin?

The sentence in Conversation 14—В Аме́рике, коне́чно, не е́ла. Но мне́ о́чень нра́вится и бо́рщ и щи.—is an illustration of the meaning of нра́виться. Mary is not saying that she has a permanent liking for borsch, but rather that she has never had it before and now that she has tried it she finds that she enjoys it.

The verb **любить** is also used to mean *love*.

Он **лю́бит** ма́ть.   He *loves* his mother.

Люби́ть is used with a following infinitive, but нра́виться is not.

Он **лю́бит** чита́ть.   He *likes* to read.

⊙ 6. Some aspect pairs

6.1 -ходи́ть and -йти́

You have already met the aspect pair of verbs meaning to come (on foot): приходи́ть (I), прийти́ (P). This verb consists of the verbs **ходи́ть** and **итти́** plus the prefix **при-**. Other such prefixed verbs composed of a basic form ходи́ть and итти́, form aspect pairs in an identical manner.

IMPERFECTIVE	PERFECTIVE	
приходи́ть	прийти́	to come (on foot)
заходи́ть	зайти́	to come by for (on foot)
находи́ться	найти́сь	to be found, be located

In general, the addition of a prefix does not change the inflection of a verb. Thus, the verbs приходи́ть, находи́ться and заходи́ть have the identical inflection:

прихо́дят,	прихожу́
захо́дят,	захожу́
нахо́дятся,	нахожу́сь

The prefixed verbs formed from the simple verb **итти́** likewise have an identical inflection, although there is a slight stem change: after all prefixes except **при** the **и-** of итти́, иду́т, иду́, etc., changes to **-й-** and the infinitive is spelled with a single **-т-**. Whereas this is true for the infinitive прийти, the other forms of this verb are: **приду́т**, **придёт** etc.

прийти́	приду́т	пришёл	пришла́
зайти	зайду́т	зашёл	зашла́
найти́сь	найду́тся	нашёлся	нашла́сь

Examples:

О́н **захо́дит** за ва́ми ка́ждый де́нь?	Does he *come by* for you every day?
О́н **зашёл** за ва́ми в ше́сть часо́в.	He *came by* for you at six o'clock.
О́н ча́сто **заходи́л** за ва́ми.	He often *used to come by* for you.
О́н **придёт** за́втра.	He *will come* tomorrow.

6.2   Prefixation

Many verbs derive a perfective form from an imperfective by the addition of a prefix.

IMPERFECTIVE	PERFECTIVE	
е́хать	пое́хать	to go
писа́ть	написа́ть	to write

The past and non-past inflection of such verbs will be the same in the perfective as in the imperfective (although of course the non-past of the perfective will have future meaning and the non-past of the imperfective will have present meaning).

The addition of a prefix may form a perfective verb without otherwise changing the basic meaning, e.g., **е́хать** (I), **пое́хать** (P) *to go* (by vehicle); or it may change the basic meaning of a verb, e.g., **е́хать** (I) *to go*, **прие́хать** (P) *to come*. Thus, for each verb it is necessary to learn which prefix forms the perfective without changing the basic meaning. The prefix **по-**, however, is used in this function more than any other prefix.

The verbs you have met so far which use the prefix **по-** to form the perfective are:

IMPERFECTIVE	PERFECTIVE	
итти́	пойти́	to go (on foot)

éхать	поéхать	to go (by vehicle)
стрóить	пострóить	to build
смотрéть	посмотрéть	to look
нрáвиться	понрáвиться	to be pleasing to
обéдать	пообéдать	to have dinner
звонúть	позвонúть	to phone
считáть	посчитáть	to count

The important verbs you have met so far which use prefixes other than **по-** to form the perfective are:

IMPERFECTIVE	PERFECTIVE	
писáть	написáть	to write
пúть	вы́пить	to drink
дéлать	сдéлать	to do, to make
читáть	прочитáть	to read

Any verb that is perfective and has the prefix **вы-** added to it will have the stress on the prefix in all of its forms, e.g., вы́пить, вы́пью, вы́пил, etc.

Я **читáл**, когдá онá вернýлась.	I *was reading* when she returned.
Вчерá я **прочитáл** кнúгу Толстóго.	Yesterday I *read* a book by Tolstoy.
Чтó вы **дéлали** вчерá?	What *were* you *doing* yesterday?
Чтó вы **сдéлали** вчерá?	What *did* you *do* yesterday? (What *did* you *get done* yesterday?)

УПРАЖНÉНИЯ

A. Make the following substitutions orally:

Óн . . . . дáл двенáдцать рублéй.

[1] me [2] you [3] them [4] us [5] her [6] him

B. Make the following substitutions orally:

Я дáл(а) . . . . нéсколько кнúг.

[1] his sister [8] my comrades [15] the writers
[2] Peter [9] my sons [16] those Russian writers
[3] Vera [10] those children [17] my interpreter
[4] Boris [11] our friends [18] that young man
[5] Olga [12] your daughter [19] those young girls
[6] Misha [13] the doctor [20] Natasha
[7] my comrade [14] his mother

175

C. Make the following substitutions orally:

. . . . о́чень понра́вился Кре́мль.

¹ that professor	⁷ my wife
² that American professor	⁸ the students
³ those tourists	⁹ my students
⁴ those American tourists	¹⁰ that student (f.)
⁵ those Americans	¹¹ those American girls
⁶ who . . .?	¹² those young girls

D. Transform orally from non-past imperfective to past perfective according to the model:

MODEL: О́н идёт на по́чту. **Вчера́** о́н **пошёл** на по́чту.

1. Вы́ пи́шете его́ бра́ту?
2. Она́ встреча́ет америка́нского тури́ста.
3. Вы́ е́дете в Москву́?
4. Они́ захо́дят в ча́с.
5. Она́ пи́шет Ива́ну.
6. Вы́ прихо́дите в пя́ть часо́в?
7. Мы́ стро́им э́тот ма́ленький кио́ск.
8. Они́ обе́дают в два́ часа́.
9. О́н ва́м звони́т.
10. О́н чита́ет статью́.
11. Что́ о́н де́лает?

E. Transform orally according to the model:

MODEL: О́н пое́хал к Ива́ну.

О́н прие́хал сюда́ от Ива́на.

1. О́н пое́хал к сестре́.
2. О́н пое́хал к нему́.
3. О́н пое́хал к кому́?
4. О́н пое́хал к моему́ това́рищу.
5. О́н пое́хал к родны́м.
6. О́н пое́хал к его́ до́чке.
7. О́н пое́хал к мое́й молодо́й сестре́.
8. О́н пое́хал к э́тому молодо́му до́ктору.
9. О́н пое́хал к ни́м.
10. О́н пое́хал к учи́тельнице.
11. О́н пое́хал к ру́сской учи́тельнице.
12. О́н пое́хал к студе́нту.
13. О́н пое́хал к америка́нскому студе́нту.
14. О́н пое́хал к хи́мику.

F. Listen to the following questions and answer them according to the model, that is, replacing the second person plural pronoun or adjective by the first person singular pronoun or adjective.

MODEL: Э́то ва́ш бра́т? **Да́, э́то мо́й бра́т.**

1. Он живёт в вашем городе?
2. Это муж вашей сестры?
3. У вас папиросы?
4. Это ваши книги?
5. Вы написали вашему брату?
6. Они знают вашего сына?
7. Это письмо от вашего профессора?
8. Они пишут о вашем университете?
9. Вам надо было поехать в Москву?
10. Вы пообедали в восемь часов?
11. Вы заходите в час?
12. Вы купите эти книги?
13. Они вам часто звонят?
14. Они говорят о вас?
15. Он пришёл к вам вчера?
16. Она из вашего штата?

G. Give the Russian equivalents:

1. What was he doing?   2. What were they talking about?   3. Who is coming?   4. Whom did you meet?   5. Who was she talking about?   6. Who is this letter from?   7. Who has my letters?   8. Where do they live? 9. Where was she going?   10. He lives here.   11. They will come here. 12. We went there yesterday.   13. They work here.

On the road in the Caucasus Mountains

CONVERSATION 15

I have to write home

John picked up stamps at the desk in the lobby, but still can't write a letter without his neighbor's aid.

179

CONVERSATION UNIT FIFTEEN ⎯⎯⎯⎯⎯⎯

ENGLISH EQUIVALENTS

JOHN   ¹ Don't you have a pen? ² I have to write home.
PETER   ³ You can take mine. ⁴ In the meantime I'll read the newspaper.
JOHN   ⁵ Thanks. I don't like to write with a pencil. ⁶ And I have such a bad pen.
PETER   ⁷ You can write with mine. It's new. ⁸ Who are you writing to?
JOHN   ⁹ To my sister. ¹⁰ Yesterday I received a letter from her.
PETER ¹¹ Do you often receive letters from her?
JOHN   ¹² Yes, every week she writes both letters and postcards. ¹³ She's very interested in my trip around the Soviet Union.
PETER ¹⁴ Has she never been here?
JOHN   ¹⁵ No, never. ¹⁶ Therefore she has a lot of questions which I am answering.
PETER ¹⁷ Do you have enough stamps?
JOHN   ¹⁸ Yes, I have stamps, envelopes, ¹⁹ everything except paper.
PETER ²⁰ Here's a sheet of paper for you.
JOHN   ²¹ Thank you.
PETER ²² Don't mention it.

NOTE

22   Note that only **не** is stressed in this expression.

NEW VERBS

TYPE I

почита́ть (P)	почита́ют	to read
отвеча́ть (I)	отвеча́ют	to answer
получа́ть (I)	получа́ют	to receive
интересова́ться (I)	интересу́ются	to be interested in
взя́ть (P)	возьму́т	to take

взя́л, взяла́, взя́ло, взя́ли

TYPE II

получи́ть (P)   полу́чат, получу́   to receive

Note that **получа́ть** (I) and **получи́ть** (P) *receive* form an aspect pair.

180

_____ Мне надо написать домой

ДЖОН	¹ Не́т ли у ва́с ру́чки? ² Мне́ на́до написа́ть домо́й.
ПЁТР	³ Вы́ мо́жете взя́ть мою́. ⁴ Я́ пока́ почита́ю газе́ту.
ДЖОН	⁵ Спаси́бо. Я́ не люблю́ писа́ть карандашо́м. ⁶ А у меня́ така́я плоха́я ру́чка.
ПЁТР	⁷ Мо́жете писа́ть мое́й. Она́ но́вая. ⁸ Кому́ вы́ пи́шете?
ДЖОН	⁹ Сестре́. ¹⁰ Я́ вчера́ получи́л от неё письмо́.
ПЁТР	¹¹ Вы́ ча́сто получа́ете от неё пи́сьма?
ДЖОН	¹² Да́, ка́ждую неде́лю она́ пи́шет и пи́сьма и откры́тки. ¹³ Она́ о́чень интересу́ется мое́й пое́здкой по Сове́тскому Сою́зу.
ПЁТР	¹⁴ Она́ зде́сь никогда́ не была́?
ДЖОН	¹⁵ Не́т, никогда́. ¹⁶ Поэ́тому у неё мно́го вопро́сов, на кото́рые я́ ей отвеча́ю.
ПЁТР	¹⁷ У ва́с доста́точно ма́рок?
ДЖОН	¹⁸ Да́, у меня́ е́сть ма́рки, конве́рты — ¹⁹ всё, кро́ме бума́ги.
ПЁТР	²⁰ Во́т ва́м ли́ст бума́ги.
ДЖОН	²¹ Спаси́бо.
ПЁТР	²² Не́ за что.

NEW NOUNS

NOMINATIVE SINGULAR	GENITIVE SINGULAR	NOMINATIVE PLURAL	

Masculine

карандáш	карандашá	карандашú	pencil
вопрóс			question
конвéрт			envelope
лúст	листá	листы́	sheet (of paper)

Feminine I

рýчка (e)	pen, handle
газéта	newspaper
недéля	week
поéздка (o)	trip
мáрка (o)	stamp
бумáга	paper
откры́тка (o)	postcard

Достáточно is another quantity word like мнóго, мáло, etc., which is followed by the genitive case.

У вáс достáточно мáрок?	Do you have enough stamps?
У меня́ достáточно врéмени.	I have enough time.

The Russian equivalent of *to answer something* requires the preposition **на** plus an accusative case form. The person answered is in the dative case.

У неё мнóго вопрóсов, **на котóрые** я éй отвечáю.	She has a lot of questions *which* I am answering.
Не отвечáйте **емý**.	Don't answer *him*.
Óн отвечáет **на её письмó**.	He is answering *her letter*.

The preposition **крóме** *except, besides* always takes a following noun or pronoun in the genitive case.

У меня́ éсть всё **крóме бумáги**.	I have everything *except paper*.
Всё пришлú **крóме Ивáна**.	Everybody came *except Ivan*.

УПРАЖНÉНИЯ

A. Transform orally according to the model:

MODEL: Óн у Ивáна. Óн **поéхал** к Ивáну.

1. Она́ у мое́й сестры́.
2. О́н у Ната́ши.
3. Мы́ у ва́шего бра́та.
4. Они́ у Петра́.
5. Мо́й му́ж у до́ктора.
6. Хи́мик у на́шего отца́.
7. Мы́ у одного́ америка́нца.
8. О́льга у э́той молодо́й де́вушки.
9. Мы́ у америка́нского учи́теля.
10. Они́ у ру́сской учи́тельницы.
11. Хи́мик у э́того молодо́го инжене́ра.
12. Бори́с у на́шего сы́на.
13. Они́ у его́ до́чки.
14. Они́ у него́.
15. О́н у ни́х.
16. О́н у ва́с?
17. Да́, о́н у меня́.
18. У кого́ о́н?

B. Make the following substitutions orally:

О́н мне́ да́л . . . .

1 envelopes	10 a sheet of paper
2 a newspaper	11 a large sheet of paper
3 a stamp	12 photographs
4 stamps	13 a photograph
5 a pen	14 the cigarettes
6 a white pen	15 a cigarette
7 a new pen	16 a Russian cigarette
8 a pencil	17 a letter
9 a small pencil	18 the first letter

C. Make the following substitutions orally:

Доста́точно ли у ва́с . . . .

1 milk	6 envelopes	12 butter
2 sugar	7 borsch	13 bread
3 stamps	8 postcards	14 books
4 paper	9 tea	15 white paper
5 cabbage	10 fruit	16 black bread
	11 coffee	

D. Give the Russian equivalents:

1. Do you have a pen? 2. I have such a bad pen. 3. He has a good pen. 4. She has a black pen. 5. He has a black pencil. 6. Does he have a pencil?

7. I have to write home. 8. He has to write a letter. 9. Who are you writing to? 10. I have to write my wife. 11. I have to write my husband.

. 12. Yesterday I received a letter from her. 13. Did you receive a letter? 14. Do you often receive letters? 15. Did you receive a letter from your sister? 16. No, I received a letter from my friend. 17. No, I received a letter from my Russian friend. 18. I received a letter from him. 19. I used to receive letters from her. 20. I used to receive letters from that young girl. 21. I used to receive letters from Moscow. 22. I used to receive letters from the Ukraine.

23. Do you want this book? 24. You can take this book. 25. He took my book. 26. She took my newspaper. 27. They will take a sheet of paper. 28. He will take everything except the stamps. 29. She will take the new pen.

CONVERSATION 16

Very glad to meet you

John meets Ivan Smirnitsky at Boris' house. Ivan is just back from Tashkent in the Uzbek republic.

CONVERSATION UNIT SIXTEEN —————

ENGLISH EQUIVALENTS

BORIS	[1] Ivan Petrovich just returned from Tashkent. [2] Do you know him?
JOHN	[3] No, I don't know him. [4] You told me that he's an acquaintance of yours.
BORIS	[5] He's supposed to be coming to my place soon. [6] I'd like to introduce you to him.
JOHN	[7] Fine. I'll be very glad [to meet him].
BORIS	[8] Here he comes. [9] Hello, Ivan Petrovich!
IVAN	[10] Good morning, Boris Ivanovich!
BORIS	[11] I want you to meet [want to introduce to you] my friend from America, John Wright. [12] Ivan Petrovich Smirnitsky, John Wright.
IVAN	[13] Very glad to meet you.
JOHN	[14] Pleased to meet you. [15] You live in Moscow too, don't you?
IVAN	[16] Yes, I live near here. [17] It's not far from the park. [18] Have you been here long?
JOHN	[19] I arrived in the Soviet Union two weeks ago.
IVAN	[20] And are you planning to travel around the Soviet Union very long?
JOHN	[21] I don't know yet.
IVAN	[22] You definitely ought to have a look at the Caucasus. [23] The mountains there are very beautiful.
JOHN	[24] I hope to go there for a week.

NOTES

1 **Петро́вич** is his patronymic and not his family name.

5 **До́лжен** when used with a following infinitive, is likely to imply obligation (I'm supposed to, expected to, obligated to, I ought to), whereas the form **на́до** when used with a following infinitive, is likely to imply necessity (I have to, I must), although in many situations either one may be used.

8 Note that **идёт** in this context equates with English *comes*.

19 **прилете́л** literally, came by plane, flew.

_____ Очень рад познакомиться

БОРИ́С ¹ Ива́н Петро́вич то́лько что верну́лся из Ташке́нта. ² Вы́ его́ зна́ете?

ДЖО́Н ³ Не́т, я́ его́ не зна́ю. ⁴ Вы́ мне́ сказа́ли, что о́н ва́ш знако́мый.

БОРИ́С ⁵ Ско́ро о́н до́лжен прийти́ ко мне́. ⁶ Я́ хоте́л бы ва́с познако́мить с ни́м.

ДЖО́Н ⁷ Хорошо́. Я́ бу́ду о́чень ра́д.

БОРИ́С ⁸ Вот о́н идёт. ⁹ Здра́вствуйте, Ива́н Петро́вич!

ИВА́Н ¹⁰ До́брое у́тро, Бори́с Ива́нович!

БОРИ́С ¹¹ Я́ хочу́ ва́с познако́мить с мои́м дру́гом из Аме́рики, Джо́ном Ра́йтом. ¹² Ива́н Петро́вич Смирни́цкий, Джо́н Ра́йт.

ИВА́Н ¹³ О́чень ра́д познако́миться.

ДЖО́Н ¹⁴ О́чень прия́тно. ¹⁵ Вы́ то́же живёте в Москве́, не та́к ли?

ИВА́Н ¹⁶ Да́, я́ живу́ бли́зко отсю́да. ¹⁷ Э́то недалеко́ от па́рка. ¹⁸ Вы́ давно́ зде́сь?

ДЖО́Н ¹⁹ Я́ прилете́л в Сове́тский Сою́з две́ неде́ли тому́ наза́д.

ИВА́Н ²⁰ И до́лго вы́ собира́етесь путеше́ствовать по Сою́зу?

ДЖО́Н ²¹ Пока́ не зна́ю.

ИВА́Н ²² Вы́ обяза́тельно должны́ уви́деть Кавка́з. ²³ Та́м о́чень краси́вые го́ры.

ДЖО́Н ²⁴ Я́ наде́юсь туда́ пое́хать на неде́лю.

NEW VERBS

Type i

сказа́ть (Р)	ска́жут, скажу́	to say, tell
путеше́ствовать (I)	путеше́ствуют	to travel
верну́ться (Р)	верну́тся	to return, come (go) back

Type ii

познако́мить (Р)	познако́мят, познако́млю	to introduce, get (someone) acquainted
познако́миться (Р)	познако́мятся, познако́млюсь	to be introduced, get (one's self) acquainted
уви́деть (Р)	уви́дят, уви́жу	to have a look at
прилсте́ть (Р)	прилети́т, прилечу́	to fly, come by plane

NEW NOUNS

NOMINATIVE
SINGULAR

Masculine

Ива́нович	Ivanovich
Петро́вич	Petrovich
Кавка́з	Caucasus
Ташке́нт	Tashkent
па́рк	park

Neuter

у́тро	morning

The noun **Кавка́з** is used with the prepositions **на** *to, in* and **с** *from*, like вокза́л, Украи́на, etc.

NEW SHORT ADJECTIVES

Ра́д *glad* and **до́лжен** *obliged* are short adjectives (cf. *Grammar Unit* **6:5**) and have the following forms:

ра́д	до́лжен
ра́да	должна́
ра́до	должно́
ра́ды	должны́

188

УПРАЖНЕ́НИЯ

A. Make the following substitutions orally:

.... на́до бы́ло пое́хать в Нью-Йо́рк.

¹ I	⁹ that young girl
² my brother	¹⁰ the new engineer
³ he	¹¹ the Russian chemists
⁴ my wife	¹² the American students (*f.*)
⁵ we	¹³ my friends
⁶ who . . .?	¹⁴ your children
⁷ the doctors	¹⁵ they
⁸ Olga	¹⁶ you

B. Listen to the following questions and answer them according to the model:

MODEL: Вы ви́дите э́ту го́ру? **Да́, я ви́жу э́ту го́ру.**

1. Вы сиди́те здесь?
2. Вы ча́сто прихо́дите сюда́?
3. Вы встре́тите Петра́ за́втра?
4. Вы лю́бите ру́сские блю́да?
5. Вы ку́пите но́вый дом?
6. Вы меня́ познако́мите с ним?

C. Replace the last word or phrase you hear with the proper form of the interrogative pronouns **кто́, что́** as if you did not catch the end of the sentence:

1. Вы зна́ете Ива́на Петро́вича? — **(Кого́?)** 2. Мы говори́ли о Кавка́зе. 3. Вы ви́дели мою́ газе́ту? 4. Она́ мне дала́ но́вую ру́чку. 5. Это сестра́ америка́нского профе́ссора. 6. Мы да́ли кни́гу э́тому молодо́му студе́нту. 7. Он взял э́ту кни́гу. 8. Они́ говори́ли о мои́х знако́мых. 9. Он живёт у сове́тского инжене́ра. 10. Я получи́л письмо́ от э́той ру́сской де́вушки. 11. Он пое́хал к моему́ бра́ту. 12. Вы зна́ете э́того челове́ка? 13. Я ничего́ не зна́ю об э́том. 14. Я ничего́ не зна́ю об Ольге. 15 Вы прилете́ли сюда́ с Ива́ном Петро́вичем?

D. Give the Russian equivalents:

1. Where are you going (on foot)? 2. I'm going to the university. 3. I have to go to the university. 4. I'm supposed to go to the university soon. 5. I intend to go to the university today. 6. You definitely ought to see the Caucasus. 7. I hope to go there soon. 8. I want to go to the Caucasus, 9. I would like to go to the Caucasus.

10. Where did he go (by vehicle)? 11. He went to the Soviet Union. 12. He came to the Soviet Union. 13. He came (by plane) to the Soviet Union.

189

14. He's traveling around the Soviet Union. 15. He returned from the Soviet Union. 16. He arrived here yesterday. 17. He arrived in the Soviet Union two weeks ago. 18. When will he return? 19. He will return tomorrow.

20. He's here now. 21. Has he been here long? 22. I want to introduce you to my friend. 23. My friend lives in America. 24. Have you been in America? 25. Yes, I was there once. 26. Have you been in the Soviet Union? 27. My sister went to the Soviet Union. 28. I want to go there very much. 29. My brother's friend is from the Soviet Union. 30. He's from America.

GRAMMAR UNIT EIGHT

1. The Instrumental Case

1.1 Instrumental forms of Nouns

INSTRUMENTAL CASE ENDINGS OF NOUNS							
SINGULAR						PLURAL	
MASC. & NEUTER		FEMININE I		FEMININE II		M., N., & F.	
Sound	Spelling	Sound	Spelling	Sound	Spelling	Sound	Spelling
-Om	**-ом, -ем**	-Oy	**-ой, -ей**	-yU	**-ью**	-Aṃi	**-ами, -ями**

SPELLING: Instrumental case endings of nouns are written according to the regular rules of spelling.

NOTE: A few nouns have an instrumental plural in /-ṃi/. The only ones you have had so far are **дети** *children* and **люди** *people:* **детьми́** and **людьми́**.

The instrumental endings of the irregular noun **вре́мя** are:

Instrumental Singular   **вре́менем**
Instrumental Plural   **времена́ми**

1.2 Instrumental forms of Adjectives

INSTRUMENTAL CASE ENDINGS OF ADJECTIVES					
SINGULAR				PLURAL	
MASC. & NEUTER		FEMININE		MASC., NEUT. & FEMIN.	
Sound	Spelling	Sound	Spelling	Sound	Spelling
-Im	**-ым, -им**	-Oy	**-ой, -ей**	-Iṃi	**-ыми, -ими**

SPELLING: Instrumental case endings of adjectives are written according to the regular rules of spelling.

SPECIAL NOTE: A comparison of Noun and Adjective Endings

	NOUNS	ADJECTIVES
LOCATIVE, DATIVE, INSTRUMENTAL *Plurals*	-*A*x, -*A*m, -*A*ɱi	-*I*x, -*I*m, -*I*ɱi

EXAMPLES:

о больши́х карандаша́х   about the big pencils
больши́м карандаша́м   to the big pencils
с больши́ми карандаша́ми   with the big pencils

-*Oy* as an ending =	Instrumental *Singular* Feminine I	Genitive, Dative, = Locative, Instrumental *Singular* all FEMININE forms

EXAMPLES:

молодо́й жены́   Genitive
молодо́й жене́   Dative or Locative
молодо́й жено́й   Instrumental

-*Om* as an ending =	Instrumental *Singular* Masc. & Neuter	Locative = *Singular* Masc. & Neuter

EXAMPLES:

Instrumental: больши́м карандашо́м   with a large pencil
Locative: о большо́м карандаше́   about a large pencil

1.3 Instrumental forms of special adjectives

The instrumental forms of special adjectives are:

Masculine and Neuter	*Feminine*	*Plural*
э́тим	э́той	э́тими
те́м	то́й	те́ми
все́м	все́й	все́ми
одни́м	одно́й	одни́ми
мои́м	мое́й	мои́ми
ва́шим	ва́шей	ва́шими
на́шим	на́шей	на́шими

SPELLING: In special adjectives the final consonant of the stem is palatalized, if possible, before adding any ending beginning with the basic vowel *I*. Thus **э́тим** instrumental singular, just as in the plural one finds э́ти, э́тих, etc.; also instrumental singular **одни́м**, plural одни́, одни́х, etc. This rule affects only the forms of these two words.

NOTE: These endings are identical to those of ordinary adjectives, with the previously mentioned exceptions which are characteristic of special adjectives, namely, **то́т** and **ве́сь** have **-е-** where **э́тот** has **-и-** and **мо́й** and **ве́сь** have stressed *Ey* (**ей**) where the others have *Oy* (**ой, ей**).

1.4 Instrumental forms of Pronouns

PERSONAL PRONOUNS

		Singular			*Plural*
1	(я́)	мно́й		(мы́)	на́ми
2	(ты́)	тобо́й		(вы́)	ва́ми
3	(о́н)	(н)и́м			
	(оно́)	(н)и́м		(они́)	(н)и́ми
	(она́)	(н)е́й			

INTERROGATIVE PRONOUNS

(кто́)	ке́м
(что́)	че́м

NOTE: Wherever the instrumental ending is *Oy* (**ой, ей**) there is also a variant ending *Oyu* (**ою, ею**). This variant is a slightly archaic form occurring more frequently in writing than in speech. Thus, either мно́й or мно́ю; е́й or е́ю; жено́й or жено́ю, etc.

💿 2. The uses of the Instrumental Case

2.1 Use of the Instrumental Case without a Preposition

(1) The instrumental, without a preposition, is used to indicate the means or instrument by which something is done.

Я́ не люблю́ писа́ть **карандашо́м**.	I don't like to write *with a pencil*.
Я́ не могу́ писа́ть **тако́й плохо́й ру́чкой**.	I can't write *with such a bad pen*.
Вы́ е́дете **по́ездом** и́ли **самолётом**?	Are you going *by train* or *by plane*?
Он пое́хал в Ки́ев **авто́бусом**.	He went to Kiev *by bus*.
(One can also say:	
Он пое́хал в Ки́ев **на авто́бусе**.)	(He went to Kiev *on the bus*.)

(2) The instrumental, without a preposition, is used as the object of certain verbs.

193

Most verbs take an object in the accusative case, as you have already learned. However, some verbs take an object in the instrumental case. So far you have met one verb of this type:

интересова́ться (I)   to be interested in

Она́ о́чень **интересу́ется мое́й пое́здкой.**   She is very *interested in my trip.*

Че́м вы **интересу́етесь**?   *What* are you *interested in?*

2.2   The Use of the Instrumental Case with the Preposition **c.**

(1) The preposition **c** *with, along with* is used with a noun or pronoun in the instrumental case to express *accompaniment*:

Мне́ моро́женое **с фру́ктами.**   I want ice cream *with fruit.*

Вы хоти́те ча́ю **с са́харом** и́ли **с**   Do you want tea *with sugar* or *with lemon?*
лимо́ном?

Он пошёл в теа́тр **с э́той молодо́й**   He went to the theater *with that young girl.*
де́вушкой.

Before the pronoun **мно́й** this preposition has the form **co.**

Он пошёл туда́ **со мно́й.**   He went there *with me.*

2.3   The Use of the Instrumental Case with the Preposition **за.**

The preposition **за** *after, behind, beyond* is used with the instrumental case in two types of situations:

(1) With verbs of motion **за** plus instrumental is used to indicate the person or thing that is *fetched*, that is *gone after* or *for.*

Она́ пошла́ **за до́ктором.**   She went *for the doctor* (after the
                                                 doctor, *to fetch* the doctor).

Че́рез де́сять мину́т я зайду́ **за ва́ми.**   I'll come by *for you* in ten minutes.

Он пошёл на по́чту **за ма́рками.**   He went to the post office *for stamps.*

(2) **За** plus instrumental is used to indicate location beyond or behind something.

Теа́тр нахо́дится **за э́тим больши́м**   The theater is located *behind that big*
зда́нием.   *building.*

Газе́та **за э́тими кни́гами.**   The newspaper is *behind those books.*

REMEMBER:

(1) When used with the genitive case, the preposition **c** means *from.* (Cf. *Grammar Unit* **6:9**).

(2) When used with the accusative case, the preposition **за** means *for, in return for.* (Cf. *Grammar Unit* **5:1.42.**)

3. тому́ наза́д (*ago*)

The Russian equivalent of *ago* is **тому́ наза́д** with a preceding accusative case form.

Óн прие́хал сюда́ **неде́лю тому́ наза́д**.	He arrived here *a week ago*.
Óн прие́хал сюда́ **ча́с тому́ наза́д**.	He arrived here *an hour ago*.
Óн прие́хал сюда́ **два́ ме́сяца тому́ наза́д**.	He arrived here *two months ago*.

In colloquial speech тому́ may be dropped.

Óн прие́хал сюда́ **неде́лю наза́д**.	He came here *a week ago*.

4. Accusative of duration

Russian distinguishes the following two situations:

(1) Duration of time subsequent to the time of the main verb: **на** plus accusative.

Я наде́юсь пое́хать туда́ **на неде́лю**.	I hope to go there *for a week* (with the intention of staying there for a week).
Óн пое́хал в Москву́ **на ме́сяц**.	He went to Moscow *for a month* (with the intention of staying there a month).

(2) Duration of time *not* subsequent to the time of the main verb: accusative without preposition.

Óн жи́л **ме́сяц** в Ленингра́де.	He lived in Leningrad *for a month*.
Óн бу́дет **неде́лю** в Ташке́нте.	He'll be in Tashkent *a week*.
Я рабо́тал **ве́сь де́нь** в лаборато́рии.	I worked *all day* in the laboratory.

The first type is expressed in English by the preposition *for* and the second type is expressed either with or without *for*. e.g., He will be in Tashkent *a week*, or he will be in Tashkent *for a week*.

The accusative case is also used in time expressions with **ка́ждый**.

Я получа́ю пи́сьма от неё **ка́ждую неде́лю**.	I receive letters from her *every week*.

5. до́лго, давно́

The forms **до́лго** and **давно́** both refer to duration of time and both are likely to equate with English *a long time, for a long time*.

Давно́ is used with an imperfective non-past verb form (or with no verb when equating with English *be*) and indicates an event lasting up to the present.

Вы́ **давно́** зде́сь в Москве́?	Have you been in Moscow *for a long time?*
Я **давно́** живу́ в Москве́.	I have been living in Moscow *for a long time*.

195

Дóлго is used with an imperfective verb referring to any time, past, present, or future, without specifying up until when.

Я **дóлго** жил в Москвé.	I lived in Moscow *a long time.*
Я **дóлго** рабóтал сегóдня.	I worked *for a long time* today.
Кáк **дóлго** вы бýдете здéсь?	How *long* will you be here?
Кáждый дéнь я **дóлго** рабóтаю.	I work *long* every day.

Давнó is also used with a past tense, but in this case it means *a long time ago.*

Óн **давнó** приéхал в Совéтский Союз.	He came to the Soviet Union *a long time ago.*

☯ 6. тáк, кáк; такóй, какóй

The forms **тáк** *so, so much* and **кáк** *how* are adverbs in Russian. They depend upon:

(1) verbs;

Кáк вы **поживáете?**	*How are you?*
Кáк вáм **понрáвилось** метрó?	*How did you like* the subway?
Крéмль мнé **тáк понрáвился**, что я зáвтра пойдý опять.	*I liked* the Kremlin *so much* that I'm going there again tomorrow.

(2) adverbs and short adjectives;

Кáк дóлго вы бýдете здéсь?	*How long* will you be here?
Óн **тáк хорошó** говорит по-рýсски!	He speaks Russian *so well!*
Онá **тáк рáда** вáс видеть!	She is *so glad* to see you!
Мы **тáк зáняты**, что не мóжем пойти с вáми.	We are *so busy* we can't go with you.

The word **кáк** also means *as.*

Óн тáк же хорошó пишет, **кáк** и я.	He writes as well *as* I do.

The forms **такóй** *so, such* and **какóй** *what, what a,* are adjectives derived from тáк and кáк and have complete adjective inflection. They depend upon:

(1) nouns;

Какáя эта ýлица?	*What* street is this?
У ни́х мнóго **таки́х** самолётов.	They have many *such* airplanes.

(2) long adjectives;

У меня **такáя** плохáя рýчка.	I have *such* a bad pen.
Америкáнские университéты не **таки́е** высóкие.	American universities aren't *so* tall.
Какóе огрóмное здáние!	*What a* huge building!

7. кото́рый

Кото́рый *which*, *who* is an ordinary adjective in form with complete adjective inflection. It is used as a relative pronoun to introduce subordinate clauses and agrees in number and gender with the noun to which it refers. Its case form is determined by the construction in which it is used.

У неё мно́го вопро́сов, на **кото́рые** я́ отвеча́ю.	She has a lot of questions *which* I am answering.
Де́вушка, **кото́рая** чита́ет газе́ту, моя́ студе́нтка.	The girl *who* is reading the paper is my student.
Го́род, в **кото́ром** о́н живёт, недалеко́ от Москвы́.	The city in *which* he lives is not far from Moscow.

8. The preposition от

The use of the preposition **от** *from* as opposed to **из** *from* and **с** *from* generally depends on the following noun (cf. *Grammar Unit* **7:3**). In some directional expressions the use of **от** is required by the preceding item regardless of the following noun. These expressions are:

бли́зко от	near to
далеко́ от	far from
нале́во от	to the left of
напра́во от	to the right of
к за́паду от	to the west (etc.) of

Рестора́н **нале́во от** музе́я.	The restaurant is *to the left of* the museum.
Смоле́нск нахо́дится **к за́паду от** Москвы́.	Smolensk is located *to the west of* Moscow.
Э́тот го́род нахо́дится **бли́зко от** Ки́ева.	This city is located *near* Kiev.
Э́то **далеко́ от** Нью-Йо́рка.	That's *far from* New York.

The following expressions illustrate the use of the preposition **от** even with those nouns which otherwise require either the preposition **с** or **из**.

О́н **из** Москвы́.	He's *from* Moscow.
But:	
Ташке́нт **далеко́ от** Москвы́.	Tashkent is *far from* Moscow.
О́н прие́хал сюда́ **с** Кавка́за.	He came here *from* the Caucasus.
But:	
Ленингра́д **далеко́ от** Кавка́за.	Leningrad is *far from* the Caucasus.

9. Some aspect pairs

9.1 -ать, -ить

Some verbs differentiate the two members of an aspect pair by having the imperfective form end in **-ать** (with type I inflection, **-ают**) and the perfective form end in **-ить** (with type II inflection, **-ят**). This differentiation is also characterized by consonant alternation of the stem final consonant; for example, where the perfective has a stem final **-т-** the imperfective forms replace the **-т-** by **-ч-**.

Imperfective	*Perfective*	
встреча́ть, встреча́ют	встре́тить, встре́тят, встре́чу	to meet
отвеча́ть, отвеча́ют	отве́тить, отве́тят, отве́чу	to answer
получа́ть, получа́ют	получи́ть, полу́чат, получу́	to receive
покупа́ть, покупа́ют	купи́ть, ку́пят, куплю́	to buy

A regular characteristic of verbs of this type is that they are formed with a prefix and that the same prefix occurs in both the imperfective and perfective members of the pair. In встреча́ть the **в-** is a prefix, in отвеча́ть the **от-** is a prefix, and in получа́ть **по-** is a prefix. The verb pair **покупа́ть** (I), **купи́ть** (P) *buy* is irregular in that it does not have the prefix **по-** in the perfective form also, but it is the only verb like this in the language.

Я **получа́л** от неё пи́сьма.	I used to *receive* letters from her.
Вчера́ я **получи́л** письмо́.	Yesterday I *received* a letter.
Он всегда́ **отвеча́л** на мои́ вопро́сы.	He always *answered* (used to answer) my questions.
Он **отве́тил** на мо́й вопро́с.	He *answered* my question.

9.2 говори́ть, сказа́ть

The verb сказа́ть (P) forms an aspect pair with говори́ть (I).

Он **говори́т** по-ру́сски.	He *speaks* Russian.
Он **говори́л**, что Ива́н придёт.	He *was saying* that Ivan will come.
Он **сказа́л**, что Ива́н придёт.	He *said* that Ivan will come.
Что́ вы́ ему́ **ска́жете**?	What *will* you *tell* him?

9.3 The prefix по-

Many imperfective verbs in Russian may have, apart from the regular perfective, an extra perfective formed with the prefix **по-**.

Imperfective	*Perfective*	*Extra Perfective*
говори́ть	сказа́ть	поговори́ть
чита́ть	прочита́ть	почита́ть

This extra perfective has the meaning of performing the action for a short period of time. The verb **почита́ть** means *to read for a little while;* **поговори́ть** means *to have a talk (with), to have a chat (with), to talk for a little while (with).*

Я **почита́ю** газе́ту.   I'll read the paper *for a while.*
Я **поговорю́** с ним.   I'll *have a chat* with him.

УПРАЖНЕ́НИЯ

A. Make the following substitutions orally:

Его́ до́м нахо́дится за . . . .

¹ университе́т   ⁵ лаборато́рия   ¹⁰ э́та больни́ца
² рестора́н   ⁶ музе́й   ¹¹ э́та высо́кая фа́брика
³ вокза́л   ⁷ собо́р   ¹² Большо́й теа́тр
⁴ по́чта   ⁸ но́вый па́рк   ¹³ но́вая по́чта
                   ⁹ э́то большо́е зда́ние

B. Transform orally according to the model. In the sentences you hear most of the nouns will be in the accusative case, but some will be in genitive (partitive usage).

Model: Е́й на́до купи́ть папиро́сы.
     Она́ пошла́ за папиро́сами.

1. Е́й на́до купи́ть молока́.
2. Е́й на́до купи́ть па́чку сигаре́т.
3. Е́й на́до купи́ть капу́сту.
4. Е́й на́до купи́ть ко́фе.
5. Е́й на́до купи́ть са́хару.
6. Е́й на́до купи́ть газе́ту.
7. Е́й на́до купи́ть ма́рки.
8. Е́й на́до купи́ть ча́ю.
9. Е́й на́до купи́ть фру́кты.
10. Е́й на́до купи́ть но́вый каранда́ш.
11. Е́й на́до купи́ть конве́рты.
12. Е́й на́до купи́ть но́вую ру́чку.
13. Е́й на́до купи́ть откры́тки.
14. Е́й на́до купи́ть Пра́вду.
15. Е́й на́до купи́ть соси́ски.
16. Е́й на́до купи́ть моро́женое.

C. Make the following substitutions orally:

Она́ пошла́ туда́ . . . .

¹ with you
² with her
³ with me
⁴ with us
⁵ with whom?
⁶ with the doctor
⁷ with my brother
⁸ with Peter
⁹ with that man
¹⁰ with your comrade
¹¹ with a Russian student (*m.*)
¹² with an acquaintance (*m.*)
¹³ with an American engineer
¹⁴ with Peter Ivanovich
¹⁵ with Olga
¹⁶ with the interpreter

[17] with my sister	[21] with the students
[18] with that girl	[22] with the Russian tourists
[19] with that beautiful girl	[23] with the American tourists
[20] with your daughter	[24] with the American writers.

D. Transform orally according to the models:

MODELS: **Óн** рабо́тает в па́рке.
Во́т челове́к, кото́рый рабо́тает в па́рке.
Я говори́л **с ни́м.**
Во́т челове́к, с кото́рым я говори́л.

1. Я да́л **ему́** четы́ре рубля́.
2. Мы́ ча́сто быва́ем **у него́.**
3. Они́ говоря́т **о нём.**
4. Вчера́ она́ **ему́** позвони́ла.
5. Она́ ча́сто получа́ет **от него́** пи́сьма.
6. Вчера́ я познако́мился **с ни́м.**
7. О́льга **ему́** напи́шет письмо́.
8. Я́ **его́** зна́ю.

E. Do this exercise as you did the preceding, but supply

Во́т де́вушка . . . .

1. **Она́** рабо́тает в па́рке.
2. Я говори́л **с не́й.**
3. Я да́л **е́й** четы́ре рубля́.
4. Мы́ ча́сто быва́ем **у неё.**
5. Они́ говоря́т **о не́й.**
6. Вчера́ о́н **е́й** позвони́л.
7. О́н ча́сто получа́ет **от неё** пи́сьма.
8. Вчера́ я познако́мился **с не́й.**
9. Ми́ша **е́й** напи́шет письмо́.
10. Я́ её зна́ю.

F. Make the following substitutions orally:

Э́то . . . .

[1] to the right of the restaurant	[5] close to the State University
[2] to the left of the post office	[6] far from that tall building
[3] to the west of Moscow	[7] not far from those tall buildings
[4] to the east of Moscow	[8] far from the Kremlin

G. Transform orally from non-past imperfective to non-past perfective according to the model:

MODEL: Я́ **отвеча́ю** на ва́ши вопро́сы.
Я́ **отве́чу** на ва́ши вопро́сы.

1. Я́ обе́даю в ше́сть часо́в.
2. Она́ звони́т ва́шей сестре́.
3. Мы́ получа́ем от ни́х пя́ть рубле́й.
4. Мы́ его́ встреча́ем в па́рке.
5. Они́ пью́т молоко́.
6. О́н стро́ит но́вый до́м.
7. О́н е́дет на Кавка́з на неде́лю.
8. Мы́ идём к до́ктору.
9. Она́ э́то говори́т.
10. О́н говори́т с де́вушкой.

REVIEW LESSON FOUR

A. Fluency Drill

1. I have to write a letter.   2. Who are you writing to?   3. I have to write to Olga.   4. I got a letter from her yesterday.   5. She wants to know when I will be in Leningrad   6. Do you intend to go to Leningrad?   7. I'm supposed to go there in a week.   8. Ivan Petrovich, whom I met yesterday, is going with me.   9. He's supposed to come here soon.   10. He intends to come here soon.   11. He had to go to Tashkent.   12. He went to Tashkent two weeks ago.   13. He returned from Tashkent yesterday.   14. He just returned from Tashkent.   15. He hopes to go to Kiev for a week.   16. I hope to get acquainted with him.   17. I want to introduce you to my friend.   18. I want to introduce you to my friend from the Soviet Union.   19. I want to introduce you to my sister.   20. I want to introduce you to Natasha.   21. He wants to introduce me to (his) sister.   22. He introduced me to her.   23. She introduced me to Olga.   24. I'll introduce you to Olga.

(Use the verb **познакóмиться** *to become acquainted with* to translate "meet" in the following sentences.)

25. Pleased to meet you.   26. I want to meet him.   27. I met him in Leningrad.   28. We met in Tashkent.   29. Have you met (each other)?   30. I met her a year ago.   31. Have you met Boris Ivanovich?

(Use the verb **встрéтить** *to meet by appointment or by accident* to translate "meet" in the following sentences.)

32. I have to meet him at the station.   33. I met him in Tashkent.   34. I met her in Tashkent a week ago.   35. Did you meet Boris Ivanovich yesterday?   36. I'll meet him at the station tomorrow.

B. Conversation topics

(1) A is trying to write a letter and has to borrow everything he needs from B. A wants a pen from B, but B has only a pencil. A also asks for paper, stamps, and envelopes. B wants to know who A is writing to, and A says it is a girl he met in New York.

(2) A orders a full meal from B, the waiter.

(3) A tells B about a meal he had in a Moscow restaurant.

(4) A tells B that he met C yesterday and tells who he is and what he does. A says that he would like B to meet him. C arrives and is introduced.

ПИСЬМО

Дорого́й Робе́рт!

Письмо́ Ва́ше[1] я получи́л. Спаси́бо Вам за него́. Я так рад, что вы все здоро́вы[2] и что дела́[3] у вас иду́т хорошо́.

Вот уже́ пять дней я в Москве́ и уже́ о́чень мно́го ви́дел. Моя́ гости́ница нахо́дится далеко́ от це́нтра го́рода, но трамва́й остана́вливается[4] как раз[5] пе́ред[6] гости́ницей. Поэ́тому, мне о́чень легко́[7] дое́хать до це́нтра.

Я здесь встре́тил одного́ америка́нского тури́ста, кото́рый путеше́ствует по Сою́зу уже́ второ́й ме́сяц. Мы реши́ли[8] осмотре́ть го́род вме́сте. Коне́чно, мы на́чали[9] с Кремля́ и побыва́ли[10] в па́рке культу́ры. Сего́дня мы обе́дали в хоро́шем рестора́не. Я Вам посыла́ю[11] меню́. Ве́чером я собира́юсь итти́ в теа́тр с Ива́ном и его́ знако́мыми.

Пока́ бо́льше[12] писа́ть мне́ не́когда,[13] но за́втра я постара́юсь[14] посла́ть[15] Вам бо́лее дли́нное[16] письмо́. Приложу́[17] к нему́ план го́рода и па́ру[18] ви́дов Москвы́.

Переда́йте, пожа́луйста, приве́т[19] всем мои́м друзья́м.

Ваш друг,
Джон

[1] All forms of **вы** and **ваш** when having the meaning *singular* are capitalized in letters.
[2] healthy, well
[3] things, affairs
[4] stops
[5] just, right
[6] in front of
[7] easy
[8] decided
[9] began
[10] spent some time, visited briefly
[11] am sending
[12] some more, any more
[13] I have no time
[14] I'll try
[15] to send
[16] long; **бо́лее дли́нное**, longer
[17] I'll add, enclose
[18] a couple, a few
[19] regards

CONVERSATION 17

In the book store

John finds that the book business is big business in Moscow.

CONVERSATION UNIT SEVENTEEN ———————

JOHN	[1] Tell [me] please, where are books on history sold?
SALESWOMAN	[2] On the second floor.
JOHN	[3] What else do you have on the second floor?
SALESWOMAN	[4] For the most part scientific literature is there: [5] chemistry, physics, mathematics, philosophy, linguistics, and so forth.
JOHN	[6] And where is the fiction department?
SALESWOMAN	[7] Right in front of you.
JOHN	[8] Please give me Tolstoy's *War and Peace*.
SALESWOMAN	[9] What edition? [10] We have it for seventy kopecks and for two rubles.
JOHN	[11] I'll take the cheaper one. [12] Here's a ruble.
SALESWOMAN	[13] You should pay at the cashier's desk.
JOHN	[14] Why not [pay] you?
SALESWOMAN	[15] Well, that's the way it's done [customary] in our country. [16] The cashier's desk is over there where the line is [standing].
JOHN	[17] OK. Then give me the book.
SALESWOMAN	[18] No, you get the book only [19] after you pay for it.
JOHN	[20] And how will you know whether I've paid?
SALESWOMAN	[21] They'll give you a ticket at the cashier's [22] and you will bring it to me.
JOHN	[23] All right.

NOTES

4 The adjective **гла́вный** literally means *main*, *principal* and the noun **о́браз** *manner*, *form*.
 Нау́чная could also be translated scholarly, since it covers a wider range of fields than the English term scientific.

5 Usually abbreviated to **и т.д.**

6 **Худо́жественная** literally, artistic.

21 **Че́к** does not refer to a railway or theater ticket.

NEW VERBS

TYPE I

продава́ться (I) продаю́тся   to be sold

TYPE II

заплати́ть (P)   запла́тят, заплачу́ to pay

_____ В книжном магазине

ДЖÓН	¹ Скажи́те, пожа́луйста, где́ продаю́тся кни́ги по исто́рии?
ПРОДАВЩИ́ЦА	² На второ́м этаже́.
ДЖÓН	³ Что́ у ва́с ещё на второ́м этаже́?
ПРОДАВЩИ́ЦА	⁴ Та́м, гла́вным о́бразом нау́чная литерату́ра: ⁵ хи́мия, фи́зика, матема́тика, филосо́фия, языкозна́ние и так да́лее.
ДЖÓН	⁶ А где́ отде́л худо́жественной литерату́ры?
ПРОДАВЩИ́ЦА	⁷ Как ра́з пе́ред ва́ми.
ДЖÓН	⁸ Да́йте мне́, пожа́луйста, « Войну́ и ми́р » Толсто́го.
ПРОДАВЩИ́ЦА	⁹ А како́е изда́ние? ¹⁰ У на́с е́сть за се́мьдесят копе́ек и за два́ рубля́.
ДЖÓН	¹¹ Я́ возьму́ бо́лее дешёвое. ¹² Во́т ва́м ру́бль.
ПРОДАВЩИ́ЦА	¹³ Вы́ должны́ заплати́ть в ка́ссу.
ДЖÓН	¹⁴ Почему́ не ва́м?
ПРОДАВЩИ́ЦА	¹⁵ А та́к у на́с при́нято. ¹⁶ Ка́сса во́н та́м, где́ стои́т о́чередь.
ДЖÓН	¹⁷ Хорошо́. Да́йте же кни́гу.
ПРОДАВЩИ́ЦА	¹⁸ Не́т, кни́гу вы́ полу́чите то́лько по́сле того́, ¹⁹ как запла́тите за неё.
ДЖÓН	²⁰ А как вы́ бу́дете зна́ть, заплати́л ли я́?
ПРОДАВЩИ́ЦА	²¹ Ва́м даду́т че́к в ка́ссе, ²² и вы́ принесёте его́ мне́.
ДЖÓН	²³ Ну́, хорошо́.

NEW NOUNS

NOMINATIVE
SINGULAR

Masculine

о́браз	form, manner
ми́р	peace
отде́л	department
че́к	ticket, check

Neuter

изда́ние	edition
языкозна́ние	linguistics

Feminine I

литерату́ра	literature
исто́рия	history
хи́мия	chemistry
фи́зика	physics
матема́тика	mathematics
филосо́фия	philosophy
война́	war
ка́сса	cashier's desk

Feminine II

о́чередь   line, queue

Plural:	Nom.	о́череди
	Gen.	очереде́й
	Dat.	очередя́м
	Acc.	о́череди
	Inst.	очередя́ми
	Loc.	очередя́х

NEW PREPOSITIONS

По́сле *after* is a preposition that always takes a following noun or pronoun in the genitive case, e.g., **по́сле войны́** *after the war*. The expression **по́сле того́, ка́к** *after* is used to introduce clauses.

Пе́ред *in front of* takes a following noun or pronoun in the instrumental case.

По with a dative case may be the equivalent of English *on* when referring to a field of study, e.g., **кни́ги по языкозна́нию** *books on linguistics*.

206

УПРАЖНЕ́НИЯ

A. Make the following substitutions orally:

О́н стои́т пе́ред . . . .

1 bus
2 cashier's desk
3 window
4 museum
5 kiosk

6 cathedral
7 that young man
8 Olga
9 that big building
10 the new post office

B. Make the following substitutions orally:

Я́ о́чень интересу́юсь . . . .

1 history
2 physics
3 linguistics
4 architecture
5 museums
6 your trip through the Soviet Union
7 the Caucasus

8 questions of philosophy
9 airplanes
10 chemistry
11 that university
12 Soviet books
13 American history
14 scientific literature

C. Transform orally according to the model:

MODEL: Я́ пошёл (пошла́) за э́той кни́гой.
Ско́лько вы́ заплати́ли за э́ту кни́гу?

1. Я́ пошёл за откры́тками.
2. Я́ пошёл за молоко́м.
3. Я́ пошёл за ча́ем.
4. Я́ пошёл за са́харом.
5. Я́ пошёл за папиро́сами.
6. Я́ пошёл за бе́лой бума́гой.
7. Я́ пошёл за ма́рками.
8. Я́ пошёл за но́вым изда́нием Толсто́го.
9. Я́ пошёл за ру́сским хле́бом.
10. Я́ пошёл за дешёвым ма́слом.
11. Я́ пошёл за америка́нской газе́той.
12. Я́ пошёл за хоро́шими фру́ктами.

D. Give the Russian equivalents:

1. I bought a new book. 2. I bought a new book on physics. 3. Where did you buy the book? 4. How much did you pay for the book? 5. I'll take the cheap book. 6. He took the expensive book. 7. Where must I pay for the book? 8. At the cashier's desk. 9. There is a line in front of the cashier's desk. 10. It's necessary to stand in line. 11. What a big line!

207

12. Do you know whether he's paid for the book? 13. Bring me that new book on mathematics. 14. She brought me a new book on linguistics. 15. Yesterday I received a new book about the war. 16. I'm very interested in new books on chemistry. 17. She writes books. 18. She writes books about the war. 19. He reads only scientific literature. 20. He's interested in scientific literature. 21. For the most part we only read books on literature. 22. He often reads books on architecture.

23. What are you interested in? 24. I'm interested in architecture. 25. What are you writing with, a pencil? 26. No, I'm writing with a pen. 27. What is he talking about? 28. He's talking about philosophy. 29. What is sold here? 30. Newspapers are sold here.

CONVERSATION 18

What time is it?

Alexis gets last-minute help on a bibliographical reference from a friend at the library.

CONVERSATION UNIT EIGHTEEN ─────────────

TATYANA	[1] That's right.
ALEXIS	[2] Thanks. I've got to go. [3] What time is it now?
TATYANA	[4] Five minutes after nine. [5] Don't you really have a watch?
ALEXIS	[6] I have a watch but it's slow. [7] By my watch it's only quarter of nine.
TATYANA	[8] Mine is fast. [9] You'd better look at that big one [clock] on the wall.
ALEXIS	[10] Oh! As a matter of fact [11] there is a clock here! [12] By that clock [There] it's exactly nine.
TATYANA	[13] It's electric and probably shows the correct time [time correctly].
ALEXIS	[14] You see, I have to be at the airport at half past ten. [15] The plane leaves [flies away] at five of eleven.
TATYANA	[16] Where are you going?
ALEXIS	[17] To Tashkent.
TATYANA	[18] Why are you going there?
ALEXIS	[19] Because there will be a convention of engineers there [20] and we all will be taking part in it.
TATYANA	[21] Will you be there long?
ALEXIS	[22] No, I'll return in a week. [23] But it's already twenty after nine. [24] It's late. It's time for me to go.
TATYANA	[25] Why are you in such a hurry? [26] The airport is quite near here.
ALEXIS	[27] Yes, but first I've got to go to a book store. [28] I want to buy a novel. Good-bye!
TATYANA	[29] Have a good trip!

NOTES

10 Literally, in very fact.

12 **Ро́вно** literally, even.

29 Literally, happy trip.

ADDITIONAL VOCABULARY

тре́тий	*third* (See below, *New Special Adjectives.*)
четвёртый	*fourth*
пя́тый	*fifth*
шесто́й	*sixth*
седьмо́й	*seventh*
восьмо́й	*eighth*
девя́тый	*ninth*
деся́тый	*tenth*
оди́ннадцатый	*eleventh*
двена́дцатый	*twelfth*

Который час?

ТАТЬЯ́НА	¹ Э́то пра́вильно.
АЛЕКСЕ́Й	² Спаси́бо. Мне на́до спеши́ть. ³ Кото́рый сейча́с ча́с?
ТАТЬЯ́НА	⁴ Пя́ть мину́т деся́того. ⁵ Ра́зве у ва́с нет часо́в?
АЛЕКСЕ́Й	⁶ Часы́ е́сть, но отстаю́т. ⁷ На мои́х часа́х ещё то́лько без че́тверти де́вять.
ТАТЬЯ́НА	⁸ Мои́ спеша́т. ⁹ Посмотри́те лу́чше на те́ больши́е на стене́.
АЛЕКСЕ́Й	¹⁰ А́х, в са́мом де́ле, ¹¹ здесь е́сть часы́! ¹² Та́м ро́вно де́вять.
ТАТЬЯ́НА	¹³ Они́ электри́ческие и, наве́рно, пока́зывают вре́мя то́чно.
АЛЕКСЕ́Й	¹⁴ Ви́дите ли, мне́ на́до бы́ть в аэропорту́ в полови́не оди́ннадцатого. ¹⁵ Самолёт отлета́ет без пяти́ оди́ннадцать.
ТАТЬЯ́НА	¹⁶ Куда́ вы́ е́дете?
АЛЕКСЕ́Й	¹⁷ В Ташке́нт.
ТАТЬЯ́НА	¹⁸ Почему́ вы́ туда́ лети́те?
АЛЕКСЕ́Й	¹⁹ Потому́ что та́м бу́дет съе́зд инжене́ров, ²⁰ и мы́ все́ бу́дем принима́ть в нём уча́стие.
ТАТЬЯ́НА	²¹ Вы́ до́лго та́м бу́дете?
АЛЕКСЕ́Й	²² Не́т, я че́рез неде́лю верну́сь. ²³ Но во́т уже́ два́дцать мину́т деся́того. ²⁴ По́здно. Мне́ пора́.
ТАТЬЯ́НА	²⁵ Почему́ вы́ та́к спеши́те? ²⁶ Аэропо́рт совсе́м бли́зко отсю́да.
АЛЕКСЕ́Й	²⁷ Да́, но сперва́ мне на́до пойти́ в кни́жный магази́н. ²⁸ Я́ хочу́ купи́ть рома́н. До свида́ния!
ТАТЬЯ́НА	²⁹ Счастли́вого пути́!

CONVERSATION UNIT EIGHTEEN

NEW VERBS

TYPE I

пока́зывать (I)	пока́зывают	to show
отлета́ть (I)	отлета́ют	to fly away
принима́ть (I)	принима́ют	to take, accept
отстава́ть (I)	отстаю́т	to lag behind

TYPE II

спеши́ть (I)	спеша́т	to hurry
лете́ть (I)	летя́т, лечу́	to fly

NEW NOUNS

NOMINATIVE SINGULAR

Masculine

магази́н	store
аэропо́рт	airport
рома́н	novel
съе́зд	convention
пу́ть (see below)	path, trip

Neuter

де́ло	fact, deed, affair
уча́стие	participation

Feminine I

полови́на	half
стена́	wall

Feminine II

че́тверть	quarter

Plural Nominative:	че́тверти
Genitive:	четверте́й
Dative:	четвертя́м
Instrumental:	четвертя́ми
Locative:	четвертя́х

Plural only: часы́	clock, watch

Пу́ть *trip, path, road* is a masculine noun with the endings of a feminine II noun except for the instrumental singular. There are no other nouns of this type.

Nominative-Accusative	пу́ть	пу́ти
Genitive	пути́	путе́й
Dative	пути́	путя́м
Instrumental	**путём**	путя́ми
Locative	пути́	путя́х

Стена́ *wall* has the same type of unusual stress pattern as рука́ *hand* and гора́ *hill, mountain* (cf. *Conversation* **11**):

Nominative	стена́	сте́ны
Genitive	стены́	сте́н
Dative	стене́	стена́м
Accusative	сте́ну	сте́ны
Instrumental	стено́й	стена́ми
Locative	стене́	стена́х

Съезд *convention* is another noun that takes the series of prepositions **на** plus Accusative, **на** plus Locative, and **с** plus Genitive to express *to, at, from*.

NEW SPECIAL ADJECTIVES

Тре́тий /tretiy/ is a special adjective with an inserted vowel in the nominative singular masculine. In the other forms the stem is тре́ть- /trety-/ and the endings are spelled the same as those of мо́й. Thus тре́тью like мою́, тре́тьего like моего́ etc.

THE VERBS, "СМОТРЕ́ТЬ" AND "ПРИНИМА́ТЬ"

To look at in Russian is usually expressed by the verb смотре́ть (I), посмотре́ть (P) followed by **на** plus an accusative case form. For example: **Посмотри́те на** те́ больши́е часы́ на стене́. In Conversation Lesson 7 the sentence Хоти́те посмотре́ть фотогра́фии мои́х родны́х? occurred, where *to look at* is expressed without the preposition **на**. When *to look at* implies taking a single glance, the preposition **на** is used. When *to look at* does not imply taking a single glance, as in the case of a series of items such as photographs, sports events, plays, etc., the preposition is not used.

In Russian *to take part in* is **принима́ть уча́стие в** plus locative case form.

УПРАЖНЕ́НИЯ

A. Make the following substitutions orally:

Когда́ о́н стоя́л пе́ред рестора́ном, о́н посмотре́л . . . .

¹ at the Kremlin
² at the park
³ at the new factory
⁴ at the clock

⁵ at the big electric clock
⁶ at the main building of the university
⁷ at the American tourist
⁸ at the children in the park.

213

B. Make the following substitutions orally:

Óн тóлько что верну́лся . . . .

¹ from the hotel	¹³ from the book store
² from the post office	¹⁴ from the Lenin Hills
³ from Moscow	¹⁵ from the state museum
⁴ from John's	¹⁶ from (his) daughter's
⁵ from the Caucasus	¹⁷ from the Ukraine
⁶ from the doctor's	¹⁸ from Natasha's
⁷ from Tashkent	¹⁹ from Peter's
⁸ from the park	²⁰ from the east
⁹ from the convention	²¹ from Kiev
¹⁰ from the new station	²² from America
¹¹ from the Soviet Union	²³ from the west
¹² from my brother's	²⁴ from the airport

C. Make the following substitutions orally:

Она́ прие́хала . . . .

¹ an hour ago	⁵ ten days ago	⁹ six weeks ago
² a week ago	⁶ three days ago	¹⁰ two weeks ago
³ a month ago	⁷ five months ago	¹¹ a quarter of an hour ago
⁴ ten minutes ago	⁸ two months ago	¹² long ago

D. Give the Russian equivalents:

1. Where are you going? 2. I'm going to Tashkent. 3. I'm going to Tashkent by airplane. 4. My friend is going to Tashkent by train. 5. He likes to go there by bus. 6. Will you be there long? 7. I'll be there a week. 8. I'll return in a month. 9. They came back after the convention. 10. When did you arrive in Tashkent? 11. I'll be in Tashkent in four hours.

12. Is the airport located near the city? 13. The airport is never located near the station. 14. How are you going to the airport? 15. I'm going to the airport by bus. 16. I have to be at the airport in an hour. 17. I have to be in Tashkent in a week. 18. I'm going to Tashkent for a week.

19. What time is it? 20. By my watch it's three o'clock. 21. What time is it by your watch? 22. I don't have a watch. 23. Do you have a watch? 24. My sister's watch is slow but mine is fast. 25. By his watch it's exactly ten o'clock. 26. That clock is electric.

27. Electric clocks show the time accurately. 28. Do you see that big electric clock on the wall? 29. I can see it from here. 30. It's time for me to go. 31. Why are you in such a hurry? 32. I have to be at the station in ten minutes. 33. Have a good trip!

214

GRAMMAR UNIT NINE

1. The inflection of cardinal numerals: 1 to 39

Nominative case forms:

1. оди́н, одна́, одно́	11. оди́ннадцать	21. два́дцать оди́н
2. два, две	12. двена́дцать	22. два́дцать два́
3. три	13. трина́дцать	23. два́дцать три́
4. четы́ре	14. четы́рнадцать	24. два́дцать четы́ре
5. пять	15. пятна́дцать	25. два́дцать пя́ть
6. шесть	16. шестна́дцать	26. два́дцать ше́сть
7. семь	17. семна́дцать	27. два́дцать се́мь
8. во́семь	18. восемна́дцать	28. два́дцать во́семь
9. де́вять	19. девятна́дцать	29. два́дцать де́вять
10. де́сять	20. два́дцать	30. три́дцать
		31. три́дцать оди́н . . .

1.1 The cardinal numeral 1

The cardinal numeral 1 is expressed by the singular forms of the special adjective **оди́н**.

	MASCULINE	NEUTER	FEMININE
Nom.	оди́н	одно́	одна́
Gen.		одного́	одно́й
Dat.		одному́	одно́й
Acc.		N/G	одну́
Inst.		одни́м	одно́й
Loc.		одно́м	одно́й

1.2 The cardinal numerals 2, 3, 4

Nom.	два́, две́	три́	четы́ре
Gen.	двух́	трёх	четырёх
Dat.	двум́	трём	четырём
Acc.	N/G	N/G	N/G
Inst.	двумя́	тремя́	четырьмя́
Loc.	двух́	трёх	четырёх

1.3 The cardinal numerals 5 to 20 and 30

The numerals 5 to 20 and also 30 have the inflection of feminine II nouns. The numerals 5-10 inclusive and the round numbers 20 and 30 have the stress on the stem in the nominative but on the ending of the other case forms. The numerals 11-19 have stress on the stem throughout, always on the same syllable as in the nominative.

215

Nominative-Accusative	пять	одиннадцать
Genitive, Locative, Dative	пяти	одиннадцати
Instrumental	пятью	одиннадцатью

1.4   Compound numerals

When cardinal numerals consist of more than one word (e.g., 21, 22, etc.), all the numerals are inflected.

Nom.	двадцать два	тридцать пять
Gen.	двадцати двух	тридцати пяти
Dat.	двадцати двум	тридцати пяти
Acc.	N/G	N/G
Inst.	двадцатью двумя	тридцатью пятью
Loc.	двадцати двух	тридцати пяти

◑ 2.   The use of cardinal numerals

The numeral **один** (and compounds ending in this numeral, e.g., 21, 31, etc.) is different from all other numerals in that it is the only that acts like an adjective. It is therefore treated separately.

2.1   The numeral **один**

The numeral **один** (and compounds ending in **один**) agrees in case and gender with the noun it modifies, just as any other adjective does. The noun is always singular, even after compounds ending in **один**.

один конверт	1 envelope
двадцать один конверт	21 envelopes
с двадцатью одним конвертом	with 21 envelopes
одна книга	1 book
о тридцати одной книге	about 31 books

2.2   Numerals other than **один**

The form of a numeral and of the accompanying noun depends on the construction in which the combination occurs.

In the following sections we will distinguish:

(1) Constructions requiring the *nominative case* (e.g., subject, complement of an equational sentence). This is by way of review—you have already been introduced to this usage in *Grammar Unit* **4:2.3** and **6:14**.

(2) Constructions requiring the *genitive, dative, locative, or instrumental case* (e.g., object of various prepositions).

(3) Constructions requiring the *accusative case* (e.g., direct object of a verb).

216

2.21 Nominative case

If the construction requires the nominative case, then only the numeral is in the nominative case; the accompanying noun is in the genitive singular after the nominative forms **два́**, **две́**, **три́**, **четы́ре** (and compound numerals ending in **два́, две́, три́, чстыре́**) and is in the genitive plural after other numerals.

Та́м **две́ кни́ги.**	There are *two books.*
Сейча́с **пя́ть часо́в.**	It is now *five o'clock.*
Три́дцать домо́в	*Thirty houses*
два́дцать **два́ конве́рта**	*22 envelopes*
два́дцать **се́мь конве́ртов**	*27 envelopes*

2.22 Genitive, dative, locative, and instrumental

If the construction requires the genitive, dative, locative or instrumental case, then both the numeral and the accompanying noun are in that case and the noun will be plural.

без десяти́ мину́т	less ten minutes
с двумя́ де́вушками	with two girls
в трёх университе́тах	in three universities
без двадцати́ пяти́ мину́т	less twenty-five minutes

In the first example above, the preposition **без** requires a genitive case form and therefore both **де́сять** and **мину́та** occur in the genitive case. The preposition **с** requires the instrumental and therefore both **две́** and **де́вушка** occur in the instrumental. The preposition **в** *in* requires the locative case and therefore both **три́** and **университе́т** occur in the locative.

2.23 Accusative

Numeral plus noun combinations in constructions requiring the accusative seem to present a complicated picture at first glance, but once the distinction between animate and inanimate categories is understood, it will be apparent that the rules for the accusative case are not new—they are the same rules you have just learned in **2.21** and **2.22**, above.

THE FORM OF THE NUMERAL (cf. *section* 1, above)

If the numeral is

(1) 2, 3, or 4, then A = N/G

Animate like genitive: дву́х, трёх, четырёх
Inanimate like nominative: два́, две́, три́, четы́ре

(2) other numerals you have had, then A = N, whether animate or inanimate, since these numerals are inflected like singular feminine II nouns.

Animate or inanimate: пя́ть, де́сять, два́дцать, etc.

217

The form of the accompanying noun

(1) If A = N, then use the rules for the nominative in 2.21, i.e., after the accusative forms **двá**, **двé**, **трú**, **четы́ре** (and compounds) the following noun is genitive singular and after the accusative forms **пя́ть**, etc., the following noun is genitive plural.

Я ви́дел **двá** собóра.	I saw two cathedrals.
Я ви́дел **пя́ть** собóров.	I saw five cathedrals.
Я ви́дел **пя́ть** дéвушек.	I saw five girls.
Я ви́дел **двáдцать двá** собóра.	I saw 22 cathedrals.

(2) If A = G, then use the rules for the genitive in 2.22, i.e., after the accusative (animate) forms двýх, трёх, четырёх (and compounds) the following noun is in genitive plural.

Я ви́дел **двýх дéвушек**.	I saw two girls.
Я ви́дел **двáдцать двýх дéвушек**.	I saw twenty two girls.

◑ 3. The second locative

A limited number of masculine nouns have a second locative singular form ending in the stressed vowel **-у** or **-ю**. This ending is used only with the prepositions **в** and **на**. The only such nouns you have had so far are **чáс** *hour* and **аэропóрт** *airport*.

В котóром **часý** óн приéдет?	*At* what *time* will he arrive?
Мнé нáдо бы́ть **в аэропортý** в чáс.	I have to be *at the airport* at one o'clock.

But:

Мы́ говори́ли **об аэропóрте**.	We were talking *about the airport*.

3.1 Telling time

In telling time (cf. *Grammar Unit* **5**:4) the even hours are expressed as follows:

Котóрый сейчáс чáс?	What time is it?
Сейчáс чáс.	It is now one o'clock.
Сейчáс три́ часá.	It is now three o'clock.
Сейчáс пя́ть часóв.	It is now five o'clock.

Time after the even hour up to and including the half hour is expressed literally as half of, quarter of, ten minutes of the next hour, with the next hour stated by the ordinal number.

Сейчáс половúна пя́того.	It is now half past four.
	(Literally, half of the fifth)
Сейчáс чéтверть вторóго.	It is now quarter after one.
	(Literally, quarter of the second.)

Сейча́с де́сять мину́т девя́того.	It is now ten after eight.
	(Literally, ten minutes of the ninth.)
Сейча́с пя́ть мину́т пе́рвого.	It is now five after twelve.
	(Literally, five minutes of the first.)

Time after the half hour is expressed literally as the hour less so much. The word **мину́т** is often omitted in this expression.

Сейча́с **без** че́тверти ше́сть.	It is now quarter of six.
	(Literally, it is six o'clock less a quarter.)
Сейча́с **без** пяти́ (мину́т) оди́ннадцать.	It is now five of eleven.
	(Literally, it is eleven o'clock less five.)
Сейча́с **без** двадцати́ пяти́ (мину́т) ча́с.	It is twenty five of one.
	(Literally, it is one o'clock less twenty five.)

3.2   At what time

The indication of "time at" basically follows the same pattern of telling time discussed above, but with the additional factor that *at* is usually expressed by the preposition **в**. Specifically, it is expressed as follows:

(1) **в** plus locative case to express *At what time?* and *at the half hour.*

В кото́ром часу́ о́н прие́дет?	*At what time* will he arrive?
О́н прие́дет **в полови́не** девя́того.	He will arrive *at half past* eight.

(2) without preposition in expressions where **без** is used.

Самолёт отлета́ет бе́з четверти два́.	The airplane leaves at quarter of two.
О́н пришёл бе́з десяти́ ше́сть.	He came at ten of six.

(3) **в** plus accusative in the other time expressions.

Она́ верну́лась в ча́с.	She returned at one o'clock.
Она́ верну́лась в два́ часа́.	She returned at two o'clock.
Она́ верну́лась в пя́ть часо́в.	She returned at five o'clock.
Она́ верну́лась в че́тверть седьмо́го.	She returned at quarter past six.
Она́ верну́лась в пя́ть мину́т· двена́д-цатого.	She returned at five after eleven.
Она́ верну́лась в два́дцать пя́ть мину́т деся́того.	She returned at twenty five after nine.

☺ 4.   Imperative

Russian has a second person singular and a second person plural imperative, which are used in giving commands and making requests. The following

219

statements of the formation of the imperative are for the second person plural, since this is the most commonly used. The second singular may be formed regularly by dropping the **-те** from the plural.

The imperative is formed on the non-past stem in the following ways:

(1) Those verbs which have a non-past stem ending in the sound /y/ form the second plural imperative by adding /-ṭi/ to the stem. In terms of Cyrillic writing, those verbs which have a vowel letter or **ь** before the third plural ending -ют/-ят replace the ending **-ют/-ят** by **-йте**.

Рабо́тают.	/rabótay-ut/	They work.
Рабо́та**йте**!	/rabótay-ṭi/	*Work!*
Чита́ют.	/čitáy-ut/	They read.
Чита́**йте**!	/čitáy-ṭi/	*Read!*
Постро́ят.	/pastróy-it/	They will build.
Постро́**йте**!	/pastróy-ṭi/	*Build!*

If a consonant immediately precedes the /y/ the inserted vowel **-e-** occurs before the /y/.

Пью́т.	/py-ut/	They drink.
П**е́йте**!	/ṗéy-ṭi/	*Drink!*

(2) Other verbs, provided that the stress occurs on the ending on any of the forms of the non-past, add **-йте** (with the **-й-** stressed) to the non-past stem.

THIRD PLURAL	FIRST SINGULAR	IMPERATIVE	
говоря́т	говорю́	Говор**и́те**!	*Speak!*
пи́шут	пишу́	Пиш**и́те**!	*Write!*

(3) Other verbs, provided that the non-past stem ends in more than one consonant, add **-ите** (unstressed) to the non-past stem. No examples of this type have occurred so far.

(4) Other verbs, i.e., those ending in any single consonant other than /y/ and not having stress on any of the non-past endings, add **-ьте**.

познако́мят	познако́млю	Познако́м**ьте**!	*Introduce!*
бу́дут	бу́ду	Бу́д**ьте**!	*Be!*

Most verbs in Russian are of the first and second types listed above. A very small number of Russian verbs are irregular in forming the imperative differently from any of the four ways described above. (Any irregularity affecting the non-prefixed form of a verb will affect the prefixed forms as well.)

да́ть, даду́т	**Да́йте**!	*Give!*
прие́хать, прие́дут	**Приезжа́йте**!	*Come!*

The imperative of any verb in **-давать**, **-ставать**, or **-знавать** is irregular in that it is formed from the infinitive as follows:

продава́ть, продаю́т	**Продава́йте**!	*Sell!*
остава́ться, остаю́тся	**Остава́йтесь**!	*Remain!*
отстава́ть, отстаю́т	**Отстава́йте**!	*Lag behind!*

The imperative of a verb will be perfective or imperfective depending upon whether it is formed from a perfective or imperfective verb. The distinction between perfective imperative and imperfective imperative is the same as that generally indicated by perfective and imperfective forms (cf. *Grammar Unit 6:4*).

Встреча́йте его́ ка́ждый де́нь в ча́с!	Meet him every day at one o'clock!
Встре́тьте его́ за́втра в ча́с!	Meet him tomorrow at one o'clock.
Пиши́те э́то письмо́!	Write this letter! (Be busy writing this letter.)
Напиши́те э́то письмо́!	Write this letter! (Get this letter written.)

Because of the meaning of the perfective aspect (completion of an event) the perfective imperative occurs more frequently in the positive and the imperfective occurs more frequently in the negative.

Позвони́те ему́!	*Phone* him!
Не звони́те ему́!	*Don't phone* him!

Here are the infinitive and third plural forms of some verbs that have previously occurred only in the imperative form:

Type i

откры́ть (P),	откро́ют	Откро́йте!	Open!
закры́ть (P),	закро́ют	Закро́йте!	Close!

Type ii

повтори́ть (P)	повторя́т	Повтори́те!	Repeat!

● 5. Reflexive verbs

Verbs with **-сь/-ся** added to them are called reflexive verbs. These verbs are all intransitive in Russian, i.e., they do not ever take an object in the accusative case. Some reflexive verbs are translatable as reciprocals (each other), some as reflexives (one's self), some as passives, some as simple intransitives, and some have no particular connection in meaning with the non-reflexive form. Which of these meanings a particular reflexive verb will have cannot be predicted and must be learned when you meet it.

221

Non-reflexive		Reflexive	
познако́мить (P)	to introduce, make acquainted with	познако́миться	to be introduced, get acquainted with
продава́ть (I)	to sell	продава́ться	to be sold
верну́ть (P)	to return (something), to give back	верну́ться	to return (intransitive), to come back
ви́деть (I)	to see	ви́деться	to see each other
собира́ть (I)	to collect, gather (something)	собира́ться	to collect, gather (intransitive); to intend
находи́ть (I)	to find	находи́ться	to be found, be located
найти́ (P)	to find	найти́сь	

Я **прода́ю** ру́сские кни́ги.	I *sell* Russian books.
Здесь **продаю́тся** сигаре́ты.	Cigarettes *are sold* here.
Я **верну́л** ру́чку моему́ дру́гу.	I *returned* the pen to my friend.
Я **верну́лся** из Москвы́.	I *returned* from Moscow.
Я **ви́дел** его́ вчера́.	I *saw* him yesterday.
Мы ча́сто **ви́димся**.	We often *see each other.*
Он **собира́ет** всё свои́ кни́ги.	He's *gathering* all his books together.
Инжене́ры **собира́ются** в Ташке́нте.	The engineers *are meeting* (gathering) in Tashkent.
Я **собира́юсь** пое́хать в Ленингра́д.	I *am planning* to go to Leningrad.
Я **нашёл** ру́чку за кни́гой.	I *found* the pen behind the book.
Москва́ **нахо́дится** в Сове́тском Сою́зе.	Moscow *is located* in the Soviet Union.

6. The verb "To meet"

The following verbs may all be translated by the English verb *to meet*, but in different senses:

познако́миться	to meet, become acquainted with
собира́ться	to meet, to hold a meeting
встреча́ть	to meet (someone by appointment or by accident)

Я **познако́мился** с ним в Ташке́нте.	I *met* him (became acquainted with him) in Tashkent.
Они́ **собира́лись** в Ташке́нте.	They *met* (had meetings) in Tashkent.

222

Я его **встретил** в Ташкенте. I *met* him (either accidentally or by appointment) in Tashkent.

🌓 7. Genitive in wishes

Many wishes are expressed in Russian by the genitive case.

Всего хорошего! Good luck!
Счастливого пути! Have a good trip!

🌓 8. Some aspect pairs

8.1 Familiar types

WITH PREFIXES

Imperfective	*Perfective*	
спешить, спешат	поспешить, поспешат	to hurry
платить, платят, плачу	заплатить, заплатят, заплачу	to pay

Я **буду платить** каждую неделю. I *will pay* every week.
Я **заплачу** завтра. I *will pay* tomorrow.

WITH **-ать, -ять, -ить**

повторять, повторяют повторить, повторят to repeat

8.2 дава́ть (I), да́ть (Р)

These two verbs form an aspect pair. Prefixed varieties bear the same relationship.

Imperfective	*Perfective*		
давать, дают	дать	(Irregular)	to give
подавать, подают	подать	(Irregular)	to serve
продавать, продают	продать	(Irregular)	to sell
продаваться, продаются	продаться	(Irregular)	to be sold

Note the stress in the past of the prefixed forms of **да́ть**:

по́дал	про́дал	прода́лся
подала́	продала́	продала́сь
по́дало	про́дало	продало́сь
по́дали	про́дали	продали́сь

Он **продава́л** книги. He *used to sell* books.
Он мне **про́дал** эту книгу. He *sold* me this book.

◐ 9. The imperfective future

The imperfective verb has a future form composed of the non-past of быть (бу́дут) plus the imperfective infinitive (cf. *Grammar Unit* 6:4).

In Conversation Lesson 18 you had the following example:

Та́м бу́дет съе́зд инжене́ров и мы́ все́ **бу́дем принима́ть** в нём уча́стие.	There will be a convention of engineers there and we *will* all *be taking* part in it.

In this sentence the use of the imperfective implies a continued taking part, whereas the perfective would imply the completion of taking part.

The following are some examples of the contrast between perfective and imperfective in the future:

Я́ **бу́ду** ча́сто **получа́ть** пи́сьма от мое́й жены́.	I *will* often *be getting* letters from my wife.
За́втра я́ наве́рно **получу́** письмо́ от мое́й жены́.	Tomorrow I *will* probably *get* a letter from my wife.
Я́ **бу́ду чита́ть** ве́сь де́нь.	I'*ll be reading* all day.
Я́ **прочита́ю** э́ту кни́гу че́рез неде́лю.	I'*ll read* this book in a week.

◐ 10. The preposition до

The preposition **до** *before, until, as far as* takes a following noun or pronoun in the genitive case.

До свида́ния!	Goodbye! (*Until* the seeing again)
до войны́	*before* the war
До Москвы́ недалеко́.	It's not far *to* Moscow.

Far (*not far*) *from* is **далеко́** (**недалеко́**) **от**; *far* (*not far*) *from... to* is **далеко́** (**недалеко́**) **от... до.**

От Москвы́ **до** Ленингра́да не о́чень далеко́.	It's not very far *from* Moscow *to* Leningrad.

The combination **до того́, как** *before* (cf. **по́сле того́, как** *after*, *Conversation 17, New Prepositions*) is used to introduce a clause.

Я́ прочита́л всю́ кни́гу **до того́, как** о́н пришёл.	I read the whole book *before* he came.

◐ 11. The particle ли *whether*

Constructions which in English may be expressed either by *if* or by *whether* are expressed in Russian by the particle **ли** immediately following the first word in the subordinate clause. If the subordinate clause contains a verb or the word **нет**, then this will be the first word in the clause. Otherwise, the word the speaker wishes to put under question occupies the first position.

Ка́к вы́ бу́дете зна́ть, **заплати́л ли** я́?	How will you know *if (whether)* I paid?
О́н не зна́ет, **придёт ли** она́ за́втра.	He doesn't know *if (whether)* she will come tomorrow.
Я́ не зна́ю, **говори́т ли** о́н по-ру́сски.	I don't know *if (whether)* he speaks Russian.
Я́ не зна́ю, **доста́точно ли** у на́с бума́ги.	I don't know *if (whether)* we have enough paper.

УПРАЖНЕ́НИЯ

A. Make the following substitutions orally:

Сейча́с . . . .

2 o'clock	2:30	10:20	11:40
6 o'clock	6:15	11:20	3:40
1 o'clock	12:15	3:25	4:50
8 o'clock	1:15	6:45	7:50
4 o'clock	8:15	2:45	1:50
7:30	9:10	12:45	6:35
3:30	4:10	10:45	12:35
11:30	5:20	8:40	

B. Transform orally from non-past perfective to imperative according to the model:

MODEL: Ива́н повтори́т э́то сло́во.
        Ива́н, **повтори́те** э́то сло́во!

1. Ива́н ему́ ска́жет э́то.
2. Бори́с запла́тит за газе́ту.
3. Ве́ра вернётся че́рез ме́сяц.
4. Ве́ра за́втра вернёт мои́ кни́ги.
5. Бори́с познако́мится с мои́м бра́том.
6. Бори́с отве́тит на моё письмо́.
7. Ве́ра спеши́т на вокза́л.
8. О́льга не забу́дет прийти́ ко мне́ за́втра.
9. О́льга за́втра прочита́ет э́ту статью́.
10. Ве́ра принесёт мою́ газе́ту.
11. Ми́ша зайдёт за мно́й в полови́не второ́го.
12. Пётр вы́пьет э́то молоко́.
13. Пётр э́то сде́лает.

225

C. Make the following substitutions orally:

Óн приéхал сюдá . . . .

> [1] after the war
> [2] after the convention in Tashkent
> [3] after (his) trip through the Soviet Union
> [4] after (his) vacation in the Caucasus
> [5] after I received his letter
> [6] after I wrote to him
> [7] after I returned from the Soviet Union
> [8] after we had dinner
> [9] after I phoned you

D. Repeat exercise C, but substitute *before* for *after*.

E. Repeat exercise A, but in the following frame:

Óн придёт   (at) . . . .

CONVERSATION 19

Weather and climate

John has run away from Moscow's spring rains only to find it is also raining in Leningrad.

CONVERSATION UNIT NINETEEN ———————

JOHN   ¹ What bad weather! Nothing but rain! ² Does it really rain all spring in Leningrad?

HELEN   ³ Right now the wind is from the sea, from the west. ⁴ It should be over soon now.

JOHN   ⁵ And how is it in your city in the summer?

HELEN   ⁶ In the summer it's very pleasant. ⁷ It's not hot, the days are clear and the nights warm. ⁸ Leningrad is near the sea and therefore the climate here is temperate.

JOHN   ⁹ In Moscow it's rather hot, isn't it?

HELEN   ¹⁰ In Moscow it is sometimes much hotter than in Leningrad. ¹¹ But in the fall and winter it's cold there, ¹² colder than in Leningrad, although Moscow lies to the south of us.

JOHN   ¹³ And is it dry there?

HELEN   ¹⁴ Yes, it's far from the sea, so it's dry.

JOHN   ¹⁵ What's the climate like in Siberia?

HELEN   ¹⁶ In the north the snow is still lying [on the ground]; the climate is severe there. ¹⁷ And to the south of Siberia there are deserts and it's hot there. ¹⁸ I can tell you a lot about the climate of Central Asia. ¹⁹ When I was a student, I traveled around Central Asia every summer.

NOTES

1   Literally: all [the time] rain and rain. **Да** is occasionally used in the meaning *and*.

2   **Ра́зве** expresses surprise. It may be translated *is it really true that..?*
As an equivalent of *it is raining, it rains* and *it is snowing, it snows* Russian uses the verb **итти́; идёт до́ждь, идёт снег.**

18   **Рассказа́ть**, in contrast with **сказа́ть**, means *to tell a story* or to tell something lengthier than would be indicated by сказа́ть.

NEW VERBS

TYPE I

рассказать (Р)   расска́жут, расскажу́   to tell

TYPE II

ко́нчиться (Р)	ко́нчатся	to end, be over, finish
лежа́ть (I)	лежа́т	to lie
е́здить (I)	е́здят, е́зжу	to go (by vehicle)

228

Погода и климат

ДЖОН   ¹ Áх, какáя плохáя погóда! Всё дóждь дá дóждь! ² Рáзве в Ленингрáде всю весну́ идёт дóждь?

ЕЛÉНА   ³ Сейчáс у нáс вéтер с мóря, с зáпада. ⁴ Скóро ужé дóлжен кóнчиться.

ДЖОН   ⁵ А кáк у вáс лéтом?

ЕЛÉНА   ⁶ Лéтом óчень прия́тно. ⁷ Не жáрко, я́сные дни́ и тёплые нóчи. ⁸ Ленингрáд бли́зко от мóря, поэ́тому кли́мат здéсь умéренный.

ДЖОН   ⁹ В Москвé довóльно жáрко, прáвда?

ЕЛÉНА   ¹⁰ В Москвé иногдá горáздо жáрче, чем в Ленингрáде. ¹¹ Нó óсенью и зимóй тáм хóлодно, ¹² холоднéе чем в Ленингрáде, хотя́ Москвá лежи́т к ю́гу от нáс.

ДЖОН   ¹³ А тáм су́хо?

ЕЛÉНА   ¹⁴ Дá, от мóря далекó, поэ́тому и су́хо.

ДЖОН   ¹⁵ А какóй кли́мат в Сиби́ри?

ЕЛÉНА   ¹⁶ На сéвере ещё лежи́т снéг, тáм óчень сурóвый кли́мат. ¹⁷ А к ю́гу от Сиби́ри — пусты́ни, и тáм жáрко. ¹⁸ Я́ вáм мнóго могу́ рассказáть о кли́мате Срéдней Áзии. ¹⁹ Когдá я́ былá студéнткой, я́ кáждое лéто éздила по Срéдней Áзии.

NEW NOUNS

	NOMINATIVE SINGULAR	GENITIVE SINGULAR	NOMINATIVE PLURAL	

Masculine

до́ждь	дождя́		rain
ве́тер (е)			wind
кли́мат			climate
ю́г			south
се́вер			north
сне́г			snow

Neuter

мо́ре	мо́ря	моря́	sea
ле́то			summer

Feminine I

пого́да			weather
весна́			spring
зима́ (Acc. зи́му)	зи́мы		winter
пусты́ня			desert
А́зия			Asia

Feminine II

но́чь		но́чи	night

Genitive plural	ноче́й
Dative plural	ноча́м
Instrumental plural	ноча́ми
Locative plural	ноча́х

о́сень			fall
Сиби́рь			Siberia

Recall that the genitive plural ending -*Ey* occurs with masculine and neuter nouns ending in /š, ž/ or in a palatalized consonant other than /y/. Thus, the genitive plural of **мо́ре** /móṛi/ is **море́й** /maṛéy/.

Note that the nouns **ю́г** *south* and **се́вер** *north* are used with the series of prepositions **на — на — с** just like **за́пад** *west* and **восто́к** *east*.

УПРАЖНЕ́НИЯ

A. Listen to the following questions and answer them according to the model:

MODEL: Ива́н **придёт**? **Я́ не зна́ю, придёт ли** Ива́н.

1. В Нью-Йо́рке идёт до́ждь?
2. Его́ сестра́ живёт в Сиби́ри?
3. Кли́мат в Росси́и уме́ренный?
4. Но́чи в Ташке́нте тёплые?
5. Ещё лежи́т сне́г в Ленингра́де?
6. О́н принима́ет уча́стие в съе́зде?
7. Самолёт отлета́ет в че́тверть второ́го?
8. О́н мно́го е́здил по Сове́тскому Сою́зу?
9. Зде́сь продаётся нау́чная литерату́ра?
10. Они́ запла́тят за всё э́ти кни́ги?
11. О́н вернёт э́ту ру́чку?
12. Они́ собира́ются пое́хать на се́вер?
13. Они́ взя́ли че́к?
14. Э́то далеко́ от музе́я?
15. Зде́сь жа́рче чем в Москве́?

B. Transform orally from non-past imperfective to negative imperative according to the model:

MODEL: Я́ **чита́ю** газе́ты. **Не чита́йте** газе́ты!

1. Я́ рабо́таю на фа́брике.
2. Я́ спешу́ на вокза́л.
3. Я́ отвеча́ю на его́ вопро́сы.
4. Я́ пью ко́фе.
5. Я́ покупа́ю папиро́сы.
6. Я́ звоню́ её друзья́м.
7. Я́ обе́даю с тури́стами.
8. Я́ пишу́ статьи́.
9. Я́ стро́ю дома́.
10. Я́ говорю́ по-англи́йски.
11. Я́ встреча́ю друзе́й в аэропорту́.
12. Я́ повторя́ю фра́зы.

C. Transform orally from non-past imperfective to future imperfective according to the model:

MODEL: **Я́ повторя́ю** всё фра́зы в кни́ге.
Я́ **бу́ду повторя́ть** всё фра́зы в кни́ге.

1. Они́ ча́сто принима́ют уча́стие в таки́х дела́х.
2. Самолёт всегда́ отлета́ет по́здно.
3. Она́ продаёт ма́рки.
4. Иногда́ о́н стои́т у вхо́да.
5. О́н всегда́ интересу́ется кни́гами по матема́тике.
6. Они́ ча́сто получа́ют кни́ги из Аме́рики.
7. Мы́ ча́сто обе́даем у отца́.
8. Я́ всегда́ захожу́ за ни́м в ча́с.
9. Они́ всегда́ прихо́дят ро́вно в ше́сть часо́в.
10. Она́ пи́шет мно́го пи́сем.
11. Я́ пью гла́вным о́бразом молоко́.
12. Ка́ждое ле́то о́н путеше́ствует по все́й Аме́рике.

D. Give the Russian equivalents:

1. What fine weather! 2. What bad weather! 3. Is it raining today? 4. Yesterday it rained. 5. Does it rain often in the summer here? 6. Sometimes it snows in the fall. 7. It snowed yesterday. 8. It was cold in Leningrad yesterday. 9. Sometimes it's colder in Leningrad than in Moscow. 10. It's hotter in Moscow.

11. It's hot in the south. 12. It's very pleasant in the south in autumn. 13. In the south the days are warm. 14. In the north the days are clear. 15. It's rather hot in Tashkent. 16. In the summer the wind is from the sea. 17. In the winter the wind is from the desert. 18. The wind is from the desert and therefore it is dry. 19. The wind is from the sea and therefore it is pleasant.

20. Tashkent is located in the south. 21. Kiev is located to the south of Moscow. 22. He lives in the south. 23. He returned from the south yesterday. 24. Is Smolensk located in the south or in the north? 25. I think that Smolensk is located in the west. 26. Although he speaks Russian rather well, he's not a Russian. 27. Although Tashkent is not a Russian city, many Russians live there. 28. Although he lived for a long time in Moscow, he doesn't like borsch.

CONVERSATION 20

Moscow's theaters

Strolling through Red Square John and Ivan talk about the theater.

CONVERSATION UNIT TWENTY _____

ENGLISH EQUIVALENTS

JOHN	[1] This evening I'm going to the Art Theater.
IVAN	[2] What's on? [3] They say they have a good repertoire this year.
JOHN	[4] Today they're putting on Chekhov's play "Three Sisters." [5] I bought two tickets for myself and for Peter Ivanovich.
IVAN	[6] When does the performance begin?
JOHN	[7] At half past seven. [8] Peter says there are some very good and famous actors playing there.
IVAN	[9] Have you already seen our opera and ballet?
JOHN	[10] I went to [listened to] the opera last week [11] and I plan on going to the ballet next week, perhaps on Tuesday.
IVAN	[12] Which opera do you like best?
JOHN	[13] My favorite opera is Boris Godunov.
IVAN	[14] I've been told that Americans like to go to the movies. [15] Do you have interesting movies in your country?
JOHN	[16] Oh, we have so many films that there are all kinds, [17] both good ones and very bad ones.

NOTES

1 Моско́вский Худо́жественный Теа́тр (often abbreviated МХАТ /mxat/) is a famous theater in Moscow.

12 Бо́льше literally, *more*.

~~ADD~~ ITIONAL VOCABULARY

~~понед~~е́льник	*Monday*	пя́тница	*Friday*
~~вто~~рник	*Tuesday*	суббо́та	*Saturday*
~~ср~~еда́	*Wednesday*	воскресе́нье	*Sunday*
четве́рг	*Thursday*		

NEW VERBS

Type I

игра́ть (I), игра́ют	to play
слу́шать (I), слу́шают	to listen to

Московские театры

ДЖОН ¹ Сегодня вечером я пойду в Художественный театр.

ИВАН ² Что там идёт? ³ В этом году, говорят, хороший репертуар.

ДЖОН ⁴ Сегодня идёт пьеса « Три сестры » Чехова. ⁵ Я купил два билета, для себя и для Петра Ивановича.

ИВАН ⁶ Когда начинается спектакль?

ДЖОН ⁷ В половине восьмого. ⁸ Пётр говорит, что там играют очень хорошие и знаменитые актёры.

ИВАН ⁹ Вы уже видели нашу оперу и балет?

ДЖОН ¹⁰ Я слушал оперу на прошлой неделе, ¹¹ а на балет собираюсь пойти на будущей неделе, может быть во вторник.

ИВАН ¹² Какая опера вам больше нравится?

ДЖОН ¹³ Моя любимая опера — « Борис Годунов ».

ИВАН ¹⁴ Мне сказали, что американцы любят ходить в кино. ¹⁵ Интересные у вас фильмы?

ДЖОН ¹⁶ О, у нас так много фильмов, что есть всякие, ¹⁷ и хорошие и совсем плохие.

NEW NOUNS

NOMINATIVE SINGULAR

Masculine

вéчер	evening	понедéльник	Monday
Чéхов	Chekhov	втóрник	Tuesday
билéт	ticket	четвéрг	Thursday
актёр	actor	репертуáр	repertoire
балéт	ballet	спектáкль	performance
Годунóв	Godunov		
фúльм	film, movie		
гóд	year		

Nominative Plural	гóды
Genitive Plural	годóв
Dative Plural	годáм
Instrumental Plural	годáми
Locative Plural	годáх

Neuter

воскресéнье	Sunday
кинó (uninflected)	movie (theater)

Feminine I

пьéса	play
óпера	opera
средá	Wednesday
пя́тница	Friday
суббóта	Saturday

Masculine family names ending in **-ов**, such as Чéхов and Годунóв (and in **-ин**, such as Лéнин), have an irregular instrumental singular in **-ым** instead of the usual **-ом**.

The feminine noun **средá** has the same stress pattern as **рукá** and **горá**.

	SINGULAR	PLURAL
Nom.	средá	срéды
Gen.	среды́	срéд
Dat.	средé	средáм
Acc.	срéду	срéды
Inst.	средóй	средáми
Loc.	средé	средáх

The noun **год** *year* has a second locative ending in **-ý** like в котóром **часý**, e.g., в э́том **годý** *this year* (cf. *Grammar Unit* **9:3**). With the numerals *two, three,* and *four, year* is expressed by the word **гóд** e.g., **двá гóда** *two years*. But with the numerals *five* and above and after quantity words such as **скóлько**, **мнóго**, etc., it is expressed by the word **лéто** e.g., **пя́ть лéт** *five years*.

Note that **балéт** *ballet* is another noun that is used with the preposition **на** *at*.

NEW PRONOUNS

The pronoun **себя́** has no nominative form. The endings of the other forms are identical to those of **ты**.

Genitive-Accusative	себя́
Dative-Locative	себé
Instrumental	собóй

This pronoun refers to the same person or persons as the subject of the sentence, may have either singular or plural meaning for any of the three persons, and may therefore be translated as *myself, ourselves, yourself, yourselves, himself, herself, itself,* or *themselves.*

Онá купи́ла билéты для **себя́**.	She bought tickets for *herself.*
Они́ купи́ли билéты для **себя́**.	They bought tickets for *themselves.*
Мы́ купи́ли билéты для **себя́**.	We bought tickets for *ourselves.*

УПРАЖНÉНИЯ

A. Transform orally from past imperfective to non-past imperfective according to the model:

MODEL: Они́ игрáли в пьéсе « Три́ сéстры́ ».
       Они́ **игрáют** в пьéсе « Три́ сéстры́ ».

1. Спектáкль начинáлся в сéмь часóв.
2. Кни́га лежáла как рáз пéред ни́м.
3. Они́ повторя́ли э́ти словá.
4. Я́ спеши́л домóй.
5. Я́ читáл пьéсу Чéхова.
6. Мы́ говори́ли с вáшими товáрищами.
7. Иногдá он покупáл рýсские сигарéты.
8. Кáждую недéлю они́ заходи́ли за мнóй.
9. О́н шёл по ýлице.
10. О́н писáл статьи́ для газéты.
11. В какóм гóроде вы́ жи́ли?
12. Онá не моглá рабóтать так пóздно.
13. Онá интересовáлась óперой.
14. Зимóй я́ путешéствовал по ю́гу.

237

15. Они́ е́ли ру́сские блю́да.
16. Они́ ча́сто быва́ли у э́того хи́мика.
17. Иногда́ я́ плати́л за биле́ты.
18. Я́ люби́л получа́ть пи́сьма.
19. Иногда́ о́н приходи́л в полови́не шесто́го.
20. О́н ча́сто мне́ дава́л интере́сные ма́рки.

B. Make the following substitutions orally:

Она́ принесла́ всё кро́ме . . . .

¹ this book
² the newspapers
³ borsch
⁴ the new Soviet stamps
⁵ the new novels
⁶ your book on linguistics
⁷ my old watch
⁸ postcards
⁹ the articles on physics
¹⁰ white envelopes

C. Make the following substitutions orally:

Сде́лайте э́то для . . . .!

¹ me
² Peter
³ Natasha
⁴ us
⁵ Boris Ivanovich
⁶ my friends
⁷ our acquaintances
⁸ the American tourists

D. Give the Russian equivalents:

1. This evening I'm going to the theater. 2. Last week I went to the movies. 3. Next week I'm going to the ballet. 4. What's on at the theater tonight? 5. They're putting on a new play. 6. This year they have a good repertoire. 7. For the most part they put on famous plays. 8. Which opera are they putting on? 9. I don't know whether that opera is on tonight. 10. Have you heard that opera? 11. Which opera do you like best?

12. When does the performance begin? 13. Formerly the performance used to begin at 7:30. 14. Now the performance begins at eight. 15. The performance will soon be over. 16. The performance ended at 11:30.

17. Do you know the actors? 18. The actors in this play are very famous. 19. The actors who are playing in this play are famous. 20. The actors play very well.

21. I lived in Moscow for two years. 22. He worked in Tashkent for five years. 23. He wrote this play ten years ago. 24. We're going to the Soviet Union for three years. 25. I've been living in Moscow for twenty-three years.

238

GRAMMAR UNIT TEN

1. Iterative aspect

It was mentioned in Grammar Unit 6:4 that the verbs **итти́** and **éхать**, although imperfective, are used in only one of the meanings of imperfective. This is because these verbs are three-aspect verbs, i.e., they have three aspect forms rather than the two that most verbs have. Each of the verbs итти́ and éхать has one perfective form and two imperfective forms. One of the imperfective forms has the meaning of a repeated event; we will call it the *iterative* imperfective. The other imperfective form has the meaning of a continuous event (cf. *Grammar Unit* **6:4**); we will call it the *actual* imperfective.

Iterative Imperfective	*Actual Imperfective*	*Perfective*
ходи́ть	итти́	пойти́
éздить	éхать	поéхать

Since both **ходи́ть** and **итти́** (likewise **éздить** and **éхать**) are imperfective verbs, the non-past forms of both have present meaning and they both form a compound future with **бýдут**.

ходи́ть, итти́, пойти́

Кáждый дéнь óн **ходи́л** в университéт в дéвять часóв.	Every day he *went* (*used to go*) to the university at nine o'clock.
Когда́ я егó встрéтил, óн **шёл** в университéт.	When I met him he *was going* (was on his way) to the university.
Вчера́ óн **пошёл** в университéт в вóсемь часóв.	Yesterday he *went* to the university at eight o'clock.

éздить, éхать, поéхать

Кáждое лéто я **éзжу** по Сиби́ри.	Every summer I *go* (*travel*) around Siberia.
Куда́ вы сейча́с **éдете**?	Where *are* you *going* now?
Они́ **поéдут** в Сиби́рь.	They *will go* to Siberia.

When the above verbs have a prefix added that changes their basic meaning (**при-**, **за-** etc.) they are two-aspect verbs rather than three. The form with -ходи́ть or -езжа́ть is the only imperfective form and has both imperfective meanings. The verb -езжа́ть never occurs without a prefix; it has regular type I inflection, -езжа́ют.

IMPERFECTIVE		PERFECTIVE
ITERATIVE	ACTUAL	
ходи́ть	итти́	пойти́
приходи́ть		прийти́
éздить	éхать	поéхать
приезжа́ть		приéхать

239

Óн чáсто **хóдит** тудá.	He often *goes* there.
Óн чáсто **прихóдит** сюдá.	He often *comes* here.
Сейчáс óн **идёт** в рестoрáн.	He *is* now *going* to the restaurant.
Сейчáс óн **прихóдит** из рестoрáна.	He *is* now *coming* from the restaurant.

Another three-aspect verb is the verb *to fly*. As with all three-aspect verbs the prefixed forms have only two aspects.

| летáть | летéть | полетéть |
| прилетáть | | прилетéть |

Óн чáсто **летáет**.	He often *flies*.
Кудá вы́ **летúте**?	Where *are* you *flying* to?
Я́ **полечу́** в Бостóн.	I *will fly* to Boston.

There are some special usages of the above verbs.

1) In the meaning *to rain*, *to snow* the verb **иттú** is the only imperfective form that occurs and it expresses both meanings of the imperfective aspect.

| Сейчáс **идёт дóждь**. | It's *raining* now. |
| Здéсь чáсто **идёт снéг**. | It often *snows* here. |

2) The verb **иттú** is used with reference to plays, movies, etc., as an equivalent of English *to be on, be playing*. In this meaning иттú is the only imperfective verb that occurs.

Сегóдня **идёт** пьéса "Трú сестры́". Today the play "The Three Sisters" *is on*.

3) The verb **ходúть** sometimes has the special meanings *to walk for pleasure* or *to be physically capable of walking*. In these meanings, ходúть is the only imperfective form that occurs.

| Ребёнок ещё не **хóдит**. | The child *doesn't walk* yet. |
| Ивáн **хóдит** в пáрке. | Ivan *is walking* (*is taking a walk*) in the park. |

◖ 2. Short adjectives

As was mentioned in Unit 6, many adjectives in Russian have both a long form and a short form. When an adjective has a short form, the masculine singular can usually be formed from the long form by dropping the ending (-ый, -ий or -óй). There are two complications to be noted here: 1) the masculine singular short form may have an inserted vowel (свобóден vs. свобóдный) and 2) the position of stress on the short form is not predictable from the long form. Although the principle of derivation is fairly simple, for several reasons it is not advisable for the student to derive short forms of the adjective from known long forms and try to use them. First of all, many long adjectives do not have a short form; second, some short adjectives have a special meaning; third, the short form may be used only in the predicate position but since for most adjectives the long form may also be used in this position instead of the short form, it is not necessary to know the short form.

Эта о́пера интере́сн**а**. ⎫
Эта о́пера интере́сн**ая**. ⎬ This opera is interesting.

Эта де́вушка краси́в**а**. ⎫
Эта де́вушка краси́в**ая**. ⎬ This girl is beautiful.

The following list includes those short forms which you should learn to use in the predicate position. With these are given the corresponding long forms.

SHORT FORM   LONG FORM

(*masculine*)

за́нят	busy, occupied	за́нятый	
свобо́ден (е)	free, vacant, unoccupied	свобо́дный	
похо́ж	similar	похо́жий	
до́лжен (е)	must, ought	до́лжный	due, proper
гото́в	ready, prepared	гото́вый	
до́рог	dear, expensive	дорого́й	
ра́д	glad	(No long form)	

The only new short form in the above list is **до́рог**, which has the following forms: **до́рог, дорога́, до́рого, до́роги.**

The neuter short form, since it is used not only as a predicate adjective, but also as an adverb, is also worth learning for many adjectives.

PREDICATIVE ADJECTIVE

Это **свобо́дно**.   That is *free* (vacant, unoccupied).

ADVERB

Он **свобо́дно** говори́т по-ру́сски.   He speaks Russian *fluently*.

The following is a list of long adjectives and their neuter short forms for all those adjectives which you have met in one form or the other.

Long form		*Neuter short form*
хоро́ший	good	хорошо́
краси́вый	beautiful	краси́во
высо́кий	high	высоко́
плохо́й	bad	пло́хо
дешёвый	cheap	дёшево
прия́тный	pleasant	прия́тно
прекра́сный	beautiful, wonderful	прекра́сно
бли́зкий	near	бли́зко
далёкий	far	далеко́
пра́вильный	correct	пра́вильно

то́чный	exact	то́чно
я́сный	clear	я́сно
тёплый	warm	тепло́
жа́ркий	hot	жа́рко
холо́дный	cold	хо́лодно
сухо́й	dry	су́хо
интере́сный	interesting	интере́сно
просто́й	simple	про́сто
обяза́тельный	obligatory	обяза́тельно
че́стный	honorable, honest	че́стно
чуде́сный	wonderful	чуде́сно
обыкнове́нный	ordinary	обыкнове́нно

3. Comparison of long adjectives

3.1 The regular comparative

The comparative of long adjectives is regularly formed by placing the word **бо́лее** before the adjective. **Бо́лее** is uninflected, while the adjective takes normal adjective inflection.

Я возьму́ **дешёвое** изда́ние.	I'll take the cheap edition.
Я возьму́ **бо́лее дешёвое** изда́ние.	I'll take *the cheaper* edition.
У нас **я́сные** дни́.	We have clear days.
У нас **бо́лее я́сные** дни́.	We have *clearer* days.
Я живу́ в **ста́ром** до́ме.	I live in an old house.
Я живу́ в **бо́лее ста́ром** до́ме.	I live in *an older* house.

3.2 Second comparative

A very small number of adjectives, have an additional irregular comparative which consists of a single word with regular adjective inflection. These *second* comparative forms usually have a specialized meaning. Note that хоро́ший lacks the regular long comparative with бо́лее.

POSITIVE	COMPARATIVE	SECOND COMPARATIVE
ста́рый	бо́лее ста́рый	ста́рший
old	*older*	*elder, eldest, senior*
молодо́й	бо́лее молодо́й	мла́дший
young	*younger*	*younger, youngest, junior*
высо́кий	бо́лее высо́кий	вы́сший
high	*higher*	*higher, highest, superior*
хоро́ший		лу́чший
good		*better, best*

Э́то **бо́лее ста́рое** зда́ние.	That's an *older* building.
Э́то мо́й **ста́рший** бра́т.	That's my *elder* brother.

3.3 Ме́нее

To express *less* tall, etc. Russian uses the uninflected form **ме́нее** before the positive form of the adjective.

Э́то **ме́нее интере́сный** рома́н чем   That's a *less interesting* novel than "War "Война́ и ми́р".   and Peace".

3.4   Superlative of long adjectives

The superlative of long adjectives is regularly formed by using the word **са́мый** before the positive form of the adjective. Both са́мый and the adjective take regular adjective inflection.

Э́то **са́мая краси́вая** де́вушка в   That's the *most beautiful* girl in town. го́роде.
Óн живёт в **са́мой большо́й**   He lives in the *biggest* hotel in town. гости́нице в го́роде.

Those adjectives which have a second comparative may form the superlative by adding **са́мый** to either the positive or comparative form.

Э́то **са́мый лу́чший** рестора́н в   That's the *best* restaurant in the city. го́роде.

☽ 4.   Days of the week

To express *on a certain day* of the week Russian uses the preposition **в** plus the accusative case.

       Óн прие́хал **в сре́ду.**   He came *on Wednesday.*
       Óн прие́хал **в четве́рг.**   He came *on Thursday.*

To ask what day it is one says **Како́й сего́дня де́нь?** and the response has a nominative case form:

       Сего́дня среда́.   *Today is Wednesday.*

☽ 5.   Week, month, year

Except when referring to duration of time (cf. *Grammar Unit* 8:4):

(1) The expressions *this week, next week, last week* are rendered by the preposition **на** plus the locative case.

(2) *This month, next month, last month* and *this year, next year, last year* are rendered by the preposition **в** plus the locative case. (The noun **го́д** has the second locative ending **-у́.**)

	week	*month*	*year*
this	**на** э́той **неде́ле**	**в** э́том **ме́сяце**	**в** э́том **году́**
next	**на** бу́дущей **неде́ле**	**в** бу́дущем **ме́сяце**	**в** бу́дущем **году́**
last	**на** про́шлой **неде́ле**	**в** про́шлом **ме́сяце**	**в** про́шлом **году́**

❂ 6. Instrumental of time

Note the use of the instrumental case in the following time expressions:

ле́т**ом**	in the summer
о́сен**ью**	in the fall
весн**о́й**	in the spring
зим**о́й**	in the winter
у́тр**ом**	in the morning
ве́чер**ом**	in the evening
но́ч**ью**	at night
днём	in the daytime, during the day

Note that where English has "this morning, this evening" Russian has literally "today in the morning, today in the evening" and cannot have any form of э́тот "this".

сего́дня у́тром	this morning
сего́дня ве́чером	this evening
за́втра у́тром	tomorrow morning
вчера́ ве́чером	yesterday evening

The word **ве́чер** normally refers to a period of time from six or seven P.M. to around midnight. The word **ночь** is reserved for the hours of darkness thereafter.

With specific hours the genitive rather than the instrumental is used:

се́мь часо́в утра́	seven o'clock in the morning
оди́ннадцать часо́в ве́чера	eleven o'clock at night

❂ 7. Instrumental complement

The noun complement of the verb **бы́ть** is usually in the instrumental case.

Когда́ я была́ **студе́нткой**, я жила́ в Москве́.	When I was a *student* I lived in Moscow.
О́н бу́дет **до́ктором**.	He will be a *doctor*.
О́н был **инжене́ром**.	He was an *engineer*.

Sometimes a noun complement is in the nominative case. The use of the nominative case in this construction should be limited to answering the question *Who was he?*

Кто́ о́н бы́л? — О́н бы́л **америка́нец**.	Who was he? — He was an *American*.

8. Some aspect pairs

8.1 Familiar types

IMPERFECTIVE	PERFECTIVE	
конча́ться, конча́ются	ко́нчиться, ко́нчатся	to end, finish, be over
лежа́ть, лежа́т	полежа́ть, полежа́т	to lie

8.2 The suffix **-ыва-/-ива-**

Some verbs form the imperfective by the addition of this suffix to the perfective form. Most verbs that have the vowel **o** in the last syllable of the stem replace it by stressed **á** when this suffix is added. Imperfective verbs with this suffix always have type I inflection of the -ают variety.

IMPERFECTIVE	PERFECTIVE	
зака́зывать, зака́зывают	заказа́ть, зака́жут, закажу́	to order
пока́зывать, пока́зывают	показа́ть, пока́жут, покажу́	to show
расска́зывать, расска́зывают	рассказа́ть, расска́жут, расскажу́	to tell
осма́тривать, осма́тривают	осмотре́ть, осмо́трят, осмотрю́	to look over

8.3 бра́ть (I), взя́ть (P)

These two verbs form an aspect pair.

бра́ть, беру́т	взя́ть, возьму́т	to take
	взя́л, взяла́, взя́ло, взя́ли	

УПРАЖНЕ́НИЯ

A. Transform orally from *actual* imperfective to *iterative* imperfective, supplying the word **ча́сто** according to the model:

MODEL: Я **иду́** в теа́тр. Я **ча́сто хожу́** в теа́тр.

1. Óн идёт в университе́т.
2. Óн шёл по у́лице.
3. Мы́ идём в лаборато́рию.
4. Она́ шла́ в музе́й.
5. Они́ иду́т в кино́.
6. Я́ е́ду в аэропо́рт.
7. Óн е́хал на ю́г.
8. Вы́ е́дете на Украи́ну.
9. Она́ е́дет в Аме́рику.
10. Они́ е́хали по Сове́тскому Сою́зу.
11. Я́ лечу́ в Сове́тский Сою́з.
12. Она́ лете́ла в Ленингра́д.
13. Мы́ лети́м в Нью-Йо́рк.

B. Read the following sentences, using the proper form of the word in parentheses:

1. Он (fluently) говори́т по-ру́сски. 2. Мои́ часы́ иду́т (correctly). 3. Я не могу́ (clearly) ви́деть. 4. Он (poorly) рабо́тал. 5. Она́ (wonderfully) говори́т по-англи́йски. 6. Он (coldly) смотре́л на меня́ и ничего́ не говори́л. 7. (It is clear), что он не придёт. 8. В Ташке́нте ле́том (it is hot). 9. Зимо́й та́м (it is cold). 10. (It is interesting), что он не принима́ет уча́стие в э́том. 11. Здесь (it is cold). 12. Здесь (it is warm).

C. Transform orally according to the model.

MODEL: Он **знамени́тый** хи́мик.
Он **бо́лее знамени́тый** хи́мик.

1. Это интере́сный язы́к.
2. Я люблю́ я́сные дни.
3. Та́м суро́вый кли́мат.
4. Он живёт в но́вом до́ме.
5. Он купи́л дешёвую кни́гу.
6. Он рабо́тает в высо́ком зда́нии.
7. Он говори́т с краси́вой де́вушкой.
8. Это дорога́я ру́чка.

D. Make the following substitutions orally:

Он прие́хал сюда́ . . . .

1 on Monday
2 on Wednesday
3 on Thursday
4 on Sunday
5 today
6 this morning
7 this evening
8 yesterday
9 yesterday morning
10 last evening
11 last year
12 last month
13 last week
14 in the spring
15 in the winter
16 in the fall

E. Make the following substitutions orally:

Он прие́дет . . . .

1 on Tuesday
2 on Friday
3 on Wednesday
4 on Saturday
5 tomorrow
6 tomorrow morning
7 tomorrow evening
8 this year
9 this month
10 this week
11 next year
12 next month
13 next week
14 in the fall
15 in the summer

F. Transform orally according to the model:

MODEL: О́н студе́нт.
О́н жи́л та́м, когда́ о́н бы́л студе́нтом.

1. Она́ студе́нтка.
2. Они́ актёры.
3. Я́ официа́нт.
4. О́льга де́вочка.
5. Ми́ша ребёнок.
6. Они́ доктора́.
7. О́н хи́мик.
8. Она́ америка́нка.
9. Мы́ писа́тели.
10. О́н профе́ссор.
11. Они́ инжене́ры.
12. Они́ перево́дчицы.

Kiev. By the Dnieper River

REVIEW LESSON FIVE

A. FLUENCY DRILL

1. Does it really rain all spring here? 2. Is it really hot in Moscow in the summer? 3. Are books really cheaper in the Soviet Union? 4. Do you really know that young girl? 5. Don't you really know that young girl who is standing at the cashier's desk? 6. Do you really like to read books on chemistry? 7. Don't you really speak Russian? 8. Are you really taking part in a play? 9. Do you really intend to go to Moscow next year? 10. I have to be at the airport at half past five. 11. I had to go to Tashkent last week. 12. I'll have to call Vera today. 13. He has to read this book. 14. He'll have to read this book next week. 15. Everybody had to be there. 16. We have to take part in a convention in Moscow. 17. He intends to be in New York for a week. 18. They built that new building last year. 19. They came to Moscow in the winter. 20. I'm going to the movies in an hour. 21. He'll return to the Soviet Union in the spring. 22. She will return to the Soviet Union for a month. 23. The plane will leave in ten minutes. 24. I'll stop by for you this evening. 25. I'll stop by in the evening. 26. I'll meet you at the station in the morning.

27. It rained all spring. 28. It snowed all winter. 29. The children played all day. 30. He traveled all year. 31. I studied all summer. 32. He wrote her every week. 33. When he was in the Soviet Union he spoke Russian every day. 34. He wrote an article every month. 35. Are you going to Kiev today? 36. Yes, I'm flying there. 37. When does your plane leave? 38. In two hours. 39. You don't have much time. 40. Enough. 41. How long will you be there? 42. I'll be there two weeks. 43. Have a good trip!

B. Conversation topics

(1) A and B are Americans. A tells B about his purchase of books in a Russian bookstore and explains the procedure involved.

(2) A and B are Russians. A asks B about the trip he just made to New York, what he did, what he saw (art museums, theaters, the opera, parks, tall buildings, etc.), when he left, how long he stayed.

(3) A and B discuss the weather in California and New York.

МОРЯ́, РÉКИ И ОЗЁРА[1] СССР

Мно́гие из са́мых больши́х рек Евро́пы и А́зии протека́ют[2] по террито́рии Сове́тского Сою́за. Сле́дующие реки впада́ют[3] в Ледови́тый[4] океа́н: Обь, Енисе́й, Ле́на, Печо́ра. В Ти́хий океа́н впада́ет Аму́р. Во́лга, са́мая дли́нная из европе́йских рек, течёт[5] на юг, к Каспи́йскому мо́рю. Днепр впада́ет в Чёрное мо́ре.

Се́верные реки не весь год приго́дны[6] для судохо́дства.[7] Они́ замерза́ют[8] уже́ в октябре́ и бо́льшую[9] часть го́да покры́ты[10] льдо́м.[11] Да и[12] впада́ют э́ти реки в Ледови́тый океа́н, кото́рый то́же закры́т для судохо́дства почти́ весь год.

Весно́й ру́сские реки выхо́дят[13] из берего́в. Наводне́ний[14] мно́го; происхо́дят[15] они́ тогда́, когда́ та́ет[16] снег. Ле́том мно́гие реки стано́вятся[17] ме́лкими[18] от недоста́тка дожде́й.

[1] lakes
[2] flow
[3] empty
[4] Arctic

[5] flows

[6] suitable
[7] navigation
[8] freeze
[9] greater
[10] covered
[11] with ice
[12] and indeed
[13] overflow
[14] floods
[15] take place
[16] melts
[17] become
[18] shallow

Тече́ние[19] ру́сских ре́к гла́вным о́бразом ро́вное и ти́хое. В ни́х о́чень мно́го хоро́шей ры́бы.[20] Ры́бная промы́шленность[21] всегда́ име́ла[22] в Росси́и большо́е значе́ние.[23]

Озёра Сове́тского Сою́за то́же бога́ты[24] ры́бой. Са́мое глубо́кое[25] о́зеро в ми́ре[26] — Байка́л. Оно́ нахо́дится в Сиби́ри, среди́[27] высо́ких го́р. Каспи́йское мо́ре — са́мое большо́е о́зеро в ми́ре. Вода́[28] в нём солёная.[29]

Большо́й интере́с для Росси́и всегда́ представля́ли[30] моря́. Ледови́тый океа́н, хотя́ о́н и ва́жен[31] для ры́бной промы́шленности, не позволя́ет[32] разви́ться[33] судохо́дству. Несмотря́ на[34] то, что ру́сские колониза́торы дошли́ до Ти́хого океа́на в середи́не[35] XVII (семна́дцатого) ве́ка,[36] о́н не игра́л большо́й ро́ли в во́дном[37] тра́нспорте, так как[38] Ти́хий океа́н нахо́дится о́чень далеко́ от европе́йской Росси́и. (Порты́ Ти́хого океа́на приобрели́[39] большо́е значе́ние по́сле постро́йки[40] транс-сиби́рской желе́зной доро́ги[41] в XX ве́ке.) А что́ каса́ется[42] Чёрного мо́ря, его́ значе́ние бы́ло ограни́чено[43] те́м, что Босфо́р бы́л в рука́х Ту́рции.

Поэ́тому приобрело́ огро́мное для Росси́и значе́ние Балти́йское мо́ре. Пётр Пе́рвый, кото́рый получи́л до́ступ[44] к нему́ по́сле войны́ со шве́дами, да́же столи́цу Росси́и перенёс из Москвы́ в Санкт-Петербу́рг, тепе́решний Ленингра́д.

[19] course
[20] fish
[21] industry
[22] had
[23] significance
[24] rich
[25] deep
[26] world
[27] among, in the midst of
[28] water
[29] salty
[30] presented
[31] important
[32] permit
[33] to be developed
[34] in spite of
[35] middle
[36] century
[37] water
[38] since
[39] attained
[40] construction
[41] railroad
[42] concerns
[43] limited
[44] access

CONVERSATION 21

Packing things

Alexis packs for a hurried trip to Kiev.

CONVERSATION UNIT TWENTY ONE ━━━━━━━

ALEXIS	[1] Please help me pack my things. [2] Today I'm going to [leaving for] Kiev, to an engineering convention.
BORIS	[3] Will you need the things that are lying in the desk? [table]
ALEXIS	[4] No, I'm leaving all those papers here. [5] If it's no trouble to you, put everything that's lying on the table into one of the drawers. [6] In the meantime I'll put the suitcase on the chair and gather my clothes together.
BORIS	[7] What things do you need from the wardrobe?
ALEXIS	[8] Only the blue suit. Go to the table; the key to the wardrobe is on it.
BORIS	[9] I don't see it. It probably fell under the table.
ALEXIS	[10] Yes, it really did! There it lies. [11] I've already packed all the clothes and I'm almost ready.
BORIS	[12] Here's your suit.
ALEXIS	[13] Thanks. I'll put it in the suitcase.
BORIS	[14] When are you leaving?
ALEXIS	[15] The train leaves at six o'clock [16] and it's already quarter after five.
BORIS	[17] At six o'clock! But why didn't you tell me anything?
ALEXIS	[18] Because I just found out today that I have to be going.
BORIS	[19] Ivan asked me if I couldn't come to his place with you this evening.
ALEXIS	[20] I'm sorry I can't. [21] Tell him to phone me in a week. [22] But now I have to hurry. So long!

NOTES

7 **Шкáф** wardrobe, cupboard, bookcase. Wardrobes are more common than closets in the USSR.

11 **Бельё** clothes, laundry refers specifically to underwear, shirts, socks, and washable items in general.

NEW VERBS

TYPE I

помóчь (P) (identical with мóчь)	to help
уезжáть (I), уезжáют	to go away, leave
оставля́ть (I), оставля́ют	leave (behind)
подойти́ (P), подойду́т	to approach, go up to
подошёл, подошлá, подошлó, подошли́	
упáсть (P), упаду́т	to fall
упáл, упáла, упáло, упáли	
узнáть (P), узнáют	to find out
спрáшивать (I), спрáшивают	to ask (a question)

Упаковка вещей

АЛЕКСЕ́Й ¹ Помоги́те мне́, пожа́луйста, уложи́ть ве́щи. ² Я́ сего́дня уезжа́ю в Ки́ев, на съе́зд инжене́ров.

БОРИ́С ³ Ва́м нужны́ бу́дут те́ ве́щи, кото́рые лежа́т в столе́?

АЛЕКСЕ́Й ⁴ Не́т, все́ э́ти бума́ги я́ оставля́ю зде́сь. ⁵ Е́сли ва́м нетру́дно, положи́те всё то́, что лежи́т на столе́, в оди́н из я́щиков. ⁶ Я́ пока́ поста́влю чемода́н на сту́л и бу́ду собира́ть оде́жду.

БОРИ́С ⁷ Каки́е ве́щи ва́м нужны́ из шка́фа?

АЛЕКСЕ́Й ⁸ То́лько си́ний костю́м. Подойди́те к столу́, та́м клю́ч от шка́фа.

БОРИ́С ⁹ Я́ его́ не ви́жу. О́н, вероя́тно, упа́л под сто́л.

АЛЕКСЕ́Й ¹⁰ Да́, действи́тельно! Во́т о́н лежи́т. ¹¹ Я́ уже́ уложи́л всё бельё и почти́ гото́в.

БОРИ́С ¹² Во́т ва́ш костю́м.

АЛЕКСЕ́Й ¹³ Спаси́бо. Я́ его́ положу́ в чемода́н.

БОРИ́С ¹⁴ Когда́ вы́ уезжа́ете?

АЛЕКСЕ́Й ¹⁵ По́езд отхо́дит в ше́сть часо́в, ¹⁶ а сейча́с уже́ че́тверть шесто́го.

БОРИ́С ¹⁷ В ше́сть часо́в! Почему́ же вы́ мне́ ничего́ не сказа́ли?

АЛЕКСЕ́Й ¹⁸ Потому́ что я́ то́лько сего́дня узна́л, что до́лжен е́хать.

БОРИ́С ¹⁹ Ива́н меня́ спра́шивал, не могу́ ли я́ прийти́ к нему́ с ва́ми сего́дня ве́чером.

АЛЕКСЕ́Й ²⁰ Жа́ль, что я́ не могу́. ²¹ Скажи́те ему́, чтобы о́н мне́ позвони́л че́рез неде́лю. ²² А тепе́рь мне́ на́до спеши́ть. Пока́!

TYPE II

уложи́ть (Р), уло́жат, уложу́	to pack
положи́ть (Р), поло́жат, положу́	to put (lying)
поста́вить (Р), поста́вят, поста́влю	to put (standing)
отходи́ть (I), отхо́дят, отхожу́	to depart

NEW NOUNS

NOMINATIVE SINGULAR	GENITIVE SINGULAR	

Masculine

я́щик		drawer, box
чемода́н		suitcase
сту́л		chair
шка́ф		wardrobe, cupboard, bookcase
костю́м		suit
клю́ч	ключа́	key

Neuter

бельё (Never occurs in the Plural)	clothes, laundry

Feminine I

оде́жда (Never in the Plural)	clothes

The noun **шка́ф**, like **ча́с** (в кото́ром часу́?) has a second locative ending in **-у́** after the prepositions **в** and **на** e.g., **в шкафу́** in the wardrobe.

NEW ADJECTIVES

LONG FORM		NEUTER SHORT FORM
тру́дный	difficult	тру́дно

NOTE: **помо́чь** to *help* is another verb that takes an object in the dative case (cf. *Grammar Unit* **7:2.2**).

УПРАЖНЕ́НИЯ

A. Transform orally according to the models:

MODELS: 1) Вы **хоти́те написа́ть** письмо́?
Я **напишу́** письмо́.

2) Óн **хóчет прийтú** с сестрóй?
   Óн **придёт** с сестрóй.

1. Вы́ хотúте узнáть, гдé óн?
2. Óн хóчет уложúть эти вéщи?
3. Онú хотя́т постáвить кнúгу сюдá?
4. Вы́ хотúте уложúть вáше бельё?
5. Вы́ хотúте емý дáть эти вéщи?
6. Óн хóчет éй дáть клю́ч от шкáфа?
7. Онú хотя́т продáть этот дóм?
8. Вы́ хотúте повторúть эту фрáзу?
9. Вы́ хотúте прочитáть это письмó от Ивáна?
10. Óн хóчет заплатúть за билéты?
11. Вы́ хотúте заплатúть за билéты?
12. Óн хóчет отвéтить на этот вопрóс?
13. Вы́ хотúте úм сказáть, гдé óн?
14. Вы́ хотúте отвéтить на этот вопрос?
15. Óн хóчет вáм рассказáть о войнé?
16. Онá хóчет полетéть в Совéтский Сою́з?
17. Вы́ хотúте полетéть в Нью-Йóрк?

B. Transform orally from perfective to imperfective past, supplying the word **чáсто** according to the model:

Model: Онú **прóдали** кнúги.
       Онú **чáсто продавáли** кнúги.

1. Онú мнé дáли папирóсы.
2. Спектáкль кóнчился в одúннадцать часóв.
3. Мы́ повторúли этот вопрóс.
4. Онá заплатúла за нáши билéты.
5. Я́ прочитáл эту статью́.
6. Óн мнé сказáл об этом.
7. Мы́ отвéтили на úх вопрóсы.
8. Онú посмотрéли на эти вéщи.
9. Я́ его встрéтил на вокзáле.
10. Óн пришёл к нáм.
11. Онá зашлá за нéй.
12. Мы́ пошлú в университéт.
13. Онú поéхали в Кúев.
14. Óн прилетéл сюдá.
15. Мы́ полетéли в Ленингрáд.
16. Онú заказáли щú.
17. Я́ емý рассказáл о нáшем товáрище.

255

C. Transform orally from perfective non-past to imperfective non-past according to the model:

MODEL: Óн вáм **дáст** клю́ч от шкáфа.
Óн вáм **даёт** клю́ч от шкáфа.

1. Они́ продаду́т э́тот чемодáн.
2. Óпера ко́нчится в оди́ннадцать.
3. Я заплачу́ за но́вый сто́л.
4. Я э́то сдéлаю на э́той недéле.
5. Óн кýпит но́вый костю́м.
6. Что́ они́ скáжут?
7. Онá полýчит от него́ ромáн Толсто́го.
8. Комý вы́ позвони́те?
9. Óн придёт ко мнé.
10. Пьéсы Чéхова нáм понрáвятся.

D. Give the Russian equivalents:

1. I'm leaving for Kiev today. 2. I'm going to (leaving for) Kiev today for a convention of engineers. 3. When are you leaving? 4. I'm leaving this evening. 5. I'm leaving next week for New York. 6. They're leaving tomorrow morning for the Caucasus. 7. When does the train leave? 8. The train leaves this evening at 10 o'clock. 9. When does the plane for Tashkent leave? 10. The plane leaves every day at 3:30. 11. When are you coming back? 12. I'm coming back on Tuesday. 13. My friends are coming back next month. 14. We came back last month. 15. He came back from Leningrad last week. 16. I have to return on Thursday.

17. Put everything that's on the table into one of the drawers. 18. I have to put all these things in a suitcase. 19. I'll put my blue suit in the suitcase. 20. He'll put the clothes in the suitcase. 21. They will put the clothes (underclothes) in the suitcase. 22. What will you put in the suitcase? 23. Put the key in the drawer! 24. He put everything in the suitcase. 25. They put the papers in the suitcase.

26. I have to pack my things. 27. My wife will pack my clothes. 28. They packed everything. 29. When did you pack your things? 30. Please pack my things.

31. Why didn't you tell me anything? 32. Why didn't you tell me about that? 33. I only found out about it today. 34. She just found out that she's supposed to go. 35. I'll find out about that in a week. 36. We'll find out when the movie begins. 37. They will find out whether he's coming.

CONVERSATION 22

Where is my wallet?

Boris is waiting for Alexis to go to the GUM department store for socks.

CONVERSATION UNIT TWENTY TWO —————

ENGLISH EQUIVALENTS

ALEXIS	[1] I don't remember where I put my wallet. [2] I can't find it, and all my money is in it. [3] I hope I haven't lost it.
BORIS	[4] But what's lying there by the table? [5] Isn't it a wallet? Take a look!
ALEXIS	[6] No, that's a book. [7] But how could that have happened?
BORIS	[8] It's not in your pocket either?
ALEXIS	[9] No, I've already looked for it there.
BORIS	[10] But where could you have put it? In the table drawer, perhaps?
ALEXIS	[11] No, it's not there. I always put things in their place, [12] but recently I've begun to lose everything.
BORIS	[13] How much money did you have, Alexis Petrovich?
ALEXIS	[14] Not much, only nine rubles.
BORIS	[15] If you want I'll give you a loan and you give it back tomorrow.
ALEXIS	[16] Thanks a lot [but] I'll take another look for my wallet. [17] I could have put it in my coat pocket.
BORIS	[18] Well? Did you find it?
ALEXIS	[19] Wait, I must find my coat first.
BORIS	[20] What next? Now you've lost your coat!
ALEXIS	[21] I've finally found it! The wallet is in the pocket. [22] I'm sorry [Pardon] you had to wait.
BORIS	[23] Oh, that's nothing. All's well that ends well.

NEW VERBS

Type i

теря́ть (I), теря́ют	to lose
потеря́ть (Р), потеря́ют	to lose
иска́ть (I), и́щут, ищу́	to look for
поиска́ть (Р), поищут, поищу́	to look for
класть (I), кладу́т	to put (lying)
клал, кла́ла, кла́ло, кла́ли	
стать (Р), ста́нут	to begin (when followed by infinitive)
жда́ть (I), жду́т	to wait
ждал, ждала́, жда́ло, жда́ли	
подожда́ть (Р), подожду́т	to wait
подожда́л, подождала́, подожда́ло, подожда́ли	
прийти́сь (Р); as impersonal verb occurs in the following forms: придётся, пришло́сь	to be necessary

258

Где мой бумажник?

АЛЕКСЕЙ	[1] Не по́мню, куда́ я положи́л сво́й бума́жник. [2] Не могу́ его́ найти́, а в нём все́ мои́ де́ньги. [3] Наде́юсь, что я́ его́ не потеря́л.
БОРИ́С	[4] А что́ лежи́т во́н та́м, о́коло стола́? [5] Э́то не бума́жник? Посмотри́те!
АЛЕКСЕ́Й	[6] Не́т, э́то кни́га. [7] И ка́к э́то могло́ случи́ться?
БОРИ́С	[8] А в карма́не его́ то́же не́т?
АЛЕКСЕ́Й	[9] Не́т, я уже́ та́м его́ иска́л.
БОРИ́С	[10] Куда́ вы́ его́ могли́ положи́ть? В я́щик стола́, что́ ли?
АЛЕКСЕ́Й	[11] Не́т, та́м его́ не́т. Я всегда́ кладу́ ве́щи на своё ме́сто, [12] но в после́днее вре́мя я ста́л всё теря́ть.
БОРИ́С	[13] Ско́лько де́нег у ва́с бы́ло, Алексе́й Петро́вич?
АЛЕКСЕ́Й	[14] Немно́го, то́лько де́вять рубле́й.
БОРИ́С	[15] Е́сли хоти́те, я ва́м да́м взаймы́ и вы́ за́втра отдади́те.
АЛЕКСЕ́Й	[16] Большо́е спаси́бо, я ещё поищу́ бума́жник. [17] Я́ мог его́ положи́ть в карма́н пальто́.
БОРИ́С	[18] Ну́, ка́к? Вы́ нашли́?
АЛЕКСЕ́Й	[19] Подожди́те, я до́лжен снача́ла найти́ пальто́.
БОРИ́С	[20] Во́т ещё! Тепе́рь вы́ пальто́ потеря́ли!
АЛЕКСЕ́Й	[21] Наконе́ц-то нашёл! Бума́жник в карма́не. [22] Извини́те, что ва́м пришло́сь жда́ть.
БОРИ́С	[23] Ничего́. Всё хорошо́, что хорошо́ конча́ется.

TYPE II

по́мнить (I), по́мнят	to remember
случи́ться (P), случа́тся	to happen

IRREGULAR

отда́ть (P); (same irregular non-past as да́ть)   to give back
о́тдал, отдала́, о́тдало, о́тдали

Note that the following verbs form aspect pairs:

теря́ть (I), потеря́ть (P)
жда́ть (I), подожда́ть (P)
иска́ть (I), поиска́ть (P)

NEW NOUNS

NOMINATIVE
SINGULAR

Masculine

бума́жник	wallet
карма́н	pocket

Neuter   NOMINATIVE PLURAL

ме́сто	места́	place
пальто́ (indeclinable)		coat

Plural only

де́ньги	money
Genitive Plural: де́нег	
Dative Plural: деньга́м	
Instrumental Plural: деньга́ми	
Locative Plural: деньга́х	

УПРАЖНЕ́НИЯ

A. Transform orally from past perfective to non-past imperfective according to the model:

MODEL: Я получи́л де́ньги от моего́ бра́та.
Я **получа́ю** де́ньги от моего́ бра́та.

1. Он да́л бра́ту пальто́.
2. О́пера ко́нчилась о́чень по́здно.

260

3. Они́ сде́лали э́то непра́вильно.
4. Она́ прочита́ла кни́гу по исто́рии.
5. Мы́ отве́тили по-ру́сски.
6. О́н встре́тил актёра в Большо́м теа́тре.
7. О́н написа́л интере́сную пье́су.
8. Они́ положи́ли де́ньги в я́щик.
9. Я́ пришёл в воскресе́нье.

B. Transform as in Exercise A, but from the perfective infinitive to the non-past perfective:

1. Мне́ на́до прие́хать во вто́рник. (Я́ **прие́ду** во вто́рник.)
2. Ему́ на́до положи́ть кни́ги в шка́ф.
3. Моему́ бра́ту на́до заплати́ть за биле́ты.
4. Е́й на́до верну́ться че́рез неде́лю.
5. И́м на́до прилете́ть в Москву́ в четве́рг.
6. Ему́ на́до бы́ть та́м в полови́не седьмо́го.
7. Мне́ на́до купи́ть но́вый костю́м.
8. Мне́ на́до поста́вить сту́л о́коло окна́.

C. Listen to the following questions and answer them according to the model:

MODEL: О ко́м вы́ говори́те? **О Петре́.**

1. С ке́м вы рабо́таете?
2. Кого́ вы́ ви́дели?
3. Кому́ вы́ позвэни́ли?
4. У кого́ вы́ живёте?
5. К кому́ вы́ пошли́?
6. За ке́м вы́ пошли́?
7. От кого́ вы́ верну́лись?
8. Кто́ та́м живёт?
9. Кому́ вы́ да́ли де́ньги?

D. Repeat Exercise C, but use the proper singular form of **моя́ сестра́.**

E. Repeat Exercise C, but use the proper plural form of **мои́ друзья́.**

F. Give the Russian equivalents:

1. Where did you put your wallet? 2. I lost my wallet. 3. I can't find my wallet. 4. My wallet isn't here. 5. My wallet isn't in my pocket. 6. All my money is in my pocket. 7. There isn't anything in my wallet. 8. He always loses his wallet. 9. Is that your wallet near those blue books? 10. No, I put it in my coat pocket. 11. Have you looked for your wallet? 12. I've already looked in my coat. 13. He's looking for his wallet, but he can't find it.

261

CONVERSATION UNIT TWENTY TWO

14. How much money do you have? 15. I only have forty rubles. 16. He has sixty-five rubles. 17. We have ninety rubles. 18. I lost seventy-five rubles. 19. My brother found twenty-four rubles. 20. I'll lend you fifty rubles. 21. I'll give you a loan. 22. He lent me eighty rubles.

23. I'll give it back to you tomorrow. 24. He gave it back to me yesterday. 25. Why didn't you give me back the money I lent you yesterday? 26. Why didn't you give me the books we were talking about? 27. Will you give me the novel you were reading yesterday? 28. Will you give me the novel after you have read it? 29. I gave him the novel.

GRAMMAR UNIT ELEVEN

1. The comparison of short adjectives

The comparative form of long adjectives (**бо́лее** + adjective) was studied in Grammar Unit 10.

What we shall call the *regular* comparative forms of short adjectives are made up of the stem of the adjective + **-ее**. Some examples are:

POSITIVE		COMPARATIVE	
холо́дный	cold	холодне́е	colder, more coldly
краси́вый	beautiful	краси́вее	more beautiful, more beautifully
тёплый	warm	тепле́е	warmer, more warmly

In these *regular* short forms of the comparative the stress sometimes falls on the suffix **-ее** even when the stem of the adjective was stressed, as in the first example above. Indeed, if the stem of the adjective consists of one syllable it is usual for the stress to shift to the suffix, as in the last example.

A limited number of adjectives use the suffix **-е**, instead of **-ее**, and most of the adjectives which do also show a change in the stem in their comparative form. We shall call the comparatives of such adjectives the *irregular* short forms. Of the adjectives you have had so far the following have *irregular* short forms in the comparative:

POSITIVE		COMPARATIVE	
жа́ркий	hot	жа́рче	hotter, more hotly
сухо́й	dry	су́ше	drier, more drily
ста́рый	old	ста́рше	older
молодо́й	young	моло́же	younger
хоро́ший	good	лу́чше	better
дорого́й	dear	доро́же	dearer, more dearly
высо́кий	high	вы́ше	higher, more highly
плохо́й	bad	ху́же	worse
дешёвый	cheap	деше́вле	cheaper, more cheaply
бли́зкий	nearby	бли́же	nearer
далёкий	far, distant	да́льше, да́лее	farther

As has been said, all short forms of the comparative are uninflected whether they be regular or irregular. E.g.

Он ста́рше чем я.   He is older than I.
Она́ ста́рше чем я.   She is older than I.

Short comparative forms are just like short positive forms in that they are used both as adjectives in predicate position and as adverbs; also, in that they may not be used attributively, i.e., directly modifying a noun. When used as adjectives in the predicate position the regular short forms may readily be

263

replaced by long form adjectives (cf. *Grammar Unit* **10:2**), but the irregular short form comparatives are not commonly replaced by long forms.

Э́та де́вушка **краси́вее,** чем моя́ сестра́.   ⎧ This girl is *more beautiful*
Э́та де́вушка **бо́лее краси́вая,** чем моя́ сестра́. ⎩   than my sister.
Дни́ здесь **жа́рче.**   The days here are *hotter.*

The following comparative short forms of adverbs are worth noting:

POSITIVE	COMPARATIVE	
ча́сто	ча́ще	oftener, more frequently
ра́но	ра́ньше	earlier, sooner, formerly
по́здно	по́зже	later

The short comparatives **бо́льше** and **ме́ньше** are each comparatives to two different forms:

POSITIVE		COMPARATIVE	
большо́й	large	**бо́льше**	larger, more
мно́го	much, many		
ма́ленький	small	**ме́ньше**	smaller, less, fewer
ма́ло	few, not much		

Нью-Йо́рк **бо́льше,** чем Босто́н.   New York is *bigger* than Boston.
Он рабо́тает **бо́льше,** чем я́.   He works *more* than I do.

The form **бо́льше не** plus a verb equates with English *no longer, not any more.*
Он **бо́льше не** рабо́тает в э́том го́роде.   He *no longer* works in this city.

The forms **бо́лее** and **ме́нее** also mean *more* and *less,* respectively, but their use is generally restricted to the formation of comparative long forms (cf. *Grammar Unit* **10:3.1** and **3.2**).

In Russian the distinction between comparative and superlative is not as clear cut as in English. In many situations where English uses the superlative, Russian uses the comparative. This is particularly true for expressions with **всего́,** **всех,** and **из,** as in the following examples.

Я зна́ю **лу́чше всех.**   I know *best of* all (*better than* anybody).
Я люблю́ борщ **бо́льше всего́.**   I like borsch *best of* all (*more than* anything).
Он **лу́чший из** на́ших инжене́ров.   He's the *best of* our engineers.

The last example above illustrates a use of the preposition **из,** which equates with English *of* when indicating one or more *of a group* of things. This usage with **из** requires the adjective to be in the long form.

◑ 2. The Russian equivalents of *than*

In Russian there are two equivalents of English *than,* one using **чем** and the other using the genitive case.

1) *Than* may be expressed by **чем**.

Эта де́вушка краси́вее, **чем** та́.　　This girl is more beautiful *than* that one.

Он ста́рше, **чем** я́.　　He's older *than* I am.

2) *Than* may be expressed without the word чем and with the following noun or pronoun in the genitive case.

Она́ краси́вее **мое́й сестры́**.　　She's more beautiful *than my sister*.
Он ста́рше **меня́**.　　He's older *than I* am.

3. Some aspect pairs

3.1 Familiar types

IMPERFECTIVE	PERFECTIVE	
случа́ться, случа́ются	случи́ться, случа́тся	to happen
оставля́ть, оставля́ют	оста́вить, оста́вят, оста́влю	to leave, leave behind
ста́вить, ста́вят, ста́влю	поста́вить, поста́вят, поста́влю	to put (standing)
жда́ть, жду́т	подожда́ть, подожду́т	to wait
отдава́ть, отдаю́т	отда́ть (Irregular non-past), о́тдал, отдала́, о́тдало, о́тдали	to give back
подходи́ть, подхо́дят, подхожу́	подойти́, подойду́т подошёл, подошла́ …	to approach
отходи́ть, отхо́дят, отхожу́	отойти́, отойду́т отошёл, отошла́ …	to depart
приходи́ться, прихо́дится, приходи́лось	прийти́сь, придётся, пришло́сь	to be necessary
уезжа́ть, уезжа́ют	уе́хать, уе́дут	to go away, leave (by vehicle)
спра́шивать, спра́шивают	спроси́ть, спро́сят, спрошу́	to ask (a question)

3.2 кла́сть (I), положи́ть (Р)

кла́сть, кладу́т　　положи́ть, поло́жат, положу́ to put (lying)
кла́л, кла́ла, кла́ло, кла́ли

3.3 The prefix -y

Some verbs form the perfective by the addition of the prefix **-y**. Perfectives of this type are likely to have a rather specialized meaning. The imperfectives of this type are likely to be used in situations where perfectives would be used for other verbs.

265

IMPERFECTIVE		PERFECTIVE	
зна́ть, зна́ют	to know	узна́ть, узна́ют	to find out
ви́деть, ви́дят, ви́жу	to see	уви́деть, уви́дят, уви́жу	to have a look at, to catch sight of

◑ 4. Verbs meaning *to put*

The verbs класть (I), положи́ть (P) and ста́вить (I) поста́вить (P) are both equivalents of English *put*. **Положи́ть** implies to put in a lying position and **поста́вить** implies to put in a standing position. In situations where the contrast between lying and standing is not significant it is customary to use **положи́ть**.

These two verbs are verbs of motion and thus are used with the prepositions **в** and **на** followed by the *accusative* case. Similarly, the adverbial forms **куда́, туда́, сюда́**, are used with these verbs.

О́н **поста́вил** кни́гу **на сто́л.**	He *put* the book *on the table*. (standing position).
О́н **положи́л** кни́гу **на сто́л.**	He *put* the book *on the table* (*lying* position).
Я́ пока́ **поста́влю** чемода́н **на сту́л.**	In the meantime I'll *put* the suitcase *on the chair* (standing position).
Я́ **положу́** ва́ш костю́м **в чемода́н.**	I'll *put* your suit *in the suitcase* (lying position).
Я́ не по́мню, **куда́** я́ **положи́л** сво́й бума́жник.	I don't remember *where* I *put* my wallet.
Куда́ вы́ **ста́вите** чемода́н?	*Where are* you *putting* (standing) the suitcase?
О́н **кладёт** бума́жник **в карма́н.**	He *is putting* the wallet *in his pocket*.

These verbs should be compared with **лежа́ть** (I) to *be* in a lying position and **стоя́ть** (I) to *be* in a standing position, which are used with **в** and **на** plus a *locative* case and with **где́, та́м, зде́сь**, since they are not verbs of motion.

Я́ **положи́л** кни́гу **на сто́л.**	I *put* (*lay*) the book *on the table*.
Кни́га **лежи́т на столе́.**	The book *is lying on the table*.
Куда́ вы́ **поста́вили** сту́л?	*Where* did you *put* (*stand*) the chair?
Где́ стои́т сту́л?	*Where is* the chair *standing*?

◑ 5. Prepositions of location and motion

You have learned that the series **в** plus accusative, **в** plus locative, **из** plus genitive is used with certain nouns to express *to, in* or *at, from* a place (cf. *Grammar Unit* 7:3); and that with other nouns the series **на** plus accusative, **на** plus locative, **с** plus genitive is used in the same meaning. In situation where there is a contrast between position *in* and *on* (e.g., *in* a bookcase versus

266

on a bookcase) the series **в — в — из** has the meaning *into, in, out of* and the series **на — на — с** has the meaning *onto, on, off of*.

Кни́га лежи́т **в** чемода́не.	The book is lying *in* the suitcase.
Кни́га лежи́т **на** чемода́не.	The book is lying *on* the suitcase.
Он положи́л оде́жду **в** чемода́н.	He put the clothes *into* the suitcase.
Он положи́л оде́жду **на** чемода́н.	He put the clothes *onto* the suitcase.
из чемода́на.	*out of* the suitcase
с чемода́на.	*off of* the suitcase

You have learned that the series **к — у — от** is used to refer to people in the meaning *to, at, from*. This series can also be used to refer to things, in which case the prepositions have the meaning *towards, near, away from*, respectively.

Он стои́т **у** окна́.	He is standing *near* (*by*) the window.
Он подошёл **к** окну́.	He went up *to* (*towards*) the window.
Он отошёл **от** окна́.	He went *away from* the window.

The uses of these prepositions can be tabulated as follows:

	INSIDE	ON TOP	NEARBY
LOCATION	в plus ⊠ Locative	на plus ✕ ☐ Locative	у plus ✕☐ Genitive
MOTION TO	в plus →☐ Accusative	на plus ⌐ ☐ Accusative	к plus →☐ Dative
MOTION FROM	из plus ☐→ Genitive	с plus ☐↘ Genitive	от plus ☐→ Genitive

● 6. Indirect speech

6.1 Indirect statements

An indirect statement is expressed by using the verb in the same tense as in the direct statement. The Russian conjunction **что** may not be omitted the way its English counterpart *that* may be.

Ива́н: Я **иду́** на вокза́л.	*Ivan:* I'*m going* to the station.
Бори́с: Ива́н сказа́л, **что** он **идёт** на вокза́л.	*Boris:* Ivan said that he *is* (*was*) *going* to the station.

267

Ивáн: Вéра **напи́шет** письмó.   *Ivan:* Vera *will write* a letter.
Борúс: Ивáн сказáл, **что** Вéра на-   *Boris:* Ivan said that Vera *will* (*would*)
пи́шет письмó.   *write* a letter.

Ивáн: Мóй брáт **приéхал** сюдá   *Ivan:* My brother *came* here yesterday.
вчерá.
Борúс: Ивáн сказáл, **что** егó брáт   *Boris:* Ivan said that his brother *came*
приéхал сюдá вчерá.   (*had come*) yesterday.

Мэ́ри: Нáм **нáдо бýдет** éхать на   *Mary:* We *will have to* go on the bus.
автóбусе.
Мэ́ри: (*Натáше*): Я́ дýмала, **что**   *Mary* (*to Natasha*): I thought we *would*
нáм **нáдо бýдет** éхать на автóбусе.   *have to* go on the bus.

6.2 Indirect questions

An indirect question is also expressed by using the verb in the same tense
as in the original question. If the original question has an interrogative word
introducing it, this interrogative word is kept in the indirect question, e.g.,

Ивáн: **Кудá** вы́ **éдете**?   *Ivan:* Where *are* you *going*?
Борúс: Ивáн меня́ спросúл, **кудá**   *Boris:* Ivan asked me where I *am* (*was*)
я́ éду.   going.

If the original question does not have an interrogative word, then the indirect
question is expressed by putting the verb at the beginning of its clause,
immediately followed by the interrogative particle **ли**. (Cf. *Grammar Unit* **9:11**).

Ивáн: Вы́ **говорúте** по-рýсски?   *Ivan: Do* you *speak* Russian?
Борúс: Ивáн спросúл, **говорю́ ли**   *Boris:* Ivan asked me *whether* (if) I *speak*
я́ по-рýсски.   (spoke) Russian.

Ивáн: Вы́ **мóжете** прийтú ко мнé?   *Ivan: Can* you come to my place?
Борúс: Ивáн спросúл, **могý ли** я́   *Boris:* Ivan asked *whether* (if) I *can*
прийтú к немý.   (could) come to his place.

Ивáн: Натáша **былá** в Амéрике?   *Ivan: Has* Natasha *been* in America?
Борúс: Ивáн спросúл, **былá ли**   *Boris:* Ivan asked *whether* (if) Natasha
Натáша в Амéрике.   *has* (had) been in America.

Ивáн: **У вáс нéт** папирóс?   *Ivan:* Don't you have any cigarettes?
Нéт ли у вáс папирóс?
Борúс: Ивáн спросúл, **нéт ли** у   *Boris:* Ivan asked *whether* (if) I didn't
меня́ папирóс.   have any cigarettes.

6.3   Indirect commands

An indirect command or request is expressed in Russian by the conjunction **чтобы** (or **чтоб**) plus the past tense of the verb.

Иван:	**Прочита́йте** э́ту кни́гу!	*Ivan:*	*Read* this book!
Бори́с:	Ива́н сказа́л, **чтобы** я **прочита́л** э́ту кни́гу.	*Boris:*	Ivan told me *to read* this book.

Иван:	**Заплати́те** за биле́ты!	*Ivan:*	*Pay* for the tickets!
Бори́с:	Ива́н хо́чет, **чтобы** я **заплати́л** за биле́ты.	*Boris:*	Ivan wants me *to pay* for the tickets.

☯ 7.   The short adjective **ну́жен**

Ну́жен is a short adjective corresponding to the English verb *to need* and has the following forms: **ну́жен, нужна́, ну́жно, нужны́** (or ну́жны).

The person who needs something is put in the dative case and the thing needed is the subject in the nominative case. Ну́жен agrees with the subject. The past and future are formed with the past and future forms of бы́ть which will then agree with the subject.

Ва́м **нужны́ бу́дут** э́ти ве́щи?	*Will* you *need* these things?
Мне́ **ну́жен** но́вый костю́м.	I *need* a new suit.
Ему́ **нужна́ была́** откры́тка.	He *needed* a postcard.

☯ 8.   The form **свой**

The form **свой** is a special adjective having an inflection identical to that of **мой**. It has a possessive meaning and refers to the same person as the subject of the sentence. If the subject of the sentence is first or second person, the form свой is interchangeable with the possessive adjectives мой, твой, наш, ваш with no difference in meaning.

Куда́ я положи́л **свой** бума́жник?	Where did I put *my* wallet?
Куда́ я положи́л **мой** бума́жник?	

Вы́ ви́дели **своего́** това́рища вчера́?	Did you see *your* comrade yesterday?
Вы́ ви́дели **ва́шего** това́рища вчера́?	

If the subject of the sentence is third person, свой is not interchangeable with the forms его́, её, их because there is a difference in meaning.

In the third person the possessive adjective (*his, her, its their*) must be свой if it refers to the *same* person as the subject of the sentence. The forms его́, её and их are used only to refer to some person *other* than the subject of the sentence.

Ивáн читáл **свою** статью.	Ivan was reading *his* (*his own*) article.
Ивáн читáл **егó** статью.	Ivan was reading *his* (*somebody else's*) article.
Онá говорила о **своём** мýже.	She was talking about *her* (*her own*) husband.
Онá говорила о **её** мýже.	She was talking about *her* (*somebody else's*) husband.

◑ 9. New prepositions: **óколо, пóд**

The preposition **óколо** is always followed by the genitive case. It has the meaning *near to*, *by* and also *approximately*.

Чтó лежит **óколо столá**?	What's lying *by the table?*
óколо десяти рублéй	*about ten* rubles

The preposition **пóд** *under* is used with the accusative case meaning motion to a place and with the instrumental meaning location in a place.

Книга упáла **под стóл**.	The book fell under the table.
Книга **под столóм**.	The book is under the table.

УПРАЖНЕ́НИЯ

A. Give the Russian equivalents:

1. It's colder in Moscow than in Tashkent. 2. She is more beautiful than her sister. 3. It's warmer here than in Leningrad. 4. The English language is harder than Russian. 5. Hotels in New York are more expensive than here. 6. In the Soviet Union books are cheaper than in America. 7. Moscow is farther from here than Leningrad. 8. Boris is older than his brother. 9. The coffee in this restaurant is worse than in that one. 10. The climate in Siberia is drier than in Leningrad. 11. Leningrad is nearer to the sea than Kiev.

B. Give the Russian equivalents:

1. He just put his suit in the suitcase. 2. He is putting his suit in the suitcase. 3. He will put his suit in the suitcase. 4. The suit is lying in the suitcase. 5. They put (stood) the books on the table. 6. She always puts (stands) the books on the table. 7. The books are standing on the table. 8. The newspaper is lying on the chair. 9. Did you put the newspaper on the chair? 10. Where did you put the newspaper? 11. I never put the newspaper on the chair. 12. He's putting the money in his pocket. 13. I'll put the book in my coat. 14. Put (stand) the coffee on the table! 15. Put the suit in the suitcase!

C. Transform orally according to the model:

MODEL: Она́ говори́т по ру́сски?
Он спроси́л, говори́т **ли** она́ по-ру́сски.

1. Они́ заплати́ли за биле́ты?
2. Он потеря́л свои́ де́ньги?
3. Он прие́дет в понеде́льник?
4. Он получи́л письмо́ в пя́тницу?
5. Он прода́ст свой дом?
6. Она́ ско́ро вернётся в Сове́тский Сою́з?
7. Стул стои́т у окна́?
8. Ива́н уложи́л свою́ оде́жду?
9. Ему́ на́до пое́хать в Ташке́нт?
10. У него́ есть чемода́н?
11. У него́ нет папиро́с?
12. Он обяза́тельно хо́чет уе́хать?
13. Он давно́ рабо́тает в Сиби́ри?
14. Э́ти ве́щи упа́ли со стола́?

271

D. Transform orally to indirect commands according to the model:

MODEL: Поста́вьте сту́л сюда́!

О́н мне́ сказа́л, что́бы я́ поста́вил сту́л сюда́.

1. Закажи́те э́то блю́до!
2. Ду́майте об э́том!
3. Вы́пейте э́то молоко́!
4. Да́йте мне́ газе́ту!
5. Заплати́те за папиро́сы!
6. Прочита́йте э́ту статью́!
7. Напиши́те моему́ дру́гу!

8. Постро́йте но́вый до́м!
9. Подожди́те меня́!
10. Спроси́те его́ о музе́ях!
11. Встре́тьте моего́ бра́та на вокза́ле!
12. Приди́те ко мне́ во вто́рник!
13. Зайди́те за мно́й!

E. Make the following substitutions orally. Use the proper form of **ну́жен:**

Мне́ (ну́жен) . . . .

1 a cheap suit
2 an expensive suitcase
3 a good pen
4 a new coat
5 money
6 a new watch

7 a Russian newspaper
8 white paper
9 an interesting novel
10 a book on mathematics
11 cheaper chairs
12 other stamps

F. Give the Russian equivalents:

1. A man was walking down the street. 2. I've never seen that man before. 3. I walked up to that man and asked him where he was going. 4. I walked along the street with that man. 5. Why are you talking about that man? (Repeat, substituting woman for man).

6. Moscow is a big city. 7. Moscow is located far from the sea. 8. The climate in Moscow is temperate. 9. The Ukraine is to the south of Moscow. 10. In the Ukraine the climate is not so severe as in Moscow. 11. Kiev is located in the Ukraine. 12. Kiev is a very old city. 13. Kiev is an older city than Moscow. 14. Kiev is not very far from the Black Sea. 15. Leningrad is closer to the White Sea than Kiev.

CONVERSATION 23

Students' conversation

Moscow University students are hurrying to their classes.

CONVERSATION UNIT TWENTY THREE ─────────

SONYA ¹ Where are you hurrying to, Kolya? ² It's still early.

KOLYA ³ I have to stop along the way. ⁴ I must find out when they are going to open the new dormitory.

SONYA ⁵ Which one is that? The one that they built next to the chemistry laboratory?

KOLYA ⁶ That's it. They say about two hundred students are going to live there.

SONYA ⁷ Are you going to classes early tomorrow?

KOLYA ⁸ [Yes, I'm going] early because on Fridays I take Professor Dobrolyubov's course in the history of English literature. ⁹ The class begins at nine in the morning.

SONYA ¹⁰ Does he give good lectures? ¹¹ I've heard about him several times.

KOLYA ¹² You've heard about him too? He's a remarkable teacher. ¹³ He gives a course not only in English literature but also in French literature. ¹⁴ But haven't you taken English?

SONYA ¹⁵ No. In school I studied German.

KOLYA ¹⁶ Don't you study in the philology department?

SONYA ¹⁷ No, I'm in the history department. My major specialty is the history of Poland.

KOLYA ¹⁸ Have you been here long?

SONYA ¹⁹ I'm in my second year ²⁰ but I came to Moscow in 1957.

NOTES

5 **Ря́дом с** literally, in a row with.

6 **То́ са́мое** literally, that very one, the same.

7 **Заня́тие** refers only to the activity, not to the room or group of students, whereas the English word *class* refers to all of these.

8 **Слу́шать ле́кции** *listen to lectures* is the usual way of saying to *take a course*.

10 **Чита́ть (ле́кции)** to *read lectures* is the usual way of saying to *give a course*, whether or not the teacher actually reads lectures.

14 **Проходи́ли** literally, went through, went past.

15 **Сре́дняя шко́ла** literally, middle school, the Soviet equivalent of grade and high school.
The reflexive verb **учи́ться** with an object in the dative case is the recommended expression for the literary language. The modern colloquial form of this sentence is **Я учи́ла неме́цкий (язы́к)**.

19 **Ку́рс** means *year of studies*. A course of study at a university or institute usually lasts five years.

Разговор студентов

СÓНЯ [1] Кудá вы́ спешúте, Кóля? [2] Ещё рáно.

КÓЛЯ [3] Мнé нáдо остановúться по дорóге. [4] Я́ дóлжен узнáть, когдá открóют нóвое общежúтие.

СÓНЯ [5] Э́то какóе? Тó, котóрое пострóили ря́дом с химúческой лаборатóрией?

КÓЛЯ [6] Тó сáмое. Тáм, говоря́т, бýдет жúть примéрно двéсти студéнтов.

СÓНЯ [7] Вы́ рáно идёте зáвтра на заня́тия?

КÓЛЯ [8] Рáно, потомý что по пя́тницам я́ слýшаю лéкции профéссора Добролю́бова по истóрии англúйской литератýры. [9] Лéкция начинáется в дéвять утрá.

СÓНЯ [10] Хорошó óн читáет? [11] Я́ слы́шала о нём ужé нéсколько рáз.

КÓЛЯ [12] Вы́ тóже о нём слы́шали? Óн замечáтельный преподавáтель. [13] Óн читáет лéкции не тóлько по англúйской литератýре, нó и по францýзской. [14] А вы́ рáзве не проходúли англúйский язы́к?

СÓНЯ [15] Нéт. В срéдней шкóле я́ учúлась немéцкому языкý.

КÓЛЯ [16] Вы́ не на филологúческом факультéте ýчитесь?

СÓНЯ [17] Нéт, я́ на историческом. Моя́ специáльность-истóрия Пóльши.

КÓЛЯ [18] Давнó вы́ здéсь?

СÓНЯ [19] Я́ учýсь на вторóм кýрсе, [20] нó приéхала в Москвý в ты́сяча девятьсóт пятьдеся́т седьмóм годý.

ADDITIONAL VOCABULARY

стó	100	шестнáдцатый	16th
двéсти	200	семнáдцатый	17th
трúста	300	восемнáдцатый	18th
четы́реста	400	девятнáдцатый	19th
пятьсóт	500	двадцáтый	20th
шестьсóт	600	тридцáтый	30th
семьсóт	700	сороковóй	40th
восемьсóт	800	пятидеся́тый	50th
девятьсóт	900	шестидеся́тый	60th
ты́сяча	1000	семидеся́тый	70th
тринáдцатый	13th	восьмидеся́тый	80th
четы́рнадцатый	14th	девянóстый	90th
пятнáдцатый	15th	сóтый	100th

NEW VERBS

TYPE II

остановúться (Р), останóвятся, остановлю́сь	to stop
слы́шать (I), слы́шат	to hear
проходúть (I), прохóдят, прохожý	to go through

NEW NOUNS

NOMINATIVE SINGULAR	NOMINATIVE PLURAL	
Masculine		
ря́д	ряды́	row, series
факультéт		department
кýрс		year (of studies)
Добролю́бов		Dobrolyubov
преподавáтель		teacher
Кóля		Kolya
Neuter		
общежúтие		dormitory
заня́тие		studies, class
Feminine I		
Сóня		Sonya
лéкция		lecture
литератýра		literature
Пóльша		Poland
дорóга		road
шкóла		school

Feminine II

специа́льность   specialty

From неме́цкий and францу́зский may be formed по-неме́цки and по-францу́зски just as from ру́сский, по-ру́сски.

УПРАЖНЕ́НИЯ

A. Transform orally according to the model;

MODEL: У меня́ **папиро́сы.   У меня́ нет папиро́с.**

1. В э́том университе́те филологи́ческий факульте́т.
2. Здесь хоро́шее общежи́тие.
3. Сего́дня у меня́ заня́тия.
4. В Нью-Йо́рке замеча́тельные актёры.
5. У нас хоро́ший репертуа́р.
6. В Сове́тском Сою́зе пусты́ни.
7. Там хоро́шие доро́ги.
8. В Ташке́нте бу́дет съезд хи́миков.
9. В э́том го́роде огро́мные аэропо́рты.
10. У нас ста́рые костю́мы.
11. У меня́ интере́сная газе́та.
12. В э́том го́роде дешёвые дома́.
13. У него́ неме́цкие знако́мые.
14. У вас францу́зские газе́ты?
15. В э́том шта́те госуда́рственный университе́т.
16. В э́том го́роде и авто́бусы и трамва́и.
17. В Нью-Йо́рке истори́ческий музе́й.

B. Transform orally, using the short form (without **бо́лее**), according to the model:

MODEL: Здесь хо́лодно.   Здесь **холодне́е.**

1. Москва́ далеко́.
2. Ру́сский язы́к тру́дный.
3. Лю́ди там счастли́вые.
4. В па́рке всё дёшево.
5. Это зда́ние высо́кое.
6. Его́ сестра́ краси́вая.
7. В э́том шта́те сигаре́ты дороги́е.
8. Эта доро́га плоха́я.
9. Этот рестора́н бли́зко отсю́да.
10. Хи́мик ста́рый.
11. Тури́ст молодо́й.

C. Make the following substitutions orally:

Он сиди́т ря́дом с . . . .

1 your professor
2 the famous actor
3 Peter Ivanovich
4 him
5 my wife
6 his (own) wife
7 our friend
8 you
9 the young engineer

10 the famous writer
11 her
12 an American (*m.*)
13 an American (*f.*)
14 teacher (*m.*)
15 teacher (*f.*)
16 me
17 a beautiful girl

D. Make the following substitutions orally:

Они́ у́чатся . . . .

1 in the philology department
2 in our school
3 in the summer
4 in the history department
5 in Moscow

6 in America
7 at our university
8 at the Moscow State University
9 in the chemistry laboratory

E. Give the Russian equivalents:

1. I have to stop along the way.   2. I'll stop along the way.   3. The bus will stop along the way.   4. The streetcar stopped.   5. I stopped right in front of his house.   6. I have to find out when they are going to open the new dorm. 7. I have to find out where they built the new dorm.   8. They built the new dorm next to the chemistry laboratory.   9. They built the new dorm in front of the chemistry lab.   10. They are building a new chemistry laboratory. 11. Is the chemistry laboratory near the new dorm?   12. Are you going to live in the new dormitory?   13. We don't have enough dormitories.

14. When does the lecture begin?   15. The lecture in English literature? 16. No, the lecture in the history of French literature.   17. It begins at nine in the morning.   18. The lecture in German literature ends at ten in the morning. 19. Do you study German in school?   20. No, I studied English in school. 21. I have begun to study German recently.   22. Many students in America study Russian.   23. He speaks German and his wife speaks French.

CONVERSATION 24

Time goes so fast!

Final exams are coming up and Boris is hard at work—talking with Alexis.

CONVERSATION UNIT TWENTY FOUR _____

ENGLISH EQUIVALENTS

ALEXIS   [1] Summer's coming already. [2] Time goes so fast!

BORIS   [3] Too fast. [4] On Thursday I have an exam. [5] I'm afraid I'll fail [it].

ALEXIS   [6] No, you'll pass! [7] On what date do exams begin?

BORIS   [8] They begin in two days. [9] Today is the twenty-fifth, and so exams begin on the twenty-seventh.

ALEXIS   [10] I still have a lot of work. [11] I've become completely lazy. [12] However, I too have to take exams and write a paper.

BORIS   [13] It seems that you're in your fifth year, aren't you?

ALEXIS   [14] Yes, I hope to finish this year. [15] Then I'd like to become a grad student and study with Professor Ilyin.

BORIS   [16] You're studying with Ilyin? I thought that the most important professor in your subject was Semyonov.

ALEXIS   [17] Don't you know that Professor Semyonov died? [18] That was in November 1958.

BORIS   [19] No, I didn't hear about his death. [20] In the summer of that year I went to the Caucasus and didn't return until the following year. [21] Therefore I don't know what happened here during that time.

ADDITIONAL VOCABULARY

янва́рь	*January*	**ию́ль**	*July*
февра́ль	*February*	**а́вгуст**	*August*
ма́рт	*March*	**сентя́брь**	*September*
апре́ль	*April*	**октя́брь**	*October*
ма́й	*May*	**ноя́брь**	*November*
ию́нь	*June*	**дека́брь**	*December*

NEW VERBS

TYPE I

наступа́ть (I), наступа́ют	to approach
нача́ться (P), начну́тся	to begin
начался́, начала́сь, начало́сь, начали́сь	
ста́ть (P), ста́нут	to become; begin
умере́ть (P), умру́т	to die
у́мер, умерла́, у́мерло, у́мерли	
произойти́ (P), произойду́т	to happen
произошёл, произошла́, произошло́, произошли́	
сдава́ть (I), сдаю́т	to take (an exam)
каза́ться (I), ка́жется, каза́лось (impersonal)	to seem

280

Время идет так быстро!

АЛЕКСЕЙ ¹ Уже наступает лето! ² Время идёт так быстро!

БОРИС ³ Слишком быстро. ⁴ В четверг у меня экзамен. ⁵ Боюсь провалиться.

АЛЕКСЕЙ ⁶ Нет, вы выдержите! ⁷ Которого числа начинаются экзамены?

БОРИС ⁸ Они начнутся через два дня. ⁹ Сегодня двадцать пятое, значит, экзамены начнутся двадцать седьмого.

АЛЕКСЕЙ ¹⁰ У меня ещё много работы. ¹¹ Я совсем обленился. ¹² Однако, и мне надо сдавать экзамены и писать работу.

БОРИС ¹³ Вы, кажется, на пятом курсе, да?

АЛЕКСЕЙ ¹⁴ Да, надеюсь кончить в этом году. ¹⁵ Потом я хотел бы стать аспирантом у профессора Ильина.

БОРИС ¹⁶ Вы у Ильина учитесь? Я думал, что по вашему предмету самый важный профессор — Семёнов.

АЛЕКСЕЙ ¹⁷ Разве вы не знаете, что профессор Семёнов умер? ¹⁸ Это было в ноябре пятьдесят восьмого года.

БОРИС ¹⁹ Нет, я не слышал о его смерти. ²⁰ Летом в том году я уехал на Кавказ, а вернулся только в следующем году. ²¹ Поэтому я не знаю, что здесь произошло за это время.

Type II

боя́ться (I), боя́тся	to be afraid
провали́ться (P), прова́лятся, провалю́сь	to fail (an exam)
вы́держать (P), вы́держат	to pass (an exam)
ко́нчить (P), ко́нчат	to finish
облени́ться (P), обле́нятся, обленю́сь	to get lazy

NEW NOUNS

NOMINATIVE SINGULAR	GENITIVE SINGULAR	NOMINATIVE PLURAL	

Masculine

экза́мен			exam
аспира́нт			grad student
предме́т			subject
Семёнов			Semyonov
Ильи́н			Ilyin
янва́рь	января́		January
февра́ль	февраля́		February
сентя́брь	сентября́		September
октя́брь	октября́		October
ноя́брь	ноября́		November
дека́брь	декабря́		December
ма́рт			March
апре́ль			April
ма́й			May
ию́нь			June
ию́ль			July
а́вгуст			August

Neuter

число́ (е)		чи́сла	date; number

Feminine I

рабо́та	work, paper

Feminine II

сме́рть	death

NEW ADJECTIVES

Long form	*Neuter short form*	
ва́жный	ва́жно	important
бы́стрый	бы́стро	fast, quick

УПРАЖНЕ́НИЯ

A. Make the following substitutions orally:

Я верну́лся . . . .

¹ in March	⁵ in April	⁹ in November
² in May	⁶ in August	¹⁰ in September
³ in June	⁷ in January	¹¹ in October
⁴ in July	⁸ in February	¹² in December

B. Make the following substitutions orally:

Он чита́л кни́гу . . . .

¹ on your subject	⁶ on mathematics
² on my specialty	⁷ on German history
³ on Russian literature	⁸ on physics
⁴ on American history	⁹ on chemistry
⁵ on Soviet linguistics	

C. Transform orally from past perfective to non-past imperfective, supplying the word **ча́сто** according to the model.

MODEL: Она́ потеря́ла свои́ де́ньги.
        Она́ **ча́сто теря́ет** свои́ де́ньги.

1. Они́ уе́хали в Сиби́рь.
2. Я прие́хал сюда́ из Нью-Йо́рка.
3. По́езд отошёл по́здно.
4. Я её подожда́л.
5. Мы поста́вили кни́ги в его́ шка́ф.
6. Я их поста́вил туда́.
7. Она́ положи́ла бума́жник в я́щик.
8. Спекта́кль начался́ ро́вно в де́вять.
9. Мы про́дали на́ши ста́рые кни́ги.
10. Ле́кция ко́нчилась без десяти́ пять.
11. Он заплати́л сли́шком мно́го за костю́м.
12. Он да́л свое́й жене́ де́ньги.
13. Она́ прочита́ла ле́кцию в на́шем университе́те.

D. Give the Russian equivalents:

1. I have an exam on Wednesday. 2. He has two exams on Wednesday. 3. When do exams begin? 4. Exams begin on Monday. 5. Exams begin in a week. 6. Exams begin in June. 7. My exam began at three o'clock. 8. He has to take an exam next week. 9. She passed the exam. 10. We failed.

283

11. They are studying under (y) Semyonov. 12. The most important professor in my subject is Semyonov. 13. The best professor in mathematics is Ilyin. 14. They are graduate students. 15. He will become a graduate student at the University of Moscow. 16. He will be a graduate student next year. 17. When they were graduate students they studied under Professor Ilyin. 18. Last year we were graduate students. 19. She hopes to finish this year.

20. Do you know that Professor Ilyin died? 21. He died soon after his wife died. 22. When did his wife die? 23. His wife died in March and he died in November. 24. I didn't know that they died. 25. I didn't hear about their death.

26. This year in the spring I went to New York. 27. It's more pleasant there in the spring than in the winter. 28. Last year in the fall I was in Detroit. 29. Last year I was in Detroit. 30. Next year I hope to be in Moscow. 31. I will be in Moscow next year in the winter. 32. I'll come back in January.

GRAMMAR UNIT TWELVE

1. Ordinal forms of compound numerals

The ordinal of a compound numeral is formed by using the ordinal of only the last member of the compound, just as in English -*th* is added only to the last member of the compound. Thus, only the last member is inflected to agree with the following noun.

пя́тый	fifth
два́дцать пя́тый	twenty-fifth
стó пя́тый	one hundred and fifth
стó два́дцать пя́тый	one hundred and twenty-fifth
тысяча девятьсóт два́дцать пя́тый	one thousand nine hundred and twenty-fifth
тысяча шестидеся́— тый	one thousand and sixtieth

2. Dates, months, years

2.1 Telling the date

In Russian the day of the month is expressed by the ordinal form of the numeral in the nominative singular neuter, followed by the name of the month in the genitive singular. When the year follows the date, the year is expressed by the ordinal form in the genitive singular masculine, agreeing with **гóда**. In colloquial Russian гóда is likely to be left out.

Какóе сегóдня **числó**?	What is the *date* today?
Сегóдня **деся́тое ию́ня**.	Today is the *tenth of June*.
Сегóдня два́дцать **четвёртое ноября́** тысяча девятьсóт шестьдеся́т **пéрвого** гóда.	Today is the twenty-*fourth of November*, 1961 (of the one thousand nine hundred and sixty-*first* year).

2.2 In a certain month

Time in a month is expressed by **в** plus locative case. When the year follows the month the year appears in the ordinal form in the genitive singular masculine, agreeing with **гóда**.

Óн у́мер **в ию́не** тысяча девятьсóт шестьдеся́т **пéрвого** гóда.	He died *in June* 1961 (of the one thousand nine hundred and sixty-*first* year).

2.3 On a date (of the month, year)

To express *on the -n*[th] *of the month*, -n[th] is the ordinal in the genitive case and the month is also in the genitive case.

If the month is not specified, the genitive of числó is used after the numeral.

If the year is specified as well as the month, it appears in the genitive case (as *above* in **2.1** and **2.2**).

If the day of the week is specified (**в** plus accusative, cf. *Grammar Unit* **10:4**) the rest of the construction is not affected.

Он прие́хал **деся́того ию́ня**.	He came *on the tenth of June*.
Он прие́хал **деся́того числа́**.	He came *on the tenth*.
Он прие́хал **деся́того ию́ня** ты́сяча девятьсо́т шестьдеся́т **пе́рвого го́да**.	He came *on the tenth of June* 1961.
Он прие́хал в сре́ду **деся́того ию́ня** ты́сяча девятьсо́т шестьдеся́т **пе́рвого го́да**.	He came on Wednesday *the tenth of June*, 1961.

2.4 "In a certain year"

To express *in a certain year*, unlike the above expressions (**2.1**, **2.2**, **2.3**), the preposition **в** is used, followed by the year in the locative case. Note that this construction is used when no preceding time expression occurs.

Он у́мер **в** ты́сяча девятьсо́т шестьдеся́т **пе́рвом году́**.	He died in 1961.

Compare the following examples illustrating the use of genitive versus locative in expressions where the year is mentioned.

Он прие́хал в э́том году́.	He came this year.
Он прие́хал в ма́рте э́того го́да.	He came in March of this year.
Он прие́хал в про́шлом году́.	He came last year.
Он прие́хал в ма́рте про́шлого го́да.	He came last March (in March of last year).
Он прие́хал в ты́сяча девятьсо́т со́рок пе́рвом году́.	He came in 1941.
Он прие́хал в ма́рте ты́сяча девятьсо́т со́рок пе́рвого го́да.	He came in March, 1941.
Он прие́хал в ты́сяча девятьсо́т деся́том году́.	He came in 1910.
Он прие́хал деся́того ма́рта ты́сяча девятьсо́т деся́того го́да.	He came on the tenth of March, 1910.

Dates are frequently abbreviated as follows:

Он прие́хал в со́рок пе́рвом году́.	He came in '41.
Он прие́хал 10 ма́рта 1960 г.	He came on March 10, 1960.
Он прие́хал в 1960 г.	He came in 1960.

◑ 3. за in time expressions

The preposition **за** is used with the accusative case in time expressions indicating up to the end of that time and is frequently translatable as *during*.

Я не знáю, чтó здéсь произошлó **за** **éто врéмя**.

I don't know what happened here *during that time.*

❷ 4. "In the morning," etc.

When the expression *in the morning* is immediately preceded by a specific time, it is expressed by the genitive form **утрá** rather than the instrumental form ýтром (cf. *Grammar Unit* **10:6**).

There is a similar contrast between **вéчера** — **вéчером** *in the evening*, **нóчи** — **нóчью** *at night*, and **дня** — **днём** *in the afternoon*.

Лéкция начинáется в **дéвять утрá (вéчера)**.

The lecture begins at nine *in the morning. (in the evening).*

Лéкция начинáется **ýтром (вéчером)**.

The lecture begins *in the morning (in the evening).*

❷ 5. по in time expressions

The preposition **по** is used with the dative plural of a number of nouns referring to time in order to indicate repeated events.

Óн рабóтает тóлько **по понедéльникам**.
Óн никогдá не рабóтает **по вечерáм**.
Óн летáет в Нью-Йóрк **по четвергáм**.

He works only *on Mondays.*
He never works *evenings.*
He flies to New York *on Thursdays.*

❷ 6. The unstressed particle бы

The unstressed particle **бы** in construction with a past tense of a verb often equates with English *would.*

Я бы хотéл (я хотéл бы) стáть аспирáнтом.

I *would like* to become a graduate student.

Бы́ло бы хорошó знáть рýсский язы́к.

It *would* be good to know Russian.

Я хотéл бы вáс познакóмить с ни́м.

I'*d like* to introduce you to him.

❷ 7. Some aspect pairs

7.1 Familiar types

IMPERFECTIVE	PERFECTIVE	
проходи́ть, прохóдят, прохожý	пройти́, пройдýт, прошёл, прошлá, ...	to go past
происходи́ть, происхóдят, происхожý	произойти́, произойдýт произошёл, произошлá, ...	to happen
сдавáть, сдаю́т	сдáть (Irregular non-past)	to take (an exam)
наступáть, наступáют	наступи́ть, настýпят, наступлю́	to approach

287

| остана́вливать, остана́вливают | останови́ть, остано́вят, остановлю́ | to stop (something) |
| остана́вливаться, остана́вливаются | останови́ться, остано́вятся, остановлю́сь | to stop (intransitive) |

7.2 станови́ться (I), ста́ть (P)

These two verbs form an aspect pair.

| станови́ться, стано́вятся становлю́сь | стать, ста́нут | to become |

7.3 начина́ться (I), нача́ться (P)

These two verbs form an aspect pair.

| начина́ться, начина́ются | нача́ться, начну́тся начался́ начало́сь начала́сь начали́сь | to begin |

7.4 -нима́ть, -ня́ть

A group of verbs have an imperfective infinitive in **-нима́ть**, and a perfective in **-ня́ть**. The imperfective has Type I inflection of the regular **-а́ют** variety. The perfective has Type I inflection also, but the non-past stem is irregular, having the shape **-ним-** after a prefix ending in a consonant (there have been no examples of these so far) and the shape **-йм-** after a prefix ending in a vowel. The verb приня́ть, при́мут is exceptional in that **й** doesn't occur in the stem.

IMPERFECTIVE	PERFECTIVE	
понима́ть, понима́ют	поня́ть, пойму́т	to understand
принима́ть, принима́ют	приня́ть, при́мут, приму́	to accept, receive

Note the stress in the past tense forms of the perfectives: по́нял, поняла́, по́няло, по́няли; при́нял, приняла́, при́няло, при́няли.

◗ 8. Some reflexive verbs

Listed below are some more pairs of reflexive and non-reflexive verbs.

NON-REFLEXIVE			REFLEXIVE		
начина́ть	(I)	to begin (something)	начина́ться	(I)	to begin (intransitive)
нача́ть	(P)		нача́ться	(P)	
конча́ть	(I)	to finish (something)	конча́ться	(I)	to finish, end (intransitive)
ко́нчить	(P)		ко́нчиться	(P)	

останáвливать (I) } to stop (something)
остановúть (P) }

останáвливаться (I) } to stop (intransitive)
остановúться (P) }

{ Лéкция **начинáется** в вóсемь часóв.	The lecture *begins* at 8 o'clock.
{ Я всегдá **начинáю рабóту** в пять часóв утрá.	I always *begin work* at 5 o'clock in the morning.

{ Óн **остановúл трамвáй.**	He *stopped the streetcar.*
{ Трамвáй **остановúлся.**	The streetcar *stopped.*

{ Войнá **кóнчилась** в иóне.	The war *ended* in June.
{ Мы **кóнчили кнúгу** этими словáми.	We *finished the book* with these words.

УПРАЖНÉНИЯ

A. Make the following substitutions orally:

Съéзд начнётся . . . .

[1] on the 10th of March
[2] on the 30th of January
[3] on the 14th of May
[4] on the 17th of October
[5] on the 25th of September
[6] on the 2nd of April
[7] on the 3rd of April
[8] on the 31st of December
[9] on the 28th of February
[10] on the 7th of June
[11] on the 10th of July
[12] on the 12th of August
[13] on the 19th of November

B. Make the following substitutions orally:

Онá умерлá в декабрé . . . .

1930	1848	1899
1961	1940	1933
1905	1945	1953
1917	1960	1492
1812		1066

C. Repeat Exercise B omitting **в декабрé.**

D. Transform orally from perfective non-past to past, according to the model:

MODEL: Óн э́то поймёт.   Óн э́то **по́нял.**

1. Она́ э́то поймёт.
2. Они́ э́то пойму́т.
3. Óн при́мет уча́стие в съе́зде.
4. Она́ при́мет уча́стие в съе́зде.
5. Óн возьмёт свою́ кни́гу.

6. Она́ возьмёт свою́ кни́гу.
7. Они́ возьму́т свои́ кни́ги.
8. Óн ва́м да́ст э́ти де́ньги.
9. Она́ ва́м да́ст э́ти де́ньги.
10. Они́ ва́м даду́т э́ти де́ньги.

E. Give the Russian equivalents:

1. When does the movie begin? 2. The movie began at eight o'clock. 3. The movie ended at eleven o'clock. 4. The movie always ends early. 5. The streetcar stopped right in front of me. 6. The streetcar usually stops here. 7. The streetcar will stop here. 8. She stopped in front of the restaurant.

9. He stopped the bus in front of the hotel. 10. He always stops the bus near the lab. 11. He'll stop the bus for you.

12. He became an engineer three years ago. 13. He'll become an American citizen in five years. 14. Yesterday it got cold. 15. In the fall it usually gets cold. 16. It'll get cold tomorrow.

REVIEW LESSON SIX

A. FLUENCY DRILL

1. In Moscow it is much hotter than here. 2. In the winter it is much colder than in the summer. 3. The second edition of this book is much more expensive than the first. 4. The buildings in New York are much higher than in Moscow. 5. Olga is much prettier than her sister.

6. He stopped in front of the store. 7. The plane stopped in front of the main building of the airport. 8. He stopped the bus in front of the post office. 9. I'll stop the bus for you. 10. Does the bus always stop here? 11. The movie ended at half past eleven. 12. He finished the article in a week. 13. He always finishes his lectures with these words. 14. His lectures always end with these words. 15. His lectures always begin with these words. 16. He always begins his lectures with these words. 17. He began the article last week. 18. The movie began at half past seven.

19. I have to look for my wallet. 20. I can't find my wallet. 21. I've lost my wallet. 22. Where could I have put my wallet? 23. Did you look in your pocket? 24. I found it in the drawer. 25. I put it on the table. 26. I usually put it in my coat.

27. I would like to become an engineer. 28. He became a doctor. 29. In Tashkent it gets hot in the summer. 30. It got cold last night. 31. He stood the suitcase on the chair. 32. He left his book at the store. 33. She always leaves her cigarettes (behind).

34. Where are you studying? 35. I'm studying at the MGU. 36. What are you studying? 37. German. 38. Where did you learn English? 39. I studied English in school. 40. I have (listen to) lectures on English every day at eight. 41. Who's your English teacher? 42. Professor Ivanov, who lived for a long time in America.

B. Conversation topics

(1) Two students discuss their courses at the university.

(2) It is the end of the year. One student is helping another pack his things to go home for the vacation. Both have trouble finding things.

(3) A and B give each other the dates on which they were born and the years that they started and finished school.

ОБРАЗОВА́НИЕ В СОВЕ́ТСКОМ СОЮ́ЗЕ

Сове́тский ребёнок начина́ет своё образова́ние[1] в во́зрасте[2] семи́ лет, когда́ он поступа́ет[3] в сре́днюю шко́лу. Там он прово́дит[4] оди́ннадцать лет. По́сле э́того часть

[1] education
[2] age
[3] enters
[4] spends

ученико́в⁵ поступа́ет на рабо́ту, други́е продолжа́ют⁶ образова́ние в ву́зах,⁷ т.е.,⁸ в институ́тах и́ли в университе́тах. Кро́ме э́тих уче́бных заведе́ний е́сть ещё мно́го разли́чных⁹ школ, наприме́р, те́хникумы, техни́ческие¹⁰ учи́лища,¹¹ вече́рние и зао́чные¹² ку́рсы, ку́рсы при фа́бриках, консервато́рии, и т.д.

Вы́сшее образова́ние, ка́к в институ́те та́к и в университе́те, продолжа́ется¹³ пя́ть ле́т.

⁵ pupil
⁶ continue
⁷ вы́сшее уче́бное заведе́ние institution of higher learning
⁸ abbreviation for **то́ есть**, *that is*.
⁹ various
¹⁰ technical
¹¹ schools
¹² correspondence
¹³ lasts

По оконча́нии уча́щийся[14] получа́ет дипло́м.

Са́мый большо́й университе́т во всём Сове́тском Сою́зе — э́то МГУ. Его́ посеща́ет[15] бо́льше двадцати́ пяти́ ты́сяч студе́нтов.

Ста́рая ча́сть университе́та нахо́дится в це́нтре Москвы́ на Мохово́й у́лице. Здесь Моско́вский университе́т был осно́ван[16] уже́ бо́льше двухсо́т лет тому́ наза́д. В настоя́щем[17] ве́ке он о́чень разро́сся[18] и нужда́лся[19] в но́вых постро́йках. В 1948 году́ на́чали стро́ить огро́мное но́вое зда́ние на Ле́нинских гора́х. Тепе́рь оно́ око́нчено и явля́ется[20] о́чень ва́жной ча́стью университе́та.

В Моско́вском университе́те мно́го факульте́тов. Ка́ждый факульте́т состои́т из не́скольких ка́федр.[21] Ка́ждая ка́федра име́ет своего́ заве́дующего.[22] Вот факульте́ты МГУ: истори́ческий, филологи́ческий, филосо́фский, э́кономи́ческий, меха́нико-математи́ческий, физи́ческий, хими́ческий, географи́ческий, геологи́ческий, биологи́ческий, и факульте́ты журнали́стики и пра́ва.[23]

Как уже́ бы́ло упомяну́то,[24] на ка́ждом факульте́те мно́го ка́федр. Так, наприме́р, филологи́ческий факульте́т состои́т из семна́дцати ка́федр. Вот предме́ты, кото́рым посвящены́[25] э́ти ка́федры: ру́сская литерату́ра, сове́тская литерату́ра, иностра́нная[26] литерату́ра, исто́рия журнали́стики, тео́рия и пра́ктика сове́тской пре́ссы, о́бщее[27] языкозна́ние, ру́сский

[14] student
[15] attends
[16] founded
[17] present
[18] grew
[19] to be in need of
[20] is
[21] department, section
[22] head, chief
[23] law
[24] mentioned
[25] are devoted
[26] foreign
[27] general

294

язы́к, рома́нская филоло́гия, герма́нская
филоло́гия, славя́нская филоло́гия, фи́н-
но-уго́рская[28] филоло́гия, класси́ческая
филоло́гия, фоне́тика, англи́йский язы́к,
неме́цкий язы́к, францу́зский язы́к, и,
наконе́ц, ру́сский язы́к для иностра́нцев.

[28] Finno-Ugric, a group of related languages, including
Finnish and Hungarian

Ка́к уже́ упомяну́то вы́ше, студе́нт у́чится в университе́те пя́ть ле́т. По́сле того́, ка́к о́н получа́ет дипло́м, о́н и́ли поступа́ет на слу́жбу[29] и́ли стано́вится аспира́нтом. Но́ то́лько тому́ разреша́ют[30] нача́ть аспиранту́ру, кто́ счита́ется[31] о́чень выдаю́щимся[32] студе́нтом.

Ка́к студе́нты, та́к и аспира́нты сове́тских уче́бных заведе́ний живу́т в общежи́тиях. Обще́ственная[33] жи́знь[34] в э́тих дома́х о́чень жива́я. Всегда́ е́сть возмо́жность[35] развле́чься.[36] О́чень ча́сто состоя́тся[37] вечера́,[38] на кото́рых студе́нты ста́вят спекта́кли, танцу́ют, пою́т.[39] Ту́т[40] же, в общежи́тии, мо́жно ви́деть и фи́льмы по це́нам бо́лее ни́зким,[41] чем в городски́х кинотеа́трах.

[29] service, work
[30] permit
[31] is considered
[32] outstanding

[33] social
[34] life
[35] possibility
[36] to have a good time
[37] are held
[38] party
[39] sing
[40] here
[41] low

PRONUNCIATION OF RUSSIAN

Pronunciation of Russian

The only way to learn Russian pronunciation is to imitate a model. Therefore it is strongly recommended that the student practice the Pronunciation Drills only by repeating or imitating each item in a Drill after hearing it from a native speaker or a recording.

● 1. The sounds of Russian

Russian is spoken with five distinctive vowels and thirty six distinctive consonants. In the transcription used in this book the vowels are represented by the symbols /i e a o u/ and the consonants by the symbols /p p̦ b b̦ m m̦ f f̦ v v̦ t ț d d̦ n n̦ s ș z z̦ l ḷ r r̦ k k̦ g g̦ x x̦ c š ž č šč y/.

The vowel sounds vary depending upon whether they are stressed or not and also depending upon what type of consonant precedes or follows them.

The consonant sounds may be subdivided into two types, a plain type and a palatalized type.

Note that the terms *vowel* and *consonant* refer throughout this section to *sounds,* not letters.

PLAIN					PALATALIZED				
/p	b	m	f	v/	/p̦	b̦	m̦	f̦	v̦/
/t	d	n	s	z/	/ț	d̦	n̦	ș	z̦/
/l	r/				/ḷ	r̦/			
/k	g	x/			/k̦	g̦	x̦/		
/c	š	ž/			/č	šč	y/		

Stress, or accent, is significant in Russian and the position of stress within a word is not predictable.

The pitch, or voice, is also significant in Russian and will be discussed in Section 6, *Intonation.*

● 2. Plain Consonants

The plain consonants are listed below with their nearest English equivalents.

/p/	like *p* in *p*in	/l/	like *ll* in pu*ll*
/b/	like *b* in *b*in	/r/	like Scottish trilled *r*
/m/	like *m* in *m*an	/k/	like *c* in *c*at
/f/	like *f* in *f*an	/g/	like *g* in *g*un
/v/	like *v* in *v*an	/x/	like *ch* in German a*ch*
/t/	like *t* in *t*in		or Scottish lo*ch*
/d/	like *d* in *d*in	/c/	like *ts* in ba*ts*
/n/	like *n* in *n*et	/š/	like *sh* in *sh*in
/s/	like *s* in *s*ink	/ž/	like *z* in a*z*ure.
/z/	like *z* in *z*inc		

299

The above equations are only near approximations and are not meant to be identities. The following statements will help the student to understand the articulation of Russian sound as he imitates his Russian instructor or the recordings. This material should be studied and practised thoroughly if the student wishes to attain an intelligible pronunciation.

2.1 /p t k/

The Russian sounds /p t k/ differ from the comparable English sounds mentioned above in that the English sounds are produced with a slight release of air after the consonant articulation, whereas there is no similar release of air in the production of the Russian sounds. This release of air can be easily perceived by putting the back of the hand a few inches from the mouth and saying the English words *tin* and *din*. The release is much stronger after the *t* of *tin* than after the d of *din*.

DRILL 1

по́нял	*understood*	/póṇil/
пого́да	*weather*	/pagóda/
по́д	*under*	/pót/
то́же	*also*	/tóži/
та́м	*there*	/tám/
ты́	*you*	/tí/
ту́т	*here*	/tút/
ка́к	*how*	/kák/
кака́я	*what, which*	/kakáya/
куда́	*where to*	/kudá/
о ко́м	*about whom*	/a kóm/

2.2 /t d n/

These consonants are made by putting the tip of the tongue against the lower part of the upper teeth, whereas the comparable English consonants are made with the tip of the tongue against the gum ridge back of the teeth.

The student should particularly note that the consonant sound /n/ when it occurs before /k g x/ is pronounced as described above; it is never pronounced like the English *ng* of '*sing*'.

DRILL 2

то́же	*also*	/tóži/
та́м	*there*	/tám/
э́то	*this*	/éta/
да́	*yes*	/dá/

всегда́	*always*	/fṣigdá/
да́ть	*to give*	/dáṭ/
но́	*but*	/nó/
она́	*she*	/aná/
жена́	*wife*	/žiná/
америка́нка	*American*	/aṃiṛikánka/
по-англи́йски	*in English*	/pa angḷíysḳi/

2.3 Voicing

The consonants /b d g v z ž/ are the voiced counterparts of /p t k f s š/.
A consonant is said to be voiced when it is produced with the vocal cords
vibrating and voiceless when the vocal cords are not vibrating. The effect of
voicing can easily be perceived by the student if he pronounces a prolonged /s/,
which is voiceless, and then a prolonged /z/, which is voiced. Voiced sounds in
Russian are produced with the voicing beginning earlier than in English, giving
the effect of being pronounced more forcefully. This applies also to the voiced
consonants /m n l r/, which, however, have no voiceless counterparts.

DRILL 3

бра́т	*brother*	/brát/
вы́	*you*	/ví/
да́	*yes*	/dá/
го́род	*city*	/górat/
ва́ш	*your*	/váš/
зову́т	*call*	/zavút/
жи́ть	*live*	/žíṭ/

2.4 /r/

This consonant has no English counterpart. It is a tongue tip trill with the tongue striking back of the upper teeth. Usually only two or three taps are necessary.

DRILL 4

напра́во	*to the right*	/napráva/
фра́зу	*sentence*	/frázu/
бра́т	*brother*	/brát/
ра́з	*time*	/rás/
рабо́тать	*work*	/rabótaṭ/
рука́	*hand*	/ruká/
Ве́ра	*Vera*	/v́éra/
го́род	*city*	/górat/
теа́тр	*theater*	/ṭiátr/
Пётр	*Peter*	/ṗótr/

2.5 /l/

The nearest equivalent to the Russian plain /l/ is the double *ll* in English
pull. However, in producing the Russian /l/ the tongue is pulled further back

in the mouth. The position of the tip of the tongue is not significant. Speakers of English are likely to have more difficulty with this sound when it occurs at the beginning of a word than when it occurs elsewhere and should therefore practice it in this position.

DRILL 5

вокзáл	*station*	/vagzál/
дáл	*gave*	/dál/
бы́л	*was*	/bíl/
ви́дел	*saw*	/yíḍil/
стóл	*table*	/stól/
стýл	*chair*	/stúl/
глáвный	*main*	/glávniy/
слóво	*word*	/slóva/
мáсло	*butter*	/másla/
клáсс	*classroom*	/klás/
плохóй	*bad*	/plaxóy/
слýшать	*listen*	/slúšiṭ/
слы́шать	*hear*	/slíšiṭ/
пожáлуйста	*please*	/pažálsta/
Толстóй	*Tolstoy*	/talstóy/
дóлжен	*should*	/dólžin/
лýчше	*better*	/lútši/
лáдно	*all right*	/ládna/
взялá	*took*	/yzilá/
молодóй	*young*	/maladóy/
человéк	*man*	/čilayék/
молокó	*milk*	/malakó/

2.6 /x/

This sound has no equivalent in English. It is produced by raising the back of the tongue close to but not touching the roof of the mouth. This is similar to the pronunciation of /k/, but differs in that there is no contact between the tongue and the roof of the mouth. The sound /x/ is similar to the *ch* of German '*ach*' but has less friction.[1]

DRILL 6

хýже	*worse*	/xúži/
хóлодно	*cold*	/xóladna/
похóж	*like*	/paxóš/
них	*them*	/ṇíx/

---

[1] In the speech of some people there is a voiced counterpart of /x/ which occurs in a very limited number of words, e.g., Бóга 'of God'.

э́тих	*these*	/éṭix/
тéх	*those*	/ṭéx/
хотя́	*although*	/xaṭá/
хорошó	*good*	/xarašó/
поéхать	*go*	/payéxaṭ/
находи́ть	*find*	/naxaḍíṭ/
сáхар	*sugar*	/sáxar/
Чéхов	*Chekhov*	/čéxaf/

2.7   /c/

Russian /c/ is like English *ts*. The student will have much more difficulty with this sound when it occurs at the beginning of a word than when it occurs in other positions.

DRILL 7

отéц	*father*	/aṭéc/
молодцы́	*fellows*	/malatcí/
америкáнец	*American*	/aṃiṛikáṇic/
гости́ница	*hotel*	/gaṣṭíṇica/
цéны	*prices*	/céni/
цéлый	*whole*	/céliy/

2.8   /š ž/

The consonant /š/ is like *sh* in English *shine* but with the tongue tip pulled further back and with the tip touching the roof of the mouth well back of the upper teeth. The acoustic effect of this is to produce a sound which is much lower in pitch than English *sh*. The consonant /ž/ is produced like /š/ but with voicing (cf. **2.3**).

DRILL 8

пишý	*write*	/pišú/
хорошó	*good*	/xarašó/
большóй	*big*	/baḷšóy/
вáши	*your*	/váši/
жéнщина	*woman*	/žénščina/
женá	*wife*	/žiná/
тóже	*also*	/tóži/
скажи́те	*tell*	/skažíṭi/

2.9   Lip rounding

All consonants before the vowels /o/ and /u/ are pronounced with considerable lip rounding.

DRILL 9

хорошо́	*good*	/xarašó/
то́же	*also*	/tóži/
письмо́	*letter*	/piṣmó/
по́чта	*post office*	/póčta/
шло	*went*	/šló/
до́ктор	*doctor*	/dóktar/
го́род	*city*	/górat/
рабо́тать	*work*	/rabótaṭ/
второ́й	*second*	/ftaróy/
му́ж	*husband*	/múš/
зову́т	*call*	/zavút/
су́п	*soup*	/súp/

🌓 3. Palatalized consonants

The palatalized consonants /p̣ ḅ ṃ f̣ ṿ ṭ ḍ ṇ ṣ z̧ ḷ ṛ ḳ g̣ x̧/ have no equivalents in English. The nearest equivalents of the other palatalized consonants are:

/č/ like *ch* in *ch*in.
/šč/ like *shch* in fre*sh ch*eese
/y/ like *y* in *y*es

Palatalized consonants are characterized by the raising of a broad area of the top front surface of the tongue to a position next to the upper teeth. This is referred to as *palatalized articulation*. The acoustic effect of many of the palatalized consonants is that of the equivalent English consonant followed by a /y/ sound, for example, as in the English word *pure*. In Russian, however, this *y*-element must be simultaneous with the articulation of the consonant rather than subsequent to it.

3.1 Palatalized /p̣ ḅ ṃ f̣ ṿ/

In the case of /p̣ ḅ ṃ f̣ ṿ/ these sounds are produced the same way as plain /p b m f v/ but with the addition of palatalized articulation.

DRILL 10

Пётр	*Peter*	/p̣ótr/
пи́сьма	*letters*	/p̣íṣma/
пе́рвый	*first*	/p̣érviy/
пя́ть	*five*	/p̣áṭ/
бе́лый	*white*	/ḅéliy/
люби́ть	*love*	/ḷuḅíṭ/
ребёнок	*child*	/ṛiḅónak/
мя́со	*meat*	/ṃása/
Аме́рика	*America*	/aṃéṛika/

возьмёт	takes	/vaẓmót/
вмéсте	together	/ỵṃéṣti/
профéссор	professor	/prafésar/
фи́зика	physics	/fízika/
фи́льм	film	/fíḷm/
ви́дите	see	/ỵíḍiṭi/
живёт	lives	/žiỵót/
о Москвé	about Moscow	/a maskỵé/
двé	two	/dỵé/
человéк	man	/čilaỵék/
девя́тый	ninth	/ḍiỵátiy/

3.2 Palatalized /ḳ g̣ x̣/

The consonants /ḳ g̣ x̣/ are produced with the central part of the tongue raised to the roof of the mouth in addition to palatalized articulation. This, it may be noted, is similar in pronunciation to English /k/ in *key*, /g/ in *geezer* and /h/ in *hue*, although English does not have the added palatalized articulation.

Palatalized /ḳ g̣ x̣/ rarely occur before the vowels /a o u/ and likewise the plain consonants /k g x/ do not occur before the vowels /i e/.

DRILL 11

Ки́ев	Kiev	/ḳíyif/
ру́сский	Russian	/rúsḳiy/
с кéм	with whom	/s ḳém/
в рукé	in the hand	/v ruḳé/
дороги́е	dear	/darag̣íya/
кни́ги	books	/kṇíg̣i/
о дру́ге	about (my) friend	/a drúg̣i/
хи́мик	chemist	/x̣íṃik/

3.3 Palatalized /ṭ ḍ ṇ ṣ ẓ ṛ/

In producing palatalized /ṭ ḍ ṇ ṣ ẓ ṛ/ the articulation characteristic of palatalization is used, i.e., a broad area of the top front surface of the tongue is raised against the upper teeth, whereas in the pronunciation of plain /t d n s z r/ it is only the tongue tip that makes contact.

DRILL 12

тёплый	warm	/ṭópliy/	о́чередь	line	/óčiṛiṭ/
отéц	father	/aṭéc/	дéлать	do	/ḍélaṭ/
хоти́те	want	/xaṭíṭi/	гдé	where	/gḍé/
хотя́	although	/xaṭá/	оди́н	one	/aḍín/
пу́ть	way	/púṭ/	дя́дя	uncle	/ḍáḍi/
мáть	mother	/máṭ/	сидя́т	sit	/ṣiḍát/

идёте	*go*	/idóti/	вся *all*	/fsá/
свадьба	*wedding*	/svádba/	здесь *here*	/ zdés/
судьба	*fate*	/sudbá/	письмó *letter*	/pismó/
нéт	*no*	/nét/	газéта *newspaper*	/gazéta/
меня	*me*	/miná/	музéй *museum*	/muźéy/
книга	*book*	/kníga/	везёт *conveys*	/yizót/
о нём	*about him*	/anóm/	взял *took*	/vzál/
меню	*menu*	/minú/	возьму́ *take*	/vazmú/
дéнь	*day*	/dén/	повторите *repeat*	/paftaríti/
óсень	*autumn*	/ósin/	турист *tourist*	/turíst/
óчень	*very*	/óčin/	говорит *speaks*	/gavarít/
дéньги	*money*	/déngi/	говорят *speak*	/gavarát/
мéньше	*less*	/ménši/	говорю́ *speak*	/gavarú/
сéвер	*north*	/séyir/	смотрéл *looked*	/smatrél/
сёстры	*sisters*	/sóstri/	тепéрь *now*	/tipér/
всю	*all*	/fsú/	Сибирь *Siberia*	/sibír/

3.4 Palatalized /ļ/

Palatalized /ļ/ is produced by placing the tongue in the characteristic position for palatalized articulation. Therefore it is the articulation with the front part of the tongue that is significant for the palatalized /ļ/, whereas for the plain /l/ it is the position of the back part of tongue that is significant.

DRILL 13

лёгкий	*easy*	/ļóxķiy/	тóлько *only*	/tóļka/
самолёт	*airplane*	/samaļót/	Óльга *Olga*	/óļga/
любит	*likes*	/ļúbit/	большóй *big*	/baļšóy/
блюдо	*dish*	/bļúda/	больница *hospital*	/baļníca/
налéво	*on the left*	/naļéva/	фильм *film*	/fíļm/
английский	*English*	/angļíyşķiy/	фильтр *filter*	/fíļtr/
знали	*knew*	/znáļi/	писáтель *writer*	/pisátiļ/
дéлали	*did*	/déļaļi/	Крéмль *Kremlin*	/ķrémļ/
говорили	*said*	/gavaríļi/		

3.5 /č/

The consonant /č/ is pronounced like the English *ch* in *cheese* but with the tongue a trifle further forward.

DRILL 14

чáсто	*often*	/částa/
дóчка	*daughter*	/dóčka/
учитель	*teacher*	/učítiļ/
óчень	*very*	/óčin/
знáчит	*means*	/znáčit/

3.6 /šč/

The Russian consonant /šč/ differs from the English *shch* in *fresh cheese* in that the tongue is further forward, as in the case of the consonant /č/, and also in that there is no pause between them. Instead of the pronunciation /šč/ many Russian speakers have for this sound only the /š/ element, and in this case it differs from the plain /š/ in two respects: first by being produced with the tongue in the front position against the teeth and second by having the articulation held longer.

DRILL 15

щи́	*cabbage soup*	/ščí/
ещё	*still, more*	/yiščó/
я́щик	*box*	/yáščik/
това́рищи	*comrades*	/tavárišči/
това́рищ	*comrade*	/tavárišč/
защища́ющий	*defending*	/zaščiščáyuščiy/

3.7 /y/

The pronunciation of this consonant is like English *y* in *yet*.

3.8 Voicing and lip rounding

What was said about voicing in Section 2.3 and about lip rounding in Section 2.9 also applies to the pertinent palatalized consonants.

🄯 4. Vowels

Russian has five vowels: /i e a o u/. The pronunciation of a particular vowel is a function of several variables. The main variables are first the position of stress, and second the particular type of consonant that precedes the vowel, or, in the case of the vowel /e/, the particular type of consonant that follows the vowel. The ensuing discussion of the pronunciation of vowels will be subdivided accordingly.

Russian vowels are generally quite short, whereas in English some vowels are long.

The student should not take the suggested English vowel equivalents too seriously, since there is a great deal of dialect variation with respect to English vowels. These equivalents are only meant as approximations and the student should rather depend upon the instructor or the recordings.

4.1 Stressed vowels after plain consonants

It is the preceding consonant which is the significant variable for the vowels /i a o u/. Although it is the following consonant which is the significant variable for the vowel /e/, this vowel will also be discussed in this section.

307

Lack of a consonant, i.e. at the beginning or end of a word, has the same effect on a vowel as a plain consonant does.

4.11 /i/ stressed after plain consonant

In this position the vowel /i/ is similar to the vowel in English *bit*, with the tip of the tongue raised fairly high in the mouth, but the Russian sound differs in that the tongue is pulled much further back.

DRILL 16

вы́	*you*	/ví/
мы́	*we*	/mí/
ты́	*you*	/tí/
сы́н	*son*	/sín/
язы́к	*language*	/yizík/
молодцы́	*fellows*	/malatcí/
жены́	*wife's*	/žiní/
родны́х	*relatives'*	/radníx/
жи́л	*lived*	/žíl/
скажи́те	*tell*	/skažíṭi/

4.12 /a/ stressed after plain consonant

In this position the vowel /a/ is similar to the *a* in English *car*.

DRILL 17

да́	*yes*	/dá/
ка́к	*how*	/kák/
та́м	*there*	/tám/
ра́з	*time*	/rás/
понима́ю	*understand*	/paṇimáyu/

4.13 /o/ stressed after plain consonant

In this position the vowel /o/ is like the *o* in English *story*, although in Russian the lips are more strongly rounded and protruded than is normally the case in English. This vowel is short and does not have the drawled or glide effect heard in English *toad*.

DRILL 18

то́же	*also*	/tóži/
сло́во	*word*	/slóva/
хорошо́	*good*	/xarašó/
напро́тив	*opposite*	/napróṭif/
свобо́дно	*freely*	/svabódna/

4.14 /u/ stressed after plain consonant

In this position the vowel /u/ is similar to *oo* in English *mooring*. As in the production of the Russian vowel /o/ the lips are more strongly rounded and protruded and the vowel is short, not having the drawled or glide effect heard in English *rude*.

DRILL 19

бу́дет	*will be*	/búḍit/
ру́сский	*Russian*	/rúṣḳiy/
у́лица	*street*	/úḷica/
живу́т	*live*	/živút/
зову́т	*call*	/zavút/

4.15 /e/ stressed before plain consonant

In this position the vowel /e/ is like the *e* of English *bet*, although with the tongue slightly lower in the mouth.

DRILL 20

э́то	*this*	/éta/
не́т	*no*	/ṇét/
нале́во	*on the left*	/naḷéva/
оте́ц	*father*	/aṭéc/
о языке́	*about language*	/a yiziḳé/

4.16 Vowels in final position

All of the Russian vowels, regardless of what type of consonant precedes, are particularly short when they occur in final position, whereas English vowels in this position are apt to be lengthened.

DRILL 21

вы́	*you*	/ví/
кафе́	*cafe*	/kafé/
языка́	*language*	/yiziká/
жена́	*wife*	/žiná/
хорошо́	*good*	/xarašó/
письмо́	*letter*	/piṣmó/
пишу́	*write*	/ṛišú/

4.2 Stressed vowels after palatalized consonant

As stated in section **4.1** it is the preceding consonant which is the significant variable for the vowels /i a o u/ but the following consonant which is the significant variable for the vowel /e/. The vowels /i a o u/ after palatalized consonants have a much fronter articulation (i.e., the tongue is farther forward in the mouth) than they do after plain consonants. When both, preceded and followed by palatalized consonants the articulation is even fronter. The vowel /e/ before palatalized consonant has a higher articulation (i.e., the tongue is raised to a higher position in the front of the mouth) than it does before a plain consonant.

4.21 /i/ stressed after palatalized consonant

In this position the vowel /i/ is similar to English *ea* in *beat*. The Russian vowel, however, is shorter and without the glide effect of the English vowel.

DRILL 22

ви́дите	*see*	/yíḍiṭi/
спаси́бо	*thanks*	/spaṣíba/
кни́га	*book*	/ḳṇíga/
мой	*my*	/mayí/
ходи́ть	*go*	/xaḍíṭ/
языки́	*languages*	/yiziḳí/

4.22 /a/ stressed after palatalized consonant

In this position the vowel /a/ is similar to the *a* in *hat*.

DRILL 23

пять	*five*	/páṭ/
взять	*take*	/ẏzáṭ/
взя́ли	*took*	/ẏzáḷi/
дя́дя	*uncle*	/ḍáḍi/
моя́	*my*	/mayá/
сидя́т	*sit*	/ṣiḍát/
говоря́т	*say*	/gavaṛát/

4.23 /o/ stressed after palatalized consonant

In this position the vowel /o/ has a fronter articulation than after plain consonant. This vowel shows less difference in pronunciation in the position after palatalized consonant as against the position after plain consonant than do the vowels /i a u/.

DRILL 24

остаётесь	*remain*	/astayóṭiṣ/
о самолёте	*about the airplane*	/a samaḷóṭi/
живёте	*live*	/žiɣóṭi/
сёстры	*sisters*	/ṣóstri/
моё	*my*	/mayó/
живёт	*lives*	/žiɣót/

4.24 /u/ stressed after palatalized consonant

In this position the vowel /u/ has a fronter articulation than after plain consonants.

DRILL 25

лю́бит	*loves*	/ḷúḅit/
люблю́	*love*	/ḷuḅḷú/
говорю́	*speak*	/gavaṛú/

4.25 /e/ stressed before palatalized consonant

In this position the vowel /e/ is similar to the *a* in English *date*. The Russian sound is a short vowel and does not have the very noticeable glide (y-sound) that the English vowel has.

DRILL 26

де́ти	*children*	/ḍéṭi/
мое́й	*my*	/mayéy/
здесь	*here*	/zḍéṣ/
Аме́рика	*America*	/améṛika/
уме́ю	*can*	/uṃéyu/

4.3 Unstressed vowels after plain consonants

All unstressed vowels in Russian are generally shorter than stressed vowels.

In the case of unstressed vowels there is an extra variable that must be taken into consideration, that is, a distinction must be made between unstressed position immediately before the stress (called *pretonic* position) and all other unstressed positions. In pretonic position vowels are shorter than in stressed position but not as short as in other unstressed positions. Also, in pretonic position the vowel /a/ has a sound quite different from that in other unstressed positions.

After plain consonants Russians generally make use of only three unstressed vowels, which will be indicated in our transcription with the symbols /i a u/. The vowels /e/ and /o/ occur only rarely in unstressed position: first, in a few items borrowed from other languages and second, in a more formal pronunciation of Russian words.

4.31 /i/ unstressed after plain consonant

In this position the vowel /i/ is similar to the *i* in English *bit*, although for Russian the tongue is pulled slightly farther back than in English.

DRILL 27

языка́	*language*	/yiziká/
была́	*was*	/bilá/
жила́	*lived*	/žilá/

311

4.32 /a/ unstressed after plain consonant

This is the vowel for which it is necessary to introduce the extra variable of pretonic position. In pretonic position the vowel /a/ is similar to the *u* in English *but* and in other unstressed positions it is similar to the *a* in English *soda*.

Drill 28

Москва́	*Moscow*	/maskvá/
второ́й	*second*	/ftaróy/
спаси́бо	*thanks*	/spaṣíba/
она́	*she*	/aná/
города́	*cities*	/garadá/
хорошо́	*good*	/xarašó/
повтори́те	*repeat*	/paftaṛíṭi/
молоко́	*milk*	/malakó/
лаборато́рия	*laboratory*	/labaratóṛiya/
го́род	*city*	/górat/
мно́го	*many*	/mnóga/
пра́вда	*truth*	/právda/
за́пад	*west*	/zápat/
ва́ша	*your*	/váša/

4.33 /u/ unstressed after plain consonant

In this position the vowel /u/ is similar to the *u* in English *put*, but with slightly more lip rounding.

Drill 29

тури́ст	*tourist*	/tuṛíst/
ви́жу	*see*	/v̧ížu/
э́ту	*this*	/étu/
фра́зу	*sentence*	/frázu/
го́роду	*city*	/góradu/

4.34 /e o/ unstressed after plain consonant

These vowels occur rarely in this position (cf. **4.3**) and when they do occur are pronounced like their stressed versions (cf. **4.15** and **4.13**).

эта́ж	*floor*	/etáš/ or /itáš/
ра́дио	*radio*	/ráḍio/

4.4   Unstressed vowels after palatalized consonants

After palatalized consonants Russians generally make use of only two unstressed vowels, which will be indicated in our transcription with the symbols /i u/. Another variable is final position after the consonant /y/; in this position there are three vowel sounds used in Russian, indicated by the symbols /i a u/.[1] As noted in section **4.3** the vowels /e/ and /o/ occur only rarely in unstressed position: in borrowed words and in formal pronunciation.

4.41   /i/ unstressed after palatalized consonant

In this position the vowel /i/ is similar to the *i* in English *bit*, but with the tongue raised slightly higher.

DRILL 30

его	*his, him*	/yivó/
её	*her*	/yiyó/
читать	*read*	/čitáṭ/
письмó	*letter*	/piṣmó/
ещё	*still*	/yiščó/
американец	*American*	/amirikáṇic/
писатель	*writer*	/pisáṭiḷ/
видите	*see*	/ víḍiṭi/
любит	*likes*	/ḷúbit/
занят	*busy*	/záṇit/

4.42   /a/ unstressed after palatalized consonant

/a/ unstressed after palatalized consonant, which is generally limited to final position after /y/ (cf. **4.4** and *footnote*) is pronounced like the *a* of English *soda*.

DRILL 31

какая	*what*	/kakáya/
какóе	*what*	/kakóya/
большáя	*big*	/baḷšáya/

4.43   /u/ unstressed after palatalized consonant

In this position the vowel /u/ has a fronter articulation than after plain consonant.

---

[1] There are always variations in the pronunciation of a language, and in the position after palatalized consonants there is a fair amount of variation in the pronunciation of Russian vowels. This is particularly true of unstressed vowels in final position after palatalized consonants, where for some speakers the pronunciation may approximate the spelling more closely than the above statements indicate.

DRILL 32

зна́ю	*know*	/znáyu/
понима́ю	*understand*	/paṇimáyu/
люби́ть	*love*	/ḷub́iṭ/

4.44 /e o/ unstressed after palatalized consonants

These vowels occur rarely in this position and when they do occur are pronounced like their stressed versions (cf. **4.15** and **4.13**).

🌓 5. Stress

Stress is to be identified for the most part with loudness of pronunciation.

Russian has both word stress and phrase stress, word stress being the stress that occurs within the limits of a word and phrase stress the stress that occurs in a group of words spoken without a pause.

5.1 Word stress

In a Russian word one syllable and only one syllable is stressed. This will be indicated in the transcription by an acute accent /'/ over the vowel of that syllable. All other syllables in a word are unstressed. The particular syllable which is stressed in a Russian word is, as in English, unpredictable and must be learned as part of the word.

In English many words occur with a primary and a secondary stress. The primary stress may occur before the secondary or vice versa. In the following English examples the primary stress is marked with an acute /'/ and the secondary with a grave /`/. Thus, in the words '*óperàte, cóncentràte, díctionàry*' the primary stress precedes the secondary. In the words '*òperátion, còncentrátion, biológical*' the primary stress follows the secondary.

In English there may or may not be a secondary stress following the primary stress (e.g., *cóncentràte, cóntinent*), whereas in Russian all syllables following the primary stress are unstressed.

DRILL 33

ви́дите	*see*	/ýíḍiṭi/
понима́ете	*understand*	/paṇimáyiṭi/
гости́ница	*hotel*	/gaṣṭíṇica/
ма́ленького	*small*	/máḷiṇkavá/
зараба́тываете	*earn*	/zarabátivayiṭi/
остана́вливаете	*stop*	/astanáyḷivayiṭi/

In English whenever the primary stress occurs three or more syllables from the beginning of the word there is always a secondary stress either two or three syllables before the primary stress (e.g., *òperátion, phỳsiólogical*), whereas in

Russian all syllables preceding the primary stress are unstressed. Of these unstressed syllables the one immediately preceding the stress (the pretonic syllable) is slightly more prominent (cf. **4.3**). Because English and Russian are so different in this aspect of stress, the student should practice this pattern diligently.

DRILL 34

хорошо́	*good*	/xarašó/
города́	*cities*	/garadá/
молоко́	*milk*	/malakó/
говори́те	*speak*	/gavaṛíṭi/
повтори́те	*repeat*	/paftaṛíṭi/
лаборато́рия	*laboratory*	/labaratóṛiya/
поживáете	*get along*	/paživáyiṭi/
рестора́н	*restaurant*	/ṛistarán/
понима́ю	*understand*	/paṇimáyu/
Ленингра́д	*Leningrad*	/ḷiṇingrát/
перево́дчица	*translator*	/piṛivótčica/
до свида́ния	*goodbye*	/da ṣyidáṇiya/
америка́нец	*American*	/aṃiṛikáṇic/

5.2 Phrase stress

Although Russian does not have a primary and secondary stress within the limits of one word, it does have a primary and one or more secondary stresses within a phrase. In this situation the stressed syllable of one word will be more prominent than the stressed syllable of the other words in the phrase. Also, a small number of words, such as prepositions, may lose their stress completely within a phrase.

The particular word within a phrase that carries primary stress is not predictable, but as in English depends upon the word the speaker wishes to emphasize. This aspect of Russian stress is very similar to English and should not cause the student much difficulty, except for the accompanying intonation pattern (cf. *section* **6**).

DRILL 35

э́та у́лица	*this street*	/èta úḷica/
Э́то—у́лица.	*This is a street.*	/éta úlica/
моя́ жена́	*my wife*	/mayà žiná/
моя́ женà	*my wife*	/mayá žinà/
Мы́ ча́сто говори́м по-ру́сски		/mì částa gavaṛìm pa rùṣḳi/
	We often speak Russian.	

[1] There is a small number of words in Russian, all of them long compound words which are spoken by some people with a secondary stress as well as a primary and by others only with a primary. E.g., желѐзнодоро́жный or железнодоро́жный 'railroad' (adjective).

315

The student should note that in a phrase beginning with a preposition consisting of a single consonant the preposition and the following word are spoken as a single word without pause. Note also the assimilations that take place in such phrases (cf. *Grammar Unit* **3:1.1**).

Drill 36

к окнý	*to the window*	/k aknú/
к отцý	*to father*	/k atcú/
к столý	*to the table*	/k stalú/
к сестрé	*to the sister*	/k șișțŗé/
к брáту	*to the brother*	/g bratú/

в óчереди	*in line*	/v óčiŗiḑi/
в э́том годý	*this year*	/v étam gadú/
в э́той гости́нице	*in this hotel*	/v étay gașțíņici/
в Москвé	*in Moscow*	/v maskvé/
в гóроде	*in town*	/v góraḑi/
в Ки́еве	*in Kiev*	/f ķíyiyi/

с Ивáном	*with Ivan*	/s ivánam/
с э́тими дéвушками	*with these girls*	/s étiṃi ḑévuškaṃi/
с фи́льтром	*with a filter*	/s fíḷtram/

с ни́ми	*with them*	/s ņíṃi/
с Бори́сом	*with Boris*	/z baŗísam/
с женóй	*with the wife*	/ž žinóy/

⏻ 6.   Intonation

In any language variations in the pitch of the voice are used to convey meanings. In English it is useful to distinguish between three pitch levels, high, mid and low; but in Russian, four pitch levels, high, mid, low, and extra high. A particular combination of pitches, hereafter called intonation *contour*, used in a sentence may have different meanings in the two languages. Therefore, the pitches used in Russian sentences should be observed carefully by the student and he should imitate them as closely as possible. In both languages there are a large number of possible intonation contours that have significance, the most important of which are discussed below. The student should listen for other contours.

6.1   Statement

In English a simple statement usually has the following intonation contour, indicated here by a line:

I work in a fáctory.

The statement begins on mid pitch, which continues up to the primary stress. At this point it jumps to high pitch and then drops sharply to end on low pitch.

In Russian a simple statement usually has the following intonation contour:

Я рабòтаю на фа́брике.

The statement begins on mid pitch, jumps to high on the syllable immediately preceding the primary stress, and then on primary stress drops to low. From here to the end of the sentence the pitch may either rise slightly or simply fade away. In English the primary stress has high pitch but in Russian primary stress has low pitch. This is the feature that the student should listen for in Russian and should try to imitate when saying things in Russian.

This contour is the usual one for citing forms.

For this contour and for all those described below, if the sentence begins with primary stress then the contour remains unchanged, i.e., the pitch variations which would otherwise precede the primary stress are simply absent.

DRILL 37

Спаси́бо.	Thank you.
Пожа́луйста.	You're welcome.
Я ви́жу.	I see.
Нале́во.	To the left.
рестора́н	restaurant
гости́ница	hotel
вокза́л	station
письмо́	letter
Это рестора́н.	This is a restaurant.
Рестора́н нале́во.	The restaurant is to the left.
Откро́йте кни́ги.	Open the books.
Гости́ница напра́во.	The hotel is to the right.
Это кафе́.	That's a cafe.
До свида́ния.	Goodbye.

DRILL 38

Я рабòтаю на фа́брике.	I work in a factory.
Я не понима́ю.	I don't understand.
(Кудà вы̀ идёте?) — На вокза́л.	(Where are you going?) — To the station.
Я иду̀ на вокза́л.	I am going to the station.
Её му́ж — профèссор ру̀сского языка́.	Her husband is a professor of Russian.
Я здèсь учи́лась.	I studied here.
Архитекту̀ра не похòжа на за́падную.	The architecture is not like western (architecture).

317

Russian also uses the intonation contour described above for English, but it then implies abruptness or contrast. Thus the Russian **спасибо** with the intonation contour described above as the normal one for Russian, i.e.,

Спасибо.

is the polite way of saying *thank you*, but spoken with the contour described as the normal one for English, i.e.,

Спасибо

implies abruptness or some degree of impoliteness.

An example showing contrast is:

Я работаю на фабрике (а не в ресторане)

The normal Russian intonation for a statement also occurs in English but it implies boredom. For example, it is the most common way of saying in English:

I don't cáre.

DRILL 39

Я работаю на фабрике (а не в ресторане).
Спасибо.
Это не ресторан, это кафе.

I work in a *factory* (not in a restaurant).
Thanks.
That's not a restaurant, that's a *cafe*.

6.2 Questions with interrogative words

Questions introduced by an interrogative word (e.g., 'where, when, how', etc.) in both English and Russian have the same intonation pattern as for a statement.

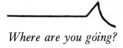

Where are you góing?

Куда́ вы́ идёте?

DRILL 40

Где́ рестора́н?	Where is the restaurant?
Ка́к вы́ пожива́ете?	How are you?
Что́ э́то нале́во?	What's that on the left?
Где́ гости́ница?	Where is the hotel?
Где́ письмо́ от Ива́на?	Where is the letter from Ivan?
Что́ э́то?	What's that?

DRILL 41

Куда́ вы́ идёте?	Where are you going?
Что́ вы́ хоти́те?	What do you want?
Ско́лько они́ сто́ят?	How much do they cost?
Когда́ вы бу́дете гото́вы?	When will you be ready?
Что́ у него́ в рука́х?	What does he have in his hands?

6.3 Questions without interrogative words

In English such a question has the following intonation contour:

Is she a téacher?

The pitch of the voice begins on mid pitch, jumps·to high on the primary stress, and at the end of the sentence there is a slight rise.

In Russian there are several contours that may occur with such questions, the most important of which is the following:

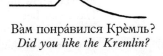

Ва̀м понра́вился Крѐмль?
Did you like the Kremlin?

319

The sentence begins on mid pitch and jumps to extra high pitch on the primary stress, thereafter falling to low pitch. Since this question contour is rather similar to a type of statement contour in English (cf. **6.1** above), it is a type that an American may interpret as a statement rather than as a question. Therefore, the student should listen to this contour carefully and practice imitating it if he is to avoid misinterpreting Russian questions or being misinterpreted.

In those cases where the last syllable in the sentence carries primary stress there is a jump to extra high pitch on that syllable, the syllable is cut off very sharply, and since there is nothing following this syllable there is no drop. Compare the following sentences, one in English and the other in Russian:

Is that só?

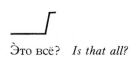

Э́то всё?   *Is that all?*

Note that the Russian stressed syllable is higher pitched than the English stressed syllable, that the pitch on that syllable is level in Russian whereas in English it continues to rise, and that in Russian the final vowel is sharply cut off, whereas in English the final vowel is long and drawled.

DRILL 42

Interrogative intonation with stressed final syllable

Э́то всё?	Is that all?
А вы́?	And you?
Э́то кафе́?	Is that a cafe?
Рестора́н та́м?	Is the restaurant there?
О́н здесь?	Is he here?
Э́то хорошо́?	Is that OK?

DRILL 43

Interrogative intonation with non-final primary stress

Ва́м понра́вился Кре́мль?	Did you like the Kremlin?
Вы́ его́ зна́ете?	Do you know him?
Вы́ давно́ здесь?	Have you been here for a long time?
Дороги́е у ва́с сигаре́ты?	Are your cigarettes expensive?
Высо́кие здесь це́ны?	Are the prices high here?

Вы видели Успенский собор?	Did you see the Uspensky cathedral?
Он живёт в Ленинграде?	Does he live in Leningrad?
Киев большой город?	Is Kiev a big city?
У вас всё ещё отпуск?	Are you still on vacation?

6.4 Other interrogative contours

There are other interrogative contours in Russian, but they do not occur with such high frequency as the one discussed above in **6.3**. The student should listen for these contours and imitate them when he hears them.

One type is the following:

Вы часто получаете от неё письма? *Do you often get letters from her?*

This contour is like the one discussed in **6.3** where there is a jump to extra high pitch on the syllable with primary stress, but differs from it in that the pitch remains on this high level instead of dropping. This contour is similar to the common English interrogative contour without a question word except that the pitch is extra high instead of high and that it does not rise at the end, as does the English contour.

Another interrogative contour is the following:

Она учительница?
Is she a teacher?

This contour is characterized by a drop on primary stress followed by a rise rather than a jump to a higher pitch followed by a level or falling pitch.

The illustrative sentences in this section can, and are very likely to be, spoken with the more frequent contour described in **6.3**.

APPENDIX

Appendix

The statements made in this appendix are true for the language as a whole but are exhaustive only for the forms occurring in the Conversation Lessons and Grammar Units of the text. Forms occurring in the Reading sections of the Review Lessons are not included in the appendix, since they are intended for passive knowledge rather than active use.

◐ 1.   Nouns and adjectives

Listed below are the endings of Russian nouns and adjectives written in terms of basic vowels. For conversational purposes it is helpful to learn this chart horizontally rather than vertically, i.e., to learn the combination of adjective and noun ending for a particular case form, since that is what must be used in conversation.

Except for feminine singular adjectives and nouns, the accusative case is identical to the genitive for animate nouns and identical to the nominative case for inanimate nouns.

Masculine and neuter nouns each have two variant endings in the genitive plural. The variant -Ey occurs with stems ending in a palatalized consonant (except /y/) or /š ž/.

Neuter differs from masculine only in the nominative singular, nominative plural, and genitive plural.

The symbol # means zero ending.

	Adj.	Noun				
Masc. Sing.						
NOM.	-*Oy*	-#				
GEN.	-*OvO*	-*A*				
DAT.	-*O*mu	-*U*				
ACC.	N/G	N/G				
INST.	-*Im*	-*O*m				
LOC.	-*O*m	;*E*				
Neut. Sing.						
NOM.	-*O*ya	-*O*				
Fem. Sing.			Fem. ii			
NOM.	-*A*ya	-*A*	-#			
GEN.	-*Oy*	-*I*	-*I*			
DAT.	-*Oy*	;*E*	-*I*			
ACC.	-*Uy*u	-*U*	-#			
INST.	-*Oy*	-*Oy*	-yu			
LOC.	-*Oy*	;*E*	-*I*			
Plural		Masc.	Neut.	Fem. i	Fem. ii	
NOM.	-*Iy*a	-*I*	-*A*	-*I*	-*I*	
GEN.	-*Ix*	-*Of*/-*Ey*	-#/-*Ey*	-#	-*Ey*	
DAT.	-*Im*		-*A*m			
ACC.	N/G		N/G			
INST.	-*I*ṃi		-*A*ṃi			
LOC.	-*Ix*		-*A*x			

1.1   Adjectives

The adjective **молодóй** *young* may serve as a typical example of the writing of the adjective endings when stressed after a non-palatalized consonant (other than **ш, ж, к, г, х**). The endings of all other adjectives are predictable from this on the basis of the spelling rules given in the Grammar Units. Such spelling variants are not considered irregularities.

	Masc.	Neut.	Fem.	Plur.
NOM.	молодóй	молодóе	молодáя	молоды́е
GEN.	молодóго		молодóй	молоды́х
DAT.	молодóму		молодóй	молоды́м
ACC.	N/G		молодýю	N/G
INST.	молоды́м		молодóй	молоды́ми
LOC.	молодóм		молодóй	молоды́х

Spelling variants

Although the spelling of the endings of all other adjectives is predictable from **молодóй**, the following examples illustrate all of the variations that may occur in the spelling of Russian adjective endings.

Нóвый *new*.   Stem final plain consonant (other than **ш, ж, к, г, х**) with unstressed ending.

NOM. SING. MASC. нóвый.

All other cases: identical to those of **молодóй**.

Си́ний *blue*.   Stem final palatalized consonant (other than **ч, щ**). This type occurs only with unstressed endings. There are very few adjectives of this type in Russian. The only ones that occur in this text are: **си́ний** *blue*, **послéдний** *last*.

	Masc.	Neut.	Fem.	Plur.
NOM.	си́ний	си́нее	си́няя	си́ние
GEN.	си́него		си́ней	си́них
DAT.	си́нему		си́ней	си́ним
ACC.	N/G		си́нюю	N/G
INST.	си́ним		си́ней	си́ними
LOC.	си́нем		си́ней	си́них

Большóй *big*.   Stressed ending with stem final **к, г, х, ч, ж, ш, щ**. The spelling of these endings is exactly like that of молодóй except that **-ы-** is replaced by **-и-**.

327

	Masc.		Neut.	Fem.	Plur.
NOM.	большо́й	большо́е		больша́я	больши́е
GEN.	большо́го			большо́й	больши́х
DAT.	большо́му			большо́й	больши́м
ACC.	N/G			большу́ю	N/G
INST.	больши́м			большо́й	больши́ми
LOC.	большо́м			большо́й	больши́х

Ру́сский *Russian.* Unstressed ending with stem final **к, г, х**. The spelling of these endings is identical to that of но́вый except that **-ы-** is replaced by **-и-**

	Masc.		Neut.	Fem.	Plur.
NOM.	ру́сский	ру́сское		ру́сская	ру́сские
GEN.	ру́сского			ру́сской	ру́сских
DAT.	ру́сскому			ру́сской	ру́сским
ACC.	N/G			ру́сскую	N/G
INST.	ру́сским			ру́сской	ру́сскими
LOC.	ру́сском			ру́сской	ру́сских

Хоро́ший *good.* Unstressed ending with stem final **ч, ж, ш, щ**. The spelling of these endings is identical to that of ру́сский except that **-о-** is replaced by **-е-**.

	Masc.		Neut.	Fem.	Plur.
NOM.	хоро́ший	хоро́шее		хоро́шая	хоро́шие
GEN.	хоро́шего			хоро́шей	хоро́ших
DAT.	хоро́шему			хоро́шей	хоро́шим
ACC.	N/G			хоро́шую	N/G
INST.	хоро́шим			хоро́шей	хоро́шими
LOC.	хоро́шем			хоро́шей	хоро́ших

1.2 Special adjectives

There is a small number of adjectives which differ from ordinary adjectives in that the nominative forms and the accusative singular feminine form have noun endings and all the other forms have adjective endings. Another characteristic of special adjectives is that the stem final consonant before the basic vowel *I* is palatalized where possible.

Э́тот *this,* **оди́н** *one.*

The main type of special adjective inflection is illustrated by the following paradigm.

	Masc.	Neut.	Fem.	Plur.
NOM.	э́тот	э́то	э́та	э́ти
GEN.	э́того		э́той	э́тих
DAT.	э́тому		э́той	э́тим
ACC.	N/G		э́ту	N/G
INST.	э́тим		э́той	э́тими
LOC.	э́том		э́той	э́тих

The endings of the special adjective **оди́н** are identical to those of **э́тот** but the stress pattern is that of **мо́й**.

Ва́ш, *your*, на́ш *our*.

These special adjectives have the same endings as those of э́тот but by the regular spelling convention replace the **-о-** of the ending by **-е-**.

	Masc.	Neut.	Fem.	Plur.
NOM.	ва́ш	ва́ше	ва́ша	ва́ши
GEN.	ва́шего		ва́шей	ва́ших
DAT.	ва́шему		ва́шей	ва́шим
ACC.	N/G		ва́шу	N/G
INST.	ва́шим		ва́шей	ва́шими
LOC.	ва́шем		ва́шей	ва́ших

Тре́тий *third*.

This special adjective has endings the same as э́тот and ва́ш which means that by regular spelling convention the endings are written like those of ва́ш, except that where **ва́ш** has **-а**, **-у**, **тре́тий** has **-я**, **-ю**.

	Masc.	Neut.	Fem.	Plur.
NOM.	тре́тий	тре́тье	тре́тья	тре́тьи
GEN.	тре́тьего		тре́тьей	тре́тьих
DAT.	тре́тьему		тре́тьей	тре́тьим
ACC.	N/G		тре́тью	N/G
INST.	тре́тьим		тре́тьей	тре́тьими
LOC.	тре́тьем		тре́тьей	тре́тьих

Мо́й *my*, тво́й *your*, сво́й *one's own*.

These special adjectives have the stressed ending *-Ey* where ordinary adjectives have *-Oy*. The rest of the endings are the same as those of э́тот but follow the regular spelling conventions.

	Masc.	Neut.	Fem.	Plur.
NOM.	мóй	моё	моя́	мóи
GEN.	моегó		моéй	мои́х
DAT.	моемý		моéй	мои́м
ACC.	N/G		мою́	N/G
INST.	мои́м		моéй	мои́ми
LOC.	моём		моéй	мои́х

Тóт *that.*

This special adjective has **-e-** where the other special adjectives have **-и-**.

	Masc.	Neut.	Fem.	Plur.
NOM.	тóт	тó	тá	тé
GEN.	тогó		тóй	тéх
DAT.	томý		тóй	тéм
ACC.	N/G		тý	N/G
INST.	тéм		тóй	тéми
LOC.	тóм		тóй	тéх

Вéсь *all.*

Like тóт this special adjective replaces **-и-** by **-e-** and in addition has stressed -*E*y instead of the regular -*O*y.

	Masc.	Neut.	Fem.	Plur.
NOM.	вéсь	всё	вся́	всé
GEN.	всегó		всéй	всéх
DAT.	всемý		всéй	всéм
ACC.	N/G		всю́	N/G
INST.	всéм		всéй	всéми
LOC.	всём		всéй	всéх

Сáм *self.*

The endings of this special adjective are identical with those of оди́н except that the accusative singular feminine, besides the regular form **самý** has the somewhat archaic variants **самоё** and **самýю**. The stress is on the ending in all forms except the nominative plural **сáми**.

There are some other adjectives that have the inflection of special adjectives. Most of them refer to animals. The spelling of the endings is identical with that of трéтий. The only one that occurs in the text is **барáний** *mutton.*

1.3   Nouns

Like in adjectives there are variations in noun endings based on spelling rules. These variations are not irregularities. Nor is the predictable occurence of the ending **-ей** (in the genitive plural of masculine and neuter nouns having a stem ending in a palatalized consonant other than /у/ or **ш, ж**) considered an irregularity.

Unlike adjectives, nouns show irregularities of various kinds. The position of stress is a special kind of irregularity which must be learned along with the noun. It will not be discussed here (cf. *Grammar Unit* **3:2.2** and **4:1.4**).

1.31   Regular nouns

The endings of the four regular noun classes are illustrated below.

	Masc.	Neut.	Fem. i	Fem. ii
Singular				
NOM.	стόл	слόво	женá	модéль
GEN.	столá	слόва	женьí	модéли
DAT.	столý	слόву	женé	модéли
ACC.	стόл	слόво	женý	модéль
INST.	столόм	слόвом	женόй	модéлью
LOC.	столé	слόве	женé	модéли
Plural				
NOM.	стольí	словá	жёны	модéли
GEN.	столόв	слόв	жён	модéлей
DAT.	столáм	словáм	жёнам	модéлям
ACC.	стольí	словá	жён	модéли
INST.	столáми	словáми	жёнами	модéлями
LOC.	столáх	словáх	жёнах	модéлях

The statements given below are simply restatements of the spelling rules given in Grammar Units 1, 2, and 3, and include no new information.

Spelling Variation in Regular Nouns

1) Stem final palatalized consonant (other than **ч, щ**, and /у/).

The first three noun types given above have variants with a stem final palatalized consonant. These variants have the same basic endings except for the genitive plural of masculines and neuters, which have the ending **-ей**. They are therefore written according to the spelling rules: **a** is replaced by **я, у** by **ю, ы** by **и, o** by **e** when unstressed and by **ё** when stressed, and **ь** written where there is no ending.

	MASC.	NEUT.	FEM.
SINGULAR			
NOM.	писа́тель	мо́ре	неде́ля
GEN.	писа́теля	мо́ря	неде́ли
DAT.	писа́телю	мо́рю	неде́ле
ACC.	писа́теля	мо́ре	неде́лю
INST.	писа́телем	мо́рем	неде́лей
LOC.	писа́теле	мо́ре	неде́ле
PLURAL			
NOM.	писа́тели	моря́	неде́ли
GEN.	писа́телей	море́й	неде́ль
DAT.	писа́телям	моря́м	неде́лям
ACC.	писа́телей	моря́	неде́ли
INST.	писа́телями	моря́ми	неде́лями
LOC.	писа́телях	моря́х	неде́лях

2) Stem final **к, г, х.**

The spelling of nouns ending in these consonants is identical to that of the first three main types except that **ы** is replaced by **и.**

E.g., **жена́** *wife*, жены́ but **кни́га** *book*, кни́ги.

3) Stem final **ц.**

The spelling of nouns ending in **ц** is identical to that of the first three types except that **o** is replaced by **e** when unstressed.

E.g., **письмо́** *letter*, письмо́м, but **со́лнце** *sun*, со́лнцем; **сто́л** *table*, столо́м and stressed **оте́ц** *father*, отцо́м.

4) Stem final **ч, ж, ш, щ.**

The spelling of nouns ending in these consonants is identical to that of the first three main types except that **o** is replaced by **e** when unstressed, and **ы** is always replaced by **и.**

E.g., **стол** *table*, столы́, столо́м but **това́рищ** *comrade*, това́рищи, това́рищем.

The spelling of nouns of feminine II ending in **чь, жь, шь,** and **щь** is like that of the main type of fem. II nouns except that **я** is replaced by **a.**

E.g., **моде́ль** *model*, моде́лями, but **ве́щь** *thing*, веща́ми.

5) Stems ending in /y/

These nouns have the genitive plural ending in -*Of* for masculines and have no ending for neuters and feminines. Therefore, those forms which do not have an ending, i.e., the nominative singular of masculines and the genitive plural of neuters and feminines, are written with **й.**

E.g., NOM. SG. MASC. трамва́**й** *streetcar*, GEN. PL. **трамва́ев.**

NOM. SG. NEUT. **зда́ние** *building*, GEN. PL. зда́ний.

NOM. SG. FEM. **лаборато́рия** *lab*, GEN. PL. лаборато́рий.

NOM. SG. FEM. **статья́** *article*, GEN. PL. стате́й

(with the inserted vowel **-e-**).

Nouns with nominative singular in **-ий**, **-ие** and **-ия** have the additional peculiarity that the locative singular of all three genders and the dative singular of feminines is spelled **-ии**.

E.g., **зда́ние** *building*, LOC. SG. зда́нии.

лаборато́рия *lab*, LOC. SG. and DAT. SG. лаборато́рии.

Otherwise the endings of nouns with a stem final /y/ are spelled like the three basic types ending in a palatalized consonant.

E.g., NOM. SG. мо́р**е** and зда́**ние**.

GEN. SG. мо́р**я** and зда́**ния**.

1.32   Irregular nouns

There is a large number of nouns that basically follow the regular pattern described above but which have one or more case forms that are irregular.

There are three types of irregularity: irregularity in stress, in the form of the stem, and in the form of the endings.

Stress may occur either on the stem of a noun or on the ending. The position in which stress occurs in one form of the singular (or of the plural) is generally the position in which it will occur in the other forms of the singular (or of the plural). The position of stress in the singular is not predictable from the position of stress in the plural or vice versa. This type of variation in stress pattern is of high frequency in the language, must be learned along with the noun, and will not here be considered an irregularity. It should be noted that from a form that has no ending, such as some nominative singulars and genitive plurals, it cannot be predicted whether the noun is a stressed stem type or a stressed ending type. (For details, see *Grammar Unit* **3:2.2** and **4:1.4**.)

Most irregularities in the form of the stem involve a plural stem different from the singular stem. However, one common variation in stem is the insertion of a vowel before the last consonant of the stem when no ending follows. This must simply be learned along with the noun. It will not be considered an irregularity here.

The irregularities in the form of the endings are limited to genitive singular, locative singular, nominative plural, genitive plural and instrumental plural.

In addition, there are a few nouns which have a radically different inflection from the regular pattern described in **1.31** above.

1.321   Irregularities in stress

1) Accusative singular of feminine I nouns

Some feminine I nouns which are basically of a stressed ending type in the singular have an accusative singular with stress on the stem, e.g., рука́ hand,

333

Acc. Sg. ру́ку. The nouns of this type which have occurred in the text are:

рука́	hand
гора́	hill, mountain
стена́	wall
зима́	winter
среда́	Wednesday

2) Nominative plural

Some nouns which are basically of the stressed ending type in the plural have the stress on the stem in the nominative plural (and in the accusative if it is like the nominative). E.g., рука́ *hand*, Nom. Pl. ру́ки, Inst. Pl. рука́ми. Nouns of this type which have occurred in the text are:

рука́	hand	че́тверть	quarter
гора́	hill, mountain	но́чь	night
стена́	wall	ма́ть	mother
среда́	Wednesday	го́д	year
ве́щь	thing	де́ньги	money
о́чередь	line, queue		

3) Genitive plural

Some nouns which are basically of the stressed stem type in the plural have the stress on the last syllable in the genitive plural, e.g., **сестра́** *sister*, Nom. Pl. сёстры, Gen. Pl. сестёр.

сестра́	sister	лю́ди	people
семья́	family	де́ти	children

Some nouns which are basically of a stressed ending type have a genitive plural with stress on the stem, but not on the last available syllable of that stem. Only one noun of this type occurs in the text:

NOM.-ACC.	де́ньги	*money*
GEN.	де́нег	
DAT.	деньга́м	
INST.	деньга́ми	
LOC.	деньга́х	

1.322 Irregularities in the form of the stem

1) Plural stem

Some nouns have a stem in the plural which is different from the stem in the singular.

Some nouns have an additional /y/ in the plural:

NOM. SG.		NOM. PL.
бра́т	brother	бра́тья

му́ж	husband	мужья́
дру́г	friend	друзья́
сы́н	son	сыновья́
сту́л	chair	сту́лья

Some nouns lose the syllable **-ин-** in the plural:

NOM. SG.		NOM. PL.
граждани́н	citizen, Mr.	гра́ждане
господи́н	Mr.	господа́

Some nouns have a singular stem which is frequently replaced by a different form in the plural:

NOM. SG.		NOM. PL.
ребёнок	child	**де́ти**
челове́к	man, person	**лю́ди** (but Gen. Pl. **челове́к** after numerals five and above)

2) Genitive Plural

One noun, **го́д**, has a stem which is replaced by an entirely different form, **ле́т**, in the genitive plural after numerals above five and quantity words.

3) Nominative and accusative singular

Some nouns have a stem in the nominative and accusative singular which is shorter than the stem in all other case forms.

NOM.-ACC. SG.	ма́ть	mother
GEN. SG.	ма́тери	

1.323 Irregularities in the form of the endings

1) Second genitive

Some masculine nouns have a second genitive in -*U* besides the regular genitive in -*A* (cf. *Conversation Lesson* **14**).

NOM. SG.		SECOND GEN.	REGULAR GEN.
су́п	soup	су́пу	су́па
ча́й	tea	ча́ю	ча́я
са́хар	sugar	са́хару	са́хара

2) Second locative

Some masculine nouns have a second locative in stressed -*U* besides the regular locative in -*E* (cf. *Grammar Unit* **9:3**).

NOM. SG.		SECOND LOC.	REGULAR LOC.
о́тпуск	vacation	отпуску́	о́тпуске
ча́с	hour	часу́	ча́се
ви́д	view	виду́	ви́де
аэропо́рт	airport	аэропорту́	аэропо́рте
го́д	year	году́	го́де
шка́ф	cupboard, wardrobe	шкафу́	шка́фе

3) Nominative plural

Some masculine nouns have a nominative plural ending *-A* instead of the regular *-I*.

NOM. SG.		NOM. PL.
учи́тель	teacher	учителя́
господи́н	Mr.	господа́
го́род	city	города́
профе́ссор	professor	профессора́
до́ктор	doctor	доктора́
до́м	house	дома́
по́езд	train	поезда́
ве́чер	evening	вечера́
бра́т	brother	бра́тья
му́ж	husband	мужья́
дру́г	friend	друзья́
сы́н	son	сыновья́
сту́л	chair	сту́лья

Some masculine nouns have the nominative plural ending *-E* instead of the regular *-I*.

NOM. SG.		NOM. PL.
граждани́н	Mr., sir, citizen	гра́ждане

4) Genitive plural

Some masculine nouns have no ending in the genitive plural where the ending *-Of* is expected. Note that when the plural stem final consonant is /y/ the vowel **-e-** is inserted.

NOM. SG.		GEN. PL.
ра́з	time	ра́з
му́ж	husband	муже́й
дру́г	friend	друзе́й
сы́н	son	сы亞́й
челове́к	man, person	челове́к
граждани́н	Mr., sir, citizen	гра́ждан
господи́н	Mr.	госпо́д

The noun **дя́дя** uncle, which has feminine forms and which would therefore be expected to have no ending in the genitive plural, has instead the ending **-ей**, **дя́дей**.

The following feminine nouns have the expected zero ending in the genitive plural. However, because they have the inserted vowel **-е-** the genitive plural is spelled **-ей**, which is confusing because this makes it look like the ending **-ей** rather than zero.

Nom. Sg.		Nom. Pl.	Gen. Pl.
статья́	article	статьи́	стате́й
семья́	family	се́мьи	семе́й

5) Instrumental plural

Some nouns have the ending /-mi/ in the instrumental plural instead of the regular /-ami/.

Nom. Pl.		Inst. Pl.
лю́ди	people	людьми́
де́ти	children	детьми́

1.324 Other inflections

Вре́мя *time*

	Singular	Plural
NOM.	вре́мя	времена́
GEN.	вре́мени	времён
DAT.	вре́мени	времена́м
ACC.	вре́мя	времена́
INST.	вре́менем	времена́ми
LOC.	вре́мени	времена́х

There is a small number of other nouns which have the above inflection. All of them are neuter.

Пу́ть *path, way*

	Singular	Plural
NOM.	пу́ть	пути́
GEN.	пути́	путе́й
DAT.	пути́	путя́м
ACC.	пу́ть	пути́
INST.	путём	путя́ми
LOC.	пути́	путя́х

The above noun has essentially the inflection of a feminine II noun but it is masculine and has a masculine instrumental singular ending. It is the only noun of this type in the language.

Family names in **-ов** and **-ин**.

The endings of these family names in the masculine singular are the same as those of a masculine noun except for the instrumental singular, which has an adjective ending. The endings in the feminine singular and in the plural are the same as those of ordinary adjectives except in the nominative and accusative feminine singular and the nominative plural, which have noun endings.

	MASC.		FEM.		PLUR.	
NOM.	Ильи́н	Mr. Ilyin	Ильина́	Mrs., Miss Ilyin	Ильины́	the Ilyins
GEN.	Ильина́		Ильино́й		Ильины́х	
DAT.	Ильину́		Ильино́й		Ильины́м	
ACC.	Ильина́		Ильину́		Ильины́х	
INST.	Ильины́м		Ильино́й		Ильины́ми	
LOC.	Ильине́		Ильино́й		Ильины́х	

☯ 2 Pronouns

The pronouns of the first and second persons are:

	I	*you* (Sg.)	*we*	*you* (Pl.)
NOM.	я	ты́	мы́	вы́
GEN.	меня́	тебя́	на́с	ва́с
DAT.	мне́	тебе́	на́м	ва́м
ACC.	меня́	тебя́	на́с	ва́с
INST.	мно́й	тобо́й	на́ми	ва́ми
LOC.	мне́	тебе́	на́с	ва́с

The reflexive pronoun is identical to the second person singular pronoun but has no nominative form.

NOM.	----
GEN.	себя́
DAT.	себе́
ACC.	себя́
INST.	собо́й
LOC.	себе́

The endings of the third person pronoun are very similar to those of adjectives.

	he, it	*it*	*she, it*	*they*
NOM.	о́н	оно́	она́	они́
GEN.		его́	её	и́х
DAT.		ему́	е́й	и́м

ACC.	егó	её	йх
INST.	йм	éй	йми
LOC.	нём	нéй	нйх

Other pronouns:

	who	*what*
NOM	ктó	чтó
GEN.	когó	чегó
DAT.	комý	чемý
ACC.	когó	чтó
INST.	кéм	чéм
LOC.	кóм	чéм

3. Verbs

The Russian verb system is composed of an infinitive; past, non-past and future tense forms; imperative mood; four participles and two gerunds. The participles and gerunds are not included in this text because for the most part they occur rarely in the spoken language.

From the infinitive and the third person non-past it is generally possible to make up all other forms of a Russian verb, and therefore these two forms should be learned for each verb. Besides this, it is necessary to know which verbs make up an aspect pair.

Compound verbs, i.e., those verbs formed from simple verbs by the addition of a prefix, normally have the same endings as the simple verbs they are made from.

Reflexive verbs are likewise inflected like their non-reflexive counterparts.

Any perfective verb with the prefix **вы-** has the stress on that prefix in all forms of the verb.

3.1 Infinitive

The infinitive is the citation form of verbs, that form which is cited in dictionaries. Most verbs have the infinitive ending **-ть**, a small number have **-тй** and a very small number **-чь**.

3.2 Past tense

The past tense form of most verbs can be formed from the infinitive by substituting the past suffixes **-л, -ла, -ло, -ли,** for the infinitive suffix **-ть**. This type will be considered regular.

There are irregularities in form and in stress.

3.21 Irregularities in form

Verbs with an infinitive in **-чь** have a stem ending in either **к** or **г** which will show up in the third person non-past. This stem is used as the stem of

339

the past tense, but with the further irregularity that the **-л** of the masculine form is absent. The only verb of this type occurring in the text is:

мо́чь *to be able*, мо́гут; мо́г, могла́, могло́, могли́.

Verbs with an infinitive ending in **-сть** or **-ти́** have a stem with a consonant which shows in the third person plural non-past. If this final consonant of stem is **-т-** or **-д-**, then the past will be formed by the addition of the usual past suffixes to the stem without the final -т- or -д-. Thus:

кла́сть *to put*, кладу́т; кла́л, кла́ла, кла́ло, кла́ли.

Other verbs of this type occurring in the text are:

упа́сть *to fall*, упаду́т; упа́л, упа́ла, упа́ло, упа́ли.

éсть *to eat*, едя́т; éл, éла, éло, éли.

If the final consonant of the stem is not -т- or -д-, then this stem is used as the stem for the past tense, but with the further irregularity that the -л of the masculine form is absent.

принести́ *to bring*, принесу́т; **принёс,** принесла́, принесло́, принесли́.

The verb **итти́** *to go* has the irregular past forms **шёл, шла́, шло́, шли́.**

Verbs with an infinitive in **-ереть** form the past stem by dropping -еть but with the additional irregularity that the -л of the masculine form is lacking.

умере́ть *to die*, у́мер, умерла́, у́мерло, у́мерли.

3.22 Irregularities in stress

Normally the stress in the past tense is on the same syllable as in the infinitive. The following irregularities occur:

1) Stress on the last syllable.

E.g., **мо́чь** *to be able*, мо́г, могла́, могло́, могли́.

Similarly:

итти́ *to go*, шёл, шла́, шло́, шли́.
принести́ *to bring*, принёс, принесла́, принесло́, принесли́.

2) Stress on the suffix in the feminine and on the stem in the other forms:

E.g., **зва́ть** *to call*, зва́л, звала́, зва́ло, зва́ли.

Similarly:

жи́ть	to live	взя́ть	to take
бы́ть	to be	жда́ть	to wait
да́ть	to give	бра́ть	to take
пи́ть	to drink		

3) Stress on the suffix in the feminine and on the prefix in the other forms:

E.g., **отда́ть** *to give back*, о́тдал, отдала́, о́тдало, о́тдали.

Similarly:

пода́ть	to serve	поня́ть	to understand
прода́ть	to sell	приня́ть	to accept
умере́ть	to die		

4) Stress on the reflexive suffix in the masculine and on the past tense suffix in the other forms:

нача́ться *to begin*, начался́, начала́сь, начало́сь, начали́сь.
прода́ться *to be sold*, продался́, продала́сь, продало́сь, продали́сь.

3.3 Non-past tense

3.31 Endings

The endings of the non-past tense can be formed from the third person plural non-past form. This holds true for all verbs of the language except four: **да́ть** *to give*, **хоте́ть** *to want*, **éсть** *to eat*, and **бежа́ть** *to run*.

There are two types of inflection for non-past tense, referred to as type I and type II. Type I is characterized by the third plural ending **-ут/-ют** and type II by the ending **-ат/-ят**.

TYPE I	STRESSED	UNSTRESSED	
1 SG.	-U	/-u/	-у (-ю)
2 SG.	⁻Oš	/⁻iš/	-ешь
3 SG.	⁻Ot	/⁻it/	-ет
1 PL.	⁻Om	/⁻im/	-ем
2 PL.	⁻Oți	/⁻iți/	-ете
3 PL.	-Ut	/-ut/	-ут (-ют)

The spelling of the vowel in the first singular is identical to that of the third plural for type I verbs. If the letter preceding the ending is a vowel letter, the third plural is always **-ют**; if a consonant, usually **-ут**, rarely **-ют**.

If the ending is stressed, the basic vowel *O* is spelled **ё** instead of **e**.

The asterisks mean that a stem final **к** or **г** will change to **ч** or **ж** respectively, and that other stem final consonants are palatalized if possible. For example, **мо́чь** *to be able*, мо́гут, мо́жете, etc.; **принести́** *to bring*, принесу́т, принесёте, etc.

TYPE II	STRESSED	UNSTRESSED	
1 SG.	⁻U	/⁻u/	-ю (-у)
2 SG.	-Iš	/-iš/	-ишь
3 SG.	-It	/-it/	-ит
1 PL.	-Im	/-im/	-им
2 PL.	-Iți	/-iți/	-ите
3 PL.	-At	/-it/	-ят (-ат)

After the letters **ч**, **ж**, **ш**, **щ** the verb forms of type II are spelled with **-у-** and **-а-** according to the spelling rules, but otherwise the spelling is **-ю-** and **-я-**.

The asterisk with the first singular ending means:

1. A stem final consonant **п**, **б**, **м**, **в**, or **ф** is replaced by that consonant plus an extra **-л-** before the first singular ending, e.g., **купи́ть** *to buy*, ку́пят, but куплю́; **люби́ть** *to love*, лю́бят but люблю́.

2. A stem final consonant **т**, **д**, **с**, **з**, **ст** is replaced by **ч**, **ж**, **ш**, **ж**, **щ** respectively. In some verbs **т** is replaced by **щ**.

E.g., **встре́тить** *to meet*, встре́тят, but встре́чу.

ходи́ть *to go*, хо́дят, but хожу́.
спроси́ть *to ask*, спро́сят, but спрошу́.

IRREGULAR VERBS.

There are four verbs in the language with irregular non-past endings. Of these all except бежа́ть have occurred in the text.

	да́ть *to give*	**éсть** *to eat*	**хоте́ть** *to want*
1 SG.	да́м	éм	хочу́
2 SG.	да́шь	éшь	хо́чешь
3 SG.	да́ст	éст	хо́чет
1 PL.	дади́м	еди́м	хоти́м
2 PL.	дади́те	еди́те	хоти́те
3 PL.	даду́т	едя́т	хотя́т

бежа́ть *to run*
бегу́
бежи́шь
бежи́т
бежи́м
бежи́те
бегу́т

3.32 Stems

Although it is generally necessary to learn two forms for a verb, the infinitive and the third person plural non-past, for many verbs the non-past form (but not the position of stress) can be predicted from the infinitive. There are four such classes of verbs:

1. Verbs with an infinitive ending in **-ить**, if they are not monosyllabic roots, have type II inflection.
говори́ть *to talk* говоря́т.

2. Verbs with an infinitive ending in **-нуть** have type I inflection.

верну́ть *to return* верну́т.

3. Verbs with an infinitive ending in **-ывать** or **-ивать** have type I inflection.

пока́зывать *to show* пока́зыва**ют**.

4. Verbs with an infinitive ending in **-овать** have type I inflection and have **-у-** in the non-past stem replacing **-ов-** in the infinitive stem.

путеше́ств**ова**ть *to travel* путеше́ств**уют**.

Further, by far the majority of verbs with an infinitive in **-ать** or **-ять** have type I inflection in **-ают** or **-яют**, respectively.

зна́ть *to know* зна́**ют**.

For all other verbs two stems must be learned. The following list includes all verbs occurring in the text except the five classes discussed above:

боя́ться, боя́тся	to be afraid
бра́ть, беру́т	to take
взя́ть, возьму́т	to take
вы́держать, вы́держат	to pass (an exam)
дава́ть, даю́т	to give
е́хать, е́дут	to go
жда́ть, ждут	to wait
заказа́ть, зака́жут, закажу́	to order
зва́ть, зову́т	to call
иска́ть, и́щут, ищу́	to look for
лежа́ть, лежа́т	to lie
каза́ться, ка́жутся, кажу́сь	to seem
наде́яться, наде́ются	to hope
нача́ть, начну́т	to begin
остава́ться, остаю́тся	to remain
отстава́ть, отстаю́т	to lag behind
писа́ть, пи́шут, пишу́	to write
поня́ть, пойму́т	to understand
приня́ть, при́мут, приму́	to accept
сказа́ть, ска́жут, скажу́	to tell
слы́шать, слы́шат	to hear
ста́ть, ста́нут	to become; begin
стоя́ть, стоя́т	to stand

343

бы́ть, бу́дут	to be
закры́ть, закро́ют	to close
откры́ть, откро́ют	to open
жи́ть, живу́т	to live
пи́ть, пью́т	to drink
ви́деть, ви́дят, ви́жу	to see
лете́ть, летя́т, лечу́	to fly
сиде́ть, сидя́т, сижу́	to sit
смотре́ть, смо́трят, смотрю́	to look at
умере́ть, умру́т	to die
уме́ть, уме́ют	to be able
итти́, иду́т	to go
кла́сть, кладу́т	to put
мо́чь, мо́гут, могу́	to be able
принести́, принесу́т	to bring
упа́сть, упаду́т	to fall

3.33 Stress

In the non-past tense there are three stress patterns:

A. Stress on the stem.

B. Stress on the ending.

C. Stress on the ending of the first person singular and on the stem of all other non-past forms.

Those verbs having pattern C which occur in the text are:

мо́чь, мо́гут, могу́	to be able
писа́ть, пи́шут, пишу́	to write
заказа́ть, зака́жут, закажу́	to order
сказа́ть, ска́жут, скажу́	to tell
люби́ть, лю́бят, люблю́	to like, love
купи́ть, ку́пят, куплю́	to buy
смотре́ть, смо́трят, смотрю́	to look at
учи́ться, у́чится, учу́сь	to study
получи́ть, полу́чат, получу́	to receive
плати́ть, пла́тят, плачу́	to pay
ходи́ть, хо́дят, хожу́	to go
уложи́ть, уло́жат, уложу́	to pack

344

положи́ть, поло́жат, положу́   to put
спроси́ть, спро́сят, спрошу́   to ask
облени́ться, обле́нятся, обленю́сь   to get lazy
наступи́ть, насту́пят, наступлю́   to approach

It is generally true, though there are a few exceptions, that the verbs of this type are those with stress on the ending of the infinitive and on the stem of the third person plural.

3.4 Future tense

The future in Russian is formed with the non-past form of **бы́ть** with the infinitive of the verb being used. This infinitive can only be an imperfective verb.

3.5 Imperative

Russian has a second person singular and a second person plural imperative. The following statements of the formation of the imperative are for the second person plural, since this is the most commonly used. The second singular may be formed regularly by dropping the **-те** from the plural.

The imperative is formed on the non-past stem in the following ways:

1) Those verbs which have a non-past stem ending in the sound /y/ form the second plural imperative by adding /-ṭi/ to the stem. In terms of Cyrillic writing, those verbs which have a vowel letter or **ь** before the third plural ending -ют/-ят replace the ending **-ют/-ят** by **йте**.

Чита́ют	/čitáy-ut/	They read.
Чита́йте!	/čitáy-ṭi/	Read!
Постро́ят	/pastróy-it/	They will build.
Постро́йте!	/pastróy-ṭi/	Build!

If a consonant immediately precedes the /y/ the inserted vowel **-e-** occurs before the /y/.

Пьют	/py-út/	They drink.
Пе́йте!	/ṗéy-ṭi/	Drink!

2) Other verbs, provided that the stress occurs on the ending on any of the forms of the non-past, add **-йте** (with the **-й-** stressed) to the non-past stem.

Third Plur.	First Sing.	Imperative	
говоря́т	говорю́	Говори́те!	Speak!
пи́шут	пишу́	Пиши́те!	Write!

3) Other verbs, provided that the non-past stem ends in more than one consonant, add **-ите** (unstressed) to the non-past stem.

ко́нчат	ко́нчу	Ко́нчите!	Finish!

4) Other verbs, i.e., those ending in any single consonant other than /y/ and not having stress on any of the non-past endings, add **-ьте**.

познако́мят	познако́млю	Познако́м**ьте**!	Introduce!
бу́дут	бу́ду	Бу́дь**те**!	Be!

Most verbs in Russian are of the first and second types listed above. A very small number of Russian verbs are irregular in not forming the imperative differently from any of the four ways described above. Irregular imperatives that have occurred in the text are:

да́ть, даду́т	**Да́йте**!	Give!
прие́хать, прие́дут	**Приезжа́йте**!	Come!

The imperative of any verb in **-давать**, **-ставать**, or **-знавать** is irregular in that it is formed from the infinitive as follows:

продава́ть, продаю́т	**Продава́йте**!	Sell!
остава́ться, остаю́тся	**Остава́йтесь**!	Remain!

3.6 Aspect

The following is a list of the aspect pairs for all verbs discussed in the Grammar Units.

IMPERFECTIVE	PERFECTIVE	
бра́ть	взя́ть	to take
быва́ть	бы́ть	to be
ви́деть	уви́деть	to see
встреча́ть	встре́тить	to meet
говори́ть	сказа́ть	to say, tell
дава́ть	да́ть	to give
де́лать	сде́лать	to do, make
е́здить (Iterative) / е́хать (Actual)	пое́хать	to go
жда́ть	подожда́ть	to wait for
зака́зывать	заказа́ть	to order
заходи́ть	зайти́	to stop by
звони́ть	позвони́ть	to phone
зна́ть	узна́ть	to know
иска́ть	поиска́ть	to look for
ходи́ть (Iterative) / итти́ (Actual)	пойти́	to go
кла́сть	положи́ть	to put (lying)
конча́ть	ко́нчить	to finish
лежа́ть	полежа́ть	to lie
лета́ть (Iterative) / лете́ть (Actual)	полете́ть	to fly
наступа́ть	наступи́ть	to approach

IMPERFECTIVE	PERFECTIVE	
находи́ть	найти́	to find
начина́ть	нача́ть	to begin
нра́виться	понра́виться	to be pleasing
обе́дать	пообе́дать	to have dinner
осма́тривать	осмотре́ть	to look over
остава́ться	оста́ться	to remain
оставля́ть	оста́вить	to leave behind
остана́вливать	останови́ть	to stop
отвеча́ть	отве́тить	to answer
отдава́ть	отда́ть	to give back
отлета́ть	отлете́ть	to fly away
отстава́ть	отста́ть	to lag behind
отходи́ть	отойти́	to leave
писа́ть	написа́ть	to write
пи́ть	вы́пить	to drink
плати́ть	заплати́ть	to pay
повторя́ть	повтори́ть	to repeat
подава́ть	пода́ть	to serve
подходи́ть	подойти́	to approach
пока́зывать	показа́ть	to show
покупа́ть	купи́ть	to buy
получа́ть	получи́ть	to receive
понима́ть	поня́ть	to understand
приезжа́ть	прие́хать	to come, arrive
прилета́ть	прилете́ть	to come by plane
принима́ть	приня́ть	to accept, receive
приходи́ть	прийти́	to come, arrive
продава́ть	прода́ть	to sell
происходи́ть	произойти́	to happen
проходи́ть	пройти́	to go past
расска́зывать	рассказа́ть	to tell
сдава́ть	сда́ть	to take (an exam)
случа́ться	случи́ться	to happen
смотре́ть	посмотре́ть	to look
спеши́ть	поспеши́ть	to hurry
спра́шивать	спроси́ть	to ask (a question)
ста́вить	поста́вить	to put (standing)
станови́ться	ста́ть	to become
стро́ить	постро́ить	to build
счита́ть	посчита́ть	to count; consider
теря́ть	потеря́ть	to lose
уезжа́ть	уе́хать	to leave
ходи́ть (see итти́)		
чита́ть	прочита́ть	to read

◑ 4. Prepositions

1) With the genitive case:

от	*from*	кро́ме	*besides, except*
из	*from, out of*	по́сле	*after*
у	*at, by, near*	до	*up, until, before*
с, со	*from, off of*	для	*for, for the benefit of*
без	*without*	о́коло	*near, about* (approximately)

2) With the dative case:

к, ко	*to, towards*
по	*according to; around; on* (e.g., on history)

3) With the accusative case:

на	*to, on, onto* (motion)
в, во	*to, in, into* (motion)
за	*for* (in return for); *behind* (motion); *during*
че́рез	*in* (at the end of); *through*
под	*under* (motion)

4) With the instrumental case:

за	*behind* (location); *after*
с, со	*with* (accompaniment)
под	*under* (location)
пе́ред	*in front of, before*

5) With the locative case:

о, об, обо	*about, concerning*
в, во	*in, at* (location)
на	*in, at, on* (location)

◑ 5. Numerals

The numeral **оди́н** has the inflection of a special adjective. The numerals 2, 3 and 4 have the following inflection:

NOM.	два́, две́	три́	четы́ре
GEN.	дву́х	трёх	четырёх
DAT.	дву́м	трём	четырём
ACC.	N/G	N/G	N/G
INST.	двумя́	тремя́	четырьмя́
LOC.	дву́х	трёх	четырёх

The numerals 5 to 20 and also 30 have the inflection of feminine II nouns. Some have stress on the stem and some on the ending.

	NOMINATIVE	GENITIVE
5	пя́ть	пяти́
6	ше́сть	шести́
7	се́мь	семи́
8	во́семь	восьми́
9	де́вять	девяти́
10	де́сять	десяти́
11	оди́ннадцать	оди́ннадцати
12	двена́дцать	двена́дцати
13	трина́дцать	трина́дцати
14	четы́рнадцать	четы́рнадцати
15	пятна́дцать	пятна́дцати
16	шестна́дцать	шестна́дцати
17	семна́дцать	семна́дцати
18	восемна́дцать	восемна́дцати
19	девятна́дцать	девятна́дцати
20	два́дцать	двадцати́
30	три́дцать	тридцати́

The numerals 40, 90 and 100 have the following inflection:

NOM.	со́рок	девяно́сто	сто́
GEN.	сорока́	девяно́ста	ста́
DAT.	сорока́	девяно́ста	ста́
ACC.	N/G	N/G	N/G
INST.	сорока́	девяно́ста	ста́
LOC.	сорока́	девяно́ста	ста́

The other tens, 50, 60, 70 and 80, have the inflection of feminine II nouns with both parts inflected.

	NOMINATIVE	GENITIVE
50	пятьдеся́т	пяти́десяти
60	шестьдеся́т	шести́десяти
70	се́мьдесят	семи́десяти
80	во́семьдесят	восьми́десяти

For compound cardinal numerals all parts are inflected. Thus, Nom. два̀дцать два́, Gen. двадцати́ дву́х, etc.

For compound ordinal numerals only the last part is inflected. Thus, Nom. два́дцать второ́й, Gen. два́дцать второ́го etc.,

APPENDIX

The form **тре́тий** has the inflection of a special adjective and all other ordinals the inflection of an ordinary adjective.

пе́рвый	оди́ннадцатый	двадца́тый
второ́й	двена́дцатый	тридца́тый
тре́тий	трина́дцатый	сороково́й
четвёртый	четы́рнадцатый	пятидеся́тый
пя́тый	пятна́дцатый	шестидеся́тый
шесто́й	шестна́дцатый	семидеся́тый
седьмо́й	семна́дцатый	восьмидеся́тый
восьмо́й	восемна́дцатый	девяно́стый
девя́тый	девятна́дцатый	со́тый
деся́тый		

VOCABULARIES

A sufficient number of forms for any given noun or verb is cited below to allow for prediction of all forms of the noun or verb according to the conventions established in the Grammar Units and Appendix. For nouns the following abbreviations are used: N — nominative, G — genitive, D — dative, A — accusative, I — instrumental, L — locative, S — singular, P — plural, indecl. — indeclinable. Masculine nouns ending in **-ь** are not marked for gender but feminine type II nouns are marked F2. Verbs with an infinitive in **-ать** and third plural non-past **-ают** are cited only in the infinitive form. The following abbreviations for verbs are used: I — imperfective, P — perfective. A letter in parenthesis (in latin alphabet) signifies an inserted vowel.

Russian-English Vocabulary

А

á and, but
а́вгуст August
авто́бус bus
азербайджа́нский Azerbaijan
А́зия Asia
актёр actor
Алексе́й Alexis
Аме́рика America
америка́нец (e) American (*m.*)
америка́нка (o) American (*f.*)
америка́нский American
Аму́р Amur (river)
англи́йский English
   по-англи́йски English, in English
апре́ль April
армя́нский Armenian
архитекту́ра architecture
аспира́нт graduate student
аспиранту́ра graduate studies
аэропо́рт 2nd L **-ý** airport

Б

Байка́л Baikal (lake)
Баку́ *indecl.* Baku
бале́т ballet
балти́йский Baltic
бара́ний *spec. adj.* mutton
баскетбо́льный basketball
бе́з without
белору́сский Belorussian
бе́лый white
бельё laundry, clothes
бе́рег 2nd L **-ý**, NP **-á** bank, shore
библиоте́ка library
биле́т ticket
биологи́ческий biological
бли́же nearer
бли́зкий near
блю́до dish
бога́тый rich
бо́лее more
больни́ца hospital
бо́льше more;
   бо́льше не no longer
бо́льший greater, larger
большо́й big
Бори́с Boris
бо́рщ GS **-á** borsch
Босто́н Boston
Босфо́р Bosporus
боя́ться I **-я́тся** to be afraid
бра́т NP **бра́тья** brother
бра́ть I беру́т; бра́л, -á, ´-о, ´-и to take
бу́дущий future, next
бума́га paper
бума́жник wallet
бы́ would, should
быва́ть I to be (frequently)
бы́стро quickly
бы́ть P бу́дут; бы́л, -á ´-о, ´-и to be **мо́жет бы́ть** maybe
бюро́ *indecl.* office;

спрáвочное бюрó information-office

В

в in, to, at
вáжный important;
  short form: вáжен
вáш your
вéк century, age
Вéра Vera
вéрно right
вернýть P вернýт to return, give back
вернýться P вернýтся to return, come back
вероя́тно probably
веснá spring
вéсь all
  всегó хорóшего good luck
  всё ещё still
  всё continually, all the time
вéтер (е) wind
вéчер NP -á evening; party
вечéрний evening
вéщь F2 NP ´-и, GP -éй, DP -áм thing
взаймы́ as a loan
взять P возьмýт; взял, -á, ´-о, ´-и to take
вид view
вúдеть I вúдят, вúжу to see
вúдеться I вúдятся to see each other
вмéсте together
водá AS ´-у, NP ´-ы water
воднóй water
возмóжность F2 possibility
вóзраст age
войнá NP ´-ы war
вокзáл railroad station
Вóлга Volga (river)

волейбóльный volleyball
вóн there, over there
вопрóс question
восемнáдцатый eighteenth
восемнáдцать eighteen
вóсемь eight
вóсемьдесят eighty
восемьсóт eight hundred
воскресéнье Sunday
востóк east
восьмидеся́тый eightieth
восьмóй eighth
вóт there, here;
  вóт как that's right
впадáть I to fall, flow into
врéмя G D L S врéмени, IS ´-ем, NP -á, GP времён, DP -áм time
всегдá always
встрéтить P ´-ят, встрéчу to meet
встречáть I to meet
вся́кий any kind of
втóрник Tuesday
вторóй second;
  на вторóе for the second course
вуз institution of higher learning
вхóд entrance
вчерá yesterday
вы́ you
выдаю́щийся outstanding
вы́держать P вы́держат to pass (an exam)
вы́пить P вы́пьют to drink
высóкий high
высокó high
вы́ставка (о) exhibit, exhibition
вы́сший higher, highest, superior
выходúть I -ят, выхожý to go out
вы́ше higher, more highly

Г

газе́та newspaper
гарни́р garnish
где́ where
географи́ческий geographical
геологи́ческий geological
герма́нский germanic
гла́вный main;
    гла́вным о́бразом mainly, for the most part
глубо́кий deep
говори́ть I **-я́т** to say, speak
говоря́ speaking;
    че́стно говоря́ to tell the truth
го́д 2nd L **-у́**, NP **⸍-ы**, GP **-о́в**, DP **-а́м** year
гора́ AS **⸍-у**, NP **⸍-ы**, DP **-а́м** mountain, hill
гора́здо much
го́род NP **-а́** city
городско́й city
Го́рький Gorky
господи́н NP **господа́** GP **госпо́д** Mr.
госпожа́ Mrs., Miss
гости́ница hotel
госуда́рственный state
гото́вый ready;
    short form: **гото́в**
граждани́н NP **гра́ждане**, GP **гра́ждан** citizen, sir, Mr.
гражда́нка (о) citizen (*f.*), Miss, Mrs.
грузи́нский Georgian
гуля́ть I to stroll

Д

да́ yes; and; but
дава́ть I **даю́т** to give

давно́ long ago; for a long time now
да́же even
да́лее further
    и та́к да́лее etc.
далёкий far, distant
далеко́ far
да́льше farther
да́ть, да́м, да́шь, да́ст, дади́м, дади́те, даду́т; да́л, -а́, ⸍-о, ⸍-и to give
два́ two
двадца́тый twentieth
два́дцать twenty
двена́дцатый twelfth
двена́дцать twelve
две́сти two hundred
де́вочка (е) girl
де́вушка (е) girl
девяно́сто ninety
девяно́стый ninetieth
девятна́дцатый nineteenth
девятна́дцать nineteen
девя́тый ninth
де́вять nine
девятьсо́т nine hundred
действи́тельно really
дека́брь GS **-я́** December
де́лать I to do, make
де́ло NP **-а́** affair, deed, fact;
    в са́мом де́ле as a matter of fact
де́нь (е) day
де́ньги (е) DP **-а́м** money
дере́вня country
деся́тый tenth
де́сять ten
де́ти GP **-е́й**, IP **детьми́** children
Детро́йт Detroit
деше́вле cheaper
дёшево cheaply
дешёвый cheap

Джо́н John
дипло́м diploma
дли́нный long
для for
Днепр GS **-а́** Dnepr (river)
до́ up to, before
    до свида́ния goodbye
    до того́, ка́к before
до́брый kind, good
дово́льно rather; enough
дое́хать P дое́дут to go as far as
до́ждь GS **-я́** rain
дойти́ P дойду́т; дошёл, дошла́, **-о́, -и́** to go as far as
до́ктор NP **-а́** doctor
до́лго long
до́лжен (e) **-а́, -о́, -ы́** ought to
до́лжный due, proper
до́м NP **-а́** house
    до́ма at home
    домо́й home(ward)
доро́га road
дорого́й expensive, dear;
    short form: **до́рог, -а́, ́-о, ́-и**
доро́же dearer, more dearly
доста́точно enough
до́ступ access
до́чка (e) daughter
драгоце́нный precious
дру́г NP друзья́, GP друзе́й friend
друго́й other
ду́мать I to think
дя́дя GP ́-ей uncle

Е

Евро́па Europe
европе́йский European
е́здить I (*Iterative*) ́-ят, е́зжу to go
Еле́на Helen

Енисе́й Yenisei (river)
е́сли if
е́сть there is, are
е́сть I е́м, е́шь, е́ст, еди́м, еди́те, едя́т; е́л, ́-а, ́-о, ́-и to eat
е́хать I (*Actual*) е́дут to go
ещё still, yet;
    ещё ра́з once more;
    ещё оди́н another;
    всё ещё still

Ж

жа́ль sorry
жа́ркий hot
жа́рче hotter
жда́ть I жду́т; жда́л, -а́, ́-о, ́-и to wait
же (*emphatic particle*)
    та́к же ка́к и just like
желе́зный iron
    желе́зная доро́га railroad
жена́ NP жёны wife
же́нщина woman
живо́й lively
жи́знь F2 life
жи́ть I живу́т; жи́л, -а́, ́-о, ́-и to live
журнали́зм journalism

З

за́ behind; for
    что́ э́то за...? what, what kind of
забы́ть P забу́дут to forget
за́втра tomorrow
зайти́ P зайду́т; зашёл, зашла́, -о́, -и́ to stop by
заказа́ть P зака́жут, -у́ to order
зака́зывать I to order
закры́тый closed
закры́ть P закро́ют to close
замерза́ть I to freeze

замеча́тельный remarkable
за́мужем married
занима́ть I to occupy
заня́тие studies, class
за́нятый busy, occupied;
    short form: за́нят, -а́, -о, -ы
зао́чный by correspondence
за́пад west
за́падный western
заплати́ть P -ят, заплачу́ to pay
зато́ on the other hand, however,
   nevertheless
заходи́ть I -ят, захожу́ to come
   by for
зва́ть I зову́т; зва́л, -а́, -о, -и
   to call
звони́ть I -ят to ring, phone
зда́ние building
здесь here
здоро́вый well, healthy
здра́вствуйте hello
зелёный green
зима́ AS -у, NP -ы winter
зна́к sign
знако́мый acquaintance
знамени́тый famous
зна́ть I to know
значе́ние significance, meaning
зна́чить I -ат to mean
золото́й gold

И

и and; also, too (*emphatic particle*)
   и... и both... and
   и та́к да́лее etc.
Ива́н Ivan
Ива́нович Ivanovich
игра́ть I to play
из from, out of
извини́те! excuse me!
изда́ние edition
изде́лие article

и́ли or
   и́ли... и́ли either... or
име́ть I име́ют to have
и́мя GS и́мени, IS -ем, NP -а́,
   GP имён, DP -а́м name;
   и́мени Го́рького named after
   Gorky
инжене́р engineer
иногда́ sometimes
иностра́нец (e) foreigner
иностра́нный foreign
институ́т institute
интере́с interest
интере́сный interesting
интересова́ться I интересу́ются
   to be interested
иска́ть I и́щут, -у́ to seek, look for
истори́ческий historical
исто́рия history
Ита́ка Ithaca
итти́ I (*Actual*) иду́т; шёл, шла́,
   шло́, шли́ to go
ию́ль July
ию́нь June

К

к towards
Кавка́з Caucasus
ка́ждый each
каза́ться I ка́жутся to seem
каза́хский Kazakh
Казбе́к Kazbek (a brand of cigarettes; a name of a mountain in the
   Caucasus)
ка́к how, as
   ка́к-то somehow;
   как ра́з right, just;
   ка́к... та́к и as well as
како́й what
ка́мень (e) NP -и, GP -ей, DP -ям
   stone
капу́ста cabbage

каранда́ш GS -а́   pencil
карма́н   pocket
каса́ться I   to touch, concern
каспи́йский   Caspian
ка́сса   cashier's desk
кафе́ *indecl.*   cafe
ка́федра   department, section
Ки́ев   Kiev
кино́ *indecl.*   motion pictures
кинотеа́тр   moving picture theater
кио́ск   kiosk
кирги́зский   Kirghiz
класс   classroom
класси́ческий   classical
класть I кладу́т; кла́л, ⸌-а, ⸌-о, ⸌-и
    to put, lay
кли́мат   climate
клуб   club
ключ GS -а́   key
кни́га   book
кни́жный   book
когда́   when
колле́кция   collection
колониза́тор   colonizer
Ко́ля   Kolya
компо́т   stewed fruit
конве́рт   envelope
коне́чно   of course
консервато́рия   conservatory
конча́ть I   to finish, end
конча́ться I   to end, finish, be over
ко́нчить P ⸌-ат   to end
ко́нчиться P ⸌-атся   to end
копе́йка (e)   kopeck
корне́льский   Cornell
корт   playing court
костю́м   suit
котле́та   chop
кото́рый   which, who
ко́фе *indecl.* (*m.*)   coffee
краси́вый   beautiful
Кре́мль GS -я́   Kremlin
кро́ме   besides, except

кто   who
куда́   where to
культу́ра   culture
купи́ть P ⸌-ят, куплю́   to buy
курс   course

Л

лаборато́рия   laboratory
Ла́йка   Eskimo dog; (cigarette
    brand name)
латви́йский   Latvian
легко́   easy, easily
лёд (ё)   ice
ледови́тый   arctic
лежа́ть I -а́т   to lie
ле́кция   lecture
Ле́на   Lena (river)
Ленингра́д   Leningrad
ле́нинский   Lenin
лета́ть I (*Iterative*)   to fly
лете́ть I (*Actual*) -я́т, лечу́   to fly
ле́то   summer
ли   (question word)
лимо́н   lemon
лист   sheet
литерату́ра   literature;
    худо́жественная   литера-
    ту́ра   fiction
лито́вский   Lithuanian
лу́чше   better
лу́чший   better, best
люби́мый   favorite
люби́ть I ⸌-ят, люблю́   to like,
    love
лю́ди GP -е́й, DP ⸌-ям, IP людьми́
    people

М

магази́н   store
май   May
ма́ленький   small

ма́ло few, not many, not much

ма́рка (о) stamp

ма́рт March

ма́сло butter

матема́тика mathematics

ма́ть F2 GS **ма́тери**, NP **ма́тери**, GP **-е́й**, DP **-я́м** mother

МГУ abbrev. for **Моско́вский госуда́рственный университе́т** Moscow State University

ме́лкий shallow

ме́нее less

ме́ньше less

меню́ *indecl.* menu

ме́сто NP **-а́** place

ме́сяц month

метро́ *indecl.* subway

меха́нико-математи́ческий mechanical-mathematical

миллио́н million

мину́та minute

мир NP **-ы́** world

мир peace

Ми́ша Misha

мла́дший younger, youngest, junior

мно́гие many

мно́го many, much

моде́ль F2 model

мой my

молда́вский Moldavian

молоде́ц (e) **-а́** young fellow

молодо́й young

моло́же younger

молоко́ milk

мо́ре NP **-я́** sea

моро́женое ice cream

Москва́ Moscow

моско́вский Moscow

Мохова́я (street name)

мочь I **мо́гут**, **-у́**; **мог, могла́, -о́, -и́** to be able; **мо́жет бы́ть** maybe

муж NP **мужья́**, GP **муже́й** husband

музе́й museum

мы we

Мэ́ри *indecl.* Mary

мя́гкий soft; **мя́гкий знак** soft sign

Н

на on, in

наве́рно probably

наводне́ние flood

наде́яться I **наде́ются** to hope

на́до it is necessary

наза́д back

называ́ться I to be called

найти́ P **найду́т**; **нашёл, нашла́, -о́, -и́** to find

найти́сь P **найду́тся**; **нашёлся, нашла́сь, -о́сь, -и́сь** to be found

наконе́ц finally

нале́во to the left

написа́ть P **напи́шут, -у́** to write

напра́во to the right

напро́тив opposite, across the way

населе́ние population

настоя́щий real; present **по-настоя́щему** really

наступа́ть I to approach

наступи́ть P **ˊ-ят, наступлю́** to approach

Ната́ша Natasha

нау́чный scientific

находи́ть I **ˊ-ят, нахожу́** to find

находи́ться I **ˊ-ятся, нахожу́сь** to be located

на́ция nation

нача́ть P **начну́т**; **на́чал, -а́, ˊ-о, ˊ-и** to begin

нача́ться P **начну́тся**; **начался́, -а́сь, -о́сь, -и́сь** to begin

начина́ть I to begin
начина́ться I to begin
наш our
не not;
   Не́ за что. Don't mention it.
неда́вно recently
неде́ля week
недоста́ток (о) lack
не́когда there is no time
неме́цкий German
немно́го a little
не́сколькие several
не́сколько some, several
несмотря́ на in spite of
нет no, there is no
ни (*negative particle*)
   ни... ни neither... nor
нигде́ nowhere
ни́зкий low
никогда́ never
никто́ nobody
никуда́ nowhere
ничего́ nothing
но but
но́вый new
ночь F2 NP ´-и, GP -е́й, DP -а́м
   night
ноя́брь GS -я́ November
нра́виться I ´-ятся, нра́влюсь to
   please
ну well
нужда́ться I to be in need
ну́жен (е), -а́, ´-о, -ы́ necessary
Нью-Йо́рк New York

О

о about
обе́дать I to have dinner
облени́ться P ´-ятся, -ю́сь to get
   lazy
о́браз way, form; **гла́вным о́бра-
   зом** mainly, for the most part

образова́ние education
общежи́тие dormitory
обще́ственный social
о́бщий general
объединённый united
обыкнове́нный usual
Обь F2 Ob (river)
обяза́тельный obligatory
ограни́ченный limited, restricted;
   short form: **ограни́чен**
огро́мный huge
оде́жда clothes
Оде́сса Odessa
оди́н one; only; alone
оди́ннадцатый eleventh
оди́ннадцать eleven
одна́ко however
о́зеро NP **озёра** lake
океа́н ocean
окно́ (о) NP ´-а window
о́коло near
оконча́ние end; completion;
   по оконча́нии upon completion, on graduating
око́нченный finished;
   short form: **око́нчен**
октя́брь GS -я́ October
О́льга Olga
он he, it
она́ she, it
оно́ it
о́пера opera
опя́ть again
организа́ция organization
оруже́йный pertaining to arms;
   оруже́йная пала́та armory
ору́жие arms
о́сень F2 fall, autumn
осма́тривать I to look over
осмо́тр inspection, looking over
осмотре́ть P ´-ят, -ю́ to look over
осно́ванный founded;
   short form: **осно́ван**

остава́ться I остаю́тся to stay, remain

оста́вить P ´-ят, оставлю́ to leave, leave behind

оставля́ть I to leave behind

остана́вливать I to stop

остана́вливаться I to stop

останови́ть P ´-ят, остановлю́ to stop

останови́ться P ´-ятся, остановлю́сь to stop

о́т from

отве́тить P ´-ят, отвечу́ to answer

отвеча́ть I to answer

отдава́ть I отдаю́т to give back

отда́ть P (non-past like да́ть) отдаду́т; о́тдал, -á, ´-о, ´-и to give back

отде́л department

о́тдых rest

оте́ц (e) GS -á father

откры́тка (o) post card

откры́ть P откро́ют open

отку́да where from

отлета́ть I to fly off

отойти́ P отойду́т; отошёл, отошла́, -ó, -и́ to depart

о́тпуск NP -á vacation

отстава́ть I отстаю́т to lag behind

отсю́да from here

отходи́ть I ´-ят, отхожу́ to depart

официа́нт waiter

о́чень very

о́чередь F2 NP ´-и, GP -éй, DP -я́м line, turn

ошиба́ться I to be mistaken

П

пала́та palace;
оруже́йная пала́та armory

пальто́ *indecl.* coat

папиро́са papirosa, cigarette

па́ра pair, couple

па́рк park

па́чка (e) pack

пе́рвый first;
на пе́рвое for the first course

перево́дчица interpreter (*f.*)

пе́ред in front of, before

переда́ть P (non-past like да́ть) пе́редал, -á, ´-о, ´-и to hand over

перенести́ P перенесу́т; перенёс, перенесла́, -ó, -и́ to transfer

Пётр GS -á Peter

Петро́вич Petrovich

пе́ть I пою́т to sing

Печо́ра Pechora (river)

писа́тель writer

писа́ть I пи́шут, -у́ to write

письмо́ (e) NP ´-а letter

пи́ть I пью́т; пи́л, -á, ´-о, ´-и to drink

пла́н map, plan

плати́ть I ´-ят, плачу́ to pay

пло́хо badly

плохо́й bad

площа́дка (o) playing court

по́ along; on

по-англи́йски (in) English

побыва́ть P to spend some time, visit briefly

повтори́ть P -я́т to repeat

повторя́ть I to repeat

поговори́ть P -я́т to have a talk (with), have a chat (with)

пого́да weather

по́д under

подава́ть I подаю́т to serve

пода́ть P (non-past like да́ть) по́дал, -á, ´-о, ´-и to serve

подожда́ть P подожду́т; подожда́л, -á, ´-о, ´-и to wait

подойти́ P подойду́т; подошёл,

xi

подошла́, -о́, -и́ to go up to, approach

подходи́ть I ´-ят, подхожу́ to approach, go up to

по́езд NP -а́ train

пое́здка (о) trip

пое́хать P пое́дут to go

пожа́луйста please, you're welcome, here you are

пожива́ете:

Ка́к вы́ пожива́ете? How are you?

позволя́ть I to permit

позвони́ть P -я́т to phone

по́здно late

по́зже later

познако́мить P ´-ят, познако́млю to acquaint, introduce

познако́миться P ´-ятся, познако́млюсь to get acquainted

поиска́ть P поищут, -у́ to look for, seek

пойти́ P пойду́т; пошёл, пошла́, -о́, -и́ to go

пока́ in the meantime; so far, yet; so long!

показа́ть P пока́жут, -у́ to show

пока́зывать I to show

покры́тый covered

покупа́тель customer

покупа́ть I to buy

поку́пка buying

полежа́ть P -а́т to lie

полете́ть P -я́т, полечу́ to fly

полови́на half

положи́ть P ´-ат, -у́ to put, lay

получа́ть I to receive

получи́ть P ´-ат, -у́ to receive

По́льша Poland

по́мнить I ´-ят to remember

помо́чь P помо́гут; -у́; помо́г, помогла́, -о́, -и́ to help

понеде́льник Monday

по-неме́цки German, in German

понима́ть I to understand

понра́виться P ´-ятся, понра́влюсь to please

поня́ть P пойму́т; по́нял, -а́, -о, ´-и to understand

пообе́дать P to dine

пора́ it is time

по́рт 2nd L -у́ port

по-ру́сски in Russian

посвящённый devoted;

short form: посвящён

посеща́ть I to attend

посла́ть P пошлю́т to send

по́сле after;

по́сле того́, как after

после́дний last

посмотре́ть P ´-ят, -ю to look at

поспеши́ть P -а́т to hurry

поста́вить P ´-ят, поста́влю to put, stand

постара́ться P to try

постро́йка (е) building, construction

постро́ить P ´-ят to build

поступа́ть I to enter

посчита́ть P to count

посыла́ть I to send

потеря́ть P to lose

пото́м then, next

потому́ for this

потому́, что because

по-францу́зски French, in French

похо́жий similar;

short form: похо́ж

почему́ why

почита́ть P to read (a little bit)

по́чта post office

почти́ almost

поэ́тому therefore

пра́вда truth

пра́вильный right, correct

пра́во law

пра́ктика practice

предме́т subject

представи́тель representative

представля́ть I to present

прекра́сный beautiful; fine

преподава́тель teacher

пре́сса press

при́ at, in the presence of, at the time of

приве́т regards

приго́дный suitable

прие́зд arrival

приезжа́ть I to come

прие́хать Р **прие́дут** to come

прийти́ Р **приду́т**; **пришёл**, **пришла́**, **-о́**, **-и́** to come

прийти́сь Р (*impersonal*) **придётся**; **пришло́сь** to be necessary

прилета́ть I to come (by plane), fly

прилете́ть Р **-я́т**, **прилечу́** to come (by plane), fly

приложи́ть Р **-а́т**, **-у́** to add, enclose

приме́р example

приме́рно approximately, about

принести́ Р **принесу́т**; **принёс**, **принесла́**, **-о́**, **-и́** to bring

принима́ть I to take, accept; **принима́ть уча́стие** to take part

при́нято customary

приня́ть Р **при́мут**, **-у́**; **при́нял**, **-а́**, **-о**, **-и** to accept, receive

приобрести́ Р **приобрету́т**; **приобрёл**, **-а́**, **-о́**, **-и́** to attain, acquire

приходи́ть I **-я́т**, **прихожу́** to come

приходи́ться I (*impersonal*) **-ится** to be necessary

прия́тный pleasant

провали́ться Р **-я́тся**, **-ю́сь** to fail (an exam)

провести́ Р **проведу́т**; **провёл, -а́, -о́, -и́** to pass, spend (time)

проводи́ть I **-я́т**, **провожу́** to pass, spend (time)

продава́ть I **продаю́т** to sell

продава́ться I **продаю́тся** to be sold

продаве́ц (e) GS **-а́** salesman

продавщи́ца saleswoman

прода́ть Р (*non-past* like **да́ть**) **про́дал, -а́, -о, -и** to sell

прода́ться Р (*non-past* like **да́ть**) **прода́лся, -а́сь, -о́сь, -и́сь** to be sold

продолжа́ть I to continue

продолжа́ться I to last, continue

продолже́ние continuation

произойти́ Р **произойду́т**; **произошёл, произошла́, -о́, -и́** to happen

происходи́ть I **-я́т**, **происхожу́** to happen

пройти́ Р **пройду́т**; **прошёл, прошла́, -о́, -и́** to go past

промы́шленность F2 industry

простира́ться I to stretch, extend

прости́те! Pardon me!

про́сто simply, just

протека́ть I to flow through

профе́ссор NP **-а́** professor

проходи́ть I **-я́т**, **прохожу́** to go through

прохо́жий passer-by

прочита́ть Р to read

про́шлый past

Пско́в Pskov

пусты́ня desert

путеше́ствовать I **путеше́ствуют** to travel

пу́ть (like F2 except IS **путём**) way, path;

Счастли́вого пути́! Have a good trip!

пье́са play

пятидеся́тый fiftieth

пятна́дцатый fifteenth

пятна́дцать fifteen

пя́тница Friday

пя́тый fifth

пять five

пятьдеся́т fifty

пятьсо́т five hundred

Р

рабо́та work; paper

рабо́тать I to work

рад glad

ра́з NP **-ы́**, GP **ра́з** time;
   ка́к ра́з right, just

ра́зве really

разви́ться Р **разовью́тся** to be developed

развле́чься Р **развлеку́тся**; **раз-
влёкся, развлекла́сь, -о́сь, -и́сь** to have a good time

разгово́р conversation

разли́чный various

разрасти́сь Р **разрасту́тся**; **раз-
ро́сся, разросла́сь, -о́сь, -и́сь** to grow, expand

разреша́ть I to permit

ра́но early

ра́ньше earlier, sooner

рассказа́ть Р **расска́жут, -у́** to tell

расска́зывать I to tell

ребёнок (о) child

револю́ция revolution

реме́сленный trade

репертуа́р repertoire

респу́блика republic

рестора́н restaurant

реши́ть Р **-а́т** to decide

ро́вный level, even, smooth, exact

роди́ться I or Р **-я́тся, рожу́сь** to be born

родно́й native, related
   родны́е relatives

ро́ль F2 role

рома́н novel

рома́нский romance

росси́йский Russian

Росси́я Russia

РСФСР RSFSR (the Russian Soviet Federated Socialist Republic)

рубль GS **-я́** ruble

рука́ AS **´-у**, NP **´-и**, DP **-а́м** hand, arm

ру́сский Russian, a Russian (male)
   ру́сская a Russian (female)
   по-ру́сски Russian, in Russian

ру́чка (e) pen

ры́ба fish

ры́бный fish

ря́д NP **-ы́** row;
   ря́дом с next to

С

с with; from

са́м one's self

самолёт airplane

са́мый the very, most

Са́нкт-Петербу́рг Saint Petersburg

са́хар 2nd G **´-у** sugar

свида́ние seeing again
   до свида́ния good-bye

свобо́дно freely, fluently

свобо́дный free, vacant, unoccupied;
   short form: **свобо́ден** (e)

сво́й one's own

сдава́ть I **сдаю́т** to take (an exam)

сда́ть P (like да́ть) to take (an exam)

сда́ча change

сде́лать P to do, make

себя́ self;
    та́к себе́ so-so

се́вер north

се́верный northern

сего́дня today

седьмо́й seventh

сейча́с now, right away

семидеся́тый seventieth

семна́дцатый seventeenth

семна́дцать seventeen

се́мь seven

се́мьдесят seventy

семьсо́т seven hundred

семья́ NP се́мьи, GP семе́й, DP се́мьям family

сентя́брь GS -я́ September

сере́брянный silver

середи́на middle

сестра́ NP сёстры, GP сестёр, DP -́ам sister

Сиби́рь F2 Siberia

сигаре́та cigarette

сиде́ть I -я́т, сижу́ to sit

си́ний blue

сказа́ть P ска́жут, -у́ to say, tell

ско́лько how many

ско́ро soon

славя́нский Slavic

сла́дкий sweet
    сла́дкое dessert

сле́дующий next, following

сли́шком too

сло́во NP -á word

слу́жба service, work

слу́чай case

случа́ться I to happen

случи́ться P -а́тся to happen

слу́шать I to listen

слы́шать I -́ат to hear

сме́рть F2 death

Смоле́нск Smolensk

смотре́ть I -́ят, -ю́ to look at

снача́ла at first

сне́г snow

собира́ть I to collect, gather

собира́ться I to intend, plan; collect, gather, meet

собо́р cathedral

сове́тский Soviet

совсе́м completely;
    совсе́м не not at all

солёный salty

Со́ня Sonya

со́рок forty

сороково́й fortieth

соси́ска (о) sausage

состоя́ть I -я́т to consist

состоя́ться I -я́тся to be held

со́тый hundredth

социалисти́ческий socialist

сою́з union

спаси́бо thank you

спекта́кль performance, show, play

сперва́ first

специа́льность F2 specialty

спеши́ть I -а́т to hurry

спра́вочный informational

спра́шивать I to ask (a question)

спроси́ть P -́ят, спрошу́ to ask

среда́ AS -́у, NP -́ы, DP -а́м Wednesday

среди́ among

сре́дний middle, central

СССР USSR

ста́вить I -́ят, ста́влю to put (standing); to put on (a play, etc.)

стадио́н stadium

станови́ться -́ятся, становлю́сь to become

ста́рше older

ста́рший elder, eldest, senior

ста́рый old

ста́ть P **ста́нут**   to begin; become
статья́   article
стена́ AS ´-у, NP ´-ы, DP -а́м   wall
сто́ hundred
сто́ить I ´-ят   to cost
сто́л GS -а́   table
столи́ца   capital
стоя́ть I -я́т   to stand
стро́ить I ´-ят   to build
студе́нт   student (*m.*)
   студе́нтка (о)   student (*f.*)
сту́л NP **сту́лья**   chair
суббо́та   Saturday
судохо́дство   navigation
су́п 2nd G ´-у   soup
суро́вый   severe
су́хо   dry
сухо́й   dry
су́ше   drier, more drily
счастли́вый   happy;
   Счастли́вого пути́!   Have a
   good trip!
счита́ть I   to count; consider
счита́ться I   to be considered
съе́зд   convention
сы́н NP **сыновья́**, GP **сынове́й**
   son
сюда́   here, to this place

T

таджи́кский   Tadjik
та́к   thus, so;
   и та́к да́лее   etc.;
   та́к как   since, because;
   ка́к... та́к и   as well as
та́кже   also
тако́й   such
та́м   there
танцова́ть I **танцу́ют**   to dance
Татья́на   Tatyana
Ташке́нт   Tashkent

та́ять I **та́ют**   to melt
твёрдый   hard
   твёрдый зна́к   hard sign
теа́тр   theater
те́ннисный   tennis
тео́рия   theory
тепе́решний   present, contem-
   porary
тепе́рь   now
тепло́   warm
тёплый   warm
террито́рия   territory
теря́ть I   to lose
те́хникум   technical school
тече́ние   course
те́чь I **теку́т; тёк, текла́, -о́, -и́**
   to flow
ти́хий   quiet, pacific
това́рищ   comrade
тогда́   then
то́же   also
то́лько   only;
   то́лько что   just
то́т   that; **то́т же** same; **тому́
   наза́д** ago; **то́ есть**   that is
то́чный   exact
трамва́й   streetcar
тра́нспорт   transport
тре́тий   third
три́   three
тридца́тый   thirtieth
три́дцать   thirty
трина́дцатый   thirteenth
трина́дцать   thirteen
три́ста   three hundred
тру́дный   difficult
туда́   there, to that place
тури́ст   tourist
туркме́нский   Turkmenian
Ту́рция   Turkey
ту́т   here
ты́   you (*sing.*)
ты́сяча   thousand

У

у at, by
уви́деть Р ´-ят, **уви́жу** to have a look at, catch sight of
уда́ться Р (*impersonal*) **уда́стся**; **удало́сь** to be successful
удово́льствие pleasure
уезжа́ть I to go away
уе́хать Р **уе́дут** to go away, leave (by vehicle)
уже́ already
узбе́кский Uzbek
узна́ть Р to find out
Украи́на Ukraine
украи́нский Ukrainian
у́лица street
уложи́ть Р ´-ат, **-у́** to pack
уме́ренный moderate
умере́ть Р **умру́т**; **у́мер, умерла́,** ´-о, ´-и to die
уме́ть I **уме́ют** to know how
университе́т university
упако́вка packing
упа́сть Р **упаду́т, упа́л,** ´-а, ´-о, ´-и to fall
упомяну́тый mentioned
упомяну́ть Р **упомя́нут, -у́** to mention
успе́нский Uspensky
у́тро morning;
   у́тром in the morning; **семь часо́в утра́** at 7 in the morning;
   по утра́м mornings
уча́стие participation;
   принима́ть уча́стие to take part
уча́щийся student
учени́к GS **-а́** pupil
учи́лище school
учи́тель NP **-я́** teacher (*m.*);

учи́тельница teacher (*f.*)
учи́ться I ´-атся, **-у́сь** to study

Ф

фа́брика factory
факульте́т department
февра́ль GS **-я́** February
федерати́вный federated
фи́зика physics
физи́ческий physical
филологи́ческий philological
филосо́фия philosophy
филосо́фский philosophical
фи́льм film
фи́льтр filter
фи́нно-уго́рский Finno-Ugric
фоне́тика phonetics
фотогра́фия photograph
фра́за sentence
францу́зский French
фру́кт fruit

Х

Ха́рьков Kharkov
хи́мик chemist
хими́ческий chemical
хи́мия chemistry
хле́б bread
ходи́ть I (*Iterative*) ´-ят, **хожу́** to go; walk
хо́лодно cold;
   Compar. **холодне́е**
холо́дный cold
хо́р chorus
хоро́ший good;
   всего́ хоро́шего good luck
хорошо́ good, well
хоте́ть I **хочу́, хо́чешь, хо́чет, хоти́м, хоти́те, хотя́т** to want
хоте́ться I (*impersonal*) **хо́чется** to want

хотя́ although
худо́жественный artistic;
худо́жественная литерату́-
ра fiction
ху́же worse

Ц

цена́ NP **⸱ы** price
це́нтр center
центра́льный central

Ч

ча́й 2nd G **⸱ю** tea
ча́с GS **-а́** o'clock; hour
часы́ clock, watch
ча́сто often
ча́сть F2 NP **⸱и**, GP **-е́й**, DP **-я́м**
part
ча́ще oftener
че́к ticket, check
челове́к (*in plural only* GP **челове́к**
occurs) man, person
чём than
чемода́н suitcase
че́рез through
чёрный black
че́стный honorable, honest;
че́стно говоря́ to tell the
truth
четве́рг GS **-а́** Thursday
четвёртый fourth
че́тверть F2 NP **⸱и**, GP **-е́й**, DP
-я́м quarter
четы́ре four
четы́реста four hundred
четы́рнадцатый fourteenth
четы́рнадцать fourteen
число́ (e) NP **⸱а** date, number
чита́ть I to read; **чита́ть ле́к-**
цию to give a lecture
что́ what; that; **что́ э́то за...?**
what, what kind of; **то́лько**
что just; **что́-ли** perhaps

что́бы, что́б in order to; that
чуде́сный wonderful

Ш

ша́хматный chess
шве́д Swede
шестидеся́тый sixtieth
шестна́дцатый sixteenth
шестна́дцать sixteen
шесто́й sixth
ше́сть six
шестьдеся́т sixty
шестьсо́т six hundred
шка́ф 2nd L **-у́** wardrobe, bookcase
шко́ла school
шта́т state

Щ

щи́ cabbage soup

Э

экза́мен exam
экономи́ческий economic
электри́ческий electric
эсто́нский Estonian
эта́ж GS **-а́** storey, floor
э́то this; that
э́тот this; that

Ю

ю́г south

Я

я́ I
явля́ться I to be
язы́к GS **-а́** language
языкозна́ние linguistics
янва́рь GS **-я́** January
я́сный clear
я́щик drawer, box

English-Russian Vocabulary

This vocabulary includes all items from the Conversation Lessons and Grammar Units but does not include items from the Reading Lessons.

A

able, be— мочь I

about примéрно, óколо, о

acquaint познакóмить Р; **get acquainted** познакóмиться Р

acquaintance знакóмый

across чéрез; **across the way** напрóтив

actor актёр

affair дéло

afraid, to be— боя́ться I

after пóсле, пóсле тогó кáк, за

ago томý назáд, назáд

airplane самолёт

airport аэропóрт

Alexis Алексéй

all весь

almost почтú

alone одúн

along по

already ужé

also тóже, тáкже, и

although хотя́

always всегдá

America Амéрика

American америкáнец (*m.*), америкáнка (*f.*), америкáнский (*adj.*)

and и, а, да

another другóй, ещё одúн

answer отвечáть I, отвéтить Р

any kind of вся́кий

approach подходúть I, подойтú Р, наступáть I, наступúть Р

approximately примéрно, óколо

April апрéль

architecture архитектýра

arm рукá

around по

arrive приходúть I, прийтú Р, приезжáть I, приéхать Р, прилетáть I, прилетéть Р

art (*adj.*) худóжественный

article статья́

artistic худóжественный

as кáк; **as well as** кáк.,. так и

Asia Áзия

ask (a question) спрáшивать I, спросúть Р

at у, в, на

August áвгуст

autumn óсень

B

back назáд

bad плохóй

badly плóхо

ballet балéт

be (frequently) бывáть I; **be** быть Р

beautiful красúвый, прекрáсный

because потомý чтó, тáк кáк

become становиться I, стать Р

before до, до того как, перед

begin начинать I, начать Р, начинаться I, начаться Р, стать Р

behind за

besides кроме

best лучший

better лучше, лучший

big большой

black чёрный

blue синий

book книга, книжный (*adj.*)

bookcase шкаф

Boris Борис

born, be— родиться I *or* Р

borsch борщ

Boston Бостон

both... and и... и

box ящик

bread хлеб

bring принести Р

brother брат

build строить I, построить Р

building здание

bus автобус

busy занятый

but но, а, да

butter масло

buy покупать I, купить Р

by у

C

cabbage капуста; **cabbage soup** щи

cafe кафé

call звать I; **to be called** называться I

can мочь I

case случай; **in that case** в таком случае

cashier's desk касса

cathedral собор

Caucasus Кавказ

central средний

chair стул

change сдача

cheap дешёвый

cheaper дешевле

cheaply дёшево

check чек

chemical химический

chemist химик

chemistry химия

child ребёнок; **children** дети

chop котлета

chorus хор

cigarette папироса, сигарета

citizen гражданин (*m.*), гражданка (*f.*)

city город

class занятие

clear ясный

climate климат

clock часы

close закрыть Р

clothes бельё, одежда

coat пальто

coffee кофе

cold холодный

collect собирать I

come приходить I, прийти Р, приезжать I, приехать Р, прилетать I, прилететь Р; **come by for** заходить I, зайти Р; **come back** вернуться

completely совсем

comrade товарищ

consider считать I, посчитать Р

convention съезд

Cornell (*adj.*) корнельский

correct правильный

cost стоить I

count считать I, посчитать Р

country деревня

course курс; **to take a—** слу́-
шать ле́кции; **to give a—** чи-
та́ть ле́кции
course, of— коне́чно
Crimea Крым
customary при́нято
customer покупа́тель

D

date число́
daughter до́чка
day день
dear дорого́й
dearer доро́же
death смерть
December дека́брь
definitely обяза́тельно
depart отходи́ть I, отойти́ Р, отле-
та́ть I
department факульте́т, отде́л
desert пусты́ня
dessert сла́дкое
Detroit Детро́йт
die умере́ть Р
difficult тру́дный
dinner, have— обе́дать I, пообе́-
дать Р
dish блю́до
distant далёкий
do де́лать I, сде́лать Р
doctor до́ктор
dormitory общежи́тие
drawer я́щик
drier су́ше
drink пить I, вы́пить Р
dry сухо́й
during за

E

each ка́ждый
earlier ра́ньше
early ра́но

east восто́к
eat есть I
edition изда́ние
eight во́семь
eight hundred восемьсо́т
eighteen восемна́дцать
eighteenth восемна́дцатый
eighth восьмо́й
eightieth восьмидеся́тый
eighty во́семьдесят
either... or и́ли... и́ли
elder ста́рший
eldest ста́рший
electric электри́ческий
eleven оди́ннадцать
eleventh оди́ннадцатый
end конча́ть I, ко́нчить Р, кон-
ча́ться I, ко́нчиться Р
engineer инжене́р
English англи́йский; **in English**
по-англи́йски
enough дово́льно, доста́точно
entrance вход
envelope конве́рт
etc. и так да́лее
evening ве́чер
everybody все
everything всё
exact то́чный, ро́вный
exam экза́мен
example приме́р; **for example**
на приме́р
except кро́ме
Excuse me! Извини́те!
expensive дорого́й

F

fact де́ло; **as a matter of fact** в
са́мом де́ле
factory фа́брика
fail (an exam) провали́ться Р
fall (*noun*) о́сень

fall (*verb*) упа́сть P
family семья́
famous знамени́тый
far далеко́; **as far as** до
farther да́лее, да́льше
father оте́ц
favorite люби́мый
February февра́ль
few ма́ло
fiction худо́жественная литерату́ра
fifteen пятна́дцать
fifteenth пятна́дцатый
fifth пя́тый
fiftieth пятидеся́тый
fifty пятьдеся́т
film фильм
filter фильтр
finally наконе́ц
find находи́ть I, найти́ P; **find out** узна́ть P
fine прекра́сно, хорошо́
finish конча́ть I, ко́нчить P, конча́ться I, ко́нчиться P
first пе́рвый; **first of all** сперва́; **at first** снача́ла; **for the first course** на пе́рвое
five пять
five hundred пятьсо́т
floor эта́ж
fluently свобо́дно
fly лета́ть I (*Iterative*), лете́ть I (*Actual*), полете́ть P; **fly off, leave** отлета́ть I; **fly here** прилета́ть I, прилете́ть P
following сле́дующий
for для, за, на
forget забы́ть P
fortieth сороково́й
forty со́рок
four четы́ре
four hundred четы́реста
fourteen четы́рнадцать

fourteenth четы́рнадцатый
fourth четвёртый
free свобо́дный
French францу́зский
frequently ча́сто
Friday пя́тница
friend друг, това́рищ
from с, от, из
front, in—of пе́ред
fruit фрукт; **stewed fruit** компо́т
future бу́дущий

G

garnish гарни́р
gather собира́ть I
German неме́цкий
girl де́вушка, де́вочка
give дава́ть I, дать P; **give back** верну́ть P, отдава́ть I, отда́ть P; **give a lecture** чита́ть ле́кцию
glad рад
go ходи́ть I (*Iterative*), итти́ (*Actual*), пойти́ P, е́здить I (*Iterative*), е́хать I (*Actual*), пое́хать P; **go away** уезжа́ть I, уе́хать P; **go past, through** проходи́ть I, пройти́ P; **go up to** подходи́ть I, подойти́ P
good хоро́ший, до́брый; **good luck** всего́ хоро́шего
good-bye до свида́ния

H

half полови́на
hand рука́
happen происходи́ть I произойти́ P, случа́ться I, случи́ться P
happy счастли́вый
hard тру́дный, твёрдый; **hard sign** твёрдый знак

hear слышать I
Helen Елéна
hello здрáвствуйте
help помóчь Р
her её, свой
here здесь, вот; **from here** отсю́да; **here (to this place)** сюдá
high высóкий
higher вы́сший, вы́ше
hill горá
his егó, свой
historical истори́ческий
history истóрия
home дом; **at home** дóма; **home(wards)** домóй
hope надéяться I
hospital больни́ца
hot жáркий
hotel гости́ница
hotter жáрче
hour час
house дом
how как; **How are you?** Кáк вы́ поживáете?; **how much, how many** скóлько
however однáко, затó
huge огрóмный
hundred стó
hundredth сóтый
hurry спеши́ть I, поспеши́ть Р
husband муж

I

I я
ice cream морóженое
if éсли; **if (whether)** ли
important вáжный
in в, на, чéрез, по
intend собирáться I
interest, be interested in интересовáться I
interesting интерéсный

interpreter перевóдчица
introduce познакóмить Р
Ithaca Итáка
its егó, её, свой
Ivan Ивáн
Ivanovich Ивáнович

J

January январь
July ию́ль
June ию́нь
just кáк рáз, тóлько чтó, прóсто

K

Kazbek Казбéк
key ключ
Kiev Ки́ев
kind дóбрый
kiosk киóск
know знать I; **know how** умéть I
Kolya Кóля
kopeck копéйка
Kremlin Крéмль

L

laboratory лаборатóрия
lag behind отставáть I
language язы́к
large большóй
last послéдний, прóшлый; **last night** вчерá вéчером
late пóздно
later пóзже
laundry бельё
lay класть I, положи́ть Р
lazy, get— облени́ться Р
leave отходи́ть I, отойти́ Р, отлетáть I, уезжáть I, уéхать Р; **leave behind** оставля́ть I, остáвить Р
lecture лéкция

left, to the— нале́во
lemon лимо́н
Lenin (adj.) ле́нинский
Leningrad Ленингра́д
less ме́ньше, ме́нее
letter письмо́
lie лежа́ть I, полежа́ть P
like (adj.) похо́жий
like (verb) люби́ть I, нра́виться I,
понра́виться P
line о́чередь
linguistics языкозна́ние
listen слу́шать I
literature литерату́ра
little ма́ленький; a little немно́го
live жить I
loan, as a— взаймы́
located, be— находи́ться I
long до́лго, давно́; long ago
давно́; no longer бо́льше не́
look at смотре́ть I, посмотре́ть P;
look for иска́ть I, поиска́ть P;
look over осма́тривать I, осмо-
тре́ть P; have a look at уви́-
деть P
lose теря́ть I, потеря́ть P
lot, a—of мно́го
love люби́ть I

M

main гла́вный; mainly, for the
most part гла́вным о́бразом
major специа́льность
make де́лать I, сде́лать P
man челове́к
many мно́го; not— ма́ло; how
— ско́лько
March март
married за́мужем
Mary Мэ́ри
mathematics матема́тика
May май

maybe мо́жет бы́ть
mean зна́чить I
meantime, in the — пока́
meet встреча́ть I, встре́тить P,
познако́миться I, собира́ться I
menu меню́
middle сре́дний
milk молоко́
minute мину́та
Misha Ми́ша
Miss гражда́нка, госпожа́
mistaken, be— ошиба́ться I
model моде́ль
moderate уме́ренный
Monday понеде́льник
money де́ньги·
month ме́сяц
more бо́лее, бо́льше; once more
ещё ра́з
morning у́тро; in the morning
у́тром; mornings по утра́м
Moscow (noun) Москва́; (adj.)
моско́вский
most са́мый; for the most part
гла́вным о́бразом
mother мать
mountain гора́
movies кино́
Mr. господи́н, граждани́н
Mrs. госпожа́, гражда́нка
much гора́здо, мно́го; not much
ма́ло; how much ско́лько
museum музе́й
mutton (adj.) бара́ний
my мой

N

name и́мя; What's your —? Ка́к
ва́с зову́т?; named after Gorky
и́мени Го́рького
Natasha Ната́ша

native родной
near близкий, около
nearer ближе
necessary нужен, надо, приходиться I, прийтись P
need нужен, надо
neither... nor ни... ни
never никогда
nevertheless зато
new новый
newspaper газета
New York Нью-Йорк
next будущий, следующий, потом; next to рядом с
night ночь
nine девять
nine hundred девятьсот
nineteen девятнадцать
nineteenth девятнадцатый
ninetieth девяностый
ninety девяносто
ninth девятый
no нет; there is no нет
nobody никто
north север
not не; not at all совсем не
nothing ничего
novel роман
November ноябрь
now сейчас, теперь
nowhere нигде, никуда
number число

O

obligatory обязательный
occupied занятый
o'clock час
October октябрь
off с
often часто
oftener чаще
old старый

older старше, старший
Olga Ольга
on на, по
one один
only один, только
open открыть P
opera опера
opposite напротив
or или; either... or или... или
order (verb) заказывать I, заказать P
order, in — to чтобы, чтоб
other другой
ought to должен
our наш
out of из

P

pack (noun) пачка
pack (verb) уложить P
paper бумага, работа
Pardon! Простите!
park парк
part, to take — принимать участие
party вечер
pass (an exam) выдержать P
passer-by прохожий
past прошлый
pay платить I, заплатить P
peace мир
pen ручка
pencil карандаш
people люди
performance спектакль
perhaps может быть, что-ли
person человек
Peter Пётр
Petrovich Петрович
philological филологический
philosophy философия
phone звонить I, позвонить P

photograph фотогра́фия
physics фи́зика
place ме́сто
plan собира́ться I
play (*noun*) пье́са, спекта́кль
play (*verb*) игра́ть I
pleasant прия́тный
please нра́виться I, понра́виться P, пожа́луйста
pleasure удово́льствие
pocket карма́н
Poland По́льша
post card откры́тка
post office по́чта
present настоя́щий
price цена́
probably вероя́тно, наве́рно
professor профе́ссор
Pskov Псков
put класть I, положи́ть P, ста́вить I, поста́вить P

Q

quarter че́тверть
question вопро́с
quickly бы́стро

R

rain дождь; it rains идёт до́ждь
rather дово́льно
read чита́ть I, прочита́ть P; read a little bit почита́ть P
ready гото́вый
real настоя́щий; really по-на-стоя́щему, действи́тельно, ра́зве
receive получа́ть I, получи́ть P
recently неда́вно
related родно́й
relatives родны́е
remain остава́ться I
remarkable замеча́тельный

remember по́мнить I
repeat повторя́ть I, повтори́ть P
repertoire репертуа́р
restaurant рестора́н
return верну́ть P, верну́ться P, отдава́ть I, отда́ть P
right ве́рно, пра́вильный; to the
right напра́во; that's right во́т ка́к; пра́вда; right (just) ка́к ра́з; right away сейча́с
ring звони́ть I, позвони́ть P
road доро́га
ruble рубль
Russia Росси́я
Russian ру́сский; Russian, in Russian по-ру́сски

S

salesman продаве́ц
saleswoman продавщи́ца
same то́т же
Saturday суббо́та
sausage соси́ска
say говори́ть I, сказа́ть P
school шко́ла
scientific нау́чный
sea мо́ре
second второ́й; for the second course на второ́е
see ви́деть I, уви́деть P; see each other ви́деться I
seek иска́ть I, поиска́ть P
seem каза́ться I
self себя́, сам
sell продава́ть I, прода́ть P; be sold продава́ться I, прода́ть-ся P
sentence фра́за
September сентя́брь
serve подава́ть I, пода́ть P
seven семь
seven hundred семьсо́т

seventeen семнáдцать

seventeenth семнáдцатый

seventh седьмóй

seventieth семидесятый

seventy сéмьдесят

several нéсколько

severe сурóвый

sheet лист

should бы, дóлжен

show (*noun*) спектáкль

show (*verb*) покáзывать I, показáть Р

Siberia Сибúрь

sign знак

similar похóжий

simply прóсто

since так как

sir граждани́н

sister сестрá

sit сидéть I

six шесть

six hundred шестьсóт

sixteen шестнáдцать

sixteenth шестнáдцатый

sixth шестóй

sixtieth шестидеся́тый

sixty шестьдеся́т

small мáленький

Smolensk Смолéнск

snow снег

so так

soft мя́гкий; soft sign мя́гкий знак

some нéсколько

somehow кáк-то

sometimes иногдá

son сын

Sonya Сóня

soon скóро

sooner рáньше

sorry жаль

so-so тáк себé

soup суп; cabbage soup щи

south юг

Soviet совéтский

speak говори́ть I

specialty специáльность

spring веснá

stamp мáрка

stand стоя́ть I, стáвить I, постáвить Р

state госудáрственный (*adj.*), штат

station, railroad — вокзáл

stay оставáться I

still ещё, всё ещё

stop останáвливать I, останови́ть Р, останáвливаться I, останови́ться Р; stop by for заходи́ть I, зайти́ Р

store магази́н

storey этáж

street у́лица

streetcar трамвáй

student студéнт, студéнтка; graduate student аспирáнт

studies заня́тие

study учи́ться I

subject предмéт

subway метрó

successful, be— удáться Р

such такóй

sugar сáхар

suit костю́м

suitcase чемодáн

summer лéто

Sunday воскресéнье

sweet слáдкий

T

table стол

take брать I, взять Р, принимáть I, приня́ть Р; take part принимáть учáстие; take (a course) проходи́ть I, пройти́ Р; take (an exam) сдавáть I, сдать Р

talk говори́ть I; **to have a talk (with)** поговори́ть Р
Tashkent Ташке́нт
Tatyana Татья́на
tea чай
teacher преподава́тель, учи́тель, учи́тельница
tell говори́ть I, сказа́ть Р, расска́зывать I, рассказа́ть Р; **to tell the truth** че́стно говоря́
ten де́сять
tenth деся́тый
than чем
thank you спаси́бо
that э́тот, тот, что, что́бы, чтоб, кото́рый
theater теа́тр
their их, свой
then пото́м, тогда́
there вон, вот, там; **to that place, to there** туда́; **over there** во́н та́м; **there is, there are** есть; **there isn't, there aren't** нет
therefore поэ́тому
thing вещь
think ду́мать I
third тре́тий
thirteen трина́дцать
thirteenth трина́дцатый
thirtieth тридца́тый
thirty три́дцать
this э́тот
thousand ты́сяча
three три
three hundred три́ста
through че́рез
Thursday четве́рг
thus так
ticket биле́т, чек
time вре́мя, раз; **it's time** пора́; **What time is it?** Кото́рый ча́с? *or* Ско́лько вре́мени?
to к, в, на

today сего́дня
together вме́сте
tomorrow за́втра
too сли́шком; **too (also)** то́же, та́кже, и
tourist тури́ст
towards к
train по́езд
travel путеше́ствовать I
trip пое́здка; **Have a good —!** Счастли́вого пути́!
truth пра́вда; **to tell the truth** че́стно говоря́
Tuesday вто́рник
turn о́чередь
twelfth двена́дцатый
twelve двена́дцать
twentieth двадца́тый
twenty два́дцать
two два
two hundred две́сти

U

Ukraine Украи́на
uncle дя́дя
under под
understand понима́ть I, поня́ть Р
union сою́з
university университе́т
unoccupied свобо́дный
until до
up to до, к
Uspensky успе́нский
usual обыкнове́нный

V

vacant свобо́дный
vacation о́тпуск
Vera Ве́ра
very о́чень; **the very** са́мый
view вид

W

wait   ждать I, подожда́ть Р
waiter   официа́нт
walk   ходи́ть I (*Iterative*)
wall   стена́
wallet   бума́жник
want   хоте́ть I, хоте́ться I
war   война́
wardrobe   шкаф
warm   тёплый
watch   часы́
we   мы
weather   пого́да
Wednesday   среда́
week   неде́ля
welcome, you're —   пожа́луйста
well   ну, хорошо́; as well as   как...
   так и
west   за́пад
western   за́падный
what   како́й, что, кото́рый; what
   kind of   что́ э́то за
when   когда́
where   где; where to   куда́;
   where from   отку́да
which   кото́рой, како́й
white   бе́лый
who   кто, кото́рый

why   почему́
wife   жена́
wind   ве́тер
window   окно́
winter   зима́
with   с
without   без
woman   же́нщина
wonderful   чуде́сный
word   сло́во
work (*noun*)   рабо́та
work (*verb*)   рабо́тать I
worse   ху́же
would   бы
write   писа́ть I, написа́ть Р
writer   писа́тель

Y

year   год
yes   да
yesterday   вчера́
yet   ещё
you   вы, ты
young   молодо́й; young fellow
   молоде́ц
younger   мла́дший, моло́же
youngest   мла́дший
your   ваш, твой

INDEX

Index

References to the Appendix and to the section on pronunciation are not included in this index.

INDEX

Photograph Credits

(By page numbers)

1. J. Allan Cash from Rapho-Guillumette   4. Eddy Posthuma de Boer from Black Star   7. Elliot Erwitt, Magnum Photos   21. Sovfoto   24. J. Allan Cash from Rapho-Guillumette   27. Sovfoto   47. Sovfoto   53. Sovfoto   70. J. Allan Cash from Rapho-Guillumette   71. Sovfoto   77. Eddy Posthuma de Boer from Black Star   98. Sovfoto   101. USSR Magazine from Sovfoto   107. Cornell Capa, Magnum Photos   126. Henri Cartier-Bresson, Magnum Photos   127. Cornell Capa, Magnum Photos   133. Lynn Pelham from Rapho-Guillumette   153. J. Allan Cash from Rapho-Guillumette   155. Henri Cartier-Bresson, Magnum Photos   161. Sovfoto   165. Sovfoto   178. J. Allan Cash from Rapho-Guillumette   179. Sovfoto   184. Henri Cartier-Bresson, Magnum Photos   185. Henri Cartier-Bresson, Magnum Photos   190. Henri Cartier-Bresson, Magnum Photos   203. Henri Cartier-Bresson, Magnum Photos   208. Sovfoto   209. Sovfoto   227. J. Allan Cash from Rapho-Guillumette   232. Brian Brake, Magnum Photos   233. J. Allan Cash from Rapho-Guillumette   247. Sovfoto   249. Henri Cartier-Bresson, Magnum Photos   251. Sovfoto   257. Erich Lessing, Magnum Photos   262. Lynn Pelham from Rapho-Guillumette   273. Sovfoto   279. Sovfoto   292. Elliott Erwitt, Magnum Photos   293. Sovfoto   295. Sovfoto   296. Henri Cartier-Bresson, Magnum Photos